SAINT LOUIS:

The Story of Catholic Evangelization of America's Heartland

A four-volume series

SAINT LOUIS:
The Story of Catholic Evangelization of
America's Heartland

Volume 1: From Canoe to Cathedral
Volume 2: The Lion and the Fourth City
Volume 3: Age of Cardinals
Volume 4: Contemporary Challenges

SAINT LOUIS:
The Story of Catholic Evangelization of America's Heartland

Volume 2: The Lion and the Fourth City

Monsignor Michael John Witt

Miriam Press
Saint Louis, Missouri

The Miriam Press
4120 West Pine Blvd.
St. Louis, MO 63108
www.hebrewcatholic.org

Front cover photo: Archbishop Peter Richard Kenrick. His motto was "Noli irritare leonem." ("Do not irritate the Lion.")

ISBN: 978-0-939409-08-2
Library of Congress Control Number: 2016904014

DEDICATION

To Fathers Henry van Der Sanden, John Rothensteiner, Frederick Holweck, Jesuit Barnaby Faherty, and Monsignor Nicholas Schneider. These priests preserved and promoted the history of the Archdiocese of Saint Louis and deserve our gratitude and praise.

"And when at last their prayers and labors began to bring victory after victory under such leaders as Du Bourg, Rosati, De Andreis, Van Quickenborne, Elet, De Smet and John Timon, Peter Richard Kenrick and the multitude of their devoted followers, penetrating into the regions of darkness, north, west, east and south, carrying the glad tidings of the gospel to the scattered fragments of many nations, it was again 'Ad Majorem Dei Gloriam.'"

Rev. John Rothensteiner

TABLE OF CONTENTS

PREFACE

Joseph A. Zumsteg was Swiss-born and arrived in the United States at the age of thirteen. He came to Saint Louis via New Orleans in 1852. His is not a household name, and yet he witnessed and participated in many of the events contained in this second volume of the history of the Archdiocese of Saint Louis. He is Everyman.

Joseph Zumsteg entered Saint Louis history on May 3, 1861. He enlisted in the Fifth Volunteer Infantry, a pro-Union militia formed shortly after Fort Sumter was fired on, ushering in the Civil War. The unit was the brain-child of Congressman Frank P. Blair, Jr., brother of Abraham Lincoln's Postmaster General, Montgomery Blair. The Fifth Volunteers and other German-dominated units provided the muscle for General Nathaniel Lyon to force the surrender of Camp Jackson on May 10, 1861. Zumsteg participated in that assault, though it is uncertain if his unit was involved in the brief firefight which left 27 Saint Louisans dead on Olive Road.

The Fifth Volunteers marched with Franz Sigel and were nearly crushed at the Battle of Carthage (July 5) when the Union force of 1,100 was counter-attacked by 6,000 State militia. Zumsteg saw more action under Sigel at the Battle of Wilson's Creek. He participated in the artillery attack on the rebel camp at Sharp's Farm. Unfortunately, he broke in a quick retreat when Sigel mistook a Confederate unit as friendly and was overrun. Fleeing to Springfield, the Fifth Volunteers and others in Sigel's command licked their wounds and returned to Saint Louis, as their ninety-day enlistment had expired.

Joseph A. Zumsteg did not sit out the war. Like so many early enrollees, he reenlisted, this time with the Fourth Missouri Cavalry. This unit was an amalgam of three companies of Holland Horse and the Hussars of flamboyant General John C. Frémont. Frémont was nicknamed "Pathfinder," as he led four explorations of the West. He was the first presidential candidate of the newly-formed Republican Party, and he was married to the equally flamboyant Jessie Benton Frémont, daughter of Senator Thomas Hart Benton. Frémont was the overall commander of the Western Department, but he soon embarrassed the Lincoln administration with unconstitutional applications of martial law. He was sacked on November 1, 1861 but received army commissions for much of the war.

Zumsteg saw action at the Battle of Pea Ridge (March 6-8, 1862), which was attended by Franz Sigel and also by the Confederate chaplain Father John Bannon, former pastor of Saint John the Evangelist Parish. He fought at Iuka and Corinth, where Father Bannon also served, though on the other side. He fought at the siege of Vicksburg, where Father Bannon also was and from where the priest was paroled after being captured. Remarkably, throughout these major battles Joseph Zumsteg was not wounded or seriously injured. It was swamp fever, caught in Arkansas, which would plague him later in life.

After the war, Zumsteg returned to Saint Louis and married Mary Koch, herself an immigrant from Bavaria. She was brought to America when she was seven years old. She was one of sixteen children, though only two survived to adulthood. The wedding was officiated by a priest who would be legendary in Archdiocesan history: Father Franz Goller of Saints Peter and Paul Parish. The Zumstegs had six children: four boys born in 1866, 1869, 1874, and 1877. Their two girls were born in late 1869 and late 1880. The children grew up, had families, and worked in breweries or tobacco plants, the woof and weave of everyday life. Joseph A. Zumsteg died on May 26, 1920, at the age of eighty. He had been a member of the St. Paul Benevolent Society and the Hassendeubel Post of the Grand Army of the Republic. He was waked at his daughter's residence at 2212 Chippewa Street, buried from Saint Anthony Church, and laid to rest at Saints Peter and Paul Cemetery.

The life of Joseph A. Zumsteg is similar to hundreds of thousands of Saint Louisans of the late nineteenth century. Their Catholic Faith fed them. They did their patriotic duty without question. They got up and went about the business of working to support a family. They raised their kids and watched them go off and form families of their own.

When Zumsteg first saw Saint Louis in 1852, it was already a growing Midwestern city with great potential. He saw it at its zenith, the Fourth City of America. And perhaps by his death in 1920, he realized that his hometown had ceased to expand and was settling into a challenging twentieth century. But perhaps not. Perhaps he was more distracted by the lingering illness which racked his five-foot, six-inch body. Perhaps living with his daughter Ida and her family after the death of his wife took most of his concentration.

The story of Volume Two is dominated by one man, The Lion, Peter Richard Kenrick. He served as Ordinary of Saint Louis for fifty years. He ordained an enormous number of priests. He consecrated dozens

•

of bishops. He touched the lives of countless laity, both Catholic and non-Catholic. Kenrick was assisted by extraordinary men: Joseph Melcher, Patrick Ryan, Henry van der Sanden, Henry Mühlsiepen, Ambrose Heim, Franz Goller. The list goes on and on.

This is the story of building parish communities and establishing schools bulging at the seams. It is the story of missionary work to the Native Americans and to the newly-arrived immigrants. In the end, it is the story of providing a Catholic milieu for the Zumstegs and families like theirs. Here is the story of the Catholic evangelization of America's heartland, once again.

MJW

ACKNOWLEDGMENTS

First to be thanked is Archbishop Robert Carlson, Archbishop of Saint Louis, who has encouraged me in this project and in the study of the history of this extraordinary Archdiocese. His constant support and interest is most appreciated.

Also of great encouragement are Tony and Teresa Holman of Covenant Network. Teresa and I have created fifty-three half-hour audio programs covering the fifty years of Archbishop Peter Richard Kenrick's episcopal service to the Archdiocese and the much shorter time of Archbishop John Kain. The period spans from 1843 to 1903, a time of incredible growth for Saint Louis and for America's heartland.

Rena Schergan, of the Archdiocesan Archives, has spent countless hours searching for the great photos, maps, and illustrations which are found in this volume. I admire her enthusiasm and tenacity. Thanks goes out to Mary Agnew, and Pam and Ed Nichols, who proofread the text and made many positive suggestions. Rena Schergan also served as a proofreader. I also thank Diane Wood for her research on the Zumsteg family and particularly the information about Joseph A. Zumsteg, whose life was a microcosm of nineteenth-century Saint Louis.

To Jennifer Brinker and Lisa Johnson go my thanks for their publicity of the first volume, *From Canoe to Cathedral*. By their efforts to get the word out, hundreds of people are now learning the vital history of the early days of exploration and settlement in America's heartland. And to David Moss, Kelly Boutross, and Miriam Press I wish to express my gratitude. They are a great team to work with in bringing these volumes to print.

MJW

Chapter One

KENRICK'S SAINT LOUIS: 1841

When Peter Richard Kenrick arrived in Saint Louis on December 28, 1841, the city was undergoing its third metamorphosis. The first change started on February 15, 1763, when Auguste Chouteau and around 40 workers took a grove of trees and underbrush on a limestone bluff twelve miles south of the confluence of the Mississippi and Missouri Rivers and laid out a village. The village grew as Creoles of Western Illinois fled British occupation and as the fur trade prospered. The Creole village was French in language, Catholic in religion, and royalist in sentiment. From the first, the village gazed westward, interested in fur trapping and trading with Indians deep in the interior. It established, early on, a comfortable commercial alliance with the Osage nation. The two communities learned each other's languages and learned each other's ways. Saint Louis was a Creole outpost, the northernmost point of the Spanish Empire in America.

The second metamorphosis took place abruptly in 1803 when, in a game of imperial territory swapping, Saint Louis and the whole of Louisiana was gifted back to France by Spain and then promptly sold to the United States. Meriwether Lewis and William Clark immediately launched their Corps of Discovery expedition up the Missouri River. Southerners moved to Missouri, coming from Kentucky and Tennessee and bringing their slaves, establishing farms and plantations in the interior of the state. Easterners, especially from Massachusetts, moved to Saint Louis to enter into commercial adventures, bringing their own critical opinions of slavery, of French Creoles, of the Catholic Faith, and of Indians. Saint Louis changed from a French Creole village to an American town in under a decade. The Creole leadership adapted and cooperated to make the transition as smooth as possible, while protecting their own commercial and property interests. Subtle changes were taking place in attitude, in governance, and in demographic composition. Saint Louis became for the United States the westernmost town and supply center for the launching of explorations and settlements further west.

The 1840s caused Saint Louis to change once again. It went from an American frontier town to a major city. That transition would not

1

be easy. Further changes in demographic composition complicated the language requirements. French fell into disuse, while German was added to English as a vital language to speak. Even the English spoken differed significantly, as the flat Midwestern speech was joined with a southern drawl and a Yankee staccato and even an Irish brogue. The change was characterized by the dismantling of a landmark in the name of commercial progress. The loss of the Chouteau House was only one small part of the urban change. Social changes brought diversity but also division to Saint Louis. In addition, disasters of pestilence, flood, fire, and riot scarred the city and left it not a single community but a myriad of interest groups, each vying for their own advantage.

In 1829, Auguste Chouteau died. He, along with Pierre Laclède, was the founder of Saint Louis. When he set the streets and blocks and lots, he carved out a whole block for Maxent, Laclède, et Compagnie. Between the Place des Armes and the Place d'Église, a stone warehouse was built which was later turned into the Laclède home, residence for the founder, as well as for Thérèse Bourgeois Chouteau and her children. After Laclède died, the Chouteaus inherited the house, the finest in Saint Louis, and added the second floor. Persons of note to visit Saint Louis were entertained in this home: the Marquis de Lafayette, Lewis, Clark, Stoddard and others.

Auguste's widow, Thérèse, built a second home west of town and announced that the historic site would be razed to make way for 32 two-story commercial buildings. Few Saint Louisans raised an eyebrow to the plan to destroy this landmark in the name of commercial progress. One who did was a newcomer to Saint Louis, Matthew Field, an actor who settled in Saint Louis in 1835 at the age of 22. He penned the following poem, *The Chouteau House*, as a protest against the impending destruction, but to no avail:

Touch not a stone!

An earlier pioneer of Christian sway founded this dwelling here, almost alone.

Touch not a stone!

Let the great West command a whole reef relic of the early land;

That after generations may not say all went for gold in our forefather's day, and of our infancy we nothing own.

Touch not a stone![1]

---

1   Lee Ann Sandweiss, ed. *Seeking St. Louis: Voices from a River City.* Saint Louis: The Missouri Historical Society. 2000. P. 104-105.

Thérèse Chouteau was not the only old Saint Louis type to cash in on real estate deals. Julia Soulard, widow of Antoine Soulard, royal surveyor for the Spanish, and daughter of Gabriele Cerré, the wealthy merchant who had brought his family and fortune to Saint Louis from Illinois, began the development of her lands immediately south of Saint Louis. Sophie Chouteau, widow of Auguste Pierre Chouteau, planned a subdivision for housing, as did another relative, Joseph Papin.

One of the more interesting developers was a Massachusetts lawyer, Thomas Allen. Arriving in Saint Louis he had the good fortune to meet and marry Ann Russell, daughter of William Russell, who was sent to Saint Louis by President Thomas Jefferson to replace Antoine Soulard as surveyor. In the process of surveying, Russell bought up lands which promised to become valuable properties.

Thomas Allen added to these Russell properties by buying land from John Cabanné, a scion of an old Creole family. He then hired William Cozzens, the city engineer, to parcel his properties into blocks and lots and to measure out the streets and alleys. By April 1848, Allen was ready to submit a plat to the city government and begin construction on housing, which was in great demand as the city population expanded.

To attract more people to his development, Thomas Allen sold a block of his first addition to Archbishop Peter Richard Kenrick for $4,809.[2] The Archbishop erected Saints Peter and Paul Parish for the growing German Catholic population. Allen required only a $100 down payment, with the rest due over the next ten years. People poured into his development, and by 1853 Thomas Allen saw an 800% profit in his original investment.

Others joined the bonanza, creating what Eric Sandweiss referred to as a "landed political elite."[3] James H. Lucas and his sister, Ann Lucas Hunt, developed an addition between Ninth and Eleventh Streets, Saint Charles and Market. Here the new Saint Louis social set made their homes. When Julia Soulard developed her land into 110 lots, she reserved four one-acre lots, set on higher ground than the rest, with fine views of the Mississippi River.

Another landmark to disappear at this time was Chouteau Pond. The pond and the mill at the far end were fed by natural springs, a

---

2   Eric Sandweiss. *St. Louis: The Evolution of an American Urban Landscape.* Philadelphia: Temple University Press. 2001. P. 55.
3   Ibid. P. 49.

site for recreation. In hot summer months, it was used for swimming and bathing. The Religious of the Sacred Heart complained to the city government about how the men were dressed for bathing, as the pond was within sight of Maison de Ville, the girls' school. But the city was powerless to act, as the pond was outside city limits at that time.

The pond was the scene of a Fourth of July celebration in 1830, which included a dinner in the grove, but the celebration fell out of favor as the city grew around it and businesses discharged their waste into the streets, which then made its way to the pond when it rained. An attempt to turn the pond into a public park failed, as the water level would have to be stabilized, and the rainwater carrying sewage would have to be deflected away from the pond. Instead, Chouteau received a directive from the city health department in 1850 to have the pond drained. He responded that it was the city's duty to deflect the waste away from the pond.

The city already had plans for the area as Julius Hutawa's map, the plan of the City of Saint Louis, 1850, showed. There, a street pattern was placed, even through parts of the pond area that was still under-water.

Saint Louis found itself divided into six wards in order to deal with the complexities of urban life, each ward having a unique character. The First Ward, south of Chouteau Pond in Mill Creek, was populated by immigrants. It was congested and dominated by day laborers. A few French homes existed, now in a ruined state. The area had a dingy air about it, sharing space with some industries, including The White Lead and Oil Company. Blacks and even a few slaves could be found there.

The Second Ward was home of most of the old Creole population, gathered from the original village and extending west along Mill Creek and the pond. Nicknamed "Frenchtown," it was filled with many of the original cabins built at the time of the city's founding.

The Third and Fourth Wards were located in the center of the city and ran from the riverfront westward up to the plateaus of Fourth Street, Twelfth Street, and Jefferson Avenue. Here the elite lived. Lucas Place, Connor, O'Fallon, and Christie additions were filled with graceful residences.[4] Here also resided 67% of the slaves of the city, no doubt employed as domestic help. Property values reflected the

---

4   James Neal Primm. *Lion of the Valley: St. Louis, Missouri, 1764 – 1980*. Saint Louis: Missouri Historical Society Press. 2010. P. 147.

elite nature of these wards: while a lot in the First Ward sold for $1-$4 per front foot, a lot in Ward Three sold for up to $200 per front foot.[5]

The one distraction from the Third and Fourth Wards was on Wharf Street. Here saloons served the boatmen from the paddle wheelers, with warehouses converted into boarding houses. North of this area was found "clappers alley," populated by free blacks as well as poor whites. Sub-neighborhoods were nicknamed "Wildcat Chute," "Happy Hollow" and "Paradise Alley."[6] To the north were the Fifth and Sixth Wards, which reflected the First Ward in the south: congested and populated by immigrant working-class families.

The census of 1850 reflected the extraordinary change and growth that came to Saint Louis in just a decade. In 1850, Saint Louis had a population of nearly 78,000, a growth of 373%. It was twice the size of Pittsburgh and over three times the size of Chicago. Though New Orleans and Cincinnati were still larger, their growth in the 1840s was only 14% and 149%, respectively.[7]

Over 40% of Saint Louis was German or Irish of the first generation. When added to the second and third generations, the Irish and German populations were over 50%. Many of these arrived penniless, seeking any kind of work they could get. Many received aid from the Sisters of Charity, administrating at the Mullanphy Hospital. When Bryan Mullanphy died in 1851, he left over a half million dollars to assist these immigrants. Other organizations included Friends of Ireland, William Greenleaf Eliot's Centenary Church, and the Ladies' Benevolent Society.

Immigrants also banded together to help themselves. At Saint Mary of Victories, Father Ambrose Heim developed a parish bank which proved so successful that the Archbishop made him his secretary at the Cathedral and developed the bank on a diocesan scale. In 1846, the German Catholic Benevolent Society was founded, and in 1850 the German Saint Vincent Orphan Society began; later, the Catholic Knights of America provided insurance and social activities, as did the Central-Verein.

Typically, Germans gathered together and formed faith commu-

---

5   James Neal Primm. *Lion of the Valley: St. Louis, Missouri, 1764 – 1980.* Saint Louis: Missouri Historical Society Press. 2010. P. 147.
6   Frederick A. Hodes. *Rising on the River: St. Louis 1822 to 1850.* Tooele, Utah. Patrice Press. P. 350.
7   James Neal Primm. *Lion of the Valley: St. Louis, Missouri, 1764 – 1980.* Saint Louis: Missouri Historical Society Press. 2010. P. 165.

nities, asking the bishops for recognition and a priest. Irish parishes tended to be formed by Irish priests who were given the task of founding a parish. In doing so, they would attract laity to constitute the parish.

Parishes, benevolent societies, and social clubs would be necessary shields for the vulnerable immigrants as they became part of an American city growing in stature, a region dominated by technological and commercial change and a social fabric that was at once welcoming and yet often hostile to these newcomers.

By 1850, Saint Louis could boast of ten Catholic parishes serving over 27,000 Catholics. The largest was no longer the Cathedral, with 4,450 members. Saint Joseph's on Biddle Street was close with a membership of 4,000. But Saint Patrick's claimed 5,000. Saint Francis Xavier, staffed by the Jesuits, had 3,000 members. Saint Mary of Victories and Saints Peter and Paul each claimed around 2,000, as did Saint Michael's. Under 2,000 parishioners were the parishes of Saint Vincent de Paul, Saint John the Apostle, and Most Holy Trinity.

Other voices were raised to the Lord. In 1839, Christ Church Cathedral was consecrated on Chestnut and Broadway for the Episcopalians. It seated 1,000. Pew sales went for as much as $500 each, and on one day $25,000 was raised. Soon Christ Church was joined by three other Episcopalian churches: Saint John, Grace, and Saint George.

The Presbyterians formed First Presbyterian in 1838, and sixty members left to form Second Presbyterian. A third church, Central Presbyterian, was erected in 1848 on Eighth and Locust. It sported a remarkable 190-foot steeple.

In 1847, the Second Baptist Church was completed, and Centenary Church was founded by the Methodists on the corner of Fifth and Pine. This congregation broke with the national Methodist Church in 1844 over the issue of slavery, favoring "the peculiar institution."

On July 2, 1850, the First Congregational Church was dedicated at the corner of Olive and Ninth Streets. Rev. William Greenleaf Eliot was pastor, despite his adherence to Unitarianism. German Lutherans flocked to America to avoid nationalization of their church in Prussia. In 1839, over 600 Saxon Germans arrived, moving to Perry County. By December 1839, Concordia Seminary was founded, and the Lutheran Missouri Synod was established under the leadership of C. F. W. Walther. Other German Protestants formed around George Wendelin Wall in 1836, but within four years doctrinal differences shattered the German Evangelical churches into various congregations.

While early Saint Louis blacks tended to be Catholic, such was not the case by the 1830s. In 1841, Rev. John Berry Meachum established the Baptist Church for Colored Peoples, with over 200 free blacks and 65 slaves as members. Meachum's enthusiastic sermons attracted crowds, and his baptisms in Chouteau Pond were sensational. Another black Baptist Church was founded on Almond Street, where many free blacks lived. Rev. Augustus Paris established a school for black girls, enrolling 100 students. But by the late 1840s, anti-black legislation in Missouri made it impossible to keep the school open, even under the guise of a Sunday school.

The changing attitude toward people of color, or even whites who spoke with a brogue, exhibited a growing ugly side to Saint Louis. Gone was the French Creole sense of tolerance and camaraderie. The interracial marriage of French and Indians was seen in a different light.

Under the French Code Noir, and adapted to Spanish norms, slaves were recognized as autonomous human beings with immortal souls. Several Catholic religious congregations owned slaves who performed domestic tasks. Philip François Renault brought slaves from Haiti to work in the lead mines near Sainte Genevieve. The code of King Louis XV placed an obligation on the slaveholder to see to the welfare of his slaves. Food, shelter, and clothing were required. The children of slaves could not be sold from their parents until puberty. Although slaves could be punished for misdeeds, they could not be imprisoned, put to death, or maimed by their owners. Female slaves were protected from sexual advances. Under the Spanish rule, interracial marriages were permitted, and all Indian slaves were to be freed upon the death of their masters. Free blacks were not to be harassed, but rather treated as free citizens.

Once the Americans were in charge, and once Kentuckians and Tennesseans flocked in with their families and slaves, the rules began to change. Severe punishments crept into everyday life. A former slave, Mary Armstrong, recalled the death of her nine-month-old sister at the hands of a slave owner's wife, while her slave owner was known to chain his slaves and whip them, rubbing salt into their wounds.

In 1846, Judge John M. Krum ruled that free blacks could not bring their cases into a court of law because they were not citizens. While many free blacks and mulattos had accumulated considerable wealth, and some had bought their own freedom, this ruling put all in jeopardy.

With time, the Missouri State legislature and State Supreme Court became even more hostile to free blacks. When blacks were refused education, even private education, many boarded their children in northern states, even though their property taxes went to support the public schools which their children were forbidden to attend. In 1847, Justice William Napton commented, "It has not been the policy of the state to favor the liberation of Negroes from that condition in which the law and usages have placed the mass of their species."[8] The use of the term "species" would have been unthinkable in either the French or the Spanish era. Earlier, Napton had observed that color raises a presumption of slavery.[9]

A state law was passed that every free black resident had to post a bond of $200 to guarantee their good behavior. This was soon raised to $500. When this law was challenged in court by Charles Lyons, a free black man, Judge John Krum denied his right to the court, rejecting the notion that a black man could be a citizen, and then defied the federal government to interfere in Missouri affairs.

A further state law forbade any free blacks from moving into Missouri. Abolitionists like Elijah Lovejoy and William Greenleaf Eliot favored colonization plans, in which free blacks and slaves would be sent to Africa. Meanwhile, Pope Gregory XVI, in *Supremo Apostolatus Fastigio*, condemned the slave trade, forbidding Catholics from participating in it. Indeed, two years earlier the Pope had beatified Martin de Porres, a sixteenth-century South American mulatto known for his sanctity and kindness to people and animals alike.

The state of racial tension in Saint Louis was demonstrated by an incident which haunts the city's history and was compounded by the press reaction to it afterwards. The incident took place at Sixth and Chestnut on April 28, 1836. Sheriff's deputies George Hammond and William Mull had arrested a steamboat steward, Francis McIntosh, a free mulatto who had interfered with the duties of a law officer on the levee. McIntosh asked what punishment he would face, and Hammond, in order to scare him, said he probably would be hanged. McIntosh panicked and stabbed Hammond to death, wounding Mull severely. Citizens witnessing the assault captured McIntosh and brought him to the jail. If he had a fair trial now, McIntosh would probably be

---

8   Frederick A. Hodes. *Rising on the River: St. Louis 1822 to 1850*. Tooele, Utah: Patrice Press. P. 329.
9   Ibid. P. 329.

hanged for sure.

Instead a mob, some say made of thousands, surrounded the jail as a dozen or two dozen men broke in and overcame the sheriff, dragging McIntosh out. What began as a lynching party turned demonic. McIntosh was chained to a tree on Tenth and Market, kindling wood was piled around him, and he was burned alive. During the eighteen-minute ordeal, an anonymous witness said an alderman walked around the spectacle, threatening to shoot anyone who interfered.

The next day Saint Louis newspapers played the role of apologists, trying to explain or justify the deed. The *Republican* called it a revolting spectacle, and worried that it would defame the fair name of Saint Louis. The *Missouri Argos* reminded the reader of the sadness of the Hammond family. Only William Weber's *Anzeiger des Westens* chided the citizenry: "Why did not the well-disposed citizens appear armed, the event being generally known, and continued for several hours? Where were the sheltered proud Gray civil guard, who at other times so handsomely paraded through the streets with their music? It is known that you gentlemen will not fight against the Indians; we have now witnessed that in your own town, you have been forced to fly to your bed chambers, by a handful of men."[10]

The reference is to an upper-middle-class militia known mostly for its fine gray uniforms and parades, which excited children and young ladies. It is, however, interesting to note that *Anzeiger des Westens* failed to mention the other militia units of the time: the National Guard, the Continental Rangers, the Irish-dominated Washington Guard, or the German Pioneer Corp.

Rage and mob violence visited the streets of Saint Louis in the years to come. Frequently it was caused by politics, poisoned by xenophobia and religious bigotry. The targets were often Irish and German immigrants and Catholic institutions. In 1848, a new political party emerged, the Native American Party, made up of members of the Whig Party who felt their old political clout was waning as immigrants swelled the ranks of the Democratic Party. The mayor's office was a key battleground. In the election of 1841, a Whig businessman, John F. Daggett, ran against the Irish Democrat, Hugh O'Neill. The contest was won by the Whigs, but it scared them enough to turn to a radical nativist in the next go-around, Joseph Charless Jr. But moderate Whigs

---

10   James Neal Primm. *Lion of the Valley: St. Louis, Missouri, 1764 – 1980*. Saint Louis: Missouri Historical Society Press. P. 176.

would not go along. Ultimately, the Democrats took advantage of the Whig disarray and elected the first Democratic mayor in Saint Louis history, George Maguire, born in Ireland.

In 1843 the Democrats won again, this time with the German, John Wimer. Violence welled up in the national election of 1844. The Democrats chose a dark horse candidate, James K. Polk, two-time governor of Tennessee, but they also found their voice in a platform based on Manifest Destiny. They declared American political and cultural institutions superior to others and that God's will was made manifest by the creation of those institutions in the cauldron of the American Revolution and in the very geography of North America. The United States was intended to go "from sea to shining sea," Atlantic to Pacific, as far north as they cared to go and as far south as they dared. And that meant annexing the Republic of Texas and demanding all of the Oregon Territory to 54/40.

The Whigs rallied behind Kentucky's Henry Clay, "the Great Compromiser." They too fired up their base with slogans and rallies and boldfaced lies about their opponents. And this played into the hands of nativists and bigots. In this prism, everything seemed different. The influx of Irish and German immigrants was no longer seen as people escaping economic or political hardship, pursuing the American dream. No: these were hordes of Catholic invaders, set to take over the country by dominating the Democratic Party, by running the cities and gobbling up the best farmland. Catholic schools, universities, even hospitals were not to be seen as raising the general standards and health of the society; rather, they were to be feared as preparing priests and laity to take over the levers of commerce, law, medicine, journalism, and politics.

Money from the Society for the Propagation of the Faith and from the Leopoldine Society was not to be viewed as aid for catechesis or evangelization. This was foreign money, Catholic money, from Catholic monarchs set on influencing American culture and aiding the ultimate Catholic takeover of America.

Such were the ravings of Samuel F. B. Morse, Lyman Beecher, Elijah Lovejoy, and Rev. Robert Baird. Their ideas devolved into near-pornographic books, like Rebecca Reed's *Six Months in a Convent* and Maria Monk's *Awful Disclosure of the Hotel Dieu Nunnery*. The nativists went into the election of 1844 with threats and intimidation. A mob of an estimated 3,000 attacked Saint Louis University's medical school, destroying laboratories and furniture. Attempts were made to keep the foreign-born from voting. That same summer of 1844 saw the torching of churches in Philadelphia (the see of Peter Richard Kenrick's brother, Francis Patrick). Saint Michael's Church, the diocesan seminary, Saint Augustine's Church and its magnificent five-thousand volume library, were all torched. Over 30 Catholic homes were destroyed.

On May 29, 1849, an anti-Irish riot erupted in Saint Louis. A fire broke out on the riverfront among several steamboats. Tensions ran high as the Great Fire of 1849 had gutted much of the old city earlier that month on May 17. While several volunteer firefighting companies battled a blaze, a lone Irishman taunted them. This led to a fistfight, and supporters on both sides joined in throwing stones as well as fists.

Irish boatmen and dockworkers joined the fray as did hundreds of anti-Irish thugs. The police intervened and arrested the ringleaders of both sides, but that did nothing to disperse the mob. The Irish, considerably outnumbered, retreated for shelter in O'Brien's Saloon. That establishment then came under attack and was destroyed, as well as four other Irish businesses in the neighborhood. The scene was finally pacified when fifty volunteer police showed up. Even so, later that evening, the nativists returned to Battle Row to renew the fight, this time with a 6- inch howitzer. The police returned and eventually captured the gun, hidden in the Missouri Volunteer Firehouse.

In 1850, the Germans felt the nativist fury. On Election Day, rumors spread that Germans had taken over voting polls in the First Ward. Whig mobs strove into the First Ward, and fist fights ensued. When a crowd gathered after the polls closed and threatened to burn down German homes, the Germans fired into the mob from the rooftops. Whigs returned fire and torched one house before retreating. Violent outbursts had become part of the urban landscape of Saint Louis.

Death visited the city in another fashion, too. In 1832, several people died in Saint Louis sharing the same symptoms: diarrhea, stomach cramps, and vomiting, all leading to mass dehydration and organ failure with a collapse of the circulatory system. Most died between October 14 and 25. On October 23 alone, thirty people died. Two of the doctors treating the ill succumbed to the disease. The Sisters of Charity treated victims, and one young nun died while ministering. Winter brought a welcomed respite.

What Saint Louis experienced was its first outbreak of cholera. Various steps were taken to defend the population; the city was cleansed, pork sales were limited, and people were advised to wash vegetables and fruits with fresh water. The sick were bled, a treatment which did further harm. People complained of stagnant and fetid waters at Chouteau's Pond and a big sinkhole in the north part of the city, dubbed Kayser's Lake after the city engineer. None of this proved very effective, as the disease was spread by fecal matter of those infected, which might be transmitted by contaminated water. It could also be spread by houseflies and cockroaches.

The first cholera outbreak started in 1817, north of Calcutta, India. It spread rapidly through South Asia east to Southeast Asia, Singapore, and even to the islands of Java and Borneo. To the west it struck the Middle East all the way to Palestine and north into southern Russia, causing over two million deaths.

The second pandemic also began in India, first reported in 1826. By 1827, Russia again was hit, and Russian armies unwittingly carried cholera to Poland during the suppression of a rebellion. From there, it appeared in the German States, of Austria and Hungary. Cases were reported in Paris in 1832. Efforts to combat the disease with a hygiene campaign came under attack by the city poor, who rioted and set up barriers, allowing the disease to spread until the public became convinced of the true nature of the disease through responsible journalism. England, Spain, and Portugal also felt the force of the disease.

In June 1832, cases of cholera appeared in Canada, carried to the Western Hemisphere by Irish immigrants. Due to the rapid mortality of the disease and its short incubation period, most victims would either die or recover on the long, slow voyage to America. With steam-powered ships, the time at sea was reduced, allowing for the quick spread of the disease. Two authors said the following about the unpreparedness of cities to defend their populations: "...Crowded slums, limited and contaminated water supplies, hopelessly ineffective methods of eliminating sewage and garbage, and city governments ill-equipped to deal with the explosive growth of population."[11]

That describes Saint Louis in 1832. It is believed that cholera arrived in Saint Louis with soldiers sent to fight the Black Hawk War, as both soldiers and Indians came to die of the disease in greater numbers than from battle wounds.

Cholera reappeared in Saint Louis in May 1833 and continued to kill during the summer months. Saint Louis University abandoned its

---

11   Geoffrey Marks and William K. Beatty. *Epidemics.* New York: Charles Scribner's Sons. 1976. P. 200.

city campus and moved everyone to the Jesuit seminary in Florissant. In August, sixty people died in Saint Charles. Sister Amelia Ann, serving as a Sister of Charity at Mullanphy Hospital, died.

A third wave of cholera was forewarned by an outbreak in New Orleans in December 1848. Immigrants carried it north to cities along the Mississippi and Ohio Rivers. The notion of quarantine had not yet been raised.

Weekly tallies of cholera deaths began on April 30, with forty-one victims. The death toll rose rapidly, and from June 18 to July 23, no fewer than 400 people died each week, 2,842 dying in a five-week period.

Public schools were turned into hospitals. Convinced that the disease was borne on fruit and vegetables, the city government forbade the sale of all produce and mandated all-meat meals. A body of doctors urged the city fathers that produce was healthier, and the city reversed itself. Three doctors died in this 1849 outbreak. Two Sisters of Charity died at their hospital treating 1,330 cases of cholera, of which 510 of the victims died. So many children were orphaned that the city hospital took them in. When the city council voted on $1,000 to temporarily house them, Mayor Barry suggested the money be given to Archbishop Kenrick, who had already begun to address the needs of the orphans.

In this epidemic, Saint Louis saw the second-largest devastation among major American cities. Only New York City, seven times larger in population, lost more people. In the midst of this calamity, as if it were not enough, the Great Fire of 1849 broke out.

On the evening of May 17, 1849, members of the crew of the *White Cloud* steamboat had just finished applying a fresh coat of paint and were waiting for the strong wind out of the Northeast to dry it. It is rumored that a passing steamboat belched fire out of its chimneys, and fiery particles were carried by the wind onto the *White Cloud,* which then caught fire around 10 PM.

The fire quickly spread to the *Edward Bates* next to the *White Cloud.* The second boat went up in flames and ignited the *Eudora.* A standard procedure for steamboat fires was to set the craft adrift to burn themselves out in the Mississippi. This was attempted by the crew of the *Edward Bates.* As it drifted out into the current, however, the strong wind from the northeast actually carried the boat back to the levee. The *Edward Bates* acted like some enemy fire ship and set ablaze thirteen other boats along the levee.

There were cases of gunpowder on several ships, and these exploded with a terrible report, sending chunks of fiery wood in all directions.

Saint Louis did not have a dock or wharf system. Instead, the boats pulled their nose first onto the levee and dropped their gangplanks for off-loading and on-loading of goods and passengers. When the river was high, as it was that May, there was less levee space between the boats and the warehouses that stood before the levee. Goods had to be piled higher and closer for the early process of embarking the next day. Just when the wind blew the fire from the steamboats onto the levee, the conflagration expanded. Two thousand bales of hemp erupted in flames and caught nearby houses on fire. Four people who had been sleeping on those bales were immediately consumed.

Once the warehouses were on fire, it spread west to Second Street and southward along Locust to Elm. As all of the English language newspapers were located in this area, the city lost temporarily any way of keeping up with events. The one newspaper to survive was a German-language paper. Commercial offices, homes, warehouses, taverns and restaurants, and hotels were all consumed. Firms like L. A. Benoist and Company, Sublette and Campbell Company, Pierre Chouteau, Junior, Cabanné, Rasin and Company, Berthold and Ewing, saw total losses. Hundreds of workers lost their jobs. By 4 AM the wind shifted, sending the fire over the burned-out ruins. Without fresh fuel, the fire could be contained. This happened around 8 AM. Pine, Chestnut, and Market Streets were in ruins. To starve the fire, some people blew up houses in the fire's path. The attempt caused the only casualty of the Great Fire, Thomas B. Targee. The volunteer firefighter carried a keg of gunpowder into a burning building to blow it up and stop the fire as it raced toward the Cathedral. The keg exploded before Targee could escape the building. Later, fifty people were arrested for looting, but most Saint Louisans acted honorably, honestly, and even heroically. The next day, as wood smoldered and stones were hot to the touch, people began to remove the rubble and prepared to rebuild the commercial center of the city. Remarkably, Bishop Rosati's Cathedral was untouched by the conflagration that had raged around it.

As shocking as the murder of Francis McIntosh by an angry crowd was, as fatal as the cholera epidemics of 1832, 1833 and 1849 were, as devastating as the Great Flood of 1844 was, when the Mississippi swelled to twelve miles wide, destroying businesses and mills to Second Street, as horrifying as the Great Fire of 1849 was, it was the collapse of a bridge in central Missouri which would be the most ruinous of the prospects of Saint Louis to be the premier city of the Midwest. It happened on the Feast of All Saints, 1855.

What happened on November 1, 1855, could be called a tale of two bridges, or a tale of two cities, or a tale of two views of slavery in America. It reeks of irony and pathos and hubris, and it set the course of development of both Saint Louis and Chicago for a century to come.

Despite its love affair with steamboats, Saint Louis was attracted to rail travel too, seeing itself as the railhead to all points west: to the West Coast and even across the Pacific to India. One historian showed the regional interests coming together in a national rail plan. Each region now specialized in a particular type of economic activity. The South raised cotton for export to New England and Europe; the West grew grain and livestock to feed southern slaves and eastern factory workers; New Englanders made machines and textiles for the other two regions.[12]

Saint Louisans bet on the Pacific Railroad as the key to the West. Secretary of War Jefferson Davis found graft among its directors, though. Regardless, a maiden trip took place from Saint Louis to Washington, Missouri, in February 1855. It was only a fifty-four mile trip, but boosters gave it an aura of the first step to the Pacific Ocean. Railroad interests lobbied for more support to extend the line to the state capital, Jefferson City, and right to the border with Kansas.

The next leg of the trip, meant to impress state legislators and encourage them to release more funds, was scheduled for November 1, 1855. A star-studded array of passengers boarded the 8:30 AM train. The arrival time in Jefferson City was 3 PM. Bands, politicians, and plenty of food and beverages were arranged to meet them at the state capital. Interestingly, no Catholic clergy attended. They had All Saints duties, a holy day of obligation.

As the train chugged along, no one on board knew that the bridge over the Gasconade River had not been completed. The firm Stone & Boomer of Chicago was behind schedule, and rather than inform the Pacific Railroad and cause a delay, they constructed a "false work bridge," that is to say, a timber construction across the piers with the

---

12   Thomas A. Bailey. *The American Pageant: A History of the Republic.* Lexington: D. C. Heath and Company. 1979. P. 286-287.

rails nailed to a pine lumber base.

The construction firm was confident the bridge would hold; the event pulled off faultlessly, no one the wiser. (Later, the firm could complete the structure properly.) They even drove a train full of gravel over it in the morning and it held. They were confident the pouring rain would not compromise their work.

As the train approached the Gasconade River Bridge, it slowed down so passengers could see the structure. What they saw was something else. Here Adam Arenson describes in *The Great Heart of the Republic* the terrible scene:

What came instead was a slow-motion horror. With 10 of the 14 cars on the false work, it gave way, sending them crashing down into the rocks and mud of the riverbed. The engine was catapulted onto the head long dive; other cars twisted and turned, many of the last being pulled down the embankment by their connectors. A survivor remembered the crash – crash – crash as each car came to the abutment and took the fatal plunge. The rain continued, the merciless pouring of the rain, as the Missouri Democrat *put it, the roar and flash of angry tempest mingling with the cries of the wounded and dying. Survivors sought out the injured and searched the rubble for their varied companions. Groans came from within the indistinguishable mass of wooden beams, seats, iron wheels and rods. The cars had come apart, revealing devastation. Some of the militia companies on board began the sad work of collecting the dead. No triumphant entry into Jefferson City would occur that day.*[13]

By late afternoon the news reached Saint Louis by way of steamboats on the Missouri River. By 5 PM, the wounded as well as the dead were transported back to Hermann, Missouri. The scene was made all the more grim as a steady downpour continued. The train station was commandeered to be used as a morgue. Names of the deceased filtered back to Saint Louis: Thomas O'Sullivan, the railroad engineer who had planned the trip, Thomas O'Flaherty, the steamboat captain who had attended early Mass that day, two state legislators, the president of the city council, the keynote speaker for the day, Reverend Artemas Bullard, and Henry Pierre Chouteau. In all, seventy were injured and thirty killed. These included Hudson E. Bridge and Wayman Crow, trustees of Washington University and the Mercantile Library.

---

13   Adam Arenson. *The Great Heart of the Republic: St. Louis and the Cultural Civil War.* Cambridge: Harvard University Press. 2011. P. 72.

Injured was Wilson Primm, local historian and lawyer.

The next several days were somber in Saint Louis and in Jefferson City. A funeral Mass was set for Henry Chouteau, whose body was so disfigured that he could only be identified by the ticket in his pocket. Archbishop Kenrick buried Thomas O'Flaherty. The *Democrat* commented on the recent tragedies which had befallen Saint Louis: "...fire and flood and pestilence they have withstood," but this Gasconade tragedy "caused a panic that we have never before witnessed."[14]

It took four months before a train could travel safely from Saint Louis to Jefferson City, but there was no ceremony that time. The momentum was lost.

It is a bitter irony for Saint Louis that the same firm which botched the railroad bridge over the Gasconade River, Stone & Boomer of Chicago, successfully built railroad bridges over the Mississippi River connecting Rock Island with both Illinois and Iowa. Four and a half months after the Gasconade disaster, a train rode for the first time over the Mississippi River, ultimately connecting Chicago with Saint Joseph, Missouri. This came by way of a line supported by Chicago financial interests, which built a trans-Missouri rail from Hannibal to Saint Joseph. It was now just a jump to Omaha and the whole Platte River Valley. This line would be the connector from Maine, through New England, across the New York canal grid, the railroad nexus of Ohio, Indiana and Illinois, across northern Missouri and Kansas, drawing in Iowa, Nebraska, the Dakotas, Montana and Wyoming, and all points west. Chicago would become the keystone of the transcontinental rail system, while Saint Louis received a spur brought down from Hannibal.

Arenson observes that hanging in the balance was not only the future of Saint Louis commerce, but also the implications of settlement of the West. Would the West be free of slavery or open to the extension of "the peculiar institution?" Was armed conflict inevitable, or could the issue so divisive between North and South be settled by a creative Western solution? The collapse of the Gasconade Bridge and the successful transit over the Rock Island Bridges removed that question forever. A creative Saint Louis solution, the one brewing in the minds of Saint Louis politicians like Thomas Hart Benson and Benjamin Gratz Brown, would not be available for serious national discourse. 1850s

---

14   Adam Arenson. *The Great Heart of the Republic: St. Louis and the Cultural Civil War.* Cambridge: Harvard University Press. 2011. P. 76.

America appeared to be on a course leading to a national train wreck called the Civil War. The Gasconade tragedy seemed an apt metaphor for what would happen to the United States in less than five years:

> *The collapse at Gasconade and the successful bridge at Rock Island symbolized how, after the passage of the Kansas-Nebraska Act, the missing rail from St. Louis prevented advocates from promoting a vision of westward expansion built on moderate antislavery in Kansas. By February 1857, the implications were obvious to St. Louis politician Benjamin Gratz Brown. He rose in the state legislature to warn that commerce now flowed "into Northern and Southern routes," bypassing St. Louis and its program for the West. The national bounty was slipping away from St. Louis. "Soon its outpost will be at Council Bluffs," Brown intoned, "and its emporium at Chicago." Brown blamed this loss on pro-slavery Missourians and their meddling in Kansas. And he proposed a radical response: a plan for gradual emancipation in Missouri.*
>
> *In arguing that slavery would ruin St. Louis and cause the loss of the railroad route, Brown was shading the truth. Inadequate financing and sheer bad luck played their parts, but Brown spoke only of the role of slaveholders. As when Horace Greeley turned the phrase and created "Bleeding Kansas," Brown pressed an image to incite action, not to document history. His immediate aim was to prevent more roadblocks from pro-slavery politicians and to secure a federal commitment to a railroad through Missouri, not necessarily to free slaves. He responded to the sense that, in the era of popular sovereignty, conflict over slavery had swallowed all other issues. Brown's slavery proposal was prescient: at that very moment, the U. S. Supreme Court was ready to decide the fate of Dred and Harriet Scott and their daughters, a St. Louis slave family. Once again a national decree would overturn the hard-won balance in St. Louis.[15]*

---

15   Adam Arenson. *The Great Heart of the Republic: St. Louis and the Cultural Civil War.* Cambridge: Harvard University Press. 2011. P. 79-81.

There is no known portrait of Father Ambrose Heim. He rests at Calvary Cemetery in north St. Louis. The epitaph on the opposite side reads, "R.I.P. Rev. Ambrose J Heim, Spiritual Director of the first conference of the St. Vincent de Paul Society founded in North America at St. Louis, Mo. Nov. 14, 1845; A tribute to his memory by the St. Louis members, May 1909." Photograph courtesy of Susan Ing.

Close-up of the Cathedral (with star icon) on Walnut between Second and Third Streets. From *Compton and Dry's Pictorial St. Louis, the Great Metropolis of the Mississippi Valley: A Topographical Survey Drawn in Perspective A.D. 1875* (St. Louis: Compton & Co., 1876).

21

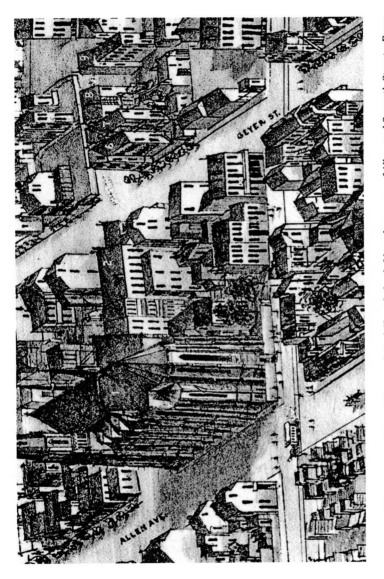

Close-up of the immense Saints Peter and Paul Church (on left) at the corner of Allen and Seventh Streets. From *Compton and Dry's Pictorial St. Louis, the Great Metropolis of the Mississippi Valley: A Topographical Survey Drawn in Perspective A.D. 1875* (St. Louis: Compton & Co., 1876).

Archbishop Peter Richard Kenrick, circa 1891. Archdiocese of
St. Louis Archives and Records.

Rt. Rev. Msgr. Francis de Sales Goller

R. I. P.

Father Francis Goller. Archdiocese of St. Louis Archives and Records.

24

Front steps and portico of the St. Louis Mullanphy Hospital. Photograph circa 1906. Image from the Bernard Becker Medical Library, Washington University School of Medicine. ID VC323012.

Saint Mary of Victories Church circa 1900 (top) and 1988 (bottom). Archdiocese of St. Louis Archives and Records.

A Sister of Charity sits with nurses at the Mullanphy Hospital, established by the Sisters of Charity in 1828. Photograph circa 1907. Image from the Bernard Becker Medical Library, Washington University School of Medicine. ID VC323035.

Lithograph depiction of the Great Fire of 1849 in St. Louis, by Currier & Ives. Image from Library of Congress Prints and Photographs Division in Washington, D.C. Digital ID: CPH 3A08625U.

Chapter Two

THE KENRICK BROTHERS

For two Catholic bishops of two of America's largest dioceses, surprisingly little is written about Francis Patrick and Peter Richard Kenrick. One of the more substantial pieces was penned by John Joseph O'Shea in his 1904 double biography of the two Kenricks. The preface, as well as the imprimatur, came by way of Patrick John Ryan, Archbishop of Philadelphia, long-time collaborator with Peter Richard Kenrick. He admitted that he himself had wanted to write the biographies, but the weight of his office kept him away from the task. Ryan lauded the efforts of the biographer, who "did not know them personally and can judge without bias."[16]

O'Shea thanked both Cardinal James Gibbons and Archbishop John Joseph Kain for their cooperation and insight, as well as access granted to diocesan archives. Several secondary sources were cited, as well as academics at Saint Charles Seminary, Overbrook, and sources in Ireland. Each biography was written separately, requiring the reader to meld the lives of the two brothers. The rhetorical style is flourishing and flowery, like many hagiographies of the day. Biographical facts are buried deep in the text and need to be mined.

The Kenrick brothers came from the sturdy, devout family of Thomas Kenrick of Number 16 Chancery Lane, Dublin. Francis Patrick was nine years older than Peter Richard. Both worked in their father's office doing scrivener's work, copying out documents with great care and in great detail. Joining them was an Irish poet, James Clarence Mangan, who took a liking to the younger brother and tutored Peter Richard in the German language.

When Francis Patrick presented himself to his bishop as a candidate for priesthood, he was selected to study in Rome at the Propaganda College. Here, John Joseph O'Shea tells us, the discerning eye of Rome saw "great qualities in the young seminarian, specifically the mind to conceive, the genius to plan, the patience to endure, and the

---

16   John J. O'Shea. *The Two Kenricks: Most Rev. Francis Patrick, Archbishop of Baltimore, and Most Rev. Peter Richard, Archbishop of Saint Louis.* Philadelphia: John J. McVey. 1903. P. vi.

charity to conquer." [17]

Francis Patrick excelled in his studies of Scripture and the early Church Fathers. When a call came from Bishop Benedict Flaget of Bardstown for missionaries to go to America, the rector of Propaganda recommended newly ordained Francis Patrick as professor of theology to Bardstown Theological Seminary.

An interesting exchange took place between the rector of the college and the newly appointed Prefect of *Propaganda Fide*, Cardinal Leta. O'Shea describes the encounter: when he saw the rector for the first time after the appointment had been made, the Prefect reproached him with some vehemence for sending one so young to a place where not only ripe experience and scholarship were demanded, but great physical endurance as well. The old rector defended vigorously the fitness of his protégé, insisting that his virtues and talents were sufficient for any requirement. Still the Prefect demurred; the extreme youth of the nominee appeared to him a fatal defect. Had he been Prefect at the time, the cardinal said, the appointment would never have been made. The rector fired up on hearing this and blurted out his sentiments unceremoniously: "Well then, Your Eminence, it was the Providence of God that prevented your appointment sooner!" The cardinal somewhat indignantly asked him to explain himself. "I mean that if you had been Prefect of Propaganda sooner," replied the sturdy old rector, "you would have deprived America of an Apostle."[18]

Francis Patrick taught for nine years at the Bardstown seminary, preparing young men for the priesthood in a land unfamiliar with and often hostile to Catholicism. One line of attack against the Church came by way of articles in local newspapers written by Protestant ministers questioning Catholic beliefs. Kenrick replied to articles written by "Omega," a pseudonym for Dr. Rev. Blackburn of Danville Presbyterian College, reducing him to silence. The Protestant cause was championed next by a Methodist minister, then an Anglican, then another Presbyterian. The last of these contests were public debates, which ended with the Protestant audience applauding the Catholic priest. Eventually the fruits of the debates became apparent with over fifty conversions.

---

17   John J. O'Shea. *The Two Kenricks: Most Rev. Francis Patrick, Archbishop of Baltimore, and Most Rev. Peter Richard, Archbishop of Saint Louis.* Philadelphia: John J. McVey. 1903. P. 32.
18   Ibid. P. 39.

In 1829, Francis Patrick Kenrick accompanied Bishop Flaget to Baltimore for the Provincial Council as his theologian. A key topic was trusteeism, which proved providential, as Rome soon selected Francis Patrick as coadjutor of the diocese of Philadelphia.

The consecration took place in Bardstown on June 6, 1830, the feast of the Holy Trinity. Present were Bishop Flaget, Bishop David, coadjutor of Louisville, John England of Charleston, South Carolina, Bishop Fenwick of Cincinnati and, of course, Bishop Conwell of Philadelphia.

When the 34-year-old Kenrick showed someone the document of his appointment, they responded, "Behold here, the certificate of the cross you will have to carry." The recent history of the Philadelphia diocese bore out the prophecy.

In 1808, Philadelphia was split from the mother diocese of Baltimore with Franciscan Michael Egan as its first bishop. There were only four parishes in the city, and the consecration was delayed until 1810 because the trustees of the four parishes refused to pay for the consecration and installation expenses and declined further to financially support their new Bishop. Only when Saint Mary's trustees set aside $400 a year for their Bishop and two other parishes agreed to pay $200 each annually did the consecration take place: in Baltimore, at the behest of Archbishop John Carroll.

Arriving at Saint Mary's Church, Bishop Egan met with the trustees, who refused to pay any part of the installation expenses and further demanded that one priest be dismissed to save a salary, as they now were obliged to pay for a bishop. Egan went over the trustees' heads and appealed to the general congregation, the pew holders, which led to a protest by the trustees and eventually an appeal to the Pennsylvania legislature for an alteration of Saint Mary's charter. That move proved unsuccessful, but conflicts continued until Bishop Egan's death in July 1814. He was a broken man, not only in his conflicts with the late trustees, but in the lack of trust between him and some of his clergy.

Philadelphia was in such disarray that the see sat vacant for nearly six years, which gave oxygen to feed the flames of an Irish priest, William Hogan. He was the darling of the Saint Mary's trustees and had great fun lampooning the diocesan administrator, a German, Father Louis de Barth.

Henry Conwell was the second Bishop of Philadelphia. He was a priest and Vicar-General of the diocese of Armagh, Ireland. He was offered the choice of Philadelphia or Madras, India. Friends tried to persuade him to refuse both. He was 63 years old, a gentle man given to academic study. Bishop Conwell chose Philadelphia and was consecrated in England in December 1820. He arrived in his new see with a young seminarian and almost immediately became the butt of Father Hogan's sarcasm.

When Bishop Conwell found that Hogan had bullied the administrator, Father de Barth, into giving him faculties, Conwell promptly removed them. The trustees of Saint Mary's parish rallied to Father Hogan's side, and Hogan wrote letters to the bishops of Boston and Cincinnati trying to build support. The trustees struck hard, dismissing clergy from their Board, electing Hogan as their pastor, and barring the Bishop from his cathedral. They even wrote an open letter to all Catholics in America encouraging the formation of an independent Catholic Church.

Bishop Conwell responded by excommunicating Hogan in 1821. Fistfights broke out on the streets in front of Saint Mary's. The police were called in. Even Pope Pius VII got involved with the letter denouncing the trustees. Amid all the tensions, Hogan and the trustees turned on each other, and in the summer of 1824, William Hogan announced that he was leaving the priesthood to marry. The rest of his life was a whirlwind: two marriages, the management of a circus, a stint as a lawyer, a U. S. government agent, and always a popular speaker on anti-Catholic topics.

Peace came between Bishop Conwell and the trustees when the Bishop agreed to a contract which recognized certain rights of the trustees. This agreement was rejected by the Roman Congregation of the Propaganda of the Faith, and Bishop Conwell was called to Rome. He returned to Philadelphia with a coadjutor, Francis Patrick Kenrick, who administrated the diocese for him until his death two years later.

Francis Patrick Kenrick inherited a diocese with four parishes, an orphanage, a few schools, and 25,000 disheartened Catholics. Outside of Philadelphia the diocese boasted several small mission parishes; few had churches, most had log cabins that doubled as chapels. Saintly Father Gallitzin, a prince from Europe, had settled down at Loretto, a remote village in the Alleghenies, where he lived out a holy life. It was estimated that the Catholic population of the rural parts of the diocese was as high as 75,000, but few had regular access to clergy.

The young prelate was not discouraged. His years in Bardstown, where he contested with Protestant ministers and academics, prepared him to counter the schismatic trustees who used many of the same Protestant arguments to justify their disobedience. Soon their side was overwhelmed by Bishop Kenrick's sheer activity. Kenrick had no sooner arrived in Philadelphia than he left for a tour of his diocese. At Wilmington, he confirmed orphans in the care of the Sisters of Charity. At Pleasant Mills, New Jersey, he consecrated a new cemetery and a church. At Reading, he confirmed many. At Pottsville, the bishop withdrew the faculties of a pastor for the offense of simony. He then continued on with more confirmations until he was overwhelmed by a fever.

In the absence of the bishop, the trustees of Saint Mary's parish asked trustees of other parishes to vote a salary for Bishop Kenrick. But this was less an olive branch than a stick to prod old Bishop Conwell mercilessly. Bishop Kenrick did not rise to the bait. Instead, he returned to Philadelphia to announce that he was appointing himself the pastor of Saint Mary's and then naming his own assistant pastor.

Upon this news the trustees revolted, and Bishop Kenrick placed the parish of Saint Mary's under interdict as the recent decree of the Baltimore Council dictated. At the last Mass offered at Saint Mary's, Bishop Kenrick made full use of the pulpit and won over most of the parishioners. The trustees called a meeting the next evening for all parishioners, but the meeting was dashed when Bishop Kenrick walked in.

With one last attempt at bravado, the trustees turned to Bishop Conwell to effect a compromise. The old bishop, previously burned by such an attempt, stayed aloof. With this the trustees gave up their fight, and Bishop Kenrick lifted the interdict on his cathedral.

This struggle became a major turning point in the history of trusteeism in the Catholic Church in America. The development of the bishop as "corporate sole" was underway, as all bequests in the future would be made in his name. When Kenrick arrived at the recently renovated Saint Paul's in Pittsburgh later that year, he found a newly elected Board of Trustees. Before the rededication ceremony began, the bishop vetoed the act. He announced that there would be no more trustees in his diocese. The congregation went silent, disapproving, but became obedient in their silence. Bishop Patrick Francis Kenrick had spoken with authority, and they knew it.

Trusteeism defeated, Bishop Kenrick turned to another challenge in his diocese: a lack of clergy. He counted a diverse crew; four French, three German, two Belgian, one Russian, one Livonian, one Englishman, three Americans, and twenty-one Irish. He needed a seminary, and he already had a building.

During the trustee controversy, Kenrick lived in a house near the church, as he was unable to occupy the rectory. He now put the house under the patronage of Saint Charles Borromeo and opened it to four young men contemplating a vocation to holy orders. The project grew and the little seminary had to be moved and then moved again. On September 30, 1833, help arrived. Newly-ordained Father Peter Richard Kenrick arrived in Philadelphia to help his brother run the seminary of ten young men.

Peter Richard Kenrick was 29 years old when he arrived in America. He shared with his brother a serious studiousness. His seminary was the famed Maynooth, outside of Dublin. After ordination, he was assigned to the cathedral in Dublin and after a few months to a parish in Rathmines. At first, he considered going to Paris to join the Vincentians, but family matters interfered; caring for his widowed mother kept them close to home.

After his mother's death, a letter from his brother, the Bishop of Philadelphia, was all Peter Richard needed to seek release from Ireland to come to America.

Father Peter Richard Kenrick served as seminary rector for two years, afterwards turning over control to two rectors in quick succession until a grant was secured from the Leopoldine Society; in 1841, Saint Charles Borromeo Seminary came under the direction of the Vincentians, with the enrollment stabilizing around 30.

In the meantime, Bishop Francis Patrick Kenrick came to rely more and more on Peter Richard, first as rector of the cathedral, then as Vicar-General of the diocese. He became editor of the diocesan newspaper, the *Catholic Herald*, and found time to publish two books, *The New Month of Mary* and *The History of the Holy House of Loretto*. Also during these years, Peter Richard Kenrick took up the question of the validity of the Anglican orders, which led to a continuing exchange of articles defining the argument.

Briefly, Peter Richard Kenrick considered joining the Society of Jesus. He traveled to Rome in 1840 without the wholehearted support of his brother. It seems Francis Patrick had written a very complimentary letter on his behalf, but Peter Richard failed to give these to the

Jesuit superior, thinking it too laudatory. As a result, Peter Richard did not use this letter and so had no recommendations from his bishop. Based on that fact, Peter Richard was refused admission to the Jesuits and quietly returned to service in Philadelphia. There he met the Bishop of Saint Louis, Joseph Rosati, attending a Baltimore Council.

Bishop Rosati pressed Peter Richard to accept the position as coadjutor for Saint Louis, and the two traveled to Rome, returning with Roman approval on November 18, 1841. Traveling from the port of Boston to Philadelphia, the two prepared for the consecration twelve days later. Bishop Rosati acted as consecrating prelate while Francis Patrick and Bishop Lefevre of Detroit were assisting bishops. Also attending was Bishop John England of Charleston.

Later, Coadjutor Peter Richard Kenrick would become Bishop Kenrick, Ordinary, and then Archbishop of Saint Louis. His brother Francis Patrick Kenrick would be transferred to become Archbishop of Baltimore, each exerting great influence on the development of the Catholic Church in America. At that point in Catholic history, the Kenrick brothers were the only two Archbishops in America.

Bishop Kenrick's initial assessment of his new realm seems not to have been all that positive. In letters to his brother, the Bishop of Philadelphia, and reports to Bishop Rosati, he painted a stark picture, especially regarding finances.

Initially, Saint Louis gave the Irish immigrant a cultural shock. French was still widely spoken, and sermons at the cathedral were delivered in French. The old Creole families still held a prominent place, but their fur trading days were numbered, and many were cashing in on real estate deals instead. More and more German and Irish were arriving, and it was not unusual to see an occasional Indian on the city streets. Almost immediately, Kenrick found himself faced with a civil suit regarding some $4,600 Rosati had borrowed for a man who disappeared with the funds. The cathedral Rosati built was the source of a huge debt, and much of the service was at high interest rates of 8% and 10%. In one letter, Kenrick complained that he was being crushed with a debt upwards of $53,000, $18,000 of which was borrowed at 10%. He estimated the annual income of the diocese to be only $7,500.

To the Bishop of Cincinnati, the Saint Louis Coadjutor described his cathedral as "an injudicious combination of ancient style and modern innovation."[19] The interior window frames had not yet been painted. Ventilation was poor, making the building damp, dark, and cold; the plaster walls were cracking. The furnace was wholly useless.

Kenrick counted his assets as liabilities. He distrusted the Jesuit community at Saint Louis University and saw their intentions to build Saint Francis Xavier Church as a naked grab to steal English-speaking parishioners from the cathedral. One of his first acts was to discontinue French sermons and adopt English, though he acknowledged "displeasing a few old ladies."

Kenrick proposed using all the monies coming from European mission societies to pay off debt, especially the high interest notes. And his appeals had their effect. In 1842, he had in hand $2,300 as a gift from the Leopoldine Society in Vienna and nearly $3,500 from the Society for the Propagation of the Faith in Lyon.

It was in 1842 that Bishop Kenrick began a tour of his diocese. He took a paddle boat south to New Madrid and explored the new State of Arkansas, but found only one priest in the whole state. He traveled through southern Missouri and arrived at the seminary at Saint Mary's of the Barrens. He marveled at the size of his diocese and remarked to his brother the need to subdivide it as soon as possible. Francis Patrick understood the sentiment well, as he too was seeking to divide his diocese of Pennsylvania into two, with Pittsburgh being the daughter to Philadelphia.

In June, Peter Richard Kenrick took another steamboat, this time up the Missouri River, and visited Westport, Kansas City, and Sugar Creek, where he confirmed three hundred Potawatomi. For the remainder of the year Kenrick continued his tours, though closer to Saint Louis.

Bishop Kenrick also complained of the lack of priests, especially those capable of speaking German, and of few seminarians. He counted only six diocesan candidates at the Barrens. A scheme to establish a diocesan seminary under the directions of the Society of Saint Viator failed, and Kenrick insisted that candidates for the "petit seminaire" pay their own way. As he put it, "we shall be spared the expensive experiment of educating at our own costs youth who afterwards—when their education is finished—discover that they have no vocation."[20]

---

19   Kenrick to Purcell. St. Louis, Feb. 2, 1842. Manuscript Collection, University of Notre Dame.
20   Kenrick to Purcell. St. Louis. August 28, 1842. Manuscript Collection, University of Notre Dame.

In all this doom and gloom, Bishop Kenrick might have counted his blessings. Unlike his brother, he was not plagued with trustee-ism. Saint Louis Catholics were docile, if not generous. He got his way about languages spoken at the cathedral without much pushback. He himself refused to use the common practice of pew rents, cutting off an easy source of revenue. Kenrick's diocese was blessed with the Society of the Sacred Heart, the Jesuits, and the Vincentians. There were among the laity those whose wealth could be tapped for the right cause. There was a pool of devout men and women whose zeal for the gospel just needed to be enkindled.

Between Peter Richard Kenrick's attendance at the Fifth Provincial Council of Baltimore in 1843 and the Sixth Provincial Council of Baltimore in 1846, several events shaped the bishop's life. One was a blessing in disguise. Kenrick suffered two carriage accidents during that time, escaping both without serious injury. He spent one winter in New Orleans to regain his strength, overcoming an illness probably caused by his exhaustive schedule. He established a Catholic periodical entitled *The Catholic Cabinet,* which his brother criticized as "a museum of curiosities," predicting it would find no readership on the East Coast. The paper folded in under two years. Peter Richard expanded his scholarship by proofreading and adding to Francis Patrick's theological works and began a study of the book of Genesis. In October 1843, he received the news of the death of Bishop Joseph Rosati.

In a letter to Bishop Purcell of Cincinnati, Kenrick admitted "experience cannot be acquired by books or observation; at least the only way I have picked up a few crumbs of it has been by blundering through excess of self-confidence."

One example of not blundering came in his acceptance and later his confidence in a gift from Bishop Rosati, Father Joseph Melcher. When Bishop Rosati began his second trip to Haiti from Rome, he got no further than Paris when his final illness overcame him. His traveling companion was Father Joseph Melcher, whom he had met in Rome. To Bishop Kenrick, Bishop Rosati wrote, "I have found an excellent traveling companion in the person of an excellent German priest, whom I met in Rome. He is so attentive to me and so full of activity and intelligence, that I have unloaded all the cares of the journey upon him."[21]

Joseph Melcher was indeed an extraordinary gift to Saint Louis.

21   Rev. John Rothensteiner. *History of the Archdiocese of St. Louis.* St. Louis: Black-well Wielandy Co. 1928. Vol. II. P. 6.

Born in Vienna in 1807, Joseph was the son of an Austrian Imperial diplomat assigned to the principality of Modena. He grew up as fluent in Italian as in German and learned Latin as a young man when he read the breviary for a partially blind priest. In 1830, Joseph Melcher was ordained a priest and earned a doctorate in divinity. For twelve years, Father Melcher led a quiet, scholarly life, serving as chaplain to the court of Modena as well as the small German-speaking community there. But his soul burned for more.

Melcher applied to *Propaganda Fide* in Rome for a mission assignment, but was told that secular priests were not to be accepted. It was on that trip to Rome that Father Melcher met Bishop Rosati, who eagerly agreed to incardinate him into the Saint Louis diocese. At first blush, Bishop Kenrick's encounter with Father Melcher was one of the bishop's blunders. Here was the German-speaking priest whom he had been begging for. Instead, Father Melcher was dispatched first to Little Rock and later to Mattese Creek, where there was no church and no residence.

Father Melcher's time there was a true test of his soul. Just a year earlier, he had served at a prince's court in Italy, with all the food, clothing, entertainment, and refinement of European nobility. Now he was pastor of a nothing-place. He befriended the neighbors. They built him a log cabin, furnished him with a box for a writing table and wood blocks for chairs. He slept on a hardwood floor and ate as a guest at parishioners' houses, each family taking turns feeding their priest. And yet, Father Melcher was happy as a clam.

In 1846, Bishop Kenrick was preparing for a trip to Baltimore for the Sixth Provincial Council. That is when he reversed his blunder. He remembered he had a priest fluent in German, Italian, and Latin, and he was rapidly learning English. This priest was a doctor of divinity. Father Melcher was invited to accompany Bishop Kenrick to the Baltimore Council, and having been made one of the Archdiocesan Vicars-General, was dispatched to Europe to find more German-speaking priests. In all, there would be three recruiting trips: 1846, 1849, and 1864. Melcher's men, at least to those who persevered in their vocations, would be leaven for Saint Louis dough.

The first trip yielded four priests and twelve seminarians, seven of whom were ordained. These included Joseph Meister, pastor at Apple Creek, Jefferson City, and Boonville. After his transfer to Indiana, Father Meister was victim of a falling tree, which killed him. Francis Rutkowski was pastor of Saint Peter's in Dardenne and built the church there. Father Francis Xavier Weiss was longtime pastor at Sainte Genevieve, 57 years. Father John Anselm served as pastor at Most Holy Trinity in north Saint Louis and later became the first resident priest at French Village. Joseph Blaarer had a wandering heart, serving one year as pastor in Jefferson City, making visits to Deep Water and Zell, and taking the post at Mattese Creek before returning to Switzerland. Lewis Rossi was the founder of Saint Philomena, which is now Saint Agnes in Bloomsdale. He drowned while crossing a creek to bring the last rites to a dying man. Francis Trojan was sent to Apple Creek and later became a professor of music at the college in Cape Girardeau. Later he was made pastor at Saint John Nepomuk in south Saint Louis and finished his priestly life in Chester, Illinois.

On his first trip to Europe, Father Melcher also secured a commitment from the Ursuline nuns in Oldenburg, Hungary. The house superior herself, Mother Madeleine Stehlin, came along with Mother Marian von Pann and Mother Augustine Stragl. Traveling through Bavaria, they stayed at an Ursuline convent and were joined by a postulant, Rosine Bruiding.

When the Ursulines arrived in Baltimore, they were surprised and enchanted to find Bishop Peter Richard Kenrick there to greet them, as well as the Baltimore Archbishop, Saint John Neumann. Coming to Saint Louis on October 4, they were guests of the Visitation sisters for a month until they found their own home and opened their school on November 2, 1848.

The next year, six more Ursulines arrived, and the King of Bavaria sent them $4,000 to found their convent and promised an annual gift of $600 from the *Ludwig Missionverein*. Ursuline success in Saint Louis led to a foundation in Alton, Illinois, and another was established in Saint Paul, Missouri.

Upon completion of the successful recruiting trip, Father Melcher was rewarded with a pastorate, replacing Father Joseph Fisher at Saint Mary of Victories. Father Fisher stayed on as the assistant. And Father Melcher needed assistance: he retained his role as Vicar-General for the German community while Father Francis Cellini was the vicar for the English-speakers.

Saint Mary's congregation proved to be less docile than might be expected. When Father Melcher planned for a large rectory, parishioners complained to the Archbishop. Kenrick ignored their pleas and approved the rectory plans. The next year Father Melcher was again engaged in building. This was the establishment of the German Orphans Home, as the two other Catholic orphanages could barely accommodate the English-speaking community after another cholera outbreak took away scores of parents.

On May 10, 1849, Father Melcher began his second recruiting tour of Europe. It would reap him ten priests, many destined to be leaders in Saint Louis.

Two years earlier, on July 20, 1847, Saint Louis was raised to the honor of an Archdiocese. This caused eyebrows to be raised in New Orleans, and even Natchez and Pittsburgh, where friend and Bishop Michael O'Connor assumed that Francis Patrick had used influence to win his brother the pallium. There is no evidence of that, though Francis Patrick did write Archbishop Cullen of Dublin to encourage the speedy dispatch of the symbol of the office of Archbishop.

In August 1847, the Archbishop-elect began a second tour of his Archdiocese, accompanied by Father Francis Rutkowski, a Melcher recruit, who acted as Kenrick's German translator. Travelling west, the two stopped at Kirkwood (then called Gravois) and on to Manchester, then to Pacific, where they stayed at Saint Bridget's Parish. In Union, they found only one Catholic. At Gallagher's Mill on the Meramec River, the Archbishop preached to an all-Protestant assembly. Another stop was at the iron forge community of Maramec Springs, where he preached to Protestant ministers, among others. One man told Kenrick he had walked eight miles to hear him preach.

At Old Mines, Potosi, Fredericktown, and Caledonia, he spoke and then went on to Iron Mountain. At Sainte Genevieve, Kenrick assisted at High Mass.

The second leg of the tour took him again up the Missouri River to Independence, Kansas City, then on to Liberty, Lexington, Marshall, and Glasgow. The whole trip took two and a half months and tested the limits of the Archbishop's German and French. This experience prompted Kenrick to observe to the Archbishop of Baltimore, on the occasion of the death of the Bishop of Vincennes, that the new bishop should speak English rather than French and that, if Chicago should be divided, the southern half of the State of Illinois would require a tri-lingual bishop, fluent in English, French, and German.   •

But the blessings of the new title of Archdiocese and the gifts of Melcher's priests would be hard-pressed in the fateful year of 1849.

In early December 1848, steamboats from New Orleans deposited immigrants along the cities of the Mississippi and Ohio Rivers. One arrived in Saint Louis with thirty cases of cholera among the travelers. Saint Louis had already experienced the disease in 1833. It suffered a debilitating flood in 1844, and in 1849 the double curse of fire and cholera would ravage its population again.

The death toll raced through the winter months and into the spring of 1849. Two died on January 9th. Thirty-four more died later that month. Seventy-eight in March! One hundred twenty-six in April! When the Great Fire of May 1849 struck, cholera took a break. Only twenty died the week after the conflagration. But in June it roared back, killing fifty-seven. In one day in July, eighty-six died.

Mayor James G. Barry, who made it a point to stay in the city during the worst months, witnessed the decimation of the city's population: one death for every ten citizens.

Archbishop Kenrick plunged himself into the work and inspired the thirty or more priests of the city to do the same. Father De Smet mentioned that every day and every night at least seven Jesuits were attending to the sick and dying. Every day the Archbishop visited the hospital. Unlike most city leaders, not a single priest fled Saint Louis. Two Sisters of Charity, Columba Long and Patricia Butler, died as they ministered to the sick. Other Sisters of Charity joined to oversee the orphanage as its population grew from seventy to one hundred and twenty, the new children orphaned due to cholera deaths. When the city of Saint Louis established its own cholera hospital, the Quarantine Hospital, through the auspices of the Committee of Safety, it was to the Sisters of Charity that they turned to run the institution, as secular help was lacking.

In the crisis of 1849, the Sisters of Saint Joseph closed their school in Saint Vincent de Paul Parish and attended to cholera victims in the neighborhood. Two Sisters, Frances Nally and Justine Mulhall, contracted the disease. Archbishop Kenrick stayed at the bedside of eighteen-year-old Sister Justine until her death at midnight. The Visitation nuns lost one Sister; the Sacred Heart Sisters lost two Sisters and two novices. Another Sister of Saint Joseph, working at the orphanage, was also carried away. The Saint Joseph Orphanage grew from eighty to one hundred and fifty boys.

To relieve the swelling population of orphans, Father Melcher organized the German Saint Vincent Orphan Society shortly before leaving on his second recruiting tour. Two weeks after its establishment, it experienced its first casualties: Sister Ignatia and fourteen children died. Not until 1888 did the Sisters of Saint Joseph give up the work of the orphanage, handing it over to a German congregation which had fled Bismarck's *Kulturkampf* in 1873. Led by their Foundress, Mother Pauline Mallinckrodt, the Sisters of Christian Charity continued the good work. By the time of publication of Father Rothensteiner's *History of the Archdiocese of Saint Louis* in 1928, the German Saint Vincent Orphanage had served hundreds of children, eleven of whom became Archdiocesan priests, ten others joining religious orders of men, and forty-three girls becoming sisters of religious orders.

Remarkably, throughout all of this turmoil, Archbishop Kenrick kept up a lively scholarly output. Prodded by an 1846 visit from his brother, Francis Kenrick, and a friend, Bishop Purcell of Cincinnati, Peter Richard began work on revising his book *Anglican Orders*, which had previously caused a stir in the Episcopalian Church.

Archbishop Kenrick was required to take a break from the cholera epidemic and the Great Fire of 1849 to attend the Seventh Provincial Council of Baltimore. Here, the American bishops recommended to the Vatican three more Archdioceses: New Orleans, New York, and Cincinnati. There was a solemn declaration of the Immaculate Conception of the Blessed Virgin Mary as patroness of America and a call for a collection to be taken up in each diocese for the relief of Pope Pius IX, who had narrowly escaped Italian revolutionaries after they imprisoned him and murdered his Secretary of State. This last measure may have galled the Archbishop of Saint Louis a bit, as he had previously made the distinction between the pope, the Vicar of Christ, as distinguished from the pope, the political ruler, which he called an accident of history.

"The Lion" was also irritated, upon his return from Baltimore, to find that the Jesuits had continued their plans to build Saint Francis Xavier Church against his specific instructions. They also defied him by establishing a boarding school, which made him all the more furious when he discovered that a building which had been designated as the chapel was temporarily rented to a German, who used it as a tavern. When forty Jesuits arrived in Saint Louis as refugees from the fearsome rebellions of 1848-49, Kenrick discerned a conspiracy to overwhelm his Archdiocese.

The Jesuits tried to use charm to disarm the situation. While Kenrick held an animus toward the Jesuit Order, he had close relations with individual Jesuits, one being his spiritual director. Father John Elet wrote the Jesuit superior asking for help, observing, "...remember that Msgr. is Irish and has a very dominant character...Woe to Catholicism if the number of Irish bishops increases in the United States; schism will come from that... the difficulties we have with Msgr. Hughes (sic), Purcell and Kenrick prove this... a Kenrick will take from us what Du Bourg and Rosati begged us to accept."[22]

In the end, all it took was a kind and apologetic letter from Father John Roothaan, the General, to smooth matters in Saint Louis. Regardless, Kenrick remained wary that the Jesuits would be drawing away potential candidates from diocesan seminarians.

And in that sphere it fell to Father Joseph Melcher to fatten the rolls. The recruitment trip of 1849 did not produce the quantity of the 1846 tour, but the quality was indisputable. Father Stephen Schweihoff became the founding pastor of Saint Liborius Parish, a daughter parish of Most Holy Trinity. His saintly life of poverty was well known. He cherished only two things, his books and his vestments. Upon his death, Father Schweihoff willed his library to the Franciscans and his vestments to his parish. Franz S. Goller was ordained in Saint Louis and was assigned as assistant at Most Holy Trinity, later as assistant and then pastor of Saints Peter and Paul. He oversaw the building of the magnificent Gothic church and its tower and the expansion of the school. Father Goller was a strong advocate of Catholic parochial education. He influenced the Fourth Baltimore Council to mandate schools in all Catholic parishes.

Caspar Doebbner was also ordained by Archbishop Kenrick. He was assigned assistant pastor at Saints Peter and Paul and became pastor of Most Holy Trinity until 1865. Christopher Wapelhorst was "one of the most learned, most zealous and efficient priests Saint Louis ever had." That is the opinion of Father John Rothensteiner, the Archdiocesan historian. Arriving in Saint Louis, Wapelhorst enrolled in the seminary to learn English but was soon employed to teach theology as well as philosophy. He served the German community at Saint Vincent de Paul in Dutzow for one year, and at Saint Peter's in Saint Charles, and in 1865 was freed to teach at the Salesianum in Milwaukee. In 1879,

---

22   Samuel J. Miller. *Peter Richard Kenrick: Bishop and Archbishop of St. Louis: 1806 – 1896*. Record of the American Catholic Historical Society of Philadelphia. Vol. 84. No. 1-3, 1973. P. 50.

Father Wapelhorst returned to Saint Louis and joined the Franciscans.

Father John Boetzkes served in Dardenne and then Scott County until the ravages of the Civil War drove him back to Saint Louis. He left the diocese to found a parish in Helena, Arkansas, and died in 1891 in Pennsylvania. Father Conrad Tinturp served small communities west of Saint Louis until he went blind and retired to become the chaplain for the Ursuline community at Arcadia College. Father Francis Rüsse served at Saint Joseph, Missouri, Deepwater, and Hermann, and became an assistant at Saints Peter and Paul.

But the prize of prizes to come from the recruiting tour of 1849 was Henry Mühlsiepen. He came to Saint Louis as a seminarian and was ordained by Archbishop Kenrick in 1857. He was assigned to Saint Mary of Victories to assist Father Joseph Melcher, pastor and Vicar-General for the Germans in the Archdiocese. Five years later, he was released from his duties to take an advanced degree in theology at a German university.

Father Mühlsiepen returned to Saint Louis and became the virtual administrator of Saint Mary's, as Father Melcher's other assignment as Vicar-General consumed most of his energies. The young assistant also found time to found a monthly journal, *The Saint Louis Pastoral-Blatt*, a rich source of information for practical theology and a great source of information on the period for later historians. He founded the *Sankt Ludwigsverein,* which encouraged Catholic readership. Later, this reading society would be absorbed into the publishing house of B. Herder. When Joseph Melcher was named the founding bishop of Green Bay, Father Mühlsiepen inherited his jobs: pastor of Saint Mary of Victories, a thriving German parish with over 350 baptisms a year, and Vicar-General for the German, Bohemian, and Polish Catholics of the Archdiocese of Saint Louis.

By the time Father Joseph Melcher returned to Saint Louis with this new brood of recruits, he found the neighborhood around the cathedral gutted by the Great Fire. He found mass graves at cemeteries dug to accommodate the cholera victims. He found his Archbishop locked in disputes with the Jesuits.

Peter Richard Kenrick had just returned from the Seventh Provincial Council of Baltimore, in which a small encounter, almost forgotten to history, represented a grand new chapter in the Archdiocese of Saint Louis as the gateway to the West. While the American bishops had petitioned Rome that New Orleans, New York, and Cincinnati be raised to the rank of Archdiocese, they also renewed a petition from 1842 asking that Pope Pius IX normalize ecclesiastical authority in the Rocky Mountains by appointing a Vicar Apostolic. Someone suggested Father De Smet for the post, but that was vetoed by Father John Elet, the Jesuit superior for Missouri. Archbishop Kenrick then suggested another Jesuit, Father Miège. Father Elet said he would neither approve nor disapprove of the appointment.

Father Miège was consecrated in March 1851 at the College Church, Saint Francis Xavier, at Saint Louis University. He was named Vicar Apostolic for East of the Rocky Mountains. His territory included everything from Canada to Texas, from the western border of Missouri to the Continental Divide of the Rocky Mountains. Bishop Miège began to make plans to move west, accompanied by Father De Smet. It was Father Peter De Smet who would play such a disproportionate role in western, Indian, and Catholic history in the years to come.

Peter De Smet was a gift to the Jesuits and to Saint Louis from Father Charles Nerinckx, co-founder of the Loretto Sisters, pioneer priest and clandestine recruiter for the American missions. In the autumn of 1815, Nerinckx journeyed to his native Belgium, fundraising for his missions in Kentucky. He crossed snow-covered France, passed over the Alps, and visited Turin and Milan before making a pilgrimage to the Holy House of Loretto. Eventually, Father Nerinckx arrived at Rome and had an audience with Pope Pius VII. The Pope remarked to him in Latin, "I have read the rule of the Sisters of Loretto, Father, and it has given me hope." The 77-year old pontiff, who had so recently returned from a five-year imprisonment at the hands of Napoleon Bonaparte, continued: "Some portions of the rule may prove to be rather rigid... I don't know. Conditions in your country are very different from those in Italy."[23]

Regardless, Father Nerinckx knew it was precisely the hard conditions and extraordinary challenges which attracted youth eager to commit themselves to the radical service of Christ as a religious Sister.

Returning to the Low Countries, Father Nerinckx found young men eager to follow him to America. There he met Peter De Smet, Peter De Meyer, and James Oliver Van de Velde, a teacher at the *petit seminaire* in Mechlin. Van de Velde convinced his friend Henry Verhaegen to come also. Henry Hendrickx, who would be Father Nerinckx' faithful

---

23   Helene Magaret. *Giant in the Wilderness: A Biography of Father Charles Nerinckx*. Milwaukee: The Bruce Publishing Company. 1952, p. 143.

companion for the rest of his life, rounded out the recruits.

Belgium was part of the Netherlands at that time, and it was against the law for these young men to leave without passports and without completing their Dutch compulsory military service. So the whole party was smuggled on a fishing boat to an island where the American brig *Mars* took them onboard for their journey to America. By the time the *Mars* docked in New York City, of the ten men Father Nerinckx brought to America, all but one had resolved to join the Society of Jesus. Only Henry Hendrickx, son of a poor Brabant farmer, remained with the Kentucky missionary.

Van de Velde became a Jesuit Superior in Missouri; Verhaegen was the first President of Saint Louis University, and Peter De Smet became, arguably, the most well-known Jesuit in American history.

Archbishop Francis Patrick Kenrick. Oil painting by artist Hinky, 1863. Owned by Archdiocese of St. Louis Archives and Records.

+ Hochw'ster Bischof Joseph Melcher. +

Bishop Joseph Melcher of the Diocese of Green Bay. Archdiocese of St. Louis Archives and Records.

Certificate of a pew rental from the Old Cathedral in 1820 to John Mullanphy. While the contract calls it a sale, it also contains fine print that ultimately retains it as property of the Church. Archdiocese of St. Louis Archives and Records.

Close-up of Saint Louis University and Saint Francis Xavier College Church on Ninth Street between Washington and Christy. From *Compton and Dry's Pictorial St. Louis, the Great Metropolis of the Mississippi Valley: A Topographical Survey Drawn in Perspective A.D. 1875* (St. Louis: Compton & Co., 1876).

48

Saint Francis Xavier College Church circa 1895 (left) and 1947 (right). The steeple was not built until 1914. Archdiocese of St. Louis Archives and Records.

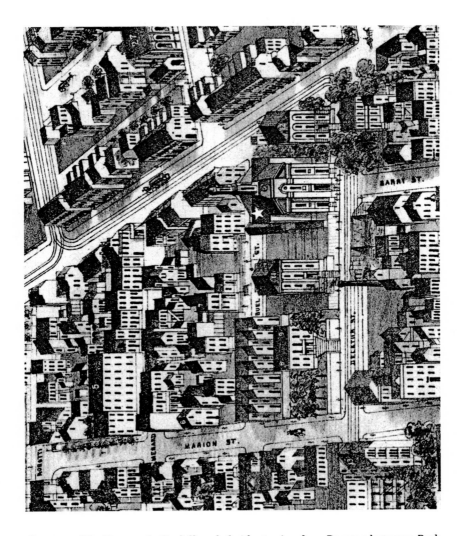

Close-up of St. Vincent de Paul Church (with star icon) on Decatur between Park and Marion Streets. To the right of the church is the parish school conducted by the Christian Brothers, and to the left is the rectory building. From *Compton and Dry's Pictorial St. Louis, the Great Metropolis of the Mississippi Valley: A Topographical Survey Drawn in Perspective A.D. 1875* (St. Louis: Compton & Co., 1876).

St. Vincent de Paul Church, circa 1910, from Souvenir Album of Catholic Churches and Institutions in the Diocese of St. Louis. Archdiocese of St. Louis Archives and Records.

Chapter Three

FATHER DE SMET

There is a long history in the relations between the Catholic Church and the Indian nations of North America. Setting aside the Hispanic contacts, in 1626 and for the next twenty years, Jesuits Jean de Brebeuf, Gabriel Lalement, and Isaac Jogues brought the Gospel of Jesus Christ to the Huron nation and were martyred by the Iroquois. Later, another Jesuit, Simon le Moyne, went to the Onondagas, a nation within the Iroquois alliance. Father Claude Jean Allouez baptized over 10,000 Indians in the Great Lakes region. Father Jacques Marquette joined Louis Jolliet in the 1673 exploration of the Mississippi River and became a close friend of the Illinois people. Layman Henri de Tonti was a hero to the Illinois people and helped them organize and defend themselves against Eastern invaders.

In the nineteenth century, Bishop William Du Bourg was visited by Osage leaders asking for priests. The earliest Jesuits to come to Saint Louis and Florissant tried to evangelize Indians. Saint Rose Philippine Duchesne came to America specifically for that intention, but was denied the opportunity until her twilight years.

But the relationship between Catholicism and the Native Americans rose to an all-new level when on May 31, 1823, a burly Belgian nicknamed "Samson" jumped from a ferryboat onto the Saint Louis levee. He was seminarian Peter John De Smet. His English was improved by a sixteen-month novitiate on the East coast.

De Smet's first Saint Louis encounter had to brighten his soul. He asked a ferryman for directions to the Cathedral, using his rudimentary English. The boatman shrugged and told him he didn't speak English, saying it in French!

As De Smet was fluent in Flemish and French, he soon found his way around the Creole town. The band of young men followed Father Charles van Quickenborne to the rectory next to the Cathedral. There they were welcomed by Father Francis Niel, the pastor as well as president of the tiny Saint Louis College. After a fine meal, the Jesuits rolled out their sleeping bags in a classroom and went to sleep surrounded by Bishop Du Bourg's 8,000-volume library.

The next day, the feast of Corpus Christi, brought a grand procession, a High Mass in Latin with a sermon in French, and a chance to meet the Creole elite of Saint Louis: Chouteaus, Cabannés, Christys, Mullanphys, General William Clark, and Mayor Lane. The next day, the band of novices moved north to Florissant, where they continued their formation.

Florissant was also the scene of an aborted attempt to found an Indian school. Father Van Quickenborne made visits to the Osage, three times in all. He was one of four priests in the Jesuit house. On September 23, 1827, the number rose to eight as Bishop Du Bourg ordained Peter John De Smet, John Baptist Elet, John Felix Verreydt, and Joducus Francis Van Asche. These would be the foundation stones of the Jesuit efforts in the Saint Louis diocese, staffing Saint Stanislaus Seminary, chartering Saint Louis University, serving in parishes, and evangelizing Indians near and far. It was in this last venture that great promise and great disappointments were to be experienced.

Father John Killoren, S. J. chronicles the events in his book *Come, Blackrobe.* The subtitle hints of what was to come: *De Smet and the Indian Tragedy.*

Father De Smet got his first full taste of Indian evangelization when he was sent with Father Verreydt and two Jesuit Brothers to the Potawatomi encampment near Council Bluffs in the summer of 1838. These were the "Prairie Potawatomi," a hodge-podge of several tribal remnants with Potawatomi in the majority. Many were Catholic, from Indiana and Illinois. Among them was Billy Caldwell, the chief who had helped Father St. Cyr found the first Catholic church in Chicago.

Colonel Kearney and his soldiers at Council Bluffs had abandoned the fort there, leaving four log cabins to be used as a school, a house for the Jesuits, and the block house as a chapel. The Jesuit mission came with permission from the federal government but with no financial support. Nearly 2,000 Indians lived there, but only thirty or so families, mostly French-Indian, were practicing Catholics. They were friendly and helpful, while the others seemed removed and resentful. They had good reason.

The Potawatomi was a proud nation, part of the Great Lakes Algonquians. They had long resisted Iroquois raids and incursions, as had all the Indians of the Midwest, and had been allied to the French in the various wars with the British. They had distinguished themselves with the capture of Fort Saint Joseph in Michigan during the French and Indian War. After that, with one notable exception of an attack by some warriors on the inhabitants of Fort Dearborn at Chicago during the War of 1812, the Potawatomi tried to live in peace, refusing to wage war against the whites, even as recently as the Black Hawk War of 1832. Many in Indiana and Illinois had converted to Catholicism and had expected to live a life of peaceful coexistence in America's Old Northwest Territory.

But that was not the intention of the federal government. When Chief Menominee was approached with an offer to sell his lands and resettle his people west of the Mississippi in 1836, he flatly refused. Under government pressure, other Potawatomi were forced out, many coming to Chief Menominee for protection. His little village grew from four dwellings to nearly one hundred in under two years. In the meantime, Abel C. Pepper, the Indian Agent for northern Indiana, had induced other Potawatomi leaders to sell out in a series of agreements called the Whiskey Treaties, as a free flow of whiskey had been used to soften up the chiefs.

The first wave was expelled and moved across Indiana, Illinois, and Missouri to be re-settled at Sugar Creek in Kansas Territory. These Indians appealed for a priest, and Jesuit Father Christian Hoeckens came to them, establishing Saint Mary's Mission there.

Other Potawatomi who resisted found assurances in a previous treaty between Chief Menominee and the federal government, in which the government promised that he and his people would not be displaced during his lifetime.

But migration pressures proved too great. New Englanders began leaving in droves as the sheep and wool industry declined. Many found work in the textile mills, but others preferred to farm. So they abandoned the rocky soil and harsh winters of New England and headed westward. In the Old South, the lands were exhausted by constant planting of tobacco and cotton. Many moved westward into Alabama, Mississippi, and Arkansas, while others sought land in Kentucky, Tennessee, and Missouri. The federal government had promised veterans of the War of 1812 land out west. These three forces, New Englanders, Southerners, and veterans put pressure on Indians. Land-hungry Americans had already begun "squatting" on Potawatomi land in several Indiana counties. When this illegal activity was reported to Indiana Governor David Wallace, he himself launched an investigation. But his conclusion came as a shock – it was the Potawatomi who must go. In August 1838, the governor called on General John Tipton to form one hundred volunteers to evict the Indians. The armed militia struck on Sunday morning, while Chief Menominee and most of the Indians were at prayer, their priest being away at the time.

When Father Benjamin Petit, ordained only a little over a year, heard about the attack and arrests, he received permission from Bishop Bruté to join the Potawatomi. The Belgian priest caught up with his flock at Danville, Illinois, and kept an account of the brutal displacement which has come to be called the Trail of Death. Father Petit said Mass each morning for the people and was assigned by the commander William Polke to care for the sick and the dying. His letters to Bishop Bruté recorded the events of the late-autumn march. An American flag led the way, carried by a mounted soldier. The officers followed, and the baggage train followed them. Behind the impedimenta was a carriage for the chiefs, with one or two chiefs riding horseback to lead over 250 horses ridden by people. Lining the trail at intervals were soldiers and armed militia to prod on stragglers. In the rear were forty baggage wagons filled with Indian luggage and the sick and dying. Father Petit counted 859 Potawatomi when he joined them. Over 150 died on the way.

The destination was Osawatomie, Kansas, where the government had promised housing and provisions for the approaching winter. When the Indians arrived on November 4, 1838, they found nothing had been prepared for them. William Polke simply abandoned them in the fields and returned his militia to Indiana.

By now the rigors of the journey had taken a toll on Father Petit. He was weak and feverish. It was decided that he should go to Saint Louis to seek treatment. He would be accompanied by Abram Burnett, a full-blood Potawatomi warrior. The others, having heard about Father Christian Hoecken's mission at Sugar Creek, decided to go there to seek help. It was a ninety-mile trek. Meanwhile, Father Petit made his way to Saint Louis University, where the Jesuit community cared for him until his death on February 10, 1839. He was twenty-seven years old. Abram Burnett took the priest's chalice and personal property to Vincennes and gave them to Bishop Bruté.

This tragedy was not the result of some terrible mistake. Something deeper and more sinister was operating here. The Potawatomi had been ideal citizens. With the sole exception of the Fort Dearborn massacre, they had lived in peace since the end of the French and Indian War. While other Indians, called the British Band, had gone into league together to fight the Americans in the War for American Independence, the War of 1812, and the Black Hawk War, the Potawatomi did not.

Father Killoren points out that it was federal policy, at least as far back as the Jefferson administration, to expel Indians from the East. Thomas Jefferson's promise and words need to be seen within the context of his own meaning. Peaceful coexistence he had never envisioned. Rather, the third president of the United States favored assimilation, as unlikely as that would be with Anglo-Saxon whites. Assimilation happened with the Spanish and the French, but that would not be the path taken by most Native Americans.

Jefferson told Native American tribal leaders, "...we will never do an unjust act to you...In time you will be as we are; you will become one people with us; your blood will mix with ours; and spread with ours over this great land."[24] With time, Jefferson came to see assimilation as a very long-term goal, perhaps taking generations. A pragmatic solution had to be found. Assimilation meant enculturation. Indians needed to become whites culturally. Putting aside hunting and trapping for farming and mining would take time. Monogamy and property rights would have to be learned. Distance could make up the time needed, and with the Louisiana Purchase, distance, real distance, was achievable.

For a while, Thomas Jefferson entertained the idea of a Red-White United States: all whites living east of the Mississippi River, all Indians west of the Mississippi. News of that idea was anything but welcomed in Saint Louis, and the scheme was soon dropped. Indeed, keeping whites out was recognized as impossible. President George Washington had warned that it would take a "Chinese wall" to accomplish that.

When Congress passed the Northwest Ordinance in 1787, Indian nations living there were assured that nothing would be done to invade or disturb them "unless in just and lawful wars authorized by Congress."[25] A year earlier, the Ordinance of 1786 furthered the Indian cause. General Henry Knox, Secretary of War, argued that peace would only be secured if the Indians knew they could rely on American treaties. He further demanded that tribes of Indians should be considered as foreign nations, not as subjects of the various states.

But American attitudes took a sinister turn with the election of the

---

24   John J. Killoren, S. J. *"Come, Blackrobe:" De Smet and the Indian Tragedy*. Norman: University of Oklahoma Press. 1994. P. 21.
25   Journal of Continental Congress, 25:602 cited in Ibid. P. 27.

third president. Jefferson wanted government trading posts called "factories" to have a monopoly on Indian trade. This would expel "unscrupulous private traders," but it had a deeper purpose. In a confidential memorandum to Congress dated January 18, 1803, the President said the factory system would drive the Indians into farming and husbandry in order to earn enough money to buy what they really craved: manufactured goods.

Earlier, Jefferson was even bolder in a letter to his Secretary of War, Henry Dearborn:

The cheapest and most effectual instrument we can use in preserving the friendship of the Indians is the establishment of training houses among them. If we could furnish goods enough to supply all their wants and sell these goods so cheap that no private trader could enter into competition with us... we should of course become objects of affection to them. There is perhaps no method more irresistible of obtaining lands from them than by letting them get in debt, which when too heavy to be paid, they are always willing to lop off by a cession of land.[26]

As Father Killoren observed, the Indian was no longer given the option to be Indian.

At this point, the question of fur trading entered in. Companies like the American Fur Company had made the Chouteaus and others wealthy. It also enriched the Indians who did the hunting, trapping, tanning, and processing of furs and hides. Many a European head was kept warm by beaver skin from the American West. Many a European library boasted of volumes bound in Missouri and Kansas deer leather. The schemes of William Ashley, Missouri's lieutenant-governor, intrigued shakers and movers like William Clark, called "the Jeffersonian man of the frontier." Clark was the territorial governor as well as part of the legendary Lewis and Clark Corps of Discovery. Ashley joined with famed fur trader Andrew Henry to form the Missouri Fur Company in 1809. Their focus was far different from the American Fur Company. They excluded Indians entirely. "Ashley men" would hunt and trap instead. Ashley needed government approval of such a move, and he used every political insider he could to get his way. He launched an advertising blitz in Saint Louis newspapers. When the Secretary of War, John C. Calhoun, objected and wrote William Clark that Ashley and the Missouri Fur Company had no legal or moral right

---

26   John J. Killoren, S. J. *"Come, Blackrobe:" De Smet and the Indian Tragedy.* Norman: University of Oklahoma Press. 1994. P. 31.

to hunt and trap on Indian lands, Clark replied that "it will be in the interest of those gentlemen to cultivate the friendship of the most distant tribes."[27]

By Clark's inaction, he violated the Trade and Intercourse Act of 1802. Further, he allowed William Sublette to bring 450 gallons of whiskey with his expedition, arguing that it was for the boatmen. That was a thinly-veiled ruse, as Sublette's route was overland. As it happened, William Clark, Federal Indian agent in Missouri, was also a founding member of the Missouri Fur Company.

But the West would not be won easily, as Ashley's men found out. Arriving at a location 150 miles north of Council Bluffs, they were attacked by Indians. Andrew Henry's expedition had been mauled similarly a month earlier, near the confluence of the Yellowstone and Missouri Rivers. Further upstream, another party suffered seven casualties. Undeterred, the Missouri Fur Company shifted its operations along the Great Platte River Road.

In a few years, the yield was enormous: in 1827, 7,000 pounds of beaver pelts were taken. In 1832, the year of the Black Hawk War, Sublette and Campbell scored over 11,000 pounds.

Chouteau's rival company introduced speed when the American Fur Company commissioned the steamboat *Yellowstone* in 1831. Its maiden voyage included Pierre Chouteau Jr. and 97 hired hands. They brought with them over $50,000 in merchandise, which included beaver traps, nearly 11,000 scalping knives, axes, hoes, blankets, and 10,000 pounds of gunpowder.

Things did not go as smoothly as expected. The Missouri River was very low that year. Beyond Council Bluffs, the steamboat encountered sandbars. After weeks of delay the *Yellowstone* arrived at Fort Tecumseh. Supplies were offloaded there and the rest of the trip was abandoned. On-loaded were buffalo robes and other signs of successful Indian hunts. Included were 10,000 pounds of buffalo tongues, evidently a real delicacy. The downside of speed was the spread of disease. In 1831, many Indians who traded with the American Fur Company were attacked by smallpox. The Pawnee experienced many deaths, while the Mandans weathered the assault, as they had accepted vaccines provided by the federal government since the days of Thomas Jefferson.

---

27   John J. Killoren, S. J. *"Come, Blackrobe:" De Smet and the Indian Tragedy.* Norman: University of Oklahoma Press. 1994. P. 42.

On the second voyage of the *Yellowstone* in 1832, it reached into the interior, even to the edge of South Dakota. Artist George Catlin was on board and described the scene of the river villages as they came into contact with modernity: "Along the route, Indians came to the shore to stare in amazement at what was passing upriver. If anything did ever literally and completely astonish (and astound) the natives, it was the appearance of our steamer, puffing and blowing and paddling and rushing by their villages...We had on board one twelve-pound cannon and three or four eight-pound swivels, which we were taking up to arm the Fur Company's Fort at the mouth of the Yellowstone; at the approach to every village, they discharge several times in rapid succession, which threw the inhabitants into utter confusion and amazement—some of them laid their faces to the ground and cried to the Great Spirit."[28]

Meanwhile, young Father De Smet was not impressed with the Prairie Potawatomi he met in Iowa. He wrote to his Saint Louis superiors: "They change wives as often as gentlemen in St. Louis change their coats." Regarding alcohol abuse, he wrote, "Their drunkenness only ceases when they have nothing more to drink." He further chronicled his experiences: "June 3. A woman with a child, a mother of four children, was murdered this morning near the issue-house. Her body presented a most horrible spectacle of savage cruelty; she was literally cut up. June 4. Burial of the unhappy woman. Among the provisions placed in her grave were several bottles of whiskey. A good idea, if all had been buried with her. June 6. Rumor. Four Iowas, three Potawatomi, one Kickapoo are said to have been killed in drunken frolics. I know from good authority that upwards of 80 barrels of whiskey are in the line ready to be brought in at the payment. No agent here seems to have the power to put the laws in execution."[29]

In another letter, Father De Smet tells of a sad tale of deprivation at Sugar Creek for all, and of the threats that the river presented:

First I will relate to you the great loss that we experienced toward the end of April. Our superior sent us from Saint Louis, goods to the amount of $500, in ornaments for the church, a tabernacle, a bell, and provisions and clothes for a year. I had been for a long time without

---

28   Shirley Christian. *Before Lewis and Clark: The Story of the Chouteaus, the French Dynasty that Ruled America's Frontier.* New York: Farrar, Straus and Giroux. P. 286.
29   Rev. John Rothensteiner. *History of the Archdiocese of Saint Louis. Volume I.* Saint Louis: Blackwell Wielandy Co. 1928. P. 657.

shoes, and from Easter we were destitute of supplies. All the Potawatomi nation were suffering from scarcity, having only acorns and a few wild roots for their whole stock of food. At last, about the 20th of April, they announced to us that the much desired boat was approaching. Already we saw it from the highest of our hills. I procured without delay two carts to go for the baggage. I reached there in time to witness a very sad sight. The vessel had struck on a sawyer, was pierced, and rapidly sinking in the waves. The confusion that reigned in the boat was great, but happily no lives were lost. The total damage was valued at $40,000. All the provisions forwarded by the government to the savages were on board her. Of our effects four articles were saved; a plow, a saw, a pair of boots and some wine. Providence was still favorable to us. With the help of the plow, we were enabled to plant a large field of corn; it was the season of furloughing. We used the saw to build a better house and enlarge our church, already too small. With my boots I can walk in the woods and prairies without fear of being bitten by serpents which throng there. And the wine permits us to offer to God every day the holy sacrifice of the Mass, a privilege that had been denied us during a long time. We therefore returned with courage and resignation to the acorns and roots until 30 May. That day another boat arrived. By the same steamer, I received news from you, as well as a letter from my family and from the good Carmelite superior.[30]

The one saving grace was the presence of the forest Potawatomi, the true Potawatomi of Indiana and Illinois. These were the ones for whom Father Benjamin Petit gave his life. His death in Saint Louis on February 10, 1839 at Saint Louis University prompted action. Rose Philippine Duchesne wrote Mother Barat in France describing the plight of the Potawatomi and the heroic death of Father Petit. Supported by Bishop Rosati, Rose Philippine finally got permission to do what had brought her to America so many years earlier: she received permission to join other Sacred Heart nuns in a mission to Sugar Creek.

Rose Philippine was eager to begin the work. She met with Father De Smet on January 6, 1841, when he urged her to try again to get permission to open the school for the Potawatomi. She brought forth from her pocket a letter sent six months earlier from Paris. It was from Bishop Rosati. It read "Go! Follow your attraction, or rather the voice

---

30   Chittenden and Richardson, De Smet, Vol. I, P.184, as cited in Rev. John Rothensteiner. *History of the Archdiocese of Saint Louis. Volume I*. Saint Louis: Blackwell Wielandy Co. 1928. Pp. 659-660.

of God. He will be with you. I beg Him to bless you."[31]

When Father Verhaegen went to City House to make plans for the journey, things did not seem quite right. Sitting in the parlor were Mother Lucille Mathevon, an Irish Sister, Mother O' Connor, and a Canadian, Louisa Amyot. Away from the others sat Rose Philippine, eyes welling with tears, fingering her rosary. The issue became obvious when Mother Mathevon, the superior, talked about reservations on the steamboat for three passengers. Father Verhaegen interrupted, "But she must come too! Even if she can use only one leg, she will come. Why, if we have to carry her all the way on our shoulders, she is coming with us. She may not be able to do much work, but she will assure success to the missions by praying for us. Her very presence will draw down all manner of heavenly favors on the work."[32]

The steamboat *Emily* departed on June 29, 1841, with four sisters, two Jesuits, and a diocesan priest onboard. Spontaneously, people at the levee took up a collection and raised $50 for the sisters, and travelers on board the boat matched that with another $40.

After a stop in Westport, the *Emily* continued on, until reaching its destination on July 9, 1841. The Indian village was eighteen miles away, and a carriage was arranged for the sisters. Along the route they were greeted by Indians, and a mile from the village a troop of 500 horsemen came, brightly arrayed, with faces painted black except for red rings around their eyes.

There was a lot of handshaking and greeting, followed by a dinner at the home of a French-Potawatomi man, Joseph Bertrand.

Within weeks, Mother O'Connor learned enough Potawatomi to begin instructing the children. So did Mother Mathevon. Sister Louise Amyot set about cooking, while Mother Duchesne grew weaker and more feeble. Regardless, the people loved "the good old lady," as she was called. Later, when they got to know her better, they called her "the woman who prays always." Indians brought her all sorts of produce, eggs, and poultry.

The winter proved to be harsh and took its toll on Mother Duchesne's health. Each day she braved the snowy path to attend morning Mass in the unheated chapel. It was her custom to return several times a day, until Mother Mathevon forbad her to leave the warmth

---

31   Paris, July 15, 1840. Louise Callan, R.S.C.J. *Philippine Duchesne: Frontier Missionary of the Sacred Heart: 1769-1852*. Westminster: The Newman Press. 1957. P. 628.
32   Ibid. P. 635.

of the convent cabin. Even otherwise healthy Indians were overcome by the weather. Varied reports came out of Sugar Creek. Rose Philippine wrote her family in February: "My heart has improved very much in this part of the country." She talked about improved eyesight and greater strength. Mother Mathevon, the very next day, wrote "Mother Duchesne is aging more and more. She is often in a very suffering condition. The life here is much too hard for a person her age."[33]

In spring, Sugar Creek was visited by Mother Galitzin, the secretary for the Sacred Heart sisters. While the visit lasted only two days, it was full of parades and demonstrations of skill and, of course, handshaking.

Rose Philippine improved with the weather. Indian girls were attracted to her, though she could not speak their language. She taught them knitting, and they loved just to be in her presence.

A second visitor came in early June who would bring this happy scene to an end. The new coadjutor, Bishop Peter Richard Kenrick, came to confirm those ready for the sacrament. But he also brought a message to Mother Duchesne: he told her he would not permit her to "lay her bones to rest in the Indian territory," turning a phrase she herself often used. It did not take long before she received an official letter from Mother Barat, recalling Rose Philippine back to Saint Louis. Father Verhaegen came from Saint Louis to accompany her back. They arrived on June 29, 1842, one year to the day after they had left Saint Louis for Sugar Creek. After a brief stay at City House, Rose Philippine moved to the Sisters' community in Saint Charles. She surrendered her will once again to the will of God as expressed by her superiors.

Father De Smet, on the other hand, had ideas beyond Sugar Creek. These would put him in complete contradiction to what seemed to be the federal government's varying policies toward Native Americans. Depending on the administration, some advocated assimilation, others concentrated on reservations, others exiled them to some far Western Indian territory, and most cynically, some preferred annihilation.

The Jesuit experience in Florissant with Saint Regis Indian School soured the Society on assimilation, and the Potawatomi experience in Indiana showed that there was no interest among American whites to accept assimilation or peaceful coexistence. But Jesuit history offered

---

33   Louise Callan, R.S.C.J. *Philippine Duchesne: Frontier Missionary of the Sacred Heart: 1769-1852.* Westminster: The Newman Press. 1957. P. 645.

a different solution, one that honored the dignity of the Native Americans: not forcing assimilation and also forestalling annihilation, and in a sense applying the reservation-in-exile option in a proactive way. This paradigm was Paraguay.

While studying the history of the Society of Jesus, the seminarians at Florissant had read about the mission work of the Jesuits among the Guarani. A textbook by Luigi Muratori entitled *A Relation of the Reductions of Paraguay* outlined how the Jesuits helped the Guarani people create a native Christian society, independent of both Spain and Portugal. This line of thought was encouraged by the superior Father Roothaan in 1829, and Father De Smet had met two Iroquois who had applied the reduction principle, demonstrating its success. Indeed, it could be argued that this was exactly the Jesuit strategy tried in the 1600s in the Great Lakes region which the French government opposed so vigorously. Other Jesuits had applied the principles: Matteo Ricci in China, Roberto de Nobili in India, and Eusebio Kino in the Southwest. Father Roothaan reassured the Jesuits that these had proven very successful. (Actually, a closer reading of each case showed them to be noble failures.) Could things turn out better this time?

The principle was called *accommodation*. The idea was to accommodate the message of Christianity to an existing culture. It could be argued that this is the pattern throughout Christian history. The faith of a dozen Palestinian Jews spread to the Hellenistic world. Hebrew or Aramaic was not forced on the Greek speakers. Indeed, Greek dominated, and Christianity found its expression enriched with Greek philosophical terms. Rome was conquered for Christ not by Hellenizing it, but by Christianizing it. Roman law and language and customs and architecture were Christianized, and Christianity's expression was enriched as a result. So with the Germans, the Vikings, the Celts, the Slavs. Why not American Indians?

The Jesuits also witnessed the disintegrating effects of contact with whites. Alcoholism, dependency on manufactured products, reliance on federal subsidies that came from surrendering lands—all these demoralized once great and noble peoples. The mighty Osage, whose empire ruled Missouri and parts of Kansas and Arkansas at the time of Laclède, now was virtually squeezed out of their Ozark redoubt; the tribe found themselves fighting other tribes and even subgroups within the Osage for mere scraps of land in Kansas and Oklahoma. The Jesuits watched the erosion of virtue even within their Potawatomi and Kickapoo missions.

A glimmer of hope came when, for the fourth time, the Flathead Indians in the faraway Rocky Mountains petitioned for a priest in 1839. The diocese of Saint Louis had no priest to send, but petitioned Rome for help. With appeals from Jesuit Father Verhaegen and from Bishop Rosati, the Society of Jesus responded.

By 1840, Fathers Gregory Mengarini and Nicholas Point arrived in Missouri. Mengarini, in particular, had great skills as a linguist and as a musician. Father De Smet was sent west to explore the possibilities, and became impressed especially with the Flathead Indians. Upon his return to Saint Louis, and bearing a favorable report, he convinced the Jesuits to assemble the manpower for an expedition: three priests led by Father De Smet and three Jesuit brothers. It was then that Father Verhaegen delivered the bad news. There was no money for the venture; it would have to be postponed indefinitely. Father De Smet took this as a challenge. He immediately launched a begging tour which took him down the Mississippi to New Orleans. There he gathered funds for his work, plus another $500 for the Sacred Heart sisters to open their school at Sugar Creek. In one fell swoop, De Smet raised $1,100 in cash and crates full of articles.

A second setback came when Joseph Nicollet announced that the U.S. expedition he was slated to lead, and that the Jesuits were to join, had been postponed indefinitely. De Smet turned to Charles Chouteau, hoping to join up with the American Fur Company party, but was told that the Wyoming rendezvous had been canceled too. No party was going west. Regardless, De Smet was relentless and in the end found a way.

The way west was under the direction of wagon-master Thomas Fitzpatrick. The Jesuits met up with Fitzpatrick and his wagons in Westport on May 10, 1841. Sixty-nine people loaded into Fitzpatrick's thirteen wagons as they headed northwest toward the Platte River. There they were joined by six more individuals, including a Protestant minister on his way to Oregon. Fitzpatrick's expedition was the first to travel what became the Oregon Trail. The route which delivered the Jesuits to the region for the reduction would eventually destroy any chance of a reduction. Five years later, 10,000 people would take this trail. Nine years after that, the count was 55,000.

The Jesuits left the Fitzpatrick party in mid-August, being greeted by a Flathead delegation. By September 1, they were in the camp of

Chief Paul, known also as "Chief Big Face." Immediately they became impressed with the geography of the Bitterroot River Valley. A chain of mountains to the south kept the hostile Blackfeet away. A chain of mountains to the north broke the worst of the winter weather while supplying a limitless amount of lumber. It was remote; the Flathead loved its location.

Father Killoren, author of *Come, Blackrobe*, noted "in these well organized and at least quasi-independent reductions the Native Americans would be able to adapt to new ways while retaining sufficient roots in their own culture. With their culture respected but modified, they could grow in dignity and health, religiously oriented as they were, into individuals prepared for the world that was changing about them."[34]

By the end of 1841 there were enough cabins built in the Bitterroot Valley, named Saint Mary's Mission, to accommodate five hundred people. Two interpreters made up for linguistic differences: Gabriel Prudhomme, a French-Indian, who was adopted by the Flathead, and another interpreter simply known as "Charles." Father Mengarini was busy developing a grammar for the Flathead language. Father Point engaged himself in paintings which were sent back to Saint Louis. Father De Smet sent these, along with glowing reports of the first year's work:

24 marriages... Had been celebrated during my absence, and 202 adults, with little boys and girls from 8 to 14 years old, had been baptized. There were still 34 couples, who awaited my return to receive the sacrament of baptism and marriage, or to renew their marriage vows.... I commenced giving three instructions daily, besides the catechism, which was taught by the other fathers. They profited so well that, in the grace of God, 115 Flatheads, with three chiefs at their head, 30 with their chief, and the Blackfoot chief and his family, presented themselves at the baptismal font on Christmas day.[35]

Notice the term "celebrated during my absence!" Father De Smet had developed a wanderlust that would take him thousands of miles on all sorts of adventures, trips to Walla Walla, to Saint Louis, and to Europe for fundraising. In 1842, Father De Smet logged 5,000 miles. In 1843, he went to Europe, and in that year he discovered a means

---

34   John J. Killoren, S. J. *Come, Blackrobe: De Smet and the Indian Tragedy.* Norman: University of Oklahoma Press. 1994. P. 73.
35   Ibid., P. 75.

of fundraising and publicity which would bear much fruit. He wrote and published a book, *Letters and Sketches, with the Narrative of the Years Residence among the Indian Tribes of the Rocky Mountains.* It was an instant success, with publications in English, German, Italian, and Dutch. De Smet was invited to speak along the eastern seaboard in places like Boston, Philadelphia, Baltimore, New York, and Washington, D. C., as well as New Orleans, Louisville, and Cincinnati.

In Europe, the Jesuit spoke in Ireland, Brussels, Lyon, Paris, Lille, and Marseille. In Rome, he met with the Jesuit General John Roothaan and had a private audience with Pope Gregory XVI. To the Pope, De Smet delivered a most surprising offer from Chief Victor of the Flathead. "If the Great Chief of the Christians is in danger, send him a message from me. I will build him a lodge in the middle of our camp; we will hunt game that he may be fed; we will be his guards to protect him from the enemy."[36]

Besides money and publicity, Father De Smet gained five more Jesuit volunteers for the reduction and a commitment of six religious sisters, of Notre Dame de Namur, for an Indian school in Wilmette. With that, Father De Smet left Europe on his fifth transatlantic voyage. This time his return took him around Cape Horn and up the Pacific coast to Vancouver. He had been at sea for eight months. De Smet wintered in the Rockies in 1844-1845. His report cites this time among the happiest years of his life.

I shall always remember with pleasure the winter of 1844-45, which I had the happiest happiness of spending among these good Indians. The place was wintry and well chosen, picturesque, agreeable, and convenient. The camp was placed near a beautiful waterfall...

The great festival of Christmas, the day on which the little band comprised of 124 adults was to be added to the number of the true children of God, will never be effaced from the memory of our good Indians. The manner in which we celebrated midnight Mass may give you an idea of our festival. The signal for rising, which was to be given a few minutes before midnight, was the firing of a pistol, announcing to the Indians that the house of prayer would soon be open. This was followed by a general discharge of guns in honor of the birth of the infant Savior, and 300 voices arose spontaneously from the midst of the forest, and intoned in the language of the Pend d'Oreilles the beautiful canticle "Du Dieu puis-

---

36   John J. Killoren, S. J. *Come, Blackrobe: De Smet and the Indian Tragedy.* Norman: University of Oklahoma Press. 1994. P. 81.

sant tout annonce la gloire." – the Almighty's glory all things proclaim. In a moment a multitude of adorers were seen wending their way to the humble temple of the Lord – resembling indeed the manger in which the Messiah was born... Of what was our little church of the wilderness constructed?... Of posts fresh cut in the woods, covered over with mats and bark; these were its only materials... The altar was neatly decorated, bespangled with stars of various brightness, covered with a profusion of ribbons – things exceedingly attractive to the eye of the Indian. At midnight I celebrated a solemn Mass as the Indians sang several canticles suitable to the occasion. That piece announced in the first verse of the angelic hymn – the Gloria – peace on earth to men of goodwill, was, I'd venture to say, literally fulfilled to the Indians of the forest. A grand banquet, according to Indian custom, followed the first Mass... The union, the contentment, the joy and charity, which predated the whole assembly, might well be compared to the agape of the primitive Christians.

Permit me to repeat here that I should be delighted could I but communicate to the zealous and fervent those pleasurable feelings – that overflowing of the heart, each one experiences on such occasions. Here indeed, the Indian missionary enjoys his greatest consolation; here he obtains his strength, his current, is sealed to labor to bring men to the knowledge of the true God, in spite of the poverty, the privations of every description, and the dangers with which he has to contend.[37]

The highlight of the Jesuit efforts in the Rocky Mountains came on September 14, 1846. The Blackfeet, who had been sworn enemies of the Flatheads, made peace with a presentation of a calumet, an Indian peace pipe. On September 15, Father De Smet celebrated Mass in a field accompanied by Flathead, the Nez Perce, Blackfeet and others: 2,000 warriors in all. Gabriel Prudhomme, the mixed-blood interpreter, and "Charles," the former interpreter for the Hudson Bay Company, translated for Father De Smet, whose facility at Indian languages never improved.

Afterwards, Father De Smet baptized some 50 Sioux children and began a winter journey back to Saint Louis. At Council Bluffs, he met an encampment of Mormons on their way West and spoke with Brigham Young, whom he referred to as "an affable and very polite gentleman."

Despite what appeared to be stable growth for the reduction, an impressive church, fourteen log homes, a large barn, and even an en-

---

37   John J. Killoren, S. J. *Come, Blackrobe: De Smet and the Indian Tragedy.* Norman: University of Oklahoma Press. 1994. P. 83-84.

closed grain field of 300 acres, as well as a herd of thirty cattle, with pigs and chickens, serious problems loomed on the horizon.

De Smet's customary discount from the Hudson Bay Company for merchandise came to an end. The company was pulling up stakes and retreating north to Canada, while Americans were moving into the area south of Puget Sound. There were rumors of war between the United States and Great Britain over the Oregon boundary. A British sloop-of-war appeared at the mouth of the Columbia River, but diplomacy won the day with the Oregon Boundary Treaty. As De Smet observed, it was agreed upon between Britain and America. The Native Americans, who alone had the right to the land, were not even consulted. And finally, with the increase of Americans in the Oregon Territory, Protestant denominations appeared eager to compete with the Jesuits.

Even so, the Jesuits found themselves pulled in various directions. Their superior, Father Roothaan in Rome, insisted that their sole duty was to establish a successful reduction for the Flathead Indians. This ran contrary to the thoughts of newly-appointed Archbishop Blanchet, who had concerns about white settlers in the area, and short of manpower, insisted the Jesuits serve those needs also. With Father De Smet always on the move, Blanchet pressured Father Roothaan to appoint another director of the reduction effort: Father John Elet.

The relationship which developed between Archbishop Francis Blanchet and the Jesuits is an interesting tale. Earlier in 1842, there were only three priests in the Oregon Territory: Fathers De Smet, Francis Blanchet, and Modeste Demers. Together, they considered a request to make the region a Vicariate Apostolic. But the erection of such an ecclesiastical authority for the area west of the Rockies would develop very differently from that of Bishop Miège and his work east of the Rockies. In the end, the creation of the second Archdiocese in the United States would result from accident rather than design.

On December 1, 1843, Oregon became a Vicariate Apostolic, and Father Blanchet was named its Bishop. This came as a surprise to the priest, as he considered himself to be too old to assume the duties of a bishop (he was only forty-eight years old). Bowing to Rome's wish, Blanchet returned to Canada for consecration and then went to Europe on a begging tour. It was in Rome that Bishop Blanchet came under the influence of two individuals who sought to manipulate his naïveté. Jean Luquet promoted the cause of the Paris Foreign Mission

Society, which encouraged the development of diocesan clergy rather than reliance on religious orders. The other intriguer was Father Augustine Theiner, a Vatican archivist and a confidant of Pope Gregory XVI.

Both Luquet and Theiner urged Blanchet to press for the establishment of a province for Oregon rather than a Vicariate Apostolic. They devised a plan to create an Archdiocese with eight suffragan, or dependent, dioceses. The idea was to short-circuit any Jesuit effort to influence events in Oregon. The scheme ran contrary to the wishes of Cardinal Giovanni Brunelli, Prefect of *Propaganda Fide*, and the intention of the American bishops, who at their May 1846 Council petitioned Rome to raise Saint Louis to the rank of Archdiocese.

Regardless, Theiner and Luquet used their influence and presented a memorandum which argued that the Franciscan missions in California had been a failure, and another failure in Oregon would be averted only if secular clergy were in charge. The argument was without basis and would prove to be incorrect; Oregon did not produce a single indigenous priestly vocation until 1895.[38]

Even so, Rome was abuzz about the Western missions, especially after Father De Smet's celebrated visit to the Eternal City in 1845. Under the influence of Luquet and Theiner, Pope Gregory XVI planned to make Oregon City an Archdiocese. The plan was temporarily suspended when the Pope died on July 23, 1846. After the 1846 conclave elected a new pontiff, Pope Pius IX, the decree was quickly signed, making Blanchet an Archbishop and Father Demes Bishop of Vancouver Island. Father Augustin Blanchet, Francis' brother, became Bishop of Walla Walla. The very same day of the papal decree, a treaty was signed between Great Britain and the United States dividing the Oregon Territory, giving Oregon City to the United States. Thus, in lightning-quick succession, Oregon City became the second Archdiocese in America, instead of Saint Louis.

The whole affair proved disastrous. Relations between Archbishop Blanchet and De Smet and the Jesuit community soured until they eventually withdrew, giving up their dream of a reduction for the Flathead. The Oblates of Mary Immaculate, laboring in the new province, were in constant battle with Blanchet, who had adopted an unbecom-

---

38   Patricia Brandt. *"'A Character of Extravagance': Establishment of the Second Archdiocese in the United States."* The Catholic Historical Review. October, 2003. P. 707.

ing air of superiority.

Thus the outdoor Mass celebrated by Father De Smet in September 1846 proved to be his last for the reduction of the Flathead. After his return to Saint Louis, De Smet set off for another European tour along with Father John Elet, who was attending meetings in Rome. Along the way, they recruited for America Father Miège, later a bishop of the Vicar Apostolic east of the Rocky Mountains, and Father Ponziglione, a remarkable frontier priest of Kansas. They also recruited Charles Elet, John Elet's brother.

Father De Smet had collected a box of letters of recommendation from bishops and political leaders, but these mattered little in the mind of Father Roothaan, who had heard criticism of De Smet and his many travels. It seems that within Jesuit circles Father De Smet's constant activity irritated some, and added to Archbishop Blanchet's concerns about his absence from the Flathead reduction, De Smet became too much for the Jesuits. When the two met, De Smet was flatly told his involvement in the reduction was at an end. One of De Smet's critics was Father Anthony Ravalli, who chafed under the Flathead expectations of Jesuit assistance. He saw the Indians' misplaced hope rooted in De Smet's unrealistic promises. He wrote, "We are expecting other distressing things to occur very soon by reason of the lavish promises which Father De Smet scattered about him everywhere in his journey, and which neither he nor others will be able to keep."[39]

Indeed, Father De Smet was an indefatigable promoter, and his promises outran his resources. In the end, Father Elet could not direct the reduction effort either, being in bad health and lingering into an early death. By April 1851, Father Ravalli sent Rome a final report: the Flathead had abandoned the reduction. Father Roothaan reflected on the failure in the following sad assessment: "It seems that the idea of renewing the miracle of Paraguay amidst those mountains was a utopia. In the first place, we could not hope for the means which our Fathers received from the crowns of Spain and Portugal. Then, it was impossible to keep the whites at a distance; then, too, the nature of the land is quite different and one cannot hope to wean the bulk of the savages from their nomadic life during a great part of the year... I

---

39   John J. Killoren, S. J. *"Come, Blackrobe:" De Smet and the Indian Tragedy.* Norman: University of Oklahoma Press. 1994. P. 97

declare, my dear Father, I don't see how one can have any success at all."[40]

The failure of the Flathead reduction was the last attempt to stave off the unpleasant alternatives of assimilation, reservation, expulsion, or annihilation. Expulsion was impossible. There was nowhere else to go. Assimilation seemed unlikely, and if accomplished, would merely alienate the Indian from his history and culture. Reservations and wars of annihilation loomed in the future.

Father Killoren opens his chapter "Mounting Confrontations on the Great Plains" with this quote from historian James C. Olson: "The shifting frontier and the changing policies presaged what was evident almost from the beginning: the permanent Indian frontier was doomed to failure.... By 1850, the Indian country was not outside the United States; it was right in the middle, a barrier that had to be removed."[41]

The trail that wagon-master Thomas Fitzpatrick first blazed when Father De Smet and his Jesuit companions went to the Flathead in 1841 had, eight years later, become the major thoroughfare for overland travel to the West Coast. It was now the Oregon Trail. The Indians who occupied the territory through which the Oregon Trail ran were now seen as hostile obstacles to be removed. Fitzpatrick himself had a low assessment of the natives, often commenting on the treachery, cunning, and great inferiority of the Indians compared with the white man. He boasted that all that was needed to bend the will of the Indians was enough merchandise to beguile them. He commented:

I will further remark that I fear the real character of the Indian can never be ascertained because it is altogether unnatural for a Christian man to comprehend how so much depravity, wickedness and folly can possibly belong to human beings.

It has always appeared to me that great error exists in the public mind, in regard to the relations between the white man and the Indian, in as much as whatever atrocities have ever been committed by the Indians are invariably attributed to their rascality and swindling operations of the white man....

I am aware that great violations of justice have been committed on both sides; but the Indians of whom I now speak (the wild tribes of the prairies) have always kept ahead of the white man in their perpetra-

---

40   John J. Killoren, S. J. *"Come, Blackrobe:" De Smet and the Indian Tragedy.* Norman: University of Oklahoma Press. 1994. P. 99.
41   Ibid. P. 103.

tion of rascality; and I believe it is only in order to keep pace, and hold his own with the Indian, that the white man is often obliged to resort to many mean practices.[42]

Soon the U.S. military became involved. As late as 1835, federal troops had protected Potawatomi located in the Platte Corner, the Northwest Panhandle, which Missouri coveted and would eventually add to its territory. The rich farmland had been given to the Potawatomi in exchange for removal from Indiana and Illinois. When whites came into the territory to steal Indian horses, a confrontation turned violent, leading to the deaths of two whites and one Indian. The Missouri governor called for 200 volunteers to drive the Potawatomi out of the Platte area, but federal troops from Fort Leavenworth stopped them.

That action displeased Missouri Senators Thomas Hart Benton and Lewis Fields Linn, and more importantly, President Andrew Jackson. Indian agent William Clark was sent to negotiate yet one more removal treaty, and Platte County was added to Missouri. The Indians were removed to parts of Kansas and Nebraska. The governor actually had the gall to petition Congress to reimburse the state for the expenses of the 200 volunteers who had been called up.

By May 1849, U.S. troops were stationed at Forts Tierney, Laramie, and Hall all the way to Fort Vancouver. What was worse was the massive slaughter of buffalo, that animal upon which the Plains Indians relied for their very culture and sustenance. It was the buffalo herds that created and sustained the nomadic lifestyle of the Plains Indians. The meat was dehydrated as jerky, which preserved it and also made it lightweight enough to carry. The buffalo provided clothing, teepee coverings, blankets, and moccasins. The sun-dried dung was used for fuel. The tongue was a delicacy.

Father De Smet addressed European readers:

The facts... reveal clearly the melancholy future which at no very remote epoch awaits these nations, if efficient means are not employed for preserving the woes with which they are threatened....

The Buffalo is disappearing and diminishing each successive year on the prairies of the upper Missouri.... The area of land that these animals frequent is becoming more and more circumscribed....

Thence arise the incursions which the Sioux make into the territory

---

42   John J. Killoren, S. J. *"Come, Blackrobe:" De Smet and the Indian Tragedy.* Norman: University of Oklahoma Press, 1994. P. 118.

of the Aricaras, the Mandans, the Minnetarees, the Crows and the Assiniboins; thence also the mutual invasions of the Crow and the Blackfeet into their respective hunts.... In the Plains, war and famine lend their aid; on the frontier of civilization, liquors, vices, and maladies carried them off by the thousands.[43]

De Smet found a sympathetic ally in David Mitchell, a trader whom the federal government sought out to help solve its Indian problem. The idea was to publicize a massive meeting of all Indian nations in the West. He published a circular promising the Indians that they would be "amply compensated for all the depredations of which they complain." He also promised annual gifts from the federal government, "their Great Father."[44]

Copies of the circular were given to traders to distribute to the tribes they visited. Father De Smet, who was about to travel to the upper Missouri River territory, was loaded down with circulars. The federal government in mid-April 1851 solicited De Smet's help officially for the first time. A date was set for the treaty conference in September 1851; the place was to be Fort Laramie. Father De Smet joined the white delegation made up of David Mitchell, the organizer of the conference, Thomas Fitzgerald, the wagon-master and father of the Oregon Trail, army officers, and Indian agents and interpreters. Encamped were as many as 10,000 Indians!

After the ceremonial sharing of the calumet, Mitchell began with the speech: "The ears of your Great Father are always open to the complaints of his Red Children." However, the Great Father "expects and will exert the right of free passage for his White Children over the roads running through your countries, and restitution for any injury they may receive from you or your people during such travels. To eliminate any connected problems caused by either whites or Indians, the Great Father's right to establish military posts, and such other posts as he may deem necessary," should be expressly acknowledged by the Indians.[45]

Mitchell promised an annual annuity to cooperating tribes of $50,000 over 50 years. All eight tribes participating in the Fort Laramie Treaty signed on September 17. The high regard Indians had for

---

43   John J. Killoren, S. J. *"Come, Blackrobe:" De Smet and the Indian Tragedy.* Norman: University of Oklahoma Press. 1994. P. 127.
44   Ibid., P. 157.
45   Ibid. P. 154.

Father De Smet impressed the federal officials. In particular, a Mass celebrated on September 14, the Feast of the Exaltation of the Cross, witnessed the remarkable coming together of various tribes, with their trappers and traders and interpreters. One of the U.S. negotiators noted the Indians regarded the Jesuit "as a great medicine man," and always treated him with marked respect and kindness.

Father De Smet himself reported baptizing 1,586 Native Americans during the conference. He added that he had been given a new Indian name, which translated as "the man who shows his love for the Great Spirit."

When the conference ended, a delegation of Indian chiefs, accompanied by Fitzpatrick and De Smet, made their way to Washington, D.C. De Smet arranged the route to pass through Saint Mary's in Kansas so they could meet the Potawatomi there, along with Bishop Miège. After a two-day visit, they continued on their way, Father De Smet ending his journey at Saint Louis University. There he concentrated on drawing a map of the territory east of the Rocky Mountains for the federal government. The map was done in great detail and measured 54" x 36." Father De Smet hoped the map would cause the Bureau of Indian Affairs to treat the tribes with fairness. In his report to the federal government, Mitchell failed to mention his promise to the Indians that Washington would protect the tribes from white incursions into their territory. When criticized for pledging $50,000 for 50 years, he argued that it was a small price to pay for removing all means of self-support in the future. Even so, Congress altered the treaty, changing 50 years to 15 years. De Smet had grave misgivings now about the future of Native Americans and the Great Father's concern for them. Mitchell went along with Congress without a word of protest.

Finally, Thomas Fitzpatrick seemed to have become aware of the enormous cost to the Indians that his Oregon Trail had caused. Arriving in Saint Louis on a trip through the Northwest, he wrote an open letter condemning the federal Indian policy. He called it the legalized murder of a whole nation. It proved to be a final *mea culpa* for Fitzpatrick, who became ill and died on February 7, 1854. That same year Father De Smet came to the same conclusion.

Further pressure was put on Indians due to the Kansas-Nebraska Act, which intended to create two new states. While Congress specifically promised the rights of the Indians there would not be impaired, the writing was on the wall. And as tensions over slavery turned violent in Kansas, Indians were victimized by both sides. A dust-up between U.S. troops and Sioux led to further hostilities. General William Harney was sent to Saint Louis, and then to Forts Leavenworth and Riley, with reinforcements. He prodded the Sioux in the battle and then beat them mercilessly, destroying all their equipment and supplies. By March 1856, seven months after the campaign began, Harney had conquered the Sioux.

Whites surged further west. By 1858, 100,000 were moving into what would become Colorado.

Meanwhile, Father De Smet busied himself with Jesuit matters. He continued working in the finance office at Saint Louis University. He did fundraising for the school and took on the task of vocation director, which caused him to travel to Europe. En route to New York, he visited Washington and met briefly with President Franklin Pierce. After visiting Rome, he returned to America with seven more Belgians eager to become Jesuits. This brought the novitiate up to forty young men. Twice he was nominated for a position as Vicar Apostolic but avoided the honor both times. He visited other Jesuit schools as the order's higher education apostolate expanded to include Saint Joseph's College in Bardstown, Saint Aloysius in Louisville, the Athenaeum in Cincinnati (which changed its name to Saint Francis Xavier College), Marquette College in Milwaukee, and Saint Ignatius College, Chicago.

With the election of James Buchanan, the climate began to shift again regarding Indian policy. Father De Smet received a letter from an Army lieutenant who spoke of meeting with the chairman of the Indian Committee in the House of Representatives. It was this congressman's intention to see to it that treaties were honored, that subsidies to tribes of the Northwest be renewed, and that a new program under Jesuit direction would be welcomed.

In March 1858, De Smet was invited by the United States Army to become a chaplain with the rank of major. With permission of the Jesuit superior in Missouri, De Smet rode out to meet General Harney in his campaign against the Mormons. By then Harney had been replaced by General Albert Sidney Johnston, a future Confederate general in the upcoming Civil War. The Mormon War came to an end before it had begun. But Father De Smet became acutely aware of the strength of the American military and was resolved to keep Indians from ever again going to war. When De Smet got back to Saint Louis University, an invitation sat on his desk from General Harney. The general was about to be placed in charge of the Oregon Territory, and he invited the Jesuit to come along. With the permission of his superiors, De Smet was again involved in Indian affairs. Harney and De Smet departed New York for the Isthmus of Panama. They crossed the land by train and then boarded a ship bound for San Francisco. It carried 1,300 passengers. After a brief stay in San Francisco, the two took another ship to the mouth of the Columbia River, though the Indian rebellion which had prompted Harney's assignment had been quelled.

With Harney's permission, Major Peter De Smet left for Indian country to spend the winter with the Coeur d'Alenes. Though the weather was brutal—forty-three days of continuous snow—Father De Smet was in his element and preached to all that would listen to him, counseling peace with the white man. Rebellion was useless. In April, he gathered nine chiefs to accompany him back to Fort Vancouver to meet with General Harney. Before returning to Saint Louis, Father De Smet left the general a detailed description of the territory and recommended a single grand reservation for all the tribes of the area, one with plenty of timber, game, and fish. This report was forwarded to the War Department with General Harney's recommendation that De Smet's plan be adopted.

But months later, the United States would be distracted by the worst war in its history.

Father de Smet's portrait is surrounded by the miles he traveled per
year from 1821 (top right) to 1870
(bottom center). From the Moses L.
Linton Album at the Jesuit Archives:
Central United States, St. Louis, MO.

Father Pierre-Jean De Smet, SJ, missionary to the Indians of the western US, 1872.
Saint Louis University Libraries Archives
and Records Management. Digital ID PER_
DeSmet, Pierre_0002.

In 1859, Father Pierre-Jean De Smet, SJ, and a deputation of Native American chiefs traveled to Fort Vancouver to meet with General Harney, then to Salem, Oregon to meet the Oregon Superintendent of Indian Affairs. The chiefs were from the nations of Kalispel, Flat Head, Coeur d'Alene, Kettle Falls, Yakima, and Spokane. Saint Louis University Libraries Archives and Records Management. Digital ID PER_DeSmet, Pierre_0006.

Chapter Four

A CATHOLIC VOICE

"Noli irritare leonem!" This was the episcopal motto of Bishop Peter Richard Kenrick. Do not irritate the lion. In his later life, the motto was posted over the front door archway of his residence like some people post a sign to beware of a dog. Even as a young coadjutor, whose Ordinary was away on a papal mission, Peter Richard Kenrick was not afraid to make decisions, hand out advice, start initiatives, and expect obedience.

Kenrick arrived in Saint Louis in the last days of 1841. The next nineteen years saw constant activity, until he went silent during the American Civil War. Most of Catholic Saint Louis got its first glimpse into the heart and mind of the new bishop just six weeks after his arrival. Bishop Kenrick penned a pastoral letter to the diocese dealing with Christian temperance.

Heavy use of alcohol was a constant target for American reformers, especially in the reform decades of the first half of the nineteenth century. This condemning attitude flared up before the arrival of the Germans and the Irish. Main stock white Americans were heavy drinkers, and, as we have seen, plied Indians with the stuff liberally to get land concessions. It was said the most efficient way to transport grain from the old Northwest was in pigs and whiskey bottles. One of the earliest challenges to the new federal government was the 1794 Whiskey Rebellion in Western Pennsylvania. Drunken brawls were common at weddings and funerals and political rallies. Untold industrial injuries resulted from a combination of unsafe machinery and impaired operators.

In 1826, the American Temperance Society was formed to address the issue. With a constant drumbeat of the temperance clubs and crusades, New England states bent to the will of the teetotalers. By 1855, Maine, Vermont, New Hampshire, Massachusetts, Rhode Island, Connecticut, and New York were totally dry. The federal government sought to do the same in the Unorganized Territory, the future Oklahoma, as well as in the Nebraska Territory. Iowa and Michigan were also dry by 1855. By that time, the 1854 novel *Ten Nights in a Barroom and What I Saw There* was a bestseller. It told the story of a once happy town destroyed by the introduction of a tavern.

Several states passed legislation allowing counties to go dry without mandating abstinence statewide. These included Mississippi, Louisiana, Texas, Missouri, Illinois, and the Kansas territory. Socially, fewer women drank intoxicating beverages when the campaign began in the 1820s. Then Irish, German, and Eastern European immigrants increased the consumption of alcoholic beverages by both sexes, but these nationalities drank as part of the cultural experience, and drunkenness was frowned upon. Typically, it was served with meals. The Germans even called their beer liquid bread!

An alternative to the total abstinence of the teetotalers was temperance, the moderate use of alcoholic beverages. It was this moderate position which Kenrick counselled in his February 16, 1842 pastoral letter. The bishop's method was to first point out the basic dignity of the human person who is loved by God. "How afflicting a spectacle, to behold a creature, endowed by God with honor and glory, and placed over the works of His Hand—a soul which has not been purchased with corruptible gold or silver, but by the precious blood of the immaculate Lamb—a soul, which by baptism, has been made the temple of the Holy Ghost, and then, perhaps, subsequently enriched with the choicest gifts of God's house—a soul which has been thus prepared to enjoy the eternal possession of God, for which alone she was drawn forth from nothing."[46]

The bishop then recounted what he referred to as the brutish pleasures of intemperance: "How afflicted to behold such a soul, unmindful of her origin, and of the glorious destinies which await her, sacrifice all the hope of happiness, in order to indulge in the brutish pleasures of intemperance; it is not necessary to dwell on the temporal evils that result from this degrading vice; the loss of character and of self-respect; the enfeeblement, no less of the physical powers of the body than of the mental faculties of the soul; the distress and ruin in which the drunkard involves his unhappy family, whom, but too often, having been taken off by the diseases engendered by excess, he leaves behind, to depend for support on the charity of strangers, or to be victims of every evil to which unprotected destitution may be exposed. Great as are these evils, and loudly as they plead for our sympathy and lamentations, they are but temporal, and therefore, not to

---

46   John Rothensteiner. *History of the Archdiocese of St. Louis. II.* Saint Louis: Blackwell Wielandy Co. 1928. P. 140.

be compared with that eternal anathema pronounced by the inspired apostle on the intemperate, when he says: drunkards shall not obtain the kingdom of heaven."[47]

Having accounted the woes of intemperance, which were physical and social and spiritual, the bishop proposed temperance rather than teetotalism, much to the relief, no doubt, of his congregation. "We should be loud and vehement in the condemnation of the vice of intemperance; but we must not involve in indiscriminate condemnation the lawful use of those creatures of God, which the intemperate man abuses to his own perdition. We must remember that such a principle is impious and irrational; that it is opposed to the direct declaration of the inspired apostle, that, 'every creature of God is good, and is to be received with thanksgiving,' that it implies an error formally condemned by the Church, and that therefore no favorable result can be expected from any system in which it is incorporated, or from any zeal to which it may give an impulse."[48]

Indeed, Saint Louis was already a significant producer of beer by the time the pastoral letter was circulated. The St. Vrain Brewery had been in business since 1810, offering table beer for five dollars a barrel. A rival brewery established by Jacob Philipson and Ezra English used caves in South Saint Louis to brew and serve beer. Adam Lemp introduced his product in 1840, just as the flood of Germans arrived. In 1852, a new brewery was financed by a German soap manufacturer, Eberhard Anheuser. When the brewery failed in 1857, Anheuser inherited the business and turned it over to his son-in-law, Adolphus Busch, to manage. The Anheuser-Busch Brewing Association resulted from the union. In short order, the company was producing nearly 30,000 barrels a year and shipping beer as far away as Texas.

Bishop Kenrick circulated a second pastoral on June 1, 1842, dealing with the persecution of Catholics in Spain. His pen flowed with eloquence as he denounced the liberal regime which sought to secularize Spain. "To perpetuate more easily these enormous evils, the sacred name of Liberty has been made use of by those whose acts show that they know not what true liberty is."[49] He saw the State seeking to bind the Church "in the degrading trammels of subservience and absolute

---

47   John Rothensteiner. *History of the Archdiocese of St. Louis. II.* Saint Louis: Blackwell Wielandy Co. 1928. Pp. 141-142.

48   Ibid. P. 142.

49   Ibid. P. 142.

subjection to the civil power." While this crisis was on the other side of the ocean, Kenrick would experience his own crisis twenty-two years later when the Missouri state legislature, burning hot with revenge for the Civil War, sought to subvert religious liberty to civil power. Kenrick the Lion resisted this usurpation and won.

A third pastoral letter followed on September 14, 1846, calling for the laity to support the clergy and religious congregations in their spiritual and apostolic work. He ended the letter with the exhortation "let us remind you that God loves a cheerful giver." The pastoral letter of February 2, 1849 had three parts: a call for serious observance for the upcoming Lent, an appeal for prayers for Pope Pius IX, who had just suffered the assault of the revolution of 1848-49 and had been forced to flee Rome, and a recognition of the support of five pious associations in Europe which had educated the clergy, funded missions, and supported diocesan administration.

In all, Peter Richard Kenrick wrote nine pastoral letters, the most important calling for civil quiet and reason in the earliest days of what spun out of control to become the Civil War.

Along with these letters, the bishop wanted to exert influence in the field of publications. After all, in Philadelphia, among his other duties, Kenrick was editor of the diocesan newspaper, *The Catholic Herald*. There had been earlier attempts at Catholic print prior to Kenrick's arrival in Saint Louis. Bishop Rosati had supported the efforts of Joseph and Deodat Taylor in founding *The Shepherd of the Valley* in 1832. It ran until July 1836. At first it appeared in English and French, but French was soon dropped. *The Shepherd* was only four pages long and contained articles of interest to Catholic readers, including an obituary of John Mullanphy. Over the years, the place of publication changed, and the editors went from Joseph Taylor to publishers Angewin and Crowe, then to Crowe alone. In the July 2, 1836 issue, there was an appeal to subscribers to pay their dues. That was probably the last hurrah. As no other papers were issued, one can assume *The Shepherd of the Valley* failed under financial burdens.

It took seven years for another publishing effort to take place; this one was started by Bishop Kenrick himself. He called it *The Catholic Cabinet*. It was to be a monthly magazine of general Catholic interest. Multiple copies were sent to Philadelphia with the hope that his brother Francis would solicit subscriptions. Instead, the Bishop of Philadelphia quipped back criticizing the title, which he said suggested "a museum of curiosities." Articles ranged from poetry to theological topics, but most especially it intended to tell the history of the events of western Catholic history. Lamenting the lack of historical interest in North American developments, the editor observed, "This inattention is inexcusable, as we believe the subject is one that has frequently suggested itself to the minds of many among our clergy, some of whom were eminently qualified to supply the acknowledged desideratum."[50]

Regardless, in just over two years, *The Catholic Cabinet* discontinued publication, "constrained by circumstances" being the explanation for its closure. *The Catholic News-Letter*, a weekly, ran for two and a half years. Again, lack of funds caused its failure.

In 1850, Bishop Kenrick revived *The Shepherd of the Valley*. He sent copies east to his brother, who congratulated him on the fine work, but added that he should not himself edit the paper, "hardly to be risked after the unfortunate attempts of the past." Kenrick took his brother's advice and hired Robert A. Bakewell to edit *The Shepherd*. This second attempt was also plagued with financial difficulties and aggravated by Bakewell's imprudent, but often correct, observations. For instance, he once argued that religious liberty in America was, for all practical purposes, the result of an accident, brought about by force of circumstances. Inasmuch as there were so many denominations and no denomination reigned supreme, the only practical way to approach civil society was to tolerate as much as could be tolerated; hence, American religious liberty. Most historians today would agree with Bakewell's assessment. But in the 1840s and 1850s, this was kindling wood for Know Nothing demagoguery and Protestant sermons. Bakewell left *The Shepherd of the Valley* in 1854 and eventually studied law.

Jedidiah Huntington ran the *St. Louis Leader* for three years, first as a weekly and finally as a daily. While holding Catholic positions, the paper was quickly seen as serving interests in one wing of the Democratic Party; that is, those Democrats who, in the days prior to the Civil War, argued to preserve the Union, but not by means of war. When Huntington left Saint Louis and *The St. Louis Leader* failed, Bishop Kenrick tried one more time to publish a Catholic periodical. *The Western Banner* operated from 1858 to 1860. Upon its failure, Kenrick gave up trying to create a diocesan newspaper.

One further venture occupied Peter Richard Kenrick's mind during

---

50   John Rothensteiner. *History of the Archdiocese of St. Louis. II.* Saint Louis: Blackwell Wielandy Co. 1928. P. 165.

the first years of his episcopacy: money. The bishop sought to reduce his inherited debt of $58,000 first by using all available funds to pay down the highest interest loans, some as high as 10%. He petitioned to restore funding from the Society for the Propagation of the Faith, which had ended in 1842, and to secure a restoration of Leopoldine Society funding by promising to use the money to build churches for the new German immigrants. The new bishop was unsuccessful in soliciting help from prominent Saint Louis Catholic families. The generous Mullanphys were unwilling to pay down diocesan debt. Mrs. Ann Mullanphy Biddle, daughter of John Mullanphy, was equally cautious, as was Mrs. Anne Hunt, daughter of James B. C. Lucas.

Money was hard to come by after the Panic of 1837, when overspeculation in Western lands set up failures for unregulated banks which, when they failed, took down depositors' money with them. Even when money was available, it often carried a 24% interest rate. The money supply was strictly tied to the gold standard, and Jacksonian finances were perpetually at war with banking concerns.

All of this made the immigrant day laborer or mechanic or shop owner very jittery. The pastor of one Saint Louis parish wanted to help his people, and in the process he solved the bishop's dilemma. Father Ambrose Heim was a German-American seminarian at Perryville, born in the diocese of Nancy, which had a Franco-German flavor of Alsace-Lorraine. He was ordained in 1837 at the age of thirty and sent immediately to become the pastor in New Madrid, replacing the pastor who had left the diocese to become a Jesuit. Father Heim proved to be an extraordinary organizer. He built a church after the previous one had been destroyed years earlier in a flood. He then went on to be pastor of a parish in Illinois as well as chaplain to the Visitation nuns in Kaskaskia. His next assignment was as assistant pastor of Saint Mary of Victories in Saint Louis. He also became the spiritual director of the first Saint Vincent de Paul conference in America.

Father Heim's concern for his struggling parishioners led him to establish a parish bank. He could assure them of safe deposits, something commercial banks of the day could not do. Father Heim collected the little accounts of the parishioners and lent the money out to only the safest projects, reaping a significant return by way of interest charged. Everyone benefited and the parish bank grew, until it caught the eye of Bishop Kenrick.

Soon after, Father Heim was transferred to the Cathedral to be the bishop's secretary. He was told to bring his bank with him. A room was set aside as an office, and when the bank went diocesan-wide, it grew significantly. Hundreds of Catholic families entrusted their meager savings with the bishop, who then lent out money, usually to parishes and religious congregations for their building projects. At one point, when the City of Saint Louis was unable to pay for public works projects, the bishop loaned the city $150,000.

Bishop Kenrick himself got involved in building. He made improvements to diocesan property and built a series of office buildings. He invested some $114,000 in this scheme, and a few years later sold it all for just under half a million dollars.

While the rest of the nation shook in the wake of the Panic of 1857 and local banks failed, the Bishop's bank weathered the storm. The largest private bank in the West, Page and Bacon, closed its doors in 1855. This prompted runs on Lucas and Simmonds Bank and on L.A. Benoist. This rippled down to Saint Louis companies with colonial pedigree, including the Chouteaus and Vallés.

In 1858, Kenrick, elevated to the rank of Archbishop in 1847, got a most pleasant surprise. Upon the death of a wealthy Catholic in Saint Louis County, a bequest was made to the Archdiocese by John Thornton for over $461,000. All of this money was directed by the Archbishop to one of four categories: charitable institutions, building improvements for religious establishments engaged in charitable work, convent expenses for religious institutions which promoted religion, especially education, and, finally, the retirement of parish debts. Over half of the distributions went to the last category. The Thornton bequest would be worth $13,500,000 in real worth in 2015. But in economic power, that is, the percentage of the gross domestic product, it would be worth $1.8 billion dollars today.

The bank continued until Archbishop Kenrick was called away to the Vatican Council in 1869. He then liquidated the bank, returning deposits to their owners, recommending their transfer to another bank of similar conservative principles run by Joseph O'Neill. The Archbishop refused to take advantage of the Legal Tender Act of 1863, which allowed him to pay in greenbacks. Instead, he returned people's deposits in gold coin.

Father John Rothensteiner, the Archdiocesan historian, makes this comment about Archbishop Kenrick's banking venture: "As the turbid waters of the Missouri and those of the crystal clear Mississippi, after their junction above St. Louis, flow on side-by-side, without mingling, yet form a faster stream that gives life to the city and the country round about, so the priestly and business life of Peter Richard Kenrick flowed on in close touch, yet uncommingled, *ad laetificandam civitatem Dei*. The Archbishop always remained the great prelate, even when seated in the counting room, for his thoughts and aspirations were always with his diocese. It was not love of money, but love of Holy Church, that urged him on. And so it was not failure that made him close his banking career. From afar he may have heard the warning voices, but there were no rapids in his business career. Of his own will, when his purpose had been accomplished, he paid back all he owed. And the Archbishop's bank ceased to exist, leaving in its wake a long trail of blessings, the Churches, Schools, Convents, Hospitals and Orphanages, that could not have been built without its ever-ready help."[51] The efforts of Archbishop Kenrick to create an Archdiocese which could address the financial needs of the Catholic community and the civic community of Saint Louis were joined by others eager to make Saint Louis "one of the finest cities of America," in the words of its founder, Pierre Laclède.

In 1841, George Taylor moved to St. Louis from Alexandria, Virginia. His training was that of a lawyer, but what struck Saint Louisans most about him was what he did to introduce himself to the community. He bought property downtown and built a six-story office building. Until then, no one built higher than two stories. Later, he financed the building of Saint Louis' premier hotel, The Barnum, at a cost of $200,000. The hotel took two years to build and became famous for its restaurant's signature dish, Barnum's Ragu Stew.

Other buildings went up, especially after the destruction of the Great Fire of 1849. Along Fourth Street on the east side between Locust and Pine, the entire block was filled with the Ten Buildings project. Each was four stories high, financed by James H. Lucas, Ann Lucas Hunt, and William M. Morrison. Along Chestnut Street between Main and Second Street, imposing two-story homes were built for prominent families, giving it the nickname Quality Row.

One indicator of growth in the city was the increase in water usage. In 1830, a reservoir was built on top of one of the Indian mounds north of the city. It held 230,000 gallons of water, which had been pumped

---

51   John Rothensteiner. *History of the Archdiocese of St. Louis. II,* Saint Louis: Blackwell Wielandy Co. 1928. P. 156.

from the Mississippi River. By 1850, it was expanded to accommodate 400,000 gallons. The city then built another reservoir west by a mile north of Cass Street, which held nearly 8,000,000 gallons. After that began construction of another reservoir containing 32,000,000 gallons. By 1850, the population of Saint Louis exceeded the hundred thousand mark. All of this caused a flurry in real estate activity and home building.

In 1841, North Saint Louis was absorbed into the City of Saint Louis. South Saint Louis, which is a geographic expression rather than a township (though some locals consider it a worldview), became more and more drawn into the realm of the city. A development called Highland, which was west of Jefferson and a few blocks to Leffingwell, was incorporated into the city. Other developments, Fairview, Lowell, Evans Place, Fairmount, Rock Point, and Rose Hill, all became part of Saint Louis expansion.

Two Saint Louis businessmen combined efforts to rationalize this real estate boom. Hiram Leffingwell and Richard Elliot published *The Real Estate Register* in 1850. Its purpose was to gather all the real estate information from newspapers, court sales, and land auctions and put them in one convenient place for potential buyers to see what was available. It seems, however, it was not an act of altruism on the part of Leffingwell and Elliot. Instead, *The Register* tended to steer buyers to properties in which they held interest.

Another extraordinary Leffingwell-Elliot scheme was to have the city construct a grand boulevard along the crest of a hill that ran directly west of the city, anticipating further growth and expansion. This crest avenue would run from Carondelet in the south all the way to Bremen in north Saint Louis. It would take advantage of the continual rises which defined the landscape of Saint Louis. One can imagine the original colonial town today buried under the Jefferson Memorial Expansion Park and the Saint Louis Arch. The first rise takes us to Broadway and the Old Courthouse. What follows is a plain once called the Saint Louis Commons. That plateau continued westward toward Jefferson Boulevard, which runs north and south, arcing toward the Mississippi both toward Bremen in the north and joining South Broadway in the south. Another plain runs westward until it becomes the rise upon which the new proposed road would be built. Leffingwell and Elliot, both civil engineers, proposed a road 120 feet wide, making it one of the great boulevards of the world. They suggested the name Lindell

Boulevard, after Peter Lindell, one of the three Lindell brothers who made a fortune in merchandising and real estate development in Saint Louis. When the authorities cut the width to 80 feet, the Lindell name was dropped and it became Grand Avenue instead.

While many newcomers to Saint Louis were from Maryland, like the Lindells, and from Virginia, like George Taylor (and others came from Kentucky and Tennessee, as well as New England), the city remained heavily Catholic, especially with the arrival of immigrants, and this necessitated the division of the city into various parishes and the erection of new Catholic churches.

We have already seen the construction of Saint Francis Xavier by the Jesuits, much to the chagrin of Bishop Kenrick, who feared it would draw English-speaking parishioners from the Cathedral. Connected to Saint Louis University, the church was completed in 1843 and opened a parish school for girls run by the Sisters of Charity. Within two years the enrollment topped 280. This was a free school called Saint Vincent's, but it was accompanied by a tuition-supported school to help fund it. A school for boys was founded as an afterthought. Boys too young and unprepared to begin classical studies at the university attended this preparatory school. Later, Archbishop Kenrick gave $1,000 from the Thornton estate to the Saint Vincent Free School for its support.

When Kenrick arrived in Saint Louis, he found Bishop Rosati had purchased property south of the Cathedral in order to build a church for German Catholics. At that time, the Germans attended Mass at the chapel of Saint Aloysius on the Saint Louis University campus, though many had begun to live in the south part of the city. So it became imperative to build a church, Saint Mary of Victories. The building cost just $8,000, but Bishop Kenrick wrote to Archbishop Vincenz Milde of the Leopoldine Society that the diocese was still $2,000 short in finishing the project. He noted that the Germans the church served were mainly working-class and unable to assume the financial burden themselves. These were the same parishioners who would turn to Father Heim to keep their meager savings safe in the banking project that would soon become diocesan-wide.

In May 1845, St. Patrick's Church was dedicated on Sixth and Biddle. The Biddle family contributed generously to the erection of the church, though it added significantly to the already indebted diocese. Six months later, Bishop Kenrick consecrated another church on the south side, Saint Vincent de Paul. The parish was put in the hands of the Vincentian fathers, who accepted the challenge of a tri-lingual congregation. Some of the old Creoles were still around and preferred their sermons in French. But the neighborhood rapidly filled with Irish and German immigrants.

The incredible generosity of these working-class families was a tribute to their deep faith and eagerness to preserve their culture. This was made evident by the establishment of a parochial school at the same time the parish was founded. Saint Vincent School was directed by Father John Uhland from 1851 until his death in 1855. As the population of the neighborhood grew and school enrollment increased, the school was divided into a boy's section under the direction of the Christian Brothers and a girl's section run by the Sisters of Charity. At its height, 900 children attended Saint Vincent School.

Father Uhland, besides being the administrator of the school, also served as rector of the German part of the parish. The founding pastor was Father Francis Xavier Dahman, a native of the Rhineland and former cavalryman in Napoleon's army. Father Dahman was a happy-go-lucky character whose administrative and financial burdens were carried by yet another resident priest, Father Blasius Raho.

With the exception of Father Uhland, priests came and went rapidly at Saint Vincent's. In 1847, Father Raho was sent to New Orleans. Father Francis Burlando was sent from the Vincentian seminary to run Saint Vincent Parish, but was transferred three years later to be replaced by Father Dahman, who returned as pastor, but only for two years. His replacement served two years and was replaced by an Irishman, Father John O'Reilly, who served two years.

Back at the Cathedral, another movement was underway. On November 20, 1845, four laymen met with Bishop Kenrick. Two doctors, Moses Linton and Thomas Anderson, Judge Bryan Mullanphy, son of John Mullanphy, founder of the Catholic hospital, and John Everhart. They received permission from Kenrick to establish a Conference of the Saint Vincent de Paul Society in Saint Louis. The Society had been founded in Paris by Frédéric Ozanam to bring relief to the poor by personal acts of charity. Ozanam was from a Christian-Jewish family and quickly attracted over 1,000 men to the cause as it spread from Paris in 1833 to all parts of France, then to Rome, Brussels, London, Dublin, and even Constantinople. The Saint Louis organization was the first in the Western Hemisphere and expanded rapidly to other parishes and then to other American dioceses. Today, Saint Louis is still the national headquarters of the Saint Vincent de Paul Society.

Bishop Kenrick appointed Father Ambrose Heim, his secretary, as the spiritual director. Dr. Moses Linton was elected as president of the Society. He taught in the medical school at Saint Louis University, authored several books, and edited the first medical journal west of the Mississippi. Bryan Mullanphy served as vice president and in 1847 was elected mayor of Saint Louis. Mullanphy's generosity extended beyond his life, as he willed a large legacy of $200,000 to aid immigrants in Saint Louis.

Other parishes soon founded their own conferences of the Saint Vincent de Paul Society as it assumed work unable to be done by the Female Charitable Society, an ecumenical effort started in 1824 by Governor Alexander McNair, the Missouri Hibernian Relief Society founded in 1827, and the lay Catholic organization known as the Society for the Diffusion of Alms founded in 1838 by Bryan Mullanphy. All these organizations were pressed to their limits as Saint Louis recovered from the Great Flood of 1844 and was about to experience the Great Fire of 1849, plus the return of cholera that same year.

On January 24, 1849, Archbishop Kenrick went to the levee to greet several Sisters of the Good Shepherd who had made their way by steamboat from Louisville, Kentucky. Four years earlier, they had arrived in Louisville at the invitation of Bishop Flaget. That foundation was firm enough to free three sisters for Saint Louis. The particular charism of the Sisters of the Good Shepherd was to aid women in vulnerable positions in society. The community was founded by Saint John Eudes in France in the 1600s. Their houses were havens for women who wanted to leave lives of prostitution, as well as young girls who were homeless and desperate. The Sisters helped restore dignity to these women.

The first house given to the Sisters had been a gift of a dying priest, who willed it as a retirement home or infirmary for diocesan priests. As there were at that time no priests in the diocese in those categories, Archbishop Kenrick let the Sisters use it. It was perfect for their needs. It had been built by Mary Alice Smith, a wealthy woman who had donated land to the diocese, first at Grand Couteau, Louisiana, then to Saint Michael's Parish in Fredericktown, Missouri, and finally this house to her private chaplain, Father Francis Cellini. As a result, she was permitted to build a chapel onto the house.

Donations flowed to the Sisters. A new facility was built on the western edge of the city between 16th and 17th Streets, bordered on the north by Pine and on the south by Chestnut. The land was donated by Ann Lucas Hunt. Kenrick donated funds from his own money and inspired others to do the same. With time, the facility housed three hundred women and girls, helping them to restore their dignity, their health, and their moral purity. Some sixty of these women opted not to return to civil life to seek employment and husbands, but to remain for the rest of their lives in contemplative prayer. They called themselves the Community of Magdalens.

The lives of these women had been horrible. These were not the courtesans who catered to high society or even the residents of the "parlour houses" where women feasted on roasts and milk and were served by maids, protected by bouncers, and given access to medical personnel, all under the careful eye of the house madam. Most likely, these women were "crib prostitutes", like their counterparts in the Wild West. They were controlled by pimps and housed in dingy frame dwellings which were "workshops" designed to process as many customers as possible. Anne Seagraves, in her excellent book *Soiled Doves: Prostitution in the Early West,* tells the story of Julia Bulette, a prostitute in Virginia City, Nevada:

She was kind and well-liked by the miners; her generosity and dona-tions to charity earned a measure of respect and gratitude. Julia nursed the sick and injured men back to health, fought a smallpox epidemic, fed the poor, and because of her help to the fire department, she became an honorary member of the Virginia City Company Number One.

But Seagraves continues the story to tell of Julia's murder: "...stran-gled, shot, suffocated and severely beaten – all of her personal posses-sions were stolen."[52]

Julia's demise was sad, but not out of the ordinary. Seagraves notes, "The majority of the soiled doves ended up with an abortionist, who usually did a bad job and left them sterile, or they attempted to abort the child themselves, which often destroyed their reproductive sys-tems. It was also discovered that 'regular use of opiates' caused dis-ruption or total cessation of menstruation and it was possible that

---

52   Anne Seagraves. *Soiled Doves: Prostitution in the Early West.* Hayden, Idaho: Wesanne Publications. P. 62.

prostitutes used opiates as form of birth control."[53] Many ended their own lives, lonely and in misery.

Very rapidly, this important women's apostolate spread. In 1859, the house was made a novitiate for young women who wished to join the Good Shepherd Sisters. Daughterhouses spread to Chicago, Kansas City, Memphis, Omaha, Milwaukee, Saint Paul, Detroit, Peoria, Sioux City, New Orleans, and Los Angeles. A reform school was even established in Havana, Cuba.

As the city commercial center grew rapidly westward and overtook the convent of the Good Shepherd Sisters, a quieter location was found when eleven acres were donated by Adolphus Busch on Gravois Road in the county; Mrs. Winifred Patterson matched that gift with a donation of $75,000.

In all, the first decade of Peter Richard Kenrick's episcopacy was very productive. And it would be followed by an even more successful second decade.

The year 1849 in St. Louis saw the Great Fire, the return of cholera, and violent anti-Irish riots. It also saw the erection of four important parishes: Saint John the Apostle and Evangelist, Saint Michael's, Most Holy Trinity, and Saints Peter and Paul. With these additions, Saint Louis entered the 1850s with nine parishes; the city would see the need for more year after year. It is hard to fathom today, but the decision to build Saint John's was an incredible act of foresight. Taking Washington Avenue west, one ended the journey at Seventh Street, where an orchard stood. Some of the surrounding land was being farmed, but much of it was still forested.

The founding pastor of Saint John's was Father Patrick O'Brien of County Cork, Ireland. His family had moved to Potosi in 1839, and young Patrick studied at the seminary in the Barrens. He was ordained in 1846, assigned to the Cathedral, and sent on a missionary tour of Missouri. Not yet ordained two years, Father O'Brien was given the assignment of founding Saint John's. The young priest immediately erected a wood frame church at the end of Washington and Seventh, and called upon his parishioners to bring him bricks. Some of his father's skills as an engineer had rubbed off on the young pastor, and he began the construction of a second, brick church. Later, this modest church would be dwarfed by a third church, the St. John's which stands

53   David Courtright. "Opiate Addiction in America: A Dissertation". Rice University, 1979, P. 93. As cited in Ibid. P. 63.

today. The little brick church was nicknamed Saint John's Library, as the next church was built for pontifical functions, in the words of Father Rothensteiner. The rectory was large enough to accommodate not only a pastor and an assistant priest, but also a coadjutor bishop and Archbishop Kenrick himself.

At Eleventh and Clinton, property was purchased and Saint Michael's Parish was established. The new parish was the eldest daughter of Saint Patrick's, itself only four years old. The founding pastor was Father John Higginbotham, a Dubliner ordained in 1845. He erected a small frame church for his 100 families and connected a small rectory to it. There was no provision for a school, so the parish children attended the public school nearby. A later pastor, Father Michael Prendergast, developed a bond of friendship with the school and was often invited to attend the public examinations and to give reflections to the students. He served as pastor only two years before his death.

Further north, the area called Bremen was being populated by Germans, especially Catholics from Westphalia. They attended St. Joseph's Church on Biddle Street, but it was a considerable walk, especially in inclement weather. The new Saint Michael's would cut the distance in half, but of course, it was an English language parish, so that would not do. After the winter of 1848, a delegation of six men who lived in Bremen met with the Vicar General Father Joseph Melcher to petition for a parish up north. When he suggested they wait for a year, they went over his head to meet with Archbishop Kenrick. The Archbishop sympathized with their plight and was pleased to know he would not have to buy property. The Mallinckrodt family donated a large lot on Eleventh and Mallinckrodt, while the Bernard Farrar family gave a similarly sized lot on Fourteenth Street.

The first church was dedicated on the feast of Holy Trinity, 1849, and received the name Most Holy Trinity. But there were difficulties from the start. The first pastor, Father Theodore Laurensen, stayed just eleven months. He was replaced by Father Joseph Blaarer, and he left within a year. Stability came in 1850 with Father John Anselm. It was during Father Anselm's pastorate that a brick church was built, baptisms rose to over 150 each year, and weddings took place nearly every week.

Father Anselm remained pastor until he developed differences with his young, very popular assistant pastor, Father Franz Goller. The assistant was later transferred, which caused such a rebellion in the

Holy Trinity congregation that Archbishop Kenrick had to transfer the pastor to restore peace. Father Anselm himself received his own peace when he was named the first resident pastor of Sainte Anne's in French Village, with a mission church, Saint Philomena, in Bloomsdale.

While three of the four new parishes were in the north, St. John's on Washington, St. Michael's on Clinton, and Most Holy Trinity on Mallinckrodt, the fourth parish was south in the Soulard addition. The addition was named for Antoine Soulard, a onetime surveyor for the Spanish during the pre-American phase of Saint Louis history. He was counted among the "junto," Creole families like the Chouteaus, the Bernard Pratte family, and others. By 1841, when the City of Saint Louis was permitted to expand sevenfold by annexing its neighbors, the Soulard Addition was swallowed up. The act gave the property owners a marvelous opportunity to make money selling their land.

Julia Soulard, daughter of Gabriele Cerré, the wealthiest man in Saint Louis, was the largest developer. She was followed by Sophie Chouteau, grand-daughter-in-law of Pierre Laclède and widow of Auguste Pierre Chouteau. Others included Joseph Papin, in-law to the Chouteaus; Bernard Pratte Junior, son of a prominent fur trader and mayor of Saint Louis in 1844; Louis Labeaume, a heavy investor in railroads; and Louis Bogy, lawyer, banker, U.S. Senator, and investor in the Pilot Knob ironworks as well as in Wiggins Ferry, which had a virtual monopoly on Illinois-Missouri transfers on the Mississippi River.

Newcomers were also engaged in the real estate boom in the south part of Saint Louis. Thomas Allen was a 34-year-old lawyer from Massachusetts. He married Ann Russell, the daughter of William Russell, whom President Thomas Jefferson named to replace Antoine Soulard as surveyor. When his father-in-law died, leaving his mansion and property to Ann, Thomas Allen bought some 30 acres contiguous to the property and hired the city engineer, William Cozzens, to lay out a plan with straight streets and uniform lots. Once the plat was filed with the City of Saint Louis, Thomas Allen became part of what researcher Eric Sandweiss refers to as "the landed political elite."

Allen sold to Archbishop Kenrick an entire block of the first addition. He gave the Archdiocese a break, asking only $100 as a down payment on the $4,809 total price. In exchange, the Archbishop established Saints Peter and Paul Parish, which served the German community in the area; more importantly, Allen attracted even more Germans. By 1853, Allen made over $50,000 on land sales, all based on an initial investment of less than $8,000.[54]

The first pastor of Saints Peter and Paul was Father Simon Sigrist, from Alsace. He had been one of Melcher's men, recruited out of the University of Strasbourg and brought to Saint Louis in 1847. A year and a half after ordination, Father Sigrist was named the founding pastor. Already a foundation for a church had been laid, but work was suspended until Father Sigrist's arrival. The brick structure was completed at a cost of $18,000.

The congregation grew rapidly, but Father Sigrist had no mind for finances, and the parish debt grew rapidly as well. Two assistant priests were replaced by one, Father Franz Goller, who had left Most Holy Trinity under unhappy circumstances. And now he walked into a similar maelstrom. Some parishioners were angry about Father Sigrist's lack of administrative skills. They turned to the new assistant and tried to get him to turn against his pastor. To Father Goller's credit, he refused to take the bait.

Nonetheless, things turned against the new assistant. The pastor felt the sting of the opposition and took it out on his young assistant. The whole rectory household treated Father Goller so badly that he finally asked for an interview with Archbishop Kenrick. There, he poured out his heart and requested yet another transfer, perhaps even outside of the Archdiocese. Instead, Archbishop Kenrick made Father Goller the pastor of Saints Peter and Paul and removed Father Sigrist. This coup was not without its controversy. Supporters of Father Sigrist mocked Father Goller and called him a mere child. Short in stature and youthful in appearance, the young priest stood in stark contrast to the stately Father Sigrist. The ousted priest himself felt slighted and even contemplated forming a new parish with his supporters. In the end, schism was avoided and Father Sigrist was invited to serve the Germans of Indianapolis. That he did with distinction until his death in 1873.

Father Franz Salesius Goller was merely 25 years old when he became pastor of Saints Peter and Paul. His mind was keen and well trained. Before coming to America, Goller studied at the University of Tübingen, intent on becoming a priest for the Paderborn diocese. Instead, he met Father Joseph Melcher and became a Melcher man for Saint Louis. It was on the fateful All Saints Day, November 1, 1855,

---

54   Eric Sandweiss. *St. Louis: The Evolution of an American Urban Landscape.* Philadelphia: Temple University Press. 2001. P. 55.

the day of the failure of the bridge over the Gasconade River which led to the deaths of so many prominent Saint Louisans, that he and Caspar Doebbner were ordained by Archbishop Kenrick. From 1858 to his death on August 18, 1910, Father Goller was pastor of Saints Peter and Paul Parish. The parishioners came to appreciate their pastor as a learned theologian, comfortable with Augustine, Aquinas, and Bonaventure. He built the present Gothic church that dominates the Soulard neighborhood. The effort cost the parish $92,000 when it was completed in 1875. Nonetheless, Father Goller led his congregation to pay off the entire debt by 1887.

More building followed, including a new rectory and a steeple tower. All this cost another $33,000. Father Goller is noted for saying, "I want this church to be as beautiful as possible, that the poor, of whom there are many among us, might also have a beautiful house which they could call their own."[55]

Hand-in-hand with Catholic worship came Catholic education. In 1859, Father Goller introduced the Sisters of Notre Dame to his parish. The school grew to 1,300 children. Father Goller experimented with forming a religious community of men to teach the boys. That failed within five years, so he turned to the Brothers of Mary in 1897. In 1898, the Brothers formed a parochial high school.

Catholic education was a passion for Father Goller. At the Third Plenary Council of Baltimore in 1884, Archbishop Kenrick invited Fathers Goller and Bonacum to act as his theologians. Father Goller was active in forming a block of bishops who favored a mandate to establish parochial schools in every parish. Such legislation was passed, and a severe penalty was placed on pastors who resisted. If a pastor, prevented by his negligence or after repeated episcopal admonition, took no steps to erect and sustain a school, he was subject to removal from his church.

The Third Plenary Council of Baltimore dealings with the school question will be considered later, but it is important to note Father Goller's role at the Council and in Catholic parochial education. When Cardinal Satolli, the Papal Nuncio, visited Saint Louis in April 1896, he visited Saints Peter and Paul and found a school of 1,300 children to greet him. The welcoming address was delivered by Father Goller in flawless Latin. He emphasized the importance of Catholic parochial

---

55   John Rothensteiner. *History of the Archdiocese of St. Louis. II.* Saint Louis: Blackwell Wielandy Co. 1928. P. 107.

education in a country where public schools had no liberty to teach religion.

By the time of his death in 1910, Father Goller, by then a Monsignor, could look with great pride on his school. During his tenure, it had produced 22 priests, 160 religious sisters, and an army of devout Catholic laity.

In May 1849, Archbishop Peter Richard Kenrick left Saint Louis to attend the Seventh Provincial Council of Baltimore. It had been called by Archbishop Eccleston to discuss Church matters, particularly the way in which priests should be recommended to Rome for elevation to the episcopacy. In the end, it was decided that the Archbishop of the province in which the diocese was vacant should recommend names to the other American Archbishops and that their opinions would be forwarded to Rome. A year later, the Sacred Congregation for the Propagation of the Faith approved of the method.

Archbishop Kenrick returned home to call his own synod. It was the second diocesan synod, the first since the one called eleven years earlier by Bishop Rosati. Forty-three priests of the forty-seven in the Archdiocese attended. Eight of the attendees had been at the first synod. The gathering began with a retreat for the diocesan priests, which lasted from Monday to Thursday, conducted by a Jesuit, Father Peter Speicher. A requiem Mass was celebrated on Friday morning for Bishop Rosati and the other deceased priests of the Archdiocese, after which diocesan business was conducted.

A state of the Archdiocese was published, showing that the Catholic population was nearly 60,000 people. There were, in 1848, 3,705 baptisms, 1,032 marriages, and 973 funerals; proofs of a very active archdiocese! In the first synod, the City of Saint Louis boasted one parish church, the Cathedral. By 1849, it was joined by Saint Mary of Victories, Saint Francis Xavier "College" Church, Saint Patrick's, Saint Michael's, Saint Joseph's, Most Holy Trinity, Saint John the Apostle, Saint Vincent de Paul, and Saints Peter and Paul. Nearby were Saints Mary and Joseph in Carondelet, Saint Ferdinand in Florissant, Saint Peter in Kirkwood, and Assumption in Matisse Creek. In Saint Charles County were Saint Peter in Dardenne, Saint Francis of Assisi in Portage de Sioux, and Saint Charles Borromeo and Saint Peter in Saint Charles City.

Further afield were parishes in these counties: Sainte Genevieve, Perry, New Madrid, St. Francois, Gasconade, Jackson, Franklin, Washington, Scott, Cape Girardeau, Henry, Madison, Monroe, Cole, Clay, Saline, Lincoln, Moniteau, Clark, Buchanan, Rolls, Platte, and Osage. The synod ended with the publication of a pastoral letter on receiving communion, on marriage, and on Catholic education.

An area of continued concern was the ongoing assault in the print media against Catholicism, especially aimed at the German immigrants. To counter these attacks, the pastor of Saint Joseph's Parish, Father Martin Seisl, S.J., joined with P. Kessel, a former employee of Francis Salers Printing Company, to introduce *Herold des Glaubens* (Herald of the Faith). The paper struggled financially for nearly two years until Francis Salers took an interest in its success. Salers used profits from his own businesses to expand *Herold* and bring in a first-rate editor, a convert, Dr. Thomas Baumstark. Unlike the previous attempts at Catholic journalism, *Herold des Glaubens* had a wide appeal into the West and Southwest of the United States.

But in Saint Louis, there was a demand for a daily newspaper, and *Herold* was only published weekly. *Tages-Chronik* addressed that need as a way to counter the stinging criticism of left-leaning dailies like *Anzeiger des Westens*. *Tages-Chronik* seems to have failed around 1861, but not before a humorous ruse was played on its editor. The story is told that the editor, a man named Meyer, was very lazy and rather than hustle for news stories, he would go downstairs where another newspaper was published, *The Republican*. Meyer made it a habit of lifting whole articles from *The Republican* and publishing them as his own. Finally, the editors of *The Republican* decided to act. They made up a false newspaper to be printed first thing in the morning. The lead article described a sensational murder in a house on Pine Street. Meyer lifted the whole story and printed it down to the last detail. The next day, the real *Republican* was printed with no mention of a Pine Street murder. Meyer was the laughingstock of Saint Louis for weeks.

The German priests circulated their own publication, *Pastoral-Blatt*. It was a monthly journal with theological, pastoral, and practical articles. This, too, was published in the shops of Francis Saler, though it did not appear until 1866.

In 1853, the Archdiocese bought what had been the Henry Clay farm, northwest of the city. More acreage contiguous to the farm was also purchased. An old mansion was located there, and Archbishop Kenrick used it as a country home from time to time. In 1854, the property was turned into Calvary Cemetery and lots were offered on

April 1, 1854; immediately reinternments began from the old cemetery at Seventeenth and Franklin, Rock Springs, and Holy Trinity. Later, remains at the Cathedral and at Saint Vincent's on Jefferson and Geyer were brought to Calvary.

In all, Calvary contained 208 acres. Archbishop Kenrick insisted that the cemetery be arranged like a park, taking advantage of the rolling landscape, with beautiful trees, shrubbery, and flowerbeds. Lawns graced the roadways and a special section was set aside for priests. It was run by the Calvary Cemetery Association, and any profits made from the cemetery would be transferred to the Catholic orphan asylum of Saint Louis.

Perhaps Kenrick was inspired by the recent developments next door. William McPherson, a prominent Saint Louis banker, brought together other Saint Louisans interested in constructing a first-class cemetery north and west of the city. They purchased 314 acres, including the Hempstead farm and much of the John O'Fallon property, and set about constructing it along the principles of the "Rural" Cemetery Movement.

Americans were rapidly abandoning crowded urban cemeteries in favor of parks for the deceased. First introduced outside Paris in 1804, the setting rapidly spread to Boston in 1831, Philadelphia in 1836, and Lowell, Massachusetts in 1841. The Bellefontaine Cemetery was to bring a spotlight to Saint Louis, showing it as a major American city on the rise. Indeed, the population had exploded in the decades before and the city was now the eighth largest in America. "Bellefontaine's founders hoped that the cemetery would become a major civic, cultural, and historical institution – a 'community classroom.' Visitors walking through the cemetery – especially newly arrived Irish and German immigrants – were meant to be inspired by notable examples of St. Louisans, bolstering a sense of community and civic identity for their adopted home. The cemetery was also to be a showcase for fine art, architecture, and horticulture."[56]

To make this dream a reality, the Bellefontaine Trustees hired Almerin Hotchkiss, a 33-year-old landscape architect who had designed other park cemeteries, including Lake Forest in Chicago. Within a year, Hotchkiss and his crew cleared 100 acres in preparation for burials. The cemetery was opened in 1849. Many of the old trees were re-

---

56   Bellefontaine Cemetery Website.

tained; others were removed and replaced with new and exotic ones as well as beds of flowering shrubs, grasses, and flower beds, both perennial and annual. Everywhere the lay of the land was preserved, including hills and valleys and glens. The main roadway was 20 feet wide with eight foot shoulders on each side. It ran to the contour of the landscape. Hotchkiss remained the Supervisor of Bellefontaine Cemetery for 46 years.

Calvary was similarly constructed under the initial leadership of John Baptist C. Lucas. When Calvary added some 240 contiguous acres of farmland, making it around 500 acres, the cemetery was the third largest in America at that time.

Father Rothensteiner, in his *History of the Archdiocese of St. Louis*, called the cemetery "one of the monuments of Archbishop Kenrick, one of the showplaces of our city: 'a thing of beauty and a joy forever.'" He then went on to quote a report from the cemetery superintendent, showing the influence the "Rural" Cemetery Movement had on the design of Calvary, as it had on Bellefontaine next door.

A modern Cemetery must be arranged on the so-called park and lawn plan, avoiding as much as possible all unnecessary accumulation of stonework, iron fencing and bars, which disfigure so many of the older Cemeteries. This plan takes nature for its model and in the trees, the shrubbery, the flowers and the neatly kept lawn, gives the burying place of our dear departed ones, the moods of peace, and longing hope, and sympathy.[57]

Although the original intent was that the profits would support all orphan institutions, the German Saint Vincent Orphan Home was excluded because the Calvary board had not received significant support from the German parishes.

In that same year, 1854, two more parishes were erected, Saint John Nepomuk and Saint Bridget of Erin. The first pastor of Saint John's was Father Henry Lipowski, the son of a Bohemian knight. After private tutoring, Henry attended school in Prague before joining and then leaving a Jesuit formation house. In 1846, he joined the Austrian army to campaign under the legendary Field Marshal Joseph Radetzky. But after two battles, military life lost its appeal. Lipowski migrated to the United States, joined the seminary in Saint Louis, and

57   Report of Superintendent Matthew P. Brazill, 1888. As cited in John Rothensteiner. *The History of the Archdiocese of St. Louis.* St. Louis: Blackwell Wielandy Co. 1928. P. 162.

completed his theological studies. He was ordained in December 1853 and was assigned as assistant at Saint Mary of Victories, where Vicar General Joseph Melcher was pastor. There, Lipowski came to edit *Herold des Glaubens*.

Unfortunately, the Bohemian noble was not a perfect fit. Father Lipowski carried himself in a military style, which alienated many of the parishioners he had gathered at Saint John's. In July 1856, he left America for his home in Europe. Leadership of the parish fell to Father Francis Trojan, himself a native of Monrovia. He was a Melcher man, among the first recruits. After service at Apple Creek, Cape Girardeau, and Chester, Illinois, Father Trojan was named pastor at Saint John Nepomuk. He served there from 1856 to 1864. His successor, Father Joseph Hessoun, would be the pastor to expand the parish, build its magnificent church, and found a Bohemian language weekly, *Hlas*.

Saint Bridget of Erin was erected at Carr and Jefferson in 1853. The cornerstone of the present church was laid in 1859. A girls' school was established, run by the Sisters of Saint Joseph. After 1871, a boys' section was opened under the leadership of the Christian Brothers. The founding pastor was Father John Christopher Fittman; but it was his successor, Father David Lillis, who built the present church. Saint Bridget became identified early on with Kerry Patch, the Irish neighborhood, as was Saint Patrick's on Sixth and Biddle.

The Irish who arrived in Saint Louis were desperately poor. They had endured lifelong hardships in Ireland at the hands of the British, who had forbidden them to use their native tongue, practice their religion openly, or seek to educate their children. Life was at least tolerable until the mid-1840s, due to the abundance of the nutritious potato. But a potato blight robbed the Irish of their staple food and drove one million to flee the country, while another estimated one million died of starvation and disease.

Many from the agricultural County Kerry migrated in "coffin ships," so named because as many as one quarter of the passengers died in transit. Their American destination was the port of New Orleans. From there, if they could afford the price, they booked passage on a steamship for Saint Louis. The poorest had to work their way north, many settling in Memphis in a neighborhood called The Pinch. A story has it that in that Irish enclave the people were so malnourished that, if you pinched one of them, there was no meat between the folds of flesh.

Saint Louis was a mecca for these Irish who had known only discrimination and hardship all their lives. They found Irish-Americans who aided their settlement in their adopted home. Millionaire John Mullanphy, of Fermanagh, set aside land north of Carr Street for them to build their shanties. His son, Bryan Mullanphy, and his daughter, Ann Mullanphy Biddle, greatly aided in their settlement and helped them find jobs. The brother and sister also strove to protect the Irish from harsh vagrancy laws the city had enacted. Bryan served as mayor of Saint Louis at one point and argued continually with the Board of Aldermen and with the chief of police over their treatment of the poor.

Parishes like Saint Bridget of Erin, Saint Patrick's, Saint Michael's, and Saint Lawrence O'Toole were true havens for these immigrants, who eventually made up more than forty percent of the city's population. Saint Lawrence O'Toole Parish was founded in 1855, just blocks away from the German church, St. Joseph's at Eighth and Biddle. The first pastor was Father James Henry, who had distinguished himself during the Know-Nothing years in his defense of Saint Patrick's Church, where he served as assistant. Alerted to an impending attack, Father Henry, a native of County Cavan, Ireland, gathered men and boys and oversaw their struggle with a Know-Nothing mob. The affair proved deadly when the leader of the anti-Catholic assault, nicknamed Violet, was killed.

Land for Saint Lawrence O'Toole was donated by Miss Jane Graham, and three years later a school was built on the adjoining lot donated by Mrs. Jane Chambers, both members of the Mullanphy family. What a Know-Nothing mob could not do to Father Henry's Saint Patrick's was done to Father Henry's Saint Lawrence O'Toole by a cyclone, which hit in 1864. It destroyed the facility entirely. Undaunted, Father Henry set about raising funds in the midst of the Civil War and had enough money to build a new church in one year.

Halfway between Saint Joseph's and Most Holy Trinity, two German parishes, and between the Irish parishes of Saint Malachy and Saint Bridget and Saint Lawrence O'Toole, the neighborhood was quickly filling with German immigrants. These people were uniformly from Westphalia in Germany, particularly the city of Paderborn. They longed for their own parish, as they were twelve blocks south of Holy Trinity and six blocks north and seven west of Saint Joseph. The driving force behind a parish formation was a layman, Liborius Musenfechter. In 1850 alone, forty German Catholic families moved into the neighborhood. Meetings were held at the Musenfechter house on Eighteenth and Monroe. When Archbishop Kenrick was unable to provide funds for the founding of a parish, Liborius Musenfechter donated his wheat field on Eighteenth and Hogan. Others pledged building materials throughout the winter of 1855.

In the meantime, during Father Melcher's second recruiting tour to Germany, he gathered ten new recruits, one being Father Stephen Schweihoff of Paderborn. Now, with Archbishop Kenrick's blessing, Father Schweihoff was sent to join Liborius Muselfechter in founding the parish of Saint Liborius. Father Schweihoff was born in 1815 and ordained for the diocese of Paderborn in 1840. The patron saint of Paderborn is Saint Liborius, and so choosing to place the parish under the patronage of this fourth-century saint was a nod both to the city and the region from which so many of these Germans had emigrated, but also to the first benefactor of the parish, Liborius Musenfechter.

Later, the parish received a financial boost from Archbishop Kenrick by way of distribution of the Thornton estate as a long-term loan. Soon a school was added to the parish, and in 1858 the Sisters of Notre Dame organized a school for seventy children. Only after a fine brick church and school were built did Father Schweihoff turn his attention to a rectory. Until then he lived in a two-room rental; the first room was used as the church, while the second room served as his bedroom and office. He lived a life of severe detachment, and when he died in 1869, he had nothing of worldly possessions except a fine library of books, which he willed to the Franciscans, and a wardrobe of vestments, which he left to the parish.

In the next four years parishes were founded annually: Saint Malachy in 1858, Annunciation in 1859, St. Boniface in 1860, and Assumption in 1861. Each in their own way spoke to the developments of the coming decade. Saint Malachy was founded by Father John O'Sullivan who, during the Civil War, would have to flee Saint Louis as the Federals condemned his southern sympathies. Annunciation would be founded by Father Patrick John Ryan, future coadjutor to Archbishop Kenrick and the Archbishop of Philadelphia, a man whose role in the second half of the nineteenth century in Saint Louis was decisive. Saint Boniface was a south side parish founded to accommodate the ballooning German population, those "damned Dutch," as Saint Louisans began to call them. The final parish in the series was Assumption on Eighth and Sidney Street, the only English-language parish on the south side. It was founded by the efforts of John Doyle and the Vincentian Father

Raphael Capezuto. The founding pastor was soon replaced by Father Bernard O'Reilly, who dedicated the church on November 30, 1862, as the nation, the state, and the city were torn asunder in the worst conflict in American history.

Father Joseph Hessoun of the Bohemian parish St. John Nepomuk, no date. Archdiocese of St. Louis Archives and Records.

Close-up of Saint John Hospital, the L-shaped building, on the corner of 22nd and Morgan. From *Compton and Dry's Pictorial St. Louis, the Great Metropolis of the Mississippi Valley: A Topographical Survey Drawn in Perspective A.D. 1875* (St. Louis: Compton & Co., 1876).

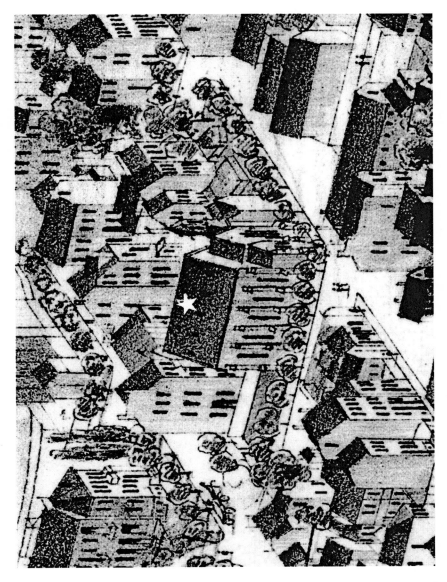

Close-up of the modest church of Saint Michael (with star icon) at the corner of 11th and Jefferson Streets. From *Compton and Dry's Pictorial St. Louis, the Great Metropolis of the Mississippi Valley: A Topographical Survey Drawn in Perspective A.D. 1875* (St. Louis: Compton & Co., 1876).

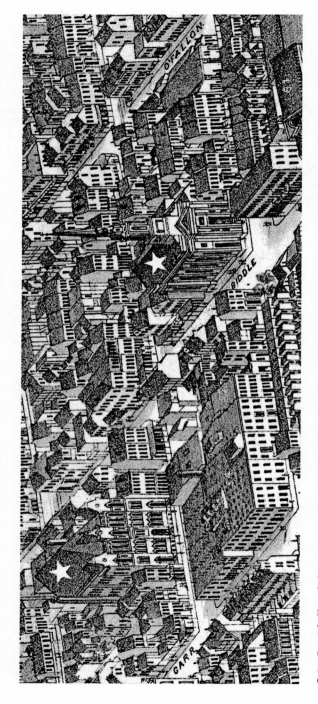

Saint Patrick Church (star icon on the right) at 6th and Biddle, and the large parish school building (star icon on the left). From *Compton and Dry's Pictorial St. Louis, the Great Metropolis of the Mississippi Valley: A Topographical Survey Drawn in Perspective A.D. 1875* (St. Louis: Compton & Co., 1876).

107

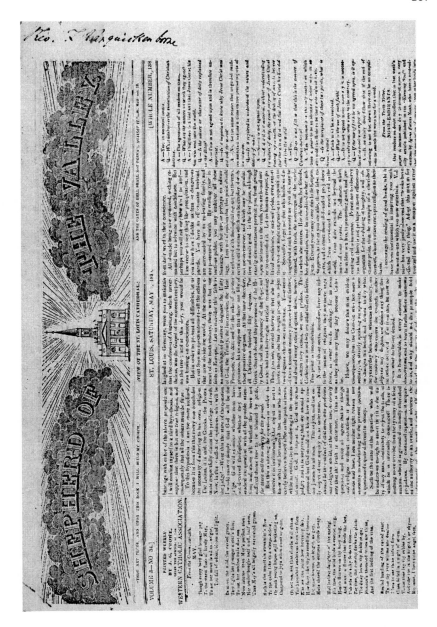

Shepherd of the Valley Newspaper, Vol. 3, No. 34, May 9, 1835 Archdiocese of St. Louis Archives and Records.

Chapter Five

DRED AND HARRIET SCOTT: NO JUSTICE, NO PEACE

Henry T. Blow was thirteen years old when his family moved to Saint Louis. He had quite a trek, beginning with his birth in Virginia in 1817. His father owned 860 acres of plantation land, but after generations of farming, it was no longer yielding fine crops. Peter Blow had a wife from an old, genteel Virginia family, a bevy of 12 children, and a handful of slaves, but little else when his older brother died, leaving his estate to two former slaves and a girl who was believed to be his daughter by a slave.

Peter Blow sold his plantation and moved the whole household to Alabama, buying 160 acres of virgin land. The move was full of hardships, but was made endurable through the kindness of one of the male slaves, a young man named Dred.

To see to it that the roads were passable, the Blows traveled in the dead of winter, adding to the discomfort of a wagon journey in which some family members rode horses and the slaves walked. They arrived in Huntsville in December 1818. To assure a successful crop, all the Blow slaves worked in the fields the first season, but all for naught. The economic downturn that came in the early 1820s drove cotton prices from $.25 a pound to $.12 a pound. Debts mounted, and Peter Blow's sole collateral was his slaves. There were but nineteen, ranging from Solomon at age 62 to Zach, age 13. Dred was around 16 years old at the time. In the end, Peter Blow found a buyer for his Alabama acreage (and probably for two slaves whose records were lost to history at the time). The family located in the town of Florence on the Tennessee River. Peter opened a hotel, the Peter Blow Inn. It was 1821.

Everyone worked. Mrs. Blow oversaw her two daughters. The boys helped out. Old Solomon ported luggage. Dred was assigned to care for the horses of the hotel clients. With time, Peter Blow bought city lots in Florence, but dreamed of bigger schemes.

In 1830, Peter Blow sold out his holdings in Florence, turning a healthy profit. The original $600 investment brought $2,000 in sales. The family moved to Saint Louis to establish the Jefferson Hotel. Again, everyone in the family pitched in. By comparison with anything the

Blows had previously experienced, Saint Louis was a big, booming city. The hotel was located on Pine Street, just west of Main. That put it within easy distance of the river levee with steamboats arriving and departing daily. It was also within walking distance of the slave markets. Dred and two other slaves were in their prime and could have been sold for top dollar. Dred already had been hired out by Peter Blow to work steamships on the Mississippi River. With the death of Mrs. Blow and the engagement of one daughter, Charlotte, life seemed all the more precarious.

Then it happened in the summer of 1831: Peter Blow entered into an agreement to sell Dred to a young Army doctor, John Emerson. After a brief period when Dred ran away and hid west of Saint Louis for a while, he returned to Dr. Emerson and moved with him to his new assignment at Fort Armstrong on Rock Island, Illinois.

Army slaves in non-slave states were called "servants," but the reality was the same. Army officers preferred Black servants to white ones. Whites were notorious for running away and laying claim to land, becoming independent farmers. Blacks, on the other hand, would be apprehended and returned, with the captors expecting a reward. Therefore, Black servants tended not to run away.

Dr. Emerson worked Dred hard, but seemed to be fair to him. For Dred, the challenge was one of climate. Northern Illinois was far colder than Saint Louis, Alabama, or Virginia, and in 1836 Dr. Emerson was posted even further north: Fort Snelling in Wisconsin territory. At Fort Snelling, Dred met Harriet. She was a 17-year-old slave of Major Lawrence Taliaferro, the Indian agent for the territory. By now Dred was in his mid-30s, but the two married soon after meeting. It is unconfirmed if the ceremony was a formal wedding or simply the custom of "jumping the broom," but it seems more likely the wedding was formal, as Major Taliaferro also served as a justice of the peace. Shortly after, Major Taliaferro sold Harriet to Dr. Emerson.

Dr. Emerson showed a concern for the couple when he requested a wood-burning stove for Dred and Harriet and their newborn Elsa during a tough winter at Fort Snelling. The quartermaster denied the request, saying that the stoves were only for officers. Even the enlisted men had to sleep with an inferior fire in their bivouac. The argument turned into a fist fight, and when Dr. Emerson went for his revolver, he had to be disarmed.

The issue of the furnace was made moot by a transfer to Florida.

That assignment did not last any longer than a previous one on the Texas-Louisiana border. In both cases, the doctor traveled alone. Dr. Emerson sent his wife, Irene, and the two slaves to Saint Louis. There, Harriet had two miscarriages, perhaps because she continued working during pregnancy. They were all joined in the summer of 1842 by Dr. Emerson, who had been dismissed from the Army, no doubt due to continual temper flares.

Earlier, Dr. Emerson had made certain land claims near Bettendorf, Iowa. Now he moved there with his wife, but left Dred and Harriet and Elsa behind in St. Louis. Iowa was a free territory, and he could no longer use the Army fiction of having "servants." Late in 1843, Dr. John Emerson died, and Irene Sanford Emerson inherited his three slaves.

For a while, Dred and Harriet were hired out to Captain Henry Bainbridge, Irene's brother-in-law. Dred traveled with the captain from Jefferson Barracks to Matamoros, Texas in 1845 and 1846 and won the captain's admiration and respect. Around this time, the couple had a second child, Lizzie. This baby differed from her seven-year-old sister in that Lizzie was born on Missouri soil, a slave state, while Elsa had been born on a steamboat on the Mississippi River in Iowa, a free state.

With the birth of Lizzie, Dred approached Irene Sanford Emerson with an offer to buy the freedom of all four. Besides working for Mrs. Emerson, Dred had been industrious and had worked further jobs. He also knew someone who would lend him more money if he needed it. Mrs. Emerson flatly refused. The Sanfords never sold their slaves unless they proved to be recalcitrant and disobedient. Then they would be "sold down the river" to the harsh life of a cotton plantation. Otherwise, the answer was no.

In the next few years, Dred and Harriet were hired out to a grocery store, Russell and Bennett. Again they won the admiration of those they worked for.

It was the love of their two daughters that brought Dred and Harriet to a crisis. They knew Mrs. Emerson, a widow, was always in need of money. They also must have known about a "baby market" operated out of a nearby house on Morgan and Garrison. There a woman bought just-weaned slave babies, raised them to childhood, and sold them in the slave market. Baby Lizzie was vulnerable. Harriet herself could fetch $1,000 and Dred was still marketable, though in his 40s. Irene Sanford Emerson's oath not to sell her slaves was only as good as economic conditions would make it.

Dred and Harriet decided on another course of action.

Harriet had joined a church, the Second African Baptist Church, led by the Rev. John R. Anderson. Anderson was a free black; his congregation was both free and slave. Harriet and Dred had also come into the acquaintance of a lawyer, Francis R. Murdoch. From him, the couple learned of a case in Missouri entitled *Winnie v. Whiteside.* It was adjudicated in 1824 and dealt with a female slave, Winnie, who had been taken to reside in Illinois in 1799. In the Saint Louis Circuit Court, she sued for her freedom, arguing that her residency in Illinois, a free state, made her free. The case made its way to the Missouri Supreme Court, which agreed with Winnie. She was a free citizen; her residency in a free state made her free.

A more recent case, *Rachel v. Walker,* had a similar outcome in 1836. This case came closer to home, as Rachel had been a slave at Fort Snelling, and her son, Jarvis, had been delivered by Dr. Emerson's predecessor. Indeed, over sixty such cases had passed through the Saint Louis Circuit Court, and all had been settled in favor of the former slaves.

Everything looked favorable for a lawsuit. The sitting judge was John M. Krum, former mayor of Alton, who had tried to reason with Elijah Lovejoy but failed to stem the mob violence which took the journalist's life. Krum was a member of the Unitarian Church founded by William Greenleaf Eliot, a quiet abolitionist. He had appointed Roswell Field to represent another female slave suing for freedom, Martha, a case that was settled for the plaintiff.

On April 6, 1846, Francis Murdoch filed with Judge Krum a petition of freedom for Dred and Harriet Scott. The use of a last name implied that Dred and Harriet were free, but they also were not wealthy, and court cases were expensive affairs. And that is how the Blow family reentered the life of Dred Scott. Dred had been sold by Peter Blow in part to pay for his wife's funeral and in part to pay for his daughter Charlotte's wedding. Charlotte Blow Charless now moved into the action. She contacted her brother, Peter Junior, a prosperous businessman who had married into the La Baume family, an old aristocratic pillar of Saint Louis. Henry Taylor Blow remembered the many kindnesses of Dred during his youth and offered to help. A sister, Patsy, was married to a lawyer who would carry the case forward. Everything appeared ready for success.

But the case rapidly grew beyond *Winnie v. Whiteside* and became a contest of wills between Mrs. Emerson, who wished to retain her slaves, and Dred and Harriet Scott, who longed for their freedom. Two families became entangled in the case. Irene Sanford Emerson's family was connected by marriage to the Pierre Chouteau Junior family, among the oldest and wealthiest of Saint Louis families, as well as the largest slaveholder in the city. John Sanford, Irene's brother, also owned slaves in Saint Charles and conducted a slave business with James H. Lucas, another prominent Saint Louisan.

This made the Blow family all the more determined to help the Scotts gain their freedom. And other allies came forward: Captain Henry Bainbridge, who had come to know and admire Dred during their time in Texas, offered to help. To add salt to the wound, Bainbridge was Mrs. Emerson's brother-in-law! Samuel Russell, co-owner of the grocery store in which Dred and Harriet had worked, also was eager to testify.

But the trial took a bizarre twist. Samuel Russell was called to testify, and when he said that Dred and Harriet had worked for him for hire and that the employment had been agreed between Mrs. Emerson and his wife, Russell could not assure the court that he knew for certain that Dred and Harriet were slaves. In the end, the 1846 trial was lost because Dred and Harriet could not prove that they had been returned to the state of slavery by Mrs. Emerson after having resided in free territory. *Winnie v. Whiteside* could not be applied in their case.

Francis Murdoch left Saint Louis for California by this time. The case had been argued by Charles D. Drake, who immediately appealed to Judge Alexander Hamilton for a new trial, noting that the reason the Scotts could not win their freedom was because they could not prove they were slaves.

It took two more years, but in January 1850, in a new case, the Scotts won their freedom, only to find the Emerson lawyers appealing to the Missouri State Supreme Court one month later. This took the case to a whole new and very ominous level. What began as a personal struggle between Irene Sanford Emerson and the Scotts escalated into a struggle between two prominent Saint Louis families. Now, in the State Supreme Court, the case took on tones of ideological, sectional, and constitutional consequences.

There were forces within the legal community in Missouri which wished to see *Winnie v. Whiteside* dismantled and abolitionism defeated. One of those was Supreme Court Justice William B. Napton. He had drafted a statement called the Jackson Resolutions, named for Claiborne Fox Jackson, leader of the pro-slavery faction of the Democratic Party in Missouri. It called upon the two Missouri U.S. Senators to support the so-called Southern Address, which defended states' rights regarding slavery against any interference by the federal government. The Southern Address had been delivered by South Carolina Senator John C. Calhoun and had become a rallying cry for those who sought to defend the institution of slavery in America. Justice Napton's intentions were revealed in a diary statement, saying he sought to use the Dred Scott case to kill *Winnie v. Whiteside*. His plans were dashed in the election of August 1851, though, when he and his fellow like-minded Justice James B. Birch were voted out of office.

The Missouri Supreme Court which would hear the Dred Scott case was mixed: Hamilton R. Gamble, a moderate, could be counted on to follow *Winnie*, William Scott, a pro-slavery Democrat, and incumbent John Ferguson Ryland, a moderate, would have been outvoted by pro-slavery Napton and Birch. But here the case took on another bizarre twist: Ryland joined pro-slavery William Scott, arguing that each state had the right to decide its future regarding slavery. That same year, in *Strader v. Graham*, the United States Supreme Court ruled that a slave's lawsuit would be governed by the laws of the state in which the suit would be filed. The majority opinion was written by Chief Justice Roger B. Taney.

This was a huge setback for the Scotts, the Blows who supported them, and for Roswell Field, their new lawyer. As he considered his options, Field, not a constitutional lawyer but a real estate lawyer, saw that *Strader v. Graham* ruled out any appeal to the federal courts from the state courts. Instead, he used a different tactic. Article 3, Section 2 of the United States Constitution specified that in controversies between citizens of different states, the federal courts would rule.

In November 1853, new litigation was submitted to the federal circuit court arguing a case between Dred Scott, a citizen of Missouri, and John Sanford of New York, Irene Sanford Emerson's brother. Dred had been listed in the 1854 and 1855 Saint Louis city directories as a resident between 10th and 11th Streets near Washington Avenue. The registry implied he was a free man.

Field expected to lose in the federal court in Saint Louis, and he did. But this allowed for the appeal that would take the case to the Supreme Court of United States. Roswell Field, a real estate lawyer, knew he was out of his league and turned for help to argue the case before the Supreme Court. He wrote to Montgomery Blair, former mayor of Saint Louis and brother of Frank Blair, an anti-slavery, pro-Union political leader. Montgomery Blair agreed to take the case. Thus developed the case of *Scott v. Sandford*, a clerical error misspelling Sanford's name. Sanford's lawyers could not argue the case on the merits of Article 3, Section 2 of the Constitution. They had to broaden their argument to question the constitutionality of the very structure of the free state/slave state divide, the 1820 Missouri Compromise. When the Supreme Court agreed to hear *Scott v. Sandford* and to consider the constitutional grounds of the Missouri Compromise, the case took on a national importance which would tear the country asunder.

The Dred Scott case was thoroughly penetrated by Catholics and Catholic ideals. Scott and his wife were not Catholic, but the Blow family, which supported them in their legal fight, was. The Chief Justice who ruled against them, Roger B. Taney, was Catholic. And Taney's greatest critic was a convert to Catholicism, Orentes Brownson. Added to this, two of the newspapers most critical of Brownson's criticism were of Catholic origin: the *New York Freeman's Journal* and the *Catholic Herald and Visitor* of Philadelphia.

Chief Justice Taney is an interesting individual. He owned ten slaves bequeathed to him by his father. In 1818 he emancipated seven and another in 1821. As a lawyer, he had no need of slaves. He could have sold them and pocketed the money. Instead, he gave them their freedom. He inherited ten and freed eight. The other two? Both were elderly and would have starved if given freedom. So Taney supported them the rest of their natural lives.

Slavery was a very complex issue in Taney's mind, considering his demeaning statement in the Dred Scott case. Taney believed the institution would die out on its own eventually. In an 1819 trial in which he joined a three-man team of lawyers to defend an abolitionist minister, Jacob Gruber, Taney commented "a hard necessity indeed compels us to endure the evil of slavery for a time." Again, this makes Taney's Dred Scott decision difficult to understand.

Another Catholic with opinions about slavery and the Dred Scott decision was the convert Orentes Brownson. He had been a Unitarian minister, scholar, author, and editor of the *Boston Quarterly Review*; he later wrote for the *Catholic World*. In 1857, Brownson wrote the article "The Slavery Question Once More" for the *New York Herald*. Slavery was a question for each state to decide, he wrote, though he personally found the institution abhorrent. He objected to it on moral grounds, but felt the federal government had no business regulating it or extending it into the territories. Brownson criticized Taney for not recognizing the human dignity of Black people and said the Chief Justice should have used natural law and religious tradition to guide them. He cited Pope Leo X condemning slavery as early as 1482.

In another article, Brownson called the Dred Scott decision "political atheism," that is, a separation of law and conscience. Too often, he argued, religious principles were not admitted to the great political, economic, and social debates of the age, and as a result, wrong, harmful, and immoral judgments are made. He concluded that Catholics had a responsibility to bring Catholic moral teaching into the national debate.

But Catholic moral teachings regarding slavery were not clear at this point. The American bishops took widely different stances on slavery. Purcell of Cincinnati wanted Catholics in his diocese to aid the Underground Railroad. So if a slave could escape from Kentucky, swim the Ohio River and make it to Ohio, he or she could be aided to get to safety in Canada. Bishop England of Charleston, South Carolina defended the practice of slavery, as did Bishop Augustine Verot of Saint Augustine, Florida. Peter Richard Kenrick never spoke on the topic, though he owned a slave who served him as a butler.

The one bishop who thought out the issue of slavery in terms of Catholic doctrine was Archbishop Francis Patrick Kenrick. His book on moral theology was widely used as a textbook in seminaries. He answered the question "May Catholics own slaves?" by writing, "The answer seems to be in the affirmative, for the defect of the title must be considered as healed by the lapses of a very long time, since the condition of society otherwise would always be uncertain."[58]

Kenrick placed the evil consequences upon the first actor but exonerates later generations. "Indeed they sin who by force take unwilling men as slaves, but it does not seem unjust to hold the descendants of these slaves in slavery, namely, a condition in which they were born and which they are not able to leave."[59] So if a person were kidnapped while farming a field and taken as a slave, that act is immoral. How-

---

58   Joseph E. Capizzi. "For What Shall We Repent? Reflections on American Bishops, Their Teaching and Slavery in the United States." *Theological Studies*. 65. 2004.
59   Francis Patrick Kenrick. Theologica Moralis 1: 107 "De Servitute." As cited in Cyprian Davis. *The History of Black Catholics in the United States.* New York: Crossroads. 1990. P. 49.

ever, if he were captured in war or born into slavery or enslaved as punishment for a crime, or even sells himself into slavery, perhaps in desperation, that is just the state of things. That is just the way things are, like being born with cancerous genes or epilepsy.

A fascinating study of Catholics owning slaves in Kentucky gives an insight into the state of affairs. Baptismal records were enlightening: between 1830 and 1849 at Saint Rose Parish in Springfield, Kentucky, 31% of all baptisms were administered to black slaves, though they made up only 25% of the population owned by Catholics. Sponsors were often other slaves or even non-slaves. Similar statistics are found for confirmations: 22%, and Christian marriages, 17%.[60] These were sacramental marriages, not "jumping over a broom!"

The Church insisted on the right to catechize Catholics slaves, but ran into violent opposition. When a Catholic school, in 1808, taught both black and white Catholic children, it was burned down the first day of classes. Similar violence was threatened in Charleston against Bishop England, and in Saint Louis when the Sisters of Saint Joseph tried to teach black children.

At Mass, segregation was the norm. Blacks, slave or free, sat in one section, typically in the back. But men and women, free and white, sat segregated also.

A quiet shame behind all of this is that, though Catholic masters often had their slaves baptized, they were not above having them beaten. Archbishop Francis Patrick Kenrick urged them "to show themselves gentle and evenhanded... and to lighten the conditions of their slaves with humanity and with zeal for their salvation."[61]

Short of emancipation, that should have worked. It did not. Again C. Walter Gollar turned to parish records. He found that between 1830 and 1865, around 25% of Christian burials were slaves who had died. After the Civil War, from 1866 to 1875, barely 5% of burials were for blacks. The same was true for other Kentucky churches.[62] Once slavery was abolished, most former Catholic slaves abandoned the Catholic Church.

The failure of the Baltimore Council of 1866 to mount an evangelical mission to these black Catholics spelled doom. The dream of Arch-

---

60   C. Walter Gollar. "Catholic Slaves and Slaveholders in Kentucky." *The Catholic Historical Review.* January 1998. P. 48.
61   Ibid. P. 53.
62   Ibid. P. 61.

bishop Martin Spalding, Francis Patrick's successor in Baltimore, was a golden opportunity to reap a harvest of souls. Neither the effort of the Mill Hill Fathers nor that of lay leaders like Daniel Rudd could stem the tide. Later, clergy and lay leaders sought to reverse what clergy and lay leaders had foolishly done a generation before.

Irene Sanford Emerson, widow of Dr. John Emerson, remarried, this time to Calvin Chaffee of Springfield, Massachusetts. He had abolitionist sentiments and in May 1857, when Mrs. Emerson's brother John Sanford died, her secret role in the enslavement of the Scotts burst on the New England newspapers. Two months earlier, the Supreme Court had handed John Sanford his victory. The Scotts were to remain slaves, and Irene became a pariah in Massachusetts society. Mr. Chaffee would not defend his wife publicly and instead made this statement to the press: "I regard slavery as a sin against God and a crime against man."[63]

Irene finally agreed to transfer ownership of the Scott family to the Blows, on the condition she could continue to draw on income from the work Dred and Harriet would do. As odious as the agreement was, all parties signed on. Dred, Harriet, Elsa, and Lizzie became free on May 26, 1857, but the damage to the nation was irreparable.

The Chief Justice of the Supreme Court, Roger B. Taney, was 80 years old and a pro-slavery southerner who had manumitted all but two old slaves earlier. He had one other feature which was extraordinary for an American in civil service of that era: he was a Catholic. He was joined by five other pro-slavery Southerner Justices and two pro-slavery Northerner Justices. Only one Justice seemed to oppose slavery.

Dred Scott had not fared well in the Saint Louis legal system. Mrs. Emerson's lawyer, Hugh Garland, would not walk into the Article 3 Section 2 trap set for him, in which a disagreement between U.S. citizens from different states would be tried in federal courts. The Sanford lawyer attacked immediately. "Dred Scott is not a citizen of the state of Missouri as alleged in his declaration, because he is a Negro of African descent; his ancestors were of pure African blood, and were brought into this country and sold as Negro slaves."[64] While Judge Robert W.

---

63   Gwyneth Swain. *Dred and Harriet Scott: A Family's Struggle for Freedom*. Minnesota: Borealis Books. 2004. P. 69.
64   Louis S. Gerteis. *Civil War Saint Louis*. Lawrence: University of Kansas Press. 2001. P. 28.

Wells agreed with Scott's lawyers that being of African descent did not disqualify one from being a U.S. citizen, he instructed the jury to rule on the case solely based on Missouri law. So Dred Scott lost in federal court due to a state interpretation of citizenship. He fared even worse in the Taney court.

Writing for the majority which had ruled for Sanford, who was by this time committed to an insane asylum, Chief Justice Taney wrote a long and rambling opinion, and it went beyond anything the previous courts had dictated. Taney wrote, "History shows that the blacks have for more than a century been regarded as beings of an inferior order, and unfit associates for the white race, either socially or politically; and had no rights which white men were bound to respect; and the black man might be reduced to slavery, bought and sold, and treated as an ordinary article of merchandise."[65]

This was March 6, 1857. This ruling was offensive to human dignity, and it also tore into shreds the Missouri Compromise when it ruled that slaves were property, and Congress had no constitutional right to regulate property. Therefore, a slaveholder could bring his slaves into the territories. That destroyed the argument for the Free Soilists, who were willing to let slavery exist in the South but not let it extend into the territories which the United States had recently acquired from Mexico and Great Britain.

Firebrands in the North, abolitionists, found a new voice of protest and threatened to ignore the Supreme Court ruling, which they called the result of "a southern debating society," noting that most of the Justices were from the south or with southern sympathies. This, in turn, inflamed the rhetoric of the South, raising the specter of secession. But it was the reflections of Frederick Douglass, an ex-slave and orator who kept audiences spellbound, that predicted the future most accurately. Regarding *Scott v. Sandford,* Douglass said, "This very attempt to blot out forever the hopes of enslaved people may be one necessary link in the chain of events preparatory to the downfall and complete overthrow of the whole slave system."[66]

But the road to the downfall and the overthrow of the slave system would be a bloody one indeed. And the first to bleed was Kansas. It would be brought about by a high-sounding principle of democracy:

---

65   Gwyneth Swain. *Dred and Harriet Scott: A Family's Struggle for Freedom.* Minnesota: Borealis Books. 2004. P. 70.

66   Ibid. P. 75.

popular sovereignty. Popular sovereignty was first introduced as a great compromise to save the Union by Senator Stephen A. Douglas of Illinois. West of Missouri and Iowa was the huge jurisdiction known as the Nebraska Territory. It ran from the south, from the Indian Territory (now Oklahoma), all the way to the Canadian border in the north and out west to the Rocky Mountains. Douglas suggested breaking this into two territories: Nebraska in the north and Kansas in the south. Each territory would, by popular sovereignty, decide if it would be free or slave. Since Kansas was north of the 36 31' line, as was Missouri, it would bend the Missouri Compromise like a pretzel.

When Congress passed the Kansas-Nebraska Act and President Franklin Pierce signed it into law, the race was on for Southerners to move to Kansas to express a pro-slave popular sovereignty; at the same time, Free Soilists, especially from New England, joined in the race to fill Kansas with anti-slave citizens. The New England Emigrant Aid Company was well organized, sending 2,000 into the Kansas territory, armed to the teeth. The 1855 election of a Kansas territorial legislature saw the balance shift back to the pro-slave side when wagonloads of "border ruffians" from Western Missouri suddenly moved to Kansas. The shenanigans won the day, as many moved from polling place to polling place, electing a pro-slave legislature which met in Shawnee Mission. In one precinct where there were just 20 registered voters, 604 votes were cast.

The Free Soilists refused to recognize the Shawnee Mission legislature and set up their own governing body in Topeka. Henry Ward Beecher, a popular preacher in New York, secretly armed them with Sharpe's rifles, smuggled west in crates marked "Bibles." These would be put to good use, as a gang of pro-slavery raiders attacked and partially burned Lawrence, Kansas, a Free Soil stronghold.

This was followed by an act of sheer madness. A fanatical abolitionist, John Brown, gathered some followers and made his way to a region known for its pro-slavery sentiments. At Potawatomi Creek, they slaughtered five innocent men in May 1856. John Brown's men assaulted their victims with swords. The act outraged southern sympathizers; all the more so when some abolitionists defended John Brown's acts.

Even as raids and counter-raids bloodied Kansas, the Shawnee Mission legislature prepared the Lecompton Constitution for a vote by popular sovereignty. Here was a truly crafty piece of legislation.

To vote for the Constitution was to make Kansas a slave state. To vote against the Constitution would protect slave owners already in Kansas. It was in reality a theoretical distinction, though, as the 1860 census found only two slaves in the whole of the Kansas territory.

The Lecompton Constitution passed and was sent to Washington for approval and permission to form as a state. The new President, James Buchanan, accepted the popular sovereignty of Kansas; but Senator Stephen A. Douglas, who had devised the popular sovereignty proposal, saw how fraudulent it was and vigorously opposed the Kansans. The Lecompton Constitution was sent back to Kansas for a revote. The Free Soilists rallied in the fair election and overturned the Constitution. Regardless, Congress was so deeply divided it did not approve of Kansas statehood until southern representatives left to join the Confederacy.

In the meantime, Kansas continued to bleed. 1855 and 1856 saw 38 murders and $2 million in property damage. Governor John Geary resigned in disgust and was replaced by Robert J. Walker, the fourth territorial government governor since the Kansas-Nebraska mess began. In 1859 Walker resigned as more Free Soilists flooded into Kansas. Among these were James Montgomery of Ohio, who organized Jayhawkers to root out pro-slavery Kansans and to launch raids into western Missouri.

Key players were now lining up for greater violence when war came. The leader of the "border ruffians" was firebrand David Rice Atchison, a Missouri Senator, who whipped up the Missouri militia into action. Claiborne Fox Jackson, educated as a lawyer, a fighter in the Black Hawk War, husband of the youngest daughter of Dr. John Sappington, a well-heeled wealthy friend of presidents and senators, sided with the southern cause. Actually, Jackson had married all three of Dr. Sappington's daughters. When the youngest died, he married the oldest. She then died and he married the middle daughter; thereupon the good doctor replied, "You can take her, but don't come back for the old woman!"[67] Later, Jackson would become Missouri's governor and try to bring the state into the Confederacy.

On the other side was James Lane from Indiana, a veteran of the Mexican War and later a Union general. While some Jayhawkers found their way into Kansas militia to fight on the Union side, others staged

---

67   James Erwin. *Guerillas in Civil War Missouri.* Charleston: The History Press. 2012. P. 16.

raids and atrocities. One such act of senseless violence came upon the Hannibal and St. Joseph Railroad Bridge over the Platte River on the night of September 3, 1861.

A priest at the scene described the gruesome act:

The railroads, because used for carrying Federal soldiers and muni-tions of war, were hated and stormed at by the other party as something wicked that should be exterminated; and civilians and con-combatants, traveling over them, were in the same predicament as the abhorred en-emy, sought to be put out of existence.

A notable example of this occurred almost at the very outset of the war, at Platte River bridge, Buchanan County, where a train full of people were sent down to death through a dark chasm, in the night; all timely notice to the approaching train, of its danger, having been prevented by the men who destroyed the bridge, and then patrolled the neighbor-hood, waiting to see the inhuman results of their cold-blooded planning. I had traveled on that train that evening from Macon City to Chillicothe. At Chillicothe, as I was leaving the train, I could not but be apprehensive of danger to those aboard it, and having to journey farther.

Being well acquainted with the conductor and brakemen in charge of the train, who were good, kind-hearted Christian men, I asked them if they thought they could go through safe that night, to their journey's end. The conductor replied to me. "Oh, yes, sir, as we have traveled safe as far as Chillicothe, we consider the danger past. You need not be ap-prehensive for our safety for the rest of the way." The train passed out from the station, and was soon on its way, speeding out of sight. Three hours later, these two good men, conductor and brakeman, Stephen Cut-ler and John Fox, were forever at their journey's end, down in the bottom of the Platte, in a heap of the dead.[68]

Father John Hogan saw firsthand the violence that spilled into Mis-souri due to the earlier violence of the Jayhawkers and the Missouri ruffians. His ministry in western Missouri was put into deep jeopardy.

Father Hogan was ordained on April 10, 1852. He was assigned to Old Mines for one year, then Potosi for two years. He was then brought back to Saint Louis. He observed that there were many young Irish girls, as many as 300, going to early morning Mass, and found out that they served as maids and servants throughout the city. Upon inquiry he found out that young Irish men were off working on the railroads,

---

68   Ed. Crystal Payton. John Joseph Hogan. *On the Mission in Missouri & Fifty Years Ago: A Memoir.* Springfield: Lens and Pen Press. 2009. P. 89-90.

living in camps, and moving with railroad construction. Father Hogan got the idea of finding these camps, building a Catholic church, and attracting young Irish Catholic women to settle down in little colonies in northwestern Missouri.

It took a lot of persuasion to convince Archbishop Kenrick to release Father Hogan from service to follow his dream. He took a train to Warrenton, the end of the line in those days. A contractor lent him a horse and Father Hogan went in search of Catholics. He refused to be discouraged. At one point he had a conversation with a local who told him, "There are no Catholics here; what then is the use of the church?" Hogan replied, "True, sir, there are no Catholics here now, but there will be here before long, and you and I may see the day, when there will be a Catholic church on every hill around here."[69]

With time, Father Hogan found a Catholic family here and a Catholic woman there. In Chillicothe, he found one Catholic woman married to a lawyer who was Protestant. The priest drew crowds to hear him at the local courthouse, and one of the town fathers, John Graves, gave him a city lot upon which to build a church.

Eventually Father Hogan founded Catholic communities in Macon City, Brookfield, Mexico, and Cameron, as well as Chillicothe. He set Mass schedules for each, dividing his Sundays accordingly: one community for each Sunday of the month. So, in January 1860, Father Hogan said Mass in Chillicothe on January 1, Macon City on January 8, Brookfield on the 15th, Mexico on the 22nd and Cameron on the fifth Sunday of the month, the 29th.

Father Hogan printed a timetable for his various parishes and included the phrase, "On days not herein stated, and accepting railroad schedule time for travel to and from places herein mentioned, the priest may be found at his place of residence in Chillicothe."[70]

Father Hogan's travels came to him gratis by the railroad company. This was partially a courtesy to this industrious Irish priest, but it was also in the interest of the railroad companies to build communities in the area and increase immigration. So the railroad subsidized Father Hogan's 10,000 miles by rail each year.

These journeys were all the more dangerous as railroads became

---

69   Rev. John Rothensteiner. *History of the Archdiocese of Saint Louis. II.* Saint Louis: Blackwell Wielandy Co. 1928. P. 51.

70   Ed. Crystal Payton. John Joseph Hogan. *On the Mission in Missouri & Fifty Years Ago: A Memoir.* Springfield: Lens and Pen Press. 2009. P. 78.

the objects of guerrilla attacks. Father Hogan survived 21 railroad wrecks, many of them the result of attacks. Others were caused by the dangers of railroading in those days. Two episodes in the life of the future Bishop of Kansas City deserve retelling in Father Hogan's own words.

Once, while on his journeys, Father Hogan stayed overnight with a lonely farmer, accepting his hospitality and conversation. As it turned out, the farmer was a Universalist and had a low opinion of Catholics. The priest did not reveal his true identity, and an interesting exchange took place when the man asked him what he thought of Papists:

"But what do you think of these people called Papists? The old priest comes along regularly, down here on the railroad, and pretends to forgive sins. The Papists confess their sins to him, and give him lots of money to be forgiven. The old priest goes away, and as soon as he is gone, the Papists are as wicked as before. What do you think of that?"

"It seems strange indeed. But, upon reflection, since the people pay their lawyers, doctors and preachers, I suppose in like manner, the Papists may be allowed to pay their priests."

"But don't you see the wickedness of cheating the people out of their money, by pretending to forgive them their sins?"

"True, in that light, it would be a wicked thing. But, it is more than likely that Papists do not see it in that light. For myself, I will not say that I am much of a religious or learned man. Nevertheless, I will say that I read a little in the Bible, and that I found there these words spoken by Christ to His Apostles: 'Whose sins ye shall forgive, they are forgiven them.' Papists believe that by these words Christ communicated power to His Apostles to forgive sins. And because Christ said that He would be with His Apostles until the end of the world, these Apostles must be in the world yet, because the world has not yet come to an end, these Apostles, that is, the ordained ministers of Christ, whoever they be, have this power today as fully as when Christ first gave it. This is the belief of the Papists in regard to their priests, and the reason no doubt, why they go to the priest to forgive them their sins. In fact it would seem to be a belief as true as the Bible itself."

"In other respects, too, it would seem a reasonable belief, and one that is practiced every day in our state affairs. For instance, the Governor of this state is Bob Stewart. Bob Stewart is said to be not a very exemplary citizen. In fact, as I believe, it is well known, that he drinks quite freely, and is often so under the influence of drink as not to be able

to attend to his official duties. Nevertheless, should Bob Stewart, governor of this state as he is, go at any time to the state penitentiary, and say to the warden of that penitentiary: 'Warden, there are three men here that I pardon, one of them is a murderer, another is a robber, and the third is a horse thief; I pardon these, let these go;' are they not by his word, then and there expressed fully pardoned, and their sins against the state forgiven them? And if the state of Missouri can, and does, give the power to forgive sins to one of its citizens, and he by no means the best or worthiest citizen, to be exercised for the purposes of mercy; why may not Almighty God give a like power for a like purpose, even to an unworthy man, such as people say the old priest is? For myself, I will say, that I have often meditated much on this matter, and the conclusion I have come to is, that this must be the reason why Catholics believe that the priests can forgive sins."

"I thank you, sir, for this explanation which is very interesting and which never occurred to my mind in such light before. Perhaps, after all, if we could understand the priests and the Papists, they might not be such as we think they are."

The next morning Hogan shared a breakfast with the Universalist farmer, harnessed his buggy, and paid a modest sum for the accommodations.

At parting I said to him, "My dear sir, I assure you, your kindness to me I will never forget, and I hope it may come to be in my power to serve you as kindly as you have served me. May the good God bless and reward you, and lead you unto all that is good. Furthermore, my dear friend, I have to say to you, not knowing how you may regard it, whether as an honor or otherwise, that you entertained a Catholic priest last night. I am the Catholic priest who attends the railroad men in the southern part of this county. My dear friend, I hope to see you again. Once more I say, God bless you. Good-bye." The horses pulled on their tugs, and moved away briskly. When I had gone quite a distance, I looked back; my host was still standing, where I left him, as if fixed to the ground, gazing steadily after me. I passed through Linneus before mid-day, and in the evening reached Chillicothe.[71]

In his memoirs, Father Hogan recounts another adventure which demonstrated his tenacity and resolve:

Saturday, September 24, 1864, I set out from Chillicothe by train to

71   Ed. Crystal Payton. John Joseph Hogan. *On the Mission in Missouri & Fifty Years Ago: A Memoir.* Springfield: Lens and Pen Press. 2009. P. 51-53.

Macon City, where I was to change cars for Mexico, in Audrain County, the point of my destination; intending to celebrate Mass there next day, Sunday, the third Sunday of the month, which I usually gave to Mexico. At Macon City where it was well known I would be on the train that day, as I was changing cars, I was met by a messenger sent to intercept me for a sick call some miles distant in the country. I could not refuse attending the sick call, though attending it would necessarily cause me to lose the train then under full steam to set out for Mexico – and the only train going there before Monday. The disappointment to the Catholics gathering from far and near at Mexico on the third Sunday of the month, which was the Sunday set apart for them, disconcerted me in my willing efforts for their sake, for they were pious good Christians. Yet to abandon them was a duty in order not to deprive the dying Christian of the last helps of religion.

The sick call attended, I returned to Macon City about sunset, with the grim determination on my features to make a night journey by hand car to Mexico, sixty miles distant. I know that I could depend on the railroad section men to carry me, by successive relays from place to place, over the distance. The Macon City section men, informed of my purpose, although tired after the day's work, hastily partook of supper, and well oiling the heavy machinery of their hand car, put it on the track and put me on it with them, and then we were away, speeding southward on our journey. In an hour we had passed over their section of the road, ten miles to Jacksonville. The Jacksonville men soon had their hand car on the track, and we rode on it, in an hour, ten miles to Allen, which place is now called Moberly. The Allen men made their run of ten miles in an hour to Renick. The Renick men, asleep when we called on them, were soon up and out on the track, and away on the course.

Instantly, in the flash of our headlight lantern, we saw armed men ahead of us, with leveled revolvers calling us to halt. We halted. A number of them mounted our handcar, and with a harsh command to us from their captain to go on, on we went. They stayed on our handcar for several miles, not saying a word the while. Again the captain cried, halt. We halted. They alighted, and ordered us to go on. We went on, glad to be free, not knowing whether they were friends or foes who had pressed us into their service. As they wore no uniforms we conjectured they were guerillas, probably belonging to the band that robbed Huntsville in the neighborhood the day previous, and now very likely reconnoitering the federal force encamped at Sturgeon, some miles before us.

We went on to the Sturgeon outpost, where we were halted by the pickets, and by them taken to camp headquarters, where, having given satisfactory account of ourselves, we got a written order to pass through the federal lines and beyond the camp. It was now midnight, and there yet remained twenty-two miles journey before us. The next relay of men took me eight miles, to Centralia. The Centralia men, aroused from their slumbers, soon had their handcar on the track, and with them I proceeded over the intervening distance, twelve miles, to Mexico; where, arriving at half past two o'clock Sunday morning, I was once again, as at Sturgeon, halted by the federal pickets, and by them taken to camp headquarters, where, having satisfactorily accounted for myself, I was again furnished with a military pass to go through the lines. I now had on my person three federal military passes, the first one having been given me a considerable time previous by Provost Marshal General McKinstry, of St. Louis, as a necessary condition to pass beyond the lines of that city.[72]

Father Hogan spent the early hours of Sunday morning at a private residence, woke early and recited his Divine Office. His parishioners streamed into the parlor where the priest heard confessions and celebrated Mass, as Mexico did not have a church at that point. Later that day, he boarded a train and continued his mission journeys.

After the Civil War, Father John Joseph Hogan would confront the state of Missouri in an issue regarding religious conscience. This was not a man to be forgotten.

The first candidate for president of the United States put forth by the new Republican Party was John C. Frémont, in 1856. Frémont's nickname was "the Pathfinder." He had led four expeditions into the West, exploring routes to Oregon and California. Frémont was married to the exceedingly capable Jessie Benton Frémont, daughter of Missouri Senator Thomas Hart Benton. But Frémont fell to James Buchanan, the Democratic candidate, under accusations that Frémont was illegitimate, which was true; that he was Catholic (actually, he was an Episcopalian); and that he had Free Soil sentiments; also true, which later grew into radical abolitionism.

In 1860, the heir apparent for the Republican Party was a lawyer from Illinois, Abraham Lincoln. Lincoln's Free Soil opinions were well known due to his senatorial debates with Stephen A. Douglas. He was

---

72   Ed. Crystal Payton. John Joseph Hogan. *On the Mission in Missouri & Fifty Years Ago: A Memoir.* Springfield: Lens and Pen Press. 2009. Pp. 97–98.

nominated with a platform that gave something to everyone, except the Southerners. Free Soilists were reassured. A protective tariff made New England manufacturers smile. For the West and Northwest, federal support was promised for the Pacific Railroad. Settlers and farmers were promised cheap and even free land from public property.

In the meantime, the Democrats imploded. James Buchanan had turned out to be a terrible president and totally inadequate to the challenges facing America. At the convention in Baltimore, the Douglas Democrats tried to keep the party unified around the call for popular sovereignty. But "cotton Democrats" saw how that was working out in Kansas and bolted the convention to nominate their own pro-slave candidate, John C. Breckenridge. His platform called for an extension of slavery into the West and South and even into Cuba, yet to be acquired. The schism sent tremors through the political landscape and yet a third party was born, made up of old Whigs and nativists calling themselves the Constitutional Union Party. They nominated James Bell of Tennessee.

With four candidates running for president in 1860, and so much split along sectional lines, national unity was the first casualty. Douglas and the Democrats got only 29% of the popular vote, 12 electoral votes. The southern Democrat Breckenridge got fewer popular votes, just 18%, but racked up 72 electoral votes, all from the South. Bell scraped by with a mere 12% of the popular vote, garnering 39 electoral votes from Virginia, Kentucky, and Tennessee.

That left the winner as Abraham Lincoln, the second Republican to run for president, with 180 electoral votes, taking every non-slave state. But ominously, he was the first president since John Quincy Adams to be elected by a *minority* of the popular vote. In the election of 1860, only 39.79% of the electorate voted for him.

The President-elect was a minority president with no support in the South and not much in the West except California and Oregon. Missouri looked like a crazy quilt with the counties in the northwest part of the state going for Douglas; Breckenridge and Bell took most of the Ozarks, except for pro-Lincoln Springfield; and Douglas was helped the most in east-central Missouri. Missouri's nine electoral votes went to the Unionist Democrat Stephen A. Douglas.

While Buchanan sat helpless, South Carolina declared a "divorce" in December 1860. In the next six weeks, six more states followed, then another four. They formed a government in Montgomery, Alabama, and fashioned themselves the Confederate States of America.

None of these events were lost on the citizens of Saint Louis. Saint Louis historian Louis S. Gerteis observed in Saint Louis, "The South and the North commingled as never before and did so at a time when events that once held significance only within the local community could generate for wider interest and impact... With communities linked together by long waterways of commerce, the passion of a locality could become the passion of a nation."[73]

The 1836 burning death of Francis McIntosh and the spirited defense of his tormentors became national news. The murder of abolitionist Elijah P. Lovejoy in 1837 in Alton, Illinois, had national implications. And the Dred Scott case had escalated from a contest between two prominent Saint Louis families to become a constitutional crisis for the nation.

By sectional standards the Saint Louis electorate was definitely not in the southern camp. Breckenridge captured only 2% of the vote. The majority voted the compromising center. 13,000 voted either for Douglas or Bell. Yet nearly 9,500 voted for Lincoln.

The Saint Louis vote of 1860, and that of Missouri, showed the electorate still longed for the ideal of Thomas Hart Benton. The bigger-than-life Missouri politician had died a painful death in 1858 due to intestinal cancer. Before that, he had lost his Senate seat as the political world radicalized and he continued to expound a vision of progress and union. He lost the affection of his favorite daughter, Jessie Frémont, when Benton refused to endorse his son-in-law John C. Frémont as Republican candidate for presidency in 1856.

Yet, in 1860, Benton's vision of America and the West's role in preserving the Union still moved Missourians. In speeches in Saint Louis, Benton inspired his audiences. The first came in November 1850 in an address at the Mercantile Library Association. It was entitled "The Progress of the Age" and saw America expanding westward with Saint Louis as the focal point. Americans would move westward and fill in the continent with cities and farms and ranches, all coming through and being supplied by Saint Louis, with great ribbons of railroads tying America together. Sectionalism would evaporate in the West as Northerners and Southerners commingled and became Westerners. Northern manufacture would find a market in the West, and by the

---

73   Louis S. Gerteis. *Civil War Saint Louis*. Lawrence: University of Kansas Press. 2001. Pp. 6-7.

railroads be brought to Pacific ports, and from there to markets in China and India. The West would feed the North, and the South would supply both cotton and tobacco. Technical innovations in agriculture would eventually make slavery obsolete and unprofitable. The scourge of slavery would quietly pass away, and the Union would be preserved.

Unfortunately, events would not wait for this peaceful evolution to happen. Instead, as southern states seceded from the Union, an incident took place on New Year's Day 1861 which showed Saint Louis as, like the rest of the nation, a tinderbox about to ignite. The city sheriff began an auction on the courthouse steps, settling an estate which included seven slaves. A large crowd gathered, dominated by a society known as the Wide Awakes. They held the bidding down to a mere three dollars, and after considerable effort the auctioneer threw in the towel at eight dollars. It was the last slave auction in Saint Louis.

Who were the Wide Awakes? They were young toughs organized by Saint Louisan Frank Blair Jr. into a paramilitary force to protect Republican gatherings from hecklers and opposition thugs. At one gathering in Ironton, Blair brought 300 Wide Awakes with him. These were dressed in uniforms and were drawn from the ranks of newly-arrived Germans. Soon they were armed, as was a second pro-Republican paramilitary outfit, *Schwarzer Jaegerkorp,* or Black Rifleman.

There was a clear militancy which was exhibited by this Republican Party/German community alliance, with both sides using the other for political advantage. At the head of the Republicans in Saint Louis were Frank Blair Jr, a founder of the Republican Party; Gratz Brown, an early collaborator and newspaper editor; and Peter Foy, who later replaced Brown as editor and served on the Saint Louis Committee of Safety, an organization that spied on and monitored secessionist activities.

Their counterparts in the German community included Henry Boernstein, Arnold Krekel, and Carl Bernays. Bernays was the editor of *Anzeiger des Westens,* a German language daily that touted Republicanism and subtle free-thinking criticism of old-school thoughts, including Catholicism. Henry Boernstein had been a refugee from the abortive 1849 revolution in Germany. He was associated with *Anzeiger des Westens* and had been deeply shocked by the accounts of the McIntosh lynching. He applauded Thomas Hart Benton, Gratz Brown, and Frank Blair with laudatory newspaper articles. Arnold Krekel was editor of the *St. Charles Demokrat,* a German language paper. Though he owned slaves on his Saint Charles farm, Krekel was a Free Soilist and Republican supporter.

The goal of these Germans was to prove their American loyalties by being loyal to the Republican Party and the federal Union. Many had fought and lost the battle for liberty and equality back in Germany. Now, in their adopted land, they would take up arms again for their ideals.

While Breckenridge did not get much support from Saint Louis in the 1860 election, there were plenty with sympathies for the southern position. The Wide Awakes had their counterpart in a group called the Minutemen. These had their headquarters at Bartholomew Berhold's residence under an umbrella group calling itself The Southern Rights Democrats. But most of the Saint Louis elite were conditional Unionists. These favored preserving the Union with slavery intact and, while not favoring secession, would not compel the seceded states to come back against their will. In this camp were the Chouteau family, banker James Lucas, George Taylor, president of the Pacific Railroad, and wholesale merchandiser, Derrick A. January.

On January 4, 1861, President Buchanan called for a day of prayer and fasting and sent an unarmed supply ship to the federal garrison at Fort Sumter, South Carolina. That same day, Claiborne Fox Jackson was sworn in as governor of Missouri. He had campaigned as a conditional Union Democrat, but his inaugural address showed his true feelings, saying Missouri's honor, her interests, and her sympathies point alike in one direction; he was determined to stand by the South.

The supply ship was turned back from Charleston harbor when it came under fire from the South Carolina militia.

To determine Missouri's position on the Union and secession, a convention was held at Mercantile Library on January 31, 1861, bringing together Union Democrats and Republicans to elect delegates for a statewide convention. Rather than let the political will have its way, both sides began maneuvering for advantage, for there was a lot at stake. For one thing, there was a depository of federal funds in Saint Louis, something in excess of $400,000, protected by a single guard. Further, the Saint Louis Arsenal was the largest cache in the West. It held 6,000 muskets, 9,000 pounds of gunpowder, forty cannons, and one million rounds of ammunition. Unionists wanted to use their paramilitary militia to bolster the defense of the arsenal. But the commander, Major William Bell, flatly refused, saying he would rely on the

Missouri State militia if the need came. That was music to the ears of Governor Jackson and his militia commander, Brigadier General Daniel M. Frost.

Before anything could be done, Major Bell was replaced as commander at the arsenal. It seems that the Saint Louis Committee of Safety had caught wind of the Bell-Frost-Jackson collusion, and Frank Blair wrote his brother Montgomery Blair, the Postmaster General of the United States, about the danger. This line of communication would often be used in the future to influence events in Saint Louis.

With Bell gone, the 48-man garrison was supplemented by a fresh company of regulars, and in February another company arrived from Kansas, under the command of Captain Nathaniel Lyon. This young Army officer caught the eye of Frank Blair and the Committee of Safety. When General Frost mustered five companies of Minutemen into the state militia and began making plans for a statewide camp in the spring in Saint Louis, the federals transferred another 203 men from Jefferson Barracks to the arsenal. On April 1, 1861, Saint Louis held an election for mayor. Daniel Taylor, the conditional Unionist Democrat, unseated Republican John How. His victory was the result of the city's disgust with and fear of the German militia, which was forming and parading around, showing its strength.

Control of the mayor's office was joined by control of the Police Board. The new Board included Basil Duke, the leader of the pro-secessionist Minutemen militia. Within a short time, the police began closing down German beer halls on Sundays and harassing German restaurant owners.

As tensions grew, the overall commander of the federal forces in the West, General William S. Harney, tried reconciliation. His hope was to build a broad understanding among Missouri and Saint Louis politicians and military leaders on the state and federal level. The one fly in the ointment was Nathaniel Lyon. Though only a Captain, Lyon had a following of powerful admirers, including Frank Blair and most of the German newspaper editors.

Nathaniel Lyon was a man of action. He was a West Pointer who fought Indians in the Seminole Wars in Florida, the Mexicans in the Mexican War, the Indians in California, and the border ruffians in Kansas. His record showed action, but also cruelty. In California, a single white man had been killed by some Native Americans. Lyon wiped out the whole village. His take-no-prisoners attitude in Kansas was also well documented. And he found his commander, General Harney, weak to the point of being treasonous.

On April 12, 1861, all bets were off. Confederate artillery shelled Fort Sumter after the Federal garrison refused to surrender. The most terrible war in American history had begun.

General Harney was not the only cool head who tried to call for peace and discussion over violence and rupture. Such were the sentiments of Archbishop Peter Richard Kenrick. On January 12, 1861, he wrote, "To the Roman Catholics of Saint Louis: Beloved brethren, in the present distressed state of the public mind, we feel it our duty to recommend you to avoid all occasions of public excitement, to obey the laws, to respect the rights of all citizens, and to keep away, as much as possible, from all assemblages where the indiscretion of a word or the impetuosity of a momentary passion might endanger public tranquility. Obey the injunction of the Apostle St. Peter: 'Follow peace with all men, and holiness, without which no man can see God.'"[74]

If Kenrick had opinions regarding the upcoming hostilities, he kept them to himself. Eventually, he even refused to preach sermons during the war for fear of exciting one side or the other. A careful reading of Father Rothensteiner's assessment of Peter Richard Kenrick during these years leads one to believe that the Archbishop would be considered a conditional Unionist, willing to protect the constitutional rights to own slaves, but looking forward to their eventual emancipation through purchase, that is, freeing the bondsman but compensating the slave owner. Kenrick himself owned a small household of slaves whom, it seems, he treated humanely. After emancipation, one man named Thomas Franklin continued to live with the Archbishop, serving him as a butler.

Once hostilities began in Charleston Harbor, war became inevitable. President Abraham Lincoln called for each state to provide militia to build a federal army 70,000 strong. He also commanded the navy to begin a blockade of Southern ports. These two actions caused many Army and Navy officers to resign their commissions and head for the Confederacy. Though having rejected the Confederacy initially, Virginia, Arkansas, and Tennessee reconsidered and joined the cause. North Carolina soon followed, bringing the Confederate States of America to eleven States. The capital was relocated to Richmond, Virginia.

---

74   John Rothensteiner. *History of the Archdiocese of St. Louis. II* St. Louis: Blackwell Wielandy Co. 1928. P. 211.

Within a week of Fort Sumter's surrender, troops were being transported to defend Washington D.C. Some moved by train to Baltimore, where they had to detrain at one station and march to another. Working their way through the streets of Baltimore, the federal troops came under fire and took casualties. They responded in kind, killing several civilians.

Maryland, and especially Baltimore, had strong southern sympathies and all the more so in the Catholic community. A local newspaper, *The Metropolitan*, had savaged *Uncle Tom's Cabin* in a book review, calling Harriet Beecher Stowe's book "fanatical and extreme." *The Catholic Mirror* saw Know-Nothings behind abolitionism and lumped the reformist movements of the era as being "evidences of a corrupt and vitiated state of society."[75]

Archbishop Francis Patrick Kenrick, the older of the two Kenrick brothers, allowed his Archdiocesan newspaper to take editorial positions from which he personally differed. Yet throughout the war, Francis Patrick would try to moderate the extremes of both sides. In the meantime, Maryland felt the heavy hand of President Lincoln as he declared martial law, sending troops and closing the State legislature.

Missouri was too far away and too fractured to be dealt with in that manner. Instead, Lincoln tried to assure the conditional Unionists that he would preserve the institution of slavery in states where it existed and try to persuade the seceded states to return, even as he raised an army against them.

When Missouri got its notice to contribute 4,000 troops to the Union effort, Governor Claiborne Fox Jackson replied within twenty-four hours. On April 17, he wrote to the War Department: "Your requisition ... is illegal, unconstitutional and revolutionary in its objects, inhuman and diabolical, and cannot be complied with."[76]

The governor then traveled to Saint Louis to meet with General Daniel Frost of the Missouri militia, as well as the President of the Police Board and Minutemen leader, Basil Duke. They devised a plan to hold a state militia camp in a few weeks and to place it directly on the bluffs south of the Arsenal. After the meeting, two emissaries were sent south to meet with Jefferson Davis, the president of the Confed-

---

75   Thomas W. Spalding. *The Premier See: A History of the Archdiocese of Baltimore, 1789 - 1989*. Baltimore: The Johns Hopkins University Press. 1989. P. 175.
76   Louis S. Gerteis. *Civil War Saint Louis*. Lawrence: University of Kansas Press. 2001. P. 93.

eracy, to request siege cannon.

That same day, Frank Blair returned from a Washington visit with authorization to arm 5,000 of his Home Guard with federal weapons from the Arsenal. Harney and Lyon clashed over federal patrols, which Lyon sent out into the neighborhoods around the Arsenal. This further weakened Harney's position at the War Department, as the Blair-Blair machinery started to work at having him removed from his post.

The state militia camp did materialize on April 22. It was meant to meet and drill for eleven days. Rather than placing it at the provocative location in South Saint Louis, General Frost arranged for it to assemble on the westernmost edge of the city, at a place called Lindell Grove. The calling of a militia camp caused several state militia officers to resign their commissions, as they saw Governor Jackson's refusal to provide state troops to the federal army as treasonous. Some of them enlisted in the regular army.

The next day, General Harney was ordered to the federal capital to give an account of his actions in Missouri. The Blair-Blair cabal was working. When Harney left Saint Louis, command of the arsenal fell to Captain Nathaniel Lyon. He immediately mustered four regiments of volunteers and armed them. He then shipped excess arms and ammunition to Illinois to keep it out of unfriendly hands. He sought and received permission from Simon Cameron, the Secretary of War, to coordinate activities with the Committee of Safety. The German Home Guard was renamed The United States Reserve Corps. As there were no federal funds for this unit, Lyon sought contributions from the business community. Several German breweries and restaurants eagerly stepped forward. They had suffered under recent police tactics to close them and their beer gardens down on Sundays. Charles G. Stifel, owner of Stifel Brewery, brewer Julius Windelmaier, and restauranteur Tony Niederwieser were among the first to contribute.

The target of all this martial might was the state militia camp, named Camp Jackson, after the governor. Around 700 men gathered there at the site bordered on the north by Olive Street, Grand Avenue to the west, Laclede Avenue on the south, and Garrison and Ewing on the east: approximately the eastern half of Saint Louis University's present campus.

But the clock was ticking. General Harney would soon return to Saint Louis, and the state militia would soon be dispersed back to their homes.

Lyon himself reconnoitered Camp Jackson on May 9. He wore the dress of Frank Blair's mother-in-law, driving a carriage through the camp, and learned that a shipment of arms had arrived there, including cannons shipped to General Frost from the captured arsenal at Baton Rouge.

That night, Captain Lyon held a council of war with the Committee of Safety. Lyon urged quick action the next day. Samuel Glover, the most cautious of the Committee, argued that a federal marshal should visit the camp first thing in the morning and demand that General Frost surrender the cannons. If the militia failed to do so, military action might then be taken. Even as Glover was convincing several members of the Committee, he was countered by arguments from Frank Blair, supporting Lyon's strike-first proposal. The Committee of Safety broke up around midnight. It seemed that action had won out over words.

The events of May 10, 1861, did not go as planned. Dawn was greeted by a severe thunderstorm, which kept Blair's men at Jefferson Barracks, unable to be transported to the city by riverboats. Instead, the soldiers had to march through the streets of Carondelet, arriving at the arsenal in early afternoon.

Then Lyon began his march to the militia campgrounds. Meanwhile, at Camp Jackson, picnickers had come, many on the Olive-Market streetcar. A federal flag flew over the encampment. Earlier, some overly enthusiastic militiamen had drawn it down and raised the Confederate Stars and Bars as an act of defiance, but General Frost quickly set things right. Early on the tenth, Frost wrote a letter to Captain Lyon outlining the legality of the camp based on the Missouri Militia Act of 1859, but Lyon refused to accept the letter.

Now seven columns of troops, 8,000 men, were marching to a confrontation. Included in these troops was an artillery battery under the command of Major Franz Backhoff, who had served with Franz Sigel in the Baden uprising of 1848. The Third U.S. Volunteers marched north on Broadway, turning west on Olive. They were commanded by Franz Sigel, a favorite of Frank Blair and soon to be a confidant of Nathaniel Lyon.

By 3:15 the camp was totally surrounded, and Frost was sent an ultimatum to surrender. He did so, under protest.

Word of the assault raced through the city like wildfire. In the German wards, the soldiers were saluted and hailed and tears of joy were shed. In the other sections, the troops were cursed, called "damned Dutch," and scorned. For many Saint Louisans it seemed that their city had been occupied by a foreign power. The Germans were not in uniform, but they carried federal muskets and took their commands in German. More than once, the Germans had ominously leveled their weapons in the face of the hostile crowds. But no shots had been fired. (Yet!)

The militia was quickly disarmed, arrested, and moved in columns onto Olive Street. Sigel's troops were sent into the camp to secure the arms and move them to the arsenal. The Union troops guarding the militiamen included Blair's own regiment and a German regiment under the command of Henry Boerstein, editor of *Anzeiger des Westens*. But the march to the arsenal did not commence. Some attribute the delay to Captain Lyon having been kicked by a horse and unable to lead for over an hour. As he alone knew the plans for the attack and arrest of the camp occupants, no one else could act. Meanwhile, tensions grew as more and more angry citizens gathered to taunt the German troops.

Suddenly, there was a burst of fire. Some reported that a drunken man with a revolver had come forward and fired the first shot. Others say that the Germans broke discipline and fired a warning volley over the heads of the gathered citizens. Regardless, there was a quick exchange of deadly gunfire between troops and citizens. Captain Constantin Blandowski fell from his horse with a gunshot wound to his leg. He would later die from that wound and receive a hero's funeral, though later investigation showed that the ball that felled him came from a federal gun. He was a casualty of friendly fire.

One witness that day was William Tecumseh Sherman, who brought his little son Willie. They dove into a ditch as they saw a stampede of wounded and dying civilians trying to flee the carnage. Twenty-seven Saint Louisans lay dead on Olive Street, including two young boys and an infant.

Ignoring the carnage, Lyon marched his troops and their prisoners to the Arsenal late that afternoon. The Captain remained unrepentant regarding his actions of that day; he also did not provide any medical relief for the wounded or dying. He pointed to three thirty-two pound cannons and a mortar, as well as shells obviously stolen from the Baton Rouge federal arsenal, as proof that Camp Jackson was more than just a state militia exercise.

Of the 700 militiamen captured, 639 were paroled the next day, along with forty-nine officers. Each had to promise not to take up arms against the United States. One officer, Captain Emmet McDonald, refused, saying that the attack on Camp Jackson was unconstitutional. His attorney, Uriel Wright, argued for a writ of *habeas corpus*, but this was ignored by General Harney, who had assumed military command; he argued that military authority trumped legal authority in time of war.

This case drove Uriel Wright, a conditional Unionist, into the Confederate camp. And so it was for former mayor John Wimer, a Benton Democrat who later joined the Republican Party. He won two terms as mayor and clearly favored the emancipation of slaves. But the Camp Jackson disaster turned him sour, and after making some unpatriotic remarks, he was arrested and sent to the Gratiot Street prison. Wimer escaped and joined the Confederate army in General Emmet McDonald's cavalry. Both were killed in action at Huntsville, Missouri, in 1863.

General Harney returned to Saint Louis, having barely survived his interrogation in Washington, D.C. Now he was presented with a perfect mess. State Militia General Daniel Frost launched a formal complaint. Harney forwarded it to the War Department on May 18. Conservative voices in Saint Louis tried to persuade Harney to discipline Lyon for his action, but Harney had learned the hard way of the powerful influences of the Blair-Blair connection and that Lyon was their darling. Harney openly endorsed the attack on Camp Jackson, but tried to disarm the German troops, which proved an impossible task because they were supported by Frank Blair.

The final undoing of General William Harney was an agreement he made on May 21 with State Militia commander Sterling Price. In essence, the Harney-Price pact assured that the federal troops would stay within the borders of Saint Louis, while state militia would patrol the rest of the state of Missouri. By May 24, Frank Blair wrote the Secretary of War, denouncing Governor Jackson as a secret Confederate and Harney as a dupe. This led to a stern warning to Harney from President Lincoln himself. On May 30th, Blair presented General Harney with his removal papers.

Captain Nathaniel Lyon was promoted to Brigadier General. There would be one meeting between Lyon and State officials, and it did not go well. The parties gathered at a neutral venue, Planter House Hotel in Saint Louis. On the state side were Governor Claiborne Fox Jackson, General Sterling Price, and his aide-de-camp, Thomas Sneed. On the federal side were General Lyon, who barely spoke for the first half hour, his aide-de-camp, Major Horace Conant, and Colonel Frank Blair.

Governor Jackson did most of the talking, proposing a mutual disarmament of the state militia and the German home guard. Missouri would remain neutral during the war, guaranteed by federal troops.

Finally, General Lyon found his voice and rose up. Sneed's account is dramatic, but considering Lyon's personality, it may be quite accurate.

He [Lyon] vehemently refused to "concede to the State of Missouri the right to demand that my Government shall not enlist troops within her limits, or bring troops into the State whenever it pleases, or move its troops at their own will into, out of, or through the State." He then rose to his feet to deliver his philippic, "Rather than concede to the State of Missouri for one single instant the right to dictate to my Government in any matter however unimportant" – as he spoke he pointed in turn to Price, Snead, Blair, and Conant – "I would see you, and you, and you, and you, and every man, woman, and child in the State dead and buried." Turning to Governor Jackson, Lyon then added, "This means war."[77]

77   Louis S. Gerteis. *Civil War Saint Louis*. Lawrence: University of Kansas Press. 2001. P. 124.

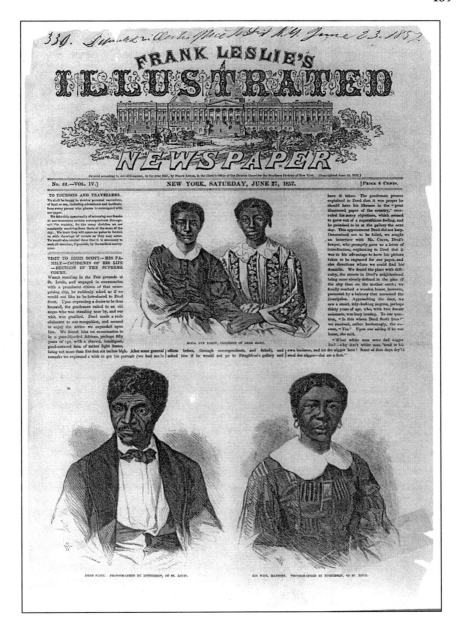

Dred and Harriet Scott and family as depicted in *Leslie's Illustrated Newspaper* on June 27, 1857. Image from Library of Congress Prints and Photographs Division in Washington, D.C. Digital ID: CPH 3B26377.

Lithograph of Camp Jackson, MO, 1861. Missouri History Museum. Digital ID N21832.

Frank P. Blair as Colonel of the First Regiment Missouri Volunteers in 1861. He was Senator from 1871 to 1873. Image from Library of Congress Prints and Photographs Division in Washington, D.C. Digital ID: PGA 04763.

Bishop John J. Hogan of the Diocese of Kansas City-St. Joseph. Image from the Diocese of Kansas City-St. Joseph Archives.

GEN! FRANZ SIGEL.

At the Battle of Pea Ridge, Ark. March 8th 1862.

General Franz Sigel at the Battle of Pea Ridge, 1862. Image from Library of Congress Prints and Photographs Division in Washington, D.C. Digital ID: CPH 3A17590.

Father John Bannon, S.J., during his service as a Confederate army chaplain, no date. Missouri History Museum. Digital ID N11749.

Chapter Six

THE CIVIL WAR AS EXPERIENCED BY
SIGEL AND BANNON

As we explore the events of the Civil War, the War Between the States, the War for Southern Independence, the War of Northern Aggression, the War to End Slavery, there is no need to chronicle the events of that conflict. There are many great histories of the Civil War that cover the events in general and in detail. Instead, we will follow the military careers of two Saint Louisans year-by-year. They are very different kinds of men. One was a German revolutionary, a free thinker and a skeptic, devoted to his German roots and to the ideals of the federal Union. He would rise to the rank of General in the Union Army. The other was an Irish Catholic priest, shocked by the violence of the Camp Jackson incident, fearful of an all-powerful federal government which closed down newspapers, suspended *habeas corpus*, and filled prisons with political prisoners. He would serve his Irish American brethren as a chaplain in the Confederate Army.

Franz Sigel and Father John Bannon were both at Camp Jackson on May 10, 1861. Each saw things differently.

Sigel was the product of the revolution of 1848-1849 in Germany. He stood for liberalism, democracy, individual rights, and popular self-government. He traveled in liberal circles, becoming friends with Italian revolutionary Giuseppe Mazzini and Hungarian Louis Kossuth. He counted Giuseppe Garibaldi as a fellow republican revolutionary. Sigel had participated in an uprising in Baden, but it was a military blunder and he was forced to flee to Switzerland. Becoming aware of Prussian spies hot on his trail, he left Switzerland for Italy, where he studied Italian and continued his radical ways. At the same time, Sigel was tutored in English.

Eventually, Sigel was found out and arrested by Swiss authorities. He was given the choice of going back to Germany to certain imprisonment or migrating to France. Sigel chose France as a jumping-off point to come to America.

While in Paris, Franz Sigel became acquainted with other German exiles, including Carl Schurz, who in the United States became a civil service reformer in the 1870s. Sigel met Karl Marx and Friedrich Engels, along with Arnold Ruge, a collaborator with Marx, though they would later part ways. Here Sigel also met his future wife, Elsie Dulon, daughter of the famous freethinker Rudolph Dulon.

On May 1, 1852, Sigel made his way to America, specifically to New York City, where many of the German "Forty-Eighters" settled. Stephen D. Engle, Sigel's biographer, says: "They viewed the United States as a constitutional republic they failed to achieve in Germany, and yet questioned their place in the American political process."[78] Most were shocked at American slavery, xenophobia, and the irrational drive to abstinence. In New York, Sigel plied his talents as a tutor in English, French, Italian, and German. He offered lessons in fencing, played piano in a German restaurant, and even established a cigar store with his brother Albert.

Two other activities would affect Franz Sigel's future. He joined the New York Turnerschaft, a social organization promoting German culture and, in 1854, he enlisted in the Fifth New York Militia. This gave Sigel the opportunity to renew and refine the military skills that had not served him well during the Baden campaign.

In August 1857, Franz Sigel moved his family to Saint Louis to assume a professorship at the *Deutsches Institut*. There he taught French, German, English, mathematics, military tactics, and even American history. By 1860, Franz Sigel was appointed district superintendent of the Saint Louis Public schools. That same year Sigel became a convicted Republican and campaigned for Abraham Lincoln. He wrote editorials condemning the secession states and called the Confederacy "an American Russia," which could not be tolerated.

During the winter of 1860-61, Sigel decided to leave his public school post and seek an officer's commission in the Union Army. He counted on his Baden experience, which had been polished up over time, and his growing popularity with the larger German population of Saint Louis. Frank Blair immediately snatched him up. He secured a rank of colonel, though the Germans always called him general. Sigel was given command of the Third Missouri Volunteers. This was the unit Sigel commanded at Camp Jackson. He was thirty-seven years old.

John B. Bannon was also at Camp Jackson on May 10, 1861. He was 32 years old, the son of an Irish grain dealer in Roscommon County.

---

78   Stephen D. Engle. *Yankee Dutchman: The Life of Franz Sigel.* Baton Rouge: Louisiana State University Press. 1993. P. 33.

John's mother, Fanny O'Farrell, came from a propertied family. The Bannons eventually moved to Dublin. When John was a mere four years old, he was enrolled in Saint Vincent College at Castleknock, a new school started by four recently ordained Dublin priests, including Peter Richard Kenrick. While Kenrick moved to America to assist his brother Bishop, John Bannon went to study theology at Maynooth near Dublin. He was ordained in 1853 by Archbishop Paul Cullen and was thereafter released to serve the Irish population in Saint Louis.

In the fall of 1855, Father John Bannon met Peter Richard Kenrick once again, now Archbishop of Saint Louis. His first assignment was as assistant pastor at Immaculate Conception Church on Eighth and Chestnut, where the pastor was Father James Duggan (who also served as vicar general of the Archdiocese). In 1857, Bannon replaced Duggan as pastor. The next year Father Bannon served as secretary for the second provincial Council of Saint Louis. This gave him a chance to meet with priests and bishops from all over the United States.

Father Bannon got involved in other affairs too. He joined the Catholic Literary Institute at Saint Louis University, was spiritual director of the Temperance Society, and served as chaplain for the Washington Blues, an Irish militia unit. He caught the eye of the state militia general Daniel Frost, a parishioner at Saint Francis Xavier Parish.

In 1858, Father Bannon became the second pastor of Saint John the Apostle and Evangelist Parish and was commissioned to construct a church truly worthy of pontifical liturgies as well as a rectory which could accommodate a bishop. Archbishop Kenrick had no particular affection for Bishop Rosati's cathedral and the surrounding neighborhood, which had become cramped and commercial. The new Saint John's would suit him well. The issue of raising funds to build the church occupied much of Father Bannon's time over the next two years, even as Archbishop Kenrick directed over $14,000 in an interest-free loan from the Thornton bequest.

In the fall of 1860, at the time of the presidential election, Jayhawk violence poured over the Missouri border, instigated by James Montgomery. At the request of residents of Vernon and Bates counties, Governor Robert Stewart sent state militia to their aid. But rather than use Western troops, the governor directed General Frost to bring state militia from Saint Louis. The troops were transported to Sedalia and then marched to the western border of the state. Many were from Irish units, and they were accompanied by their chaplain, Father John

Bannon.

The campaign was a success, as state militia coordinated sweeps with federal troops under General William Harney. Several of Montgomery's men were arrested; the area was pacified. The Kansans returned home. When a state militia muster was called for in late April and early May 1861 on the outskirts of Saint Louis, Father Bannon naturally took part.

The camp had an air of celebration and lighthearted fun, but some toyed with more serious matters. At one point a "Stars and Bars" flag of the Confederacy was hoisted on a flagpole. Streets were named after P. G. T. Beauregard and Jefferson Davis and other southern notables. All that came to an end when Captain Kelly took his Washington Blues to Jefferson City for drill at the state capital. They alone displayed secessionist feelings. As one militia man once stated, his regiment, the First Missouri Volunteers, would have enlisted in the Union Army, except for what happened to them on May 10.

There is little doubt that Father Bannon had been arrested that day, along with the rest of the Missouri militia at Camp Jackson. The name Bannon appears on a prisoner list and there were only three Bannons named in that year's city directory. The other two Bannons were not involved in the state militia and would have had no reason to be at Camp Jackson the day it was attacked.[79] Father Bannon would have had a front-row view of the carnage that day and would have felt the humiliation all the more with his detention at the arsenal.

Later, Father Bannon was returned to his parish, but under parole. As the paroles of many of his parishioners and other militiamen expired, they slipped out of Saint Louis to join General Frost, whose parole also had expired. These were joining Sterling Price in the field. Father Bannon longed to join them, as they had no chaplain. The priest feared going to the Archbishop to seek permission to serve as a Confederate chaplain. He knew the answer would be no. Already Frank Blair had tried to get Father De Smet relieved of his duties to serve as a federal chaplain, but this was blocked by Archbishop Kenrick.

Kenrick adopted a strict neutrality during the war. He refused to ring church bells when General Frost requested it. He refused to fly a federal flag over the Cathedral. But he never interfered with Father Bannon's activities as a militia chaplain. Nevertheless, serving as a

---

79   William Barnaby Faherty. *Exile in Erin: A Confederate Chaplain's Story. The Life of Father John B. Bannon.* Saint Louis: Missouri Historical Society Press. 2002. P. 36.

Confederate chaplain would be beyond what Kenrick could sanction.

In the following months of summer and fall, Father Bannon kept his opinions to himself, with one brief exception. In an unguarded moment, the priest commented to some parishioners that the Confederacy was much like his native Ireland in that it was rural and was being oppressed by an industrial neighbor; thus, he compared the North to Great Britain. A further motive could be seen in the words of Jesuit Father Barnaby Faherty, Bannon's biographer: "The priest saw the war as a contest between the remnant of Christian civilization yet living in the South and the domineering materialism of the age personified by the amalgamation of Yankee descendants of Oliver Cromwell and recent German immigrants."[80]

One should be cautious in dismissing such musings. We've seen already that Franz Sigel was no friend of religion, instead reflecting the attitude of the Forty-Eighter revolutionaries. Nathaniel Lyon, the commander of the assault on Camp Jackson, was an open skeptic regarding religion and even questioned the existence of God. Henry Boernstein, the commander of another German regiment, was the most documented freethinker of them all. Boernstein was editor of *Anzeiger des Westens,* which regularly ran articles attacking the Catholic Church and especially the Jesuits. He was hostile to the German Lutherans also. Boernstein had traveled in Parisian radical circles along with Marx, Engels, and Ruge. He had edited a radical journal for Marx called *Vorwärts,* extolling the virtues of scientific socialism, and he continued his agenda after coming to Saint Louis.

There is no doubt that Father Bannon was not a subscriber to *Anzeiger des Westens,* but he would have heard of the dangerous positions the paper advocated. The Church should have to pay taxes like everyone else. It should be held accountable for property restrictions. Religious instruction should be strictly forbidden in public schools and bishops should have no authority over individual congregations.

To titillate readers of *Anzeiger,* Boernstein filled the paper with dubious articles about misdeeds behind convent walls, kidnappings, and sexual exploitations. This German immigrant made a strange bedfellow for nativist Know-Nothings who sold the same propaganda.

By early December 1861, Father Bannon could endure inaction no longer. He gathered a small group of men at St. John's, men for whom

---

80   William Barnaby Faherty. *Exile in Erin: A Confederate Chaplain's Story. The Life of Father John B. Bannon.* Saint Louis: Missouri Historical Society Press. 2002. P. 133.

he had the highest regard. Many had helped him build and finance his magnificent Italian Renaissance church. He told them of his determination to leave Saint Louis and to join Sterling Price's army as a chaplain. Some tried to reason with the young priest. Such an act would be a career killer for him. He was destined to be a bishop, they said. He would hear of none of it.

On December 15, 1861, Father Bannon said Mass at the parish, then attended an open house at the Lucas home on Locust Street. He left there by the back door in disguise and joined two young men, Robert Bakewell and P. B. Garesché. They slipped the reins of martial law and made their way to southwest Missouri. Before leaving, Father Bannon penned a letter to his Archbishop, no doubt asking belatedly for a temporary leave of duty. When the letter was delivered to Archbishop Kenrick, he refused to take it or read it. He simply told his secretary, "Keep it. The message was never delivered."

By the time Father Bannon arrived at the Confederate camp, Franz Sigel had already seen action at Boonville in June, Carthage in July, and Wilson's Creek in August. After surveying briefly Sigel's role in each of these engagements, we will turn our attention to the battle of Pea Ridge, where, as at Camp Jackson, both the radical German general and the pious Catholic priest would share the same battlefield.

Less than a month after the Camp Jackson affair, Franz Sigel's Missouri volunteers were ordered to head to the southwest of the state. Joining General Thomas Sweeney, the Union force came to around 3,000, while Nathaniel Lyon took 2,000 to Jefferson City. Governor Jackson had fled the capital for Boonville, where Lyon caught him and gave the Missouri forces a severe thrashing. That was on June 17th, the same day Sigel arrived by train in Rolla. From there, Sigel marched his men southwest to Springfield, hoping to intercept Governor Jackson's troops in retreat.

Based on faulty intelligence, Sigel moved his men to Carthage, believing that the rebel force was quite small. His informants, two civilians arrested and detained by him, went directly to Governor Jackson when they were released. Jackson had a force of 6,000 to face off against Sigel's 1,100. Though badly outnumbered, Sigel had two advantages. The rebel force of 6,000 included 2,000 men who were not yet armed. Such was the chronic shortage of Confederate supplies. Sigel also had eight field guns to further the firepower.

Around 11 A.M. on July 5, the battle of Carthage commenced with a cannonade from the Union side. The fighting was so furious that at one point the Union cannons overheated and could not be used. Sigel's men were exhausted from the forced march a day earlier, from living off half rations due to the supply problems, and from the blistering heat. Sigel ordered his men to slowly withdraw. This became a rout as the Confederates pursued, and their cavalry, under Captain Joseph Shelby, pressed on Sigel's flank. Sigel directed his cannons to hold off the cavalry, but in doing so they relieved the advancing rebel infantry of that danger.

While Sigel's execution of the battle of Carthage left a lot to be desired, his retreat was flawless and he escaped with all of his artillery and supplies. He could boast that he suffered only 44 casualties to the Confederate's 170.

After Carthage, Sigel continued to move his troops southwest, anticipating the arrival of Lyon and the rest of the Union forces. By July 14, the federal troops were joined at Springfield. But time was running out. Many of the Union troops were 90-day volunteers, and they were fast losing the initial enthusiasm of signing up. Worse, Lyon now had a superior back in Saint Louis to answer to, John C. Frémont, who was none too eager to share his supplies or manpower with Nathaniel Lyon.

By now Lyon was in command of an army of 6,000 men. They required over 15 tons of food and 6 tons of fodder each day. And as supplies were slow to arrive at Springfield from the railhead at Rolla, local supplies were purchased at inflated prices. Men suffered from chronic diarrhea. There was a typhoid outbreak. And then came word that the Confederates were converging as near as seven miles away. Sterling Price had rallied the Missouri militia, which was being joined by General Ben McCulloch and his army from northern Arkansas, though the logistics of supply were even more critical in the Confederate camp.

In essence, the two armies, both starving, were about to disintegrate if they were not used in the next two weeks.

There were tensions in the Confederate camp over the question of command; Sterling Price thought his superior rank, experience, and age would win the day. McCulloch argued that a commission in the regular army outranked a militia commission. For unity's sake, Price agreed to follow McCulloch's command, but, interestingly, did not bind his troops to the same agreement. That settled, McCulloch gave orders for a general assault to begin at midnight, August 5. But Confederates caught nothing more than a few federal scouts in retreat. At midday McCullough called off the attack, as both sides were exhausted by the heat.

McCulloch's force of 12,000 settled in for the night, making camps along Wire Road near a peaceful, cool creek named after an early settler, James Wilson. In this setting were fresh water, fields of grain and corn, melons and vegetable gardens, chickens, and cattle. Some troops stretched out along farmer Sharp's cornfield south of Wilson Creek. McCulloch's headquarters were north of the creek and east of Wire Road, while Price was located south and west of both the creek and Wire Road, up to a small rise called Oak Hill. McCulloch intended to rest his troops for a day or so and then renew his assault, driving to Springfield.

At Lyon's headquarters all options were on the table. Clearly the Union force was outnumbered. The logical course would have been to retreat back to Rolla, where supplies would be available by rail. Frémont had made it clear that he would not reinforce Lyon, who knew that his army of 30-day volunteers was about to evaporate. He hated the idea of abandoning the campaign without a fight and of abandoning pro-Union Springfield to Confederate occupation. It was Sigel who offered Lyon a path forward. Why not strike the Confederates before they knew what was coming? They certainly would not expect an attack from a smaller Federal force. Sigel suggested further to split this small force into two columns and to launch simultaneous attacks on the Confederate camps from the west and from the east. The objective would be to paralyze the Confederates long enough to make an orderly withdrawal back to Rolla, with a field victory in hand! Lyon was impressed with Sigel's strategic acumen and began to finalize the plan. Federal troops would march in silence throughout the night and attack at dawn.

Interestingly, McCullough had devised a similar attack plan of his own, a pre-dawn assault on the Federals. If the weather had not intervened, the Battle of Wilson's Creek might well have been fought between two blind armies in the middle of the night. As it was, that night it began to rain. By all accounts it was just a summer shower, but worse threatened. The Confederates could not afford to fight in the rain. Their ammunition was in paper cartridges. They had no ammunition boxes, but carried the cartridges in their pockets. If the cartridges got damp, the ammunition was useless. So McCulloch called off the attack and the Confederates slept the night away. Shockingly, they forgot to set up pickets that night. The Federals had leather ammunition boxes, so the rain did not affect them.

In late afternoon on August 9, Lyon's 4,300 men began to move out into columns. Sigel's brigade was made up of 1,100 men and officers, including Backhoff's artillery, now just two brass six-pounders and four 12-pound howitzers. They were 85 artillerymen, but the best had already left for Saint Louis, as their 90 days had expired.

At early dawn on August 10, a Saturday, Sigel's artillery opened up on the Confederates sleeping in the Sharp family fields. The attack spread panic, achieving the early victory Sigel had predicted. On the western side, Lyon's attack was also successful, driving Sterling Price's men back. Price and McCulloch had been caught off guard. The failure to post sentries, combined with a refusal to believe early reports of a Union assault, were compounded by a local phenomenon called "acoustic shadow". The surprise was complete. Because of the rolling hills and the stands of forests, even the sound of the cannons could not be heard in the rebel headquarters. In the first part of the battle, it looked like a stunning victory for Lyon and Sigel.

Then the tide turned as a single Confederate battery spotted Lyon's charge and turned its guns on the Union artillery. Without the Union cannons to add firepower, the Union lines became vulnerable and Price's men rallied, storming up Oak Hill.

A Union force of 300 regulars and 200 Missouri volunteers charged McCulloch's Pulaski battery, but Arkansas and Louisiana units intervened and drove them back, outnumbering the Union troops 3 to 1.

On the western side of the battle, the numbers were having an effect. Price's Missouri militia could not be lodged off of Oak Hill, now dubbed Bloody Hill, despite charges by Missouri and Kansas infantry.

Meanwhile, everyone was asking, "Where is Sigel?" After his initial success, Sigel broke off his attack and waited to hear the sounds of battle in the west. It was 8 A.M. by now and the acoustic shadow phenomenon, combined with a lull in fighting, gave Sigel the false impression that the battle was over and Lyon was victorious.

Just then a column of gray uniforms came running at Sigel's position. The Germans assumed these were from a Union unit called the Greyhounds, known for their grey uniforms and their swiftness of movement whenever they maneuvered. But Sigel was wrong. They were McCulloch's Confederates, and in the success of their attack, they routed the Germans and captured their field guns. In a panic, Sigel and his men ran northeast and did not stop until they reached Springfield. Lyon launched one last desperate charge with the Second Kansas. He had been wounded twice, his horse killed from under him, and now, around 9:30 A.M., General Nathaniel Lyon fell in battle, the first Union general to die in combat.

The Union charge was met with an overwhelming Confederate counter-attack of nearly 5,000 men. These were only halted by Federal cannons. A lull fell over the battlefield around 11 A.M. The day was hot and both sides were exhausted. Taking advantage of the break in fighting, Samuel Sturgis, now in command of Lyon's forces, loaded up his artillery and led his men off the field and back to Springfield.

The Battle of Wilson's Creek was over: a Confederate victory to be added to the Confederate victory at Manassas Junction in Virginia on July 21.

As Sigel and Sturgis abandoned Springfield and returned to Rolla, the two victors, Price and McCulloch, could not agree on a common strategy. Instead, the Western Army broke up as McCulloch took his Confederate troops back to Arkansas and Price resumed command of the Missouri militia to lay siege to the Union position at Lexington, Missouri. Regardless, they would meet again to fight as comrades at Pea Ridge in Arkansas. And at that battle, both Franz Sigel and Father Bannon would be present.

Once Father John Bannon made his way to the Confederate camp of General Sterling Price, he met many men he had ministered to in Saint Louis. He met General Price and his staff. Captain William Wade and his artillerymen formed the Missouri Light Artillery with its three Irish-born lieutenants. There, Father Bannon began his service by hearing thirty confessions.

After the confessions, Father Bannon went on to another artillery unit, the Henry Guibor battery. Though Guibor was Alsatian, many of his men were Irish. He was himself a graduate of Saint Louis University. Father Bannon estimated that around 1,500 Catholics served in Price's army. With the First Missouri brigade, Father Bannon reconnected with members of the old Washington Blues. There he was adopted as their unofficial chaplain. Unlike Protestant ministers in the Confederate Army or the Missouri militia, Father Bannon carried no weapons, organized no fighting unit, and drew no salary.

Father Barnaby Faherty, in his biography of Father Bannon,

summed up his credentials in the following manner: "Father Bannon came to Price's camp with unsurpassed credentials. He had graduated from one of the most prestigious seminaries in the English-speaking world. The great Archbishop of the American West, Peter Richard Kenrick, had called him to shepherd a growing congregation of devout people. He had built an impressive church for the service of God. He had a command of the English language at a fluency of expression that would bring him wide acclaim as a preacher in years to come. His sermons showed a mastery of Scripture and of ancient Christian traditions. His voice resonated with an Irish lilt. His men knew him from the days of peace and during the southwest campaign of late 1860. He had shared their distressing surrender at Camp Jackson. While most of the other chaplains had been rural pastors, he came from the metropolis of the trans-Mississippi. He had to slip through hostile lines to reach his men."[81]

A fight was brewing as General Samuel R. Curtis was dispatched to southern Missouri with 10,000 Union troops from Missouri, Illinois, Indiana, Ohio, and Iowa. The objective was to retake Springfield and pursue Sterling Price. With Curtis marched Germans under Brigadier General Franz Sigel and his regimental colonels Osterhaus, Asboth, cavalryman Eugene Carr, and Jefferson C. Davis, a relative of the Confederate president.

But Curtis would have to deal with more than just the Missouri militia. The Confederacy sent Major General Earl Van Dorn, a dapper Mississippian, to oversee the command of Price's Missourians, McCulloch's Arkansans and Texans, Hébert's Louisiana troops, and Alfred Sidney Pike's Cherokee regiments from the Indian territories. Curtis pursued the Missourians into Arkansas and now found himself outnumbered. He dug his men in for a fight facing Sugar Creek with Pea Ridge to his back. Curtis figured the Union field fortifications would help even the odds.

Confederate General Van Dorn refused to take the bait. Instead of a frontal assault, he planned to send the whole army of the trans-Mississippi north around Curtis' army, taking the Bentonville Detour north of Pea Ridge and come down a broad valley on Curtis's left flank. This would restore the numerical advantage to the Confederates, and

---

81   William Barnaby Faherty, S. J. *Exile in Erin: A Confederate Chaplain's Story: The Life of Father John B. Bannon*. Saint Louis: Missouri Historical Society Press. 2002. P. 48.

if Curtis were defeated, he would have no retreat route back to Missouri. His army would be annihilated.

So Van Dorn set out on the detour with some 13,000 men and 60 cannons, leaving 3,000 behind to guard his baggage train. The pre-dawn maneuver did not go as smoothly as planned. The troops had to cross Sugar Creek and it was early March, so the water was cold. The Confederates built an unsteady bridge and crossed one by one, causing considerable delay. Once on the Bentonville Detour, they found that Curtis had felled trees across the road and these had to be removed before the artillery could pass.

It was already 10 A.M. by the time Price and Van Dorn arrived at Wire Road, which ran through the valley to the Union rear. The Confederates had lost the element of surprise. Two hours earlier, when Curtis discovered that they had abandoned their camp before him, he began to re-deploy his troops, making his rear now his front.

As Price deployed his 5,000 men and eight cannons, it was obvious that the Confederate units under McCulloch would not make it over Pea Ridge to join in the fight. Instead, McCulloch got Van Dorn's permission to cut short the march and to attack the Union lines on the west side of Pea Ridge while Price attacked on the east side. As McCulloch smashed into the Union troops under Franz Sigel, the Cherokee regiments scored an early victory, overrunning a Union artillery battery. But rather than press their advantage, they stopped to celebrate by scalping the dead Union men. This gave another Union battery time to zero in on the Cherokee and barrage them. Thrown into a panic, the Cherokee fled into the woods and were no longer involved in the battle.

McCulloch exposed himself to enemy fire as he sought to reconnoiter the terrain in front of him. This gave an Illinois squirrel hunter a perfect opportunity to show his skills. With a single shot to the chest, General Ben McCulloch was killed by Peter Pelican. When General Macintosh ran to the aid of his fallen commander, Pelican killed him, too.

A Union counterattack drove the Confederates down the Bentonville Detour until the dark of night brought an end to the first day of battle. In the panic and disorder, someone sent the ammunition train back to Bentonville rather than to Van Dorn. Price had broken off the fight around 8 P.M.

The Confederates had taken Elkhorn Tavern and turned it into a field hospital. Father Bannon spent much of the night there visiting the wounded.

The next morning the battle began all over again at 7 A.M. Curtis opened with an artillery barrage on his right flank, but Sigel's troops did not join in. Curtis rode over to Sigel with great agitation. He had felt that Sigel did not fight as aggressively as he might the day before. Sigel had even advocated an orderly retreat back to Missouri after Mc-Culloch and Macintosh had been killed. Now he seemed to procrastinate again. General Curtis cried out to Sigel, "I have opened the battle; it will be a hard fight... Please bring your troops in line as quickly as possible."

Sigel replied, "I have taken my position, General Curtis." Curtis went into a rage, but Sigel remained firm. "I have taken my position, General Curtis... And we will never surrender while I am Sigel."[82] Sigel's assessment of the activities of the day before was quite different than Curtis'. He had conducted a very fine offense against McCulloch's troops and had caused them to fall back eastward along the Bentonville Detour. This opened up the opportunity to move north, back to Missouri and out of this Arkansas trap. But Curtis refused to abandon the field. Sigel began with a barrage from cannons he had moved closer to the front. This knocked out some Confederate cannons, but what did the most to silence them was the lack of ammunition caused by the mistaken withdrawal of the ammunition train the day before.

Sigel sent Osterhaus forward in a flanking motion to turn Price's right. The Confederates were caught in a crossfire. There was nothing more to do than retreat, and the only way out was to flee southeast on the Huntsville Road, even as Pike's Cherokee regiments fled north on Wire Road toward Tanyard Township.

Father Bannon joined the rout, attending to the wounded General William Slack; he also baptized a dying soldier. That night he slept in the woods, his eyes wide open to the carnage of war. The Confederates lost 800 to 1,000 killed, wounded, or captured. What was left of the trans-Mississippi Army was reorganized at Van Buren and taken to join forces east of the Mississippi River. The Union army lost around 1,000 dead, wounded, and missing. But it held the field, and on March 7 and 8, it saved Missouri for the Union.

One veteran of the Pea Ridge battle reflected on the role Father John Bannon played those two days. Colonel R. S. Musser had this to

---

82   Stephen D. Engle. *Yankee Dutchman: The Life of Franz Sigel*. Baton Rouge. Louisiana State University Press. 1993. P. 114.

say at an 1885 reunion:

*I ought not to forget to mention the gallant and meritorious con-
duct of Father Bannon.... He had the general care of souls throughout
the whole army. He was everywhere in the midst of battle when the fire
was heaviest and bullets thickest. He was armed with the tourniquet
and a bottle of whiskey. Whenever there was a wounded or dying man,
Father Bannon was at his side, supporting his head; with his tourniquet
he would stanch the blood flow, with the spirits he sustained his strength
till his confession would be told, or if necessary, till he could baptize him
from the waters of the nearest brook.... Father Bannon was an Irishman
of splendid physique, full of grace and personal manliness, learned and
eloquent, social and genial....*[83]

Another veteran said this:

*His influence, in a religious sense, was felt by all who associated with
him, and his presence wherever he went repressed the rude manners of
the camp. Not that he objected to gaiety and mirthful pleasure, as he
had most affable manners and genial nature, but he always frowned
upon the soldiers' unrestrained expression and rude jests.*

*He was physically large, handsome, dignified, refined and cultured.
While his mission was one of peace, he became noted for his bravery
in the field and attending the wounded and dying in various exposed
places. He was both a pious and practical man, and became that ministering angel wherever broken and bruised humanity needed help and
consolation.*[84]

Neither Sigel nor Bannon would find rest in 1862. In April, the
priest attended the battles of Iuka and Corinth, and in August the German would participate in the Second Battle of Manassas. 1862 was
marked in the east by the peninsular campaign, in which General
George McClellan's Army of the Potomac moved with glacial speed between the York and James Rivers toward Richmond, the Confederate
capital. This movement was countered by Confederate General Robert E. Lee, who sent 70,000 rebels against McClellan, driving him back
down the peninsula. The Union army then returned to Washington,
D.C., where "Little Mac" was replaced by General John Pope.

Meanwhile, further west, Ulysses S. Grant took Cairo, Illinois, and

---

83   William Barnaby Faherty, S. J. *Exile in Erin: A Confederate Chaplain's Story: The
Life of Father John B. Bannon.* Saint Louis: Missouri Historical Society Press. 2002. P.
67.
84   Ibid. P. 72.

moved up the Tennessee River against Forts Henry and Donelson, which fell one month before the battle of Pea Ridge. One month after Pea Ridge, Grant scored a bloody but decisive victory at Shiloh on the Tennessee River. This opened up the upper South, causing Van Dorn's men to be sent east of the Mississippi River to strengthen Confederate defenses there. For the rest of the war, the Missourians in the Confederate Army would see nothing of their home state.

Before joining the trans-Mississippi Confederate Army, now on the east side of the great river, Father Bannon spent time in Arkansas in the company of a fellow Irishman. When Arkansas was created as a diocese out of the southern portion of the Saint Louis archdiocese, it received its first bishop from County Meath, Ireland. Bishop Andrew Byrne succeeded where the Saint Louis bishops failed by importing Irish clergy and religious. One of these was Father Patrick Riley, with whom Father Bannon celebrated Saint Patrick's Day that year. The Confederate chaplain then moved down the Arkansas River with Wade's and Guibor's artillery, celebrating Mass with these units. At Little Rock, Father Bannon visited the convent of the Sisters of Mercy, fellow Irish, and celebrated Mass for them on April 4 and 5.

There, Father Bannon again came face-to-face with the grim residue of battle. The Sisters were caring for some twenty-five wounded soldiers. The Sisters of Mercy were founded to run schools for poor children, but soon found themselves engaged in hospital work too. During the Crimean War, 1854 to 1856, two Mercy Sisters had accompanied an Irish unit in the British Army and cared for the wounded. Later, the same sisters came to America and cared for the sick in a Cincinnati hospital; during the Civil War, they would be pressed into service as nurses for the Union Army of the Cumberland.

The residue of battle was terrible human carnage. At Pea Ridge, hundreds of men died on both sides. The Union counted 980, while the Confederacy suffered similar casualties. Moreover, some 300 Confederates were captured in the battle. Caring for the wounded and housing the captives proved a daunting task.

These casualties were minor in comparison to the butcher's bill exacted at Forts Henry and Donelson and at the bloodiest battle, to that date, in American history: the battle of Shiloh or Pittsburgh's Landing. Historian Shelby Foote added up the casualties of the War for American Independence, the War of 1812, and the Mexican War, and counted to 23,273 American casualties. At Shiloh alone, the North and South combined to equal 23,741 dead and wounded.

Saint Louis got an early taste of having to deal with large numbers of wounded soldiers. After the Battle of Wilson's Creek, nearly 1,000 casualties were transported on rough wagons from the field to the railroads at Rolla. Then they came to Saint Louis by train. Saint Louis Hospital, run by the Sisters of Charity, was instantly filled, as was the City Municipal Hospital. A volunteer organization, the Ladies Union Aid Society, provided amateur comfort, but they too were overwhelmed when the Union abandoned Springfield and brought another 500 wounded to Saint Louis.

An organized approach was instituted when William Greenleaf Eliot, founder of Washington University, joined banker James Yeatman, Carlos Greely, grocer George Partridge, and Dr. John B. Johnston in persuading General John Frémont to establish the Western Sanitary Commission. In short order the Commission systematized the beds at Saint Louis Hospital, Municipal Hospital, the City Quarantine facility, and a new military hospital at Benton Barracks.

Much of the manpower assisting in these hospitals came from women volunteering and learning on the job. Said one such volunteer, Sarah Hill: "We were called on to assist the surgeons in their operations and to nurse the patients. There were no regular nurses then and volunteer nurses were scarce."[85] This adds testimony to Father Barnaby Faherty's assertion that the only professional nurses on either side at the start of the Civil War were a cohort of some 600 Catholic nuns.[86]

While on the Confederate side the work of the Sister-nurses was fully appreciated and had multiple requests for nurses from the Sisters of Charity Hospital in New Orleans, in the North, the Sister-nurses were met with prejudice from such quarters as Dorothea Dix, the director of the federal nurse program. While the Confederate government paid the expenses of the Sister-nurses, the Federals only did when circumstances demanded it.

One example of this Federal reluctance to employ Catholic Sisters is found in the story of Dr. Simon Pollak. A native of Bohemia, Dr. Pol-

---

85   Louis S. Gerteis. *Civil War St. Louis.* Lawrence: University Press of Kansas. 2001. P. 208.
86   William Barnaby Faherty, S. J. *Exile in Erin: A Confederate Chaplain's Story: The Life of Father John B. Bannon.* Saint Louis: Missouri Historical Society Press. 2002. P. 77.

lak studied at universities in Prague and Vienna, even traveling with a medical commission to study an outbreak of cholera in Russia. But he was determined to come to America, perhaps hoping to escape the viral anti-Semitic attitudes in central Europe. After starting in New York, then New Orleans, Pollak eventually moved to Saint Louis.

In Saint Louis, Pollak found his home. He developed friendships with Doctors McPheeters and Gratz Moses, though these friends grew distant after the Camp Jackson affair. Both held strong southern sympathies, while Pollak favored the Union. Pollak became the first Saint Louis doctor to specialize in ophthalmology, making Saint Louis a leader in education for the blind. He helped open the Missouri School for the Blind, introduced Braille as a teaching tool, and was the first to use the newly invented ophthalmoscope to study diseases of the eye.

Pollak's split with McPheeters and Moses led him to abandon Saint Louis and move to New York. But fate would draw him back again. After he joined the United States Sanitary Commission, Pollak was assigned to lead a medical team with General Ulysses S. Grant during his attack on Forts Henry and Donelson on the Tennessee River. He served on the steamboat which was outfitted as a floating hospital and was assisted by volunteers of the Ladies Union Aid Society. With two exceptions, he found the ladies to be useless in performing their duties. He complained bitterly. The rest of the lot he called "society imps."

This criticism got Dr. Pollak into trouble with the Western Sanitary Commission and its founder, William Greenleaf Elliot. Regardless, the medical doctor was too valuable to dispense with, and Dr. Pollak found himself on the hospital steamship *Continental*. Whether he had any control over naming his assistants, it is not known. But gone from the ship were the "society imps," and with him were the two women volunteers he had found valuable, as well as six Sisters of Charity. The Jewish ophthalmologist would have good reason to want these Sisters with him, as earlier he had contracted cholera and had been successfully treated by Sisters of Charity at their hospital.

Antagonism between Elliot and Pollak escalated over the role of the Sisters in nursing the wounded. When the *Continental* arrived in Saint Louis, sending the Union wounded to City Hospital, the Confederate wounded to the Sisters of Charity Hospital, and non-wounded Confederates to the Gratiot Street prison, Dr. Pollak rented a carriage to send the Sisters of Charity to their convent and charged the expense to the Western Sanitary Commission. Elliott was livid. Elliott again complained when Dr. Pollak sent Sisters to visit and to minister to wounded Catholics in the City Hospital and to make visits to the Gratiot Street prison. Elliott countered by getting all the members of the commission to sign a letter of protest demanding of the War Department that no Catholic Sisters be allowed in the City Hospitals or federal prisons. Elliott's anti-Catholic bias spilled over into accusations that the Catholic Sisters had southern sympathies and could not be trusted. In the end, Dr. Pollak declared he could no longer work with the Western Sanitary Commission, but stayed on to serve in Saint Louis as a member of the United States Sanitary Commission. Dr. Pollak stayed in Saint Louis after the war and remained one of its most prominent citizens until his death in 1903. While he was best known as a pioneer in the study of diseases of the eye and in education for the blind, the Catholic community might well remember this Jewish physician for his chivalrous defense of Catholic Sisters during the Civil War.

If those who were motivated by anti-Catholic biases tried to keep the Sisters out of the hospitals and prisons, they had good reason. Father John Bannon, chaplain to the Confederate Army, estimated that when the Sisters got involved, 80% of those treated became Catholic. He records one such encounter found in Father Faherty's book, *Exile in Erin.*

One of the Sisters told me that she had a patient willing to become a Catholic, that she had given him some instructions, but that it would be better if I saw him at once. I went to his bedside, and after a few introductory questions, I asked if he had ever professed any religion.

"No," he said, "I have not: but I have made arrangements about that now; I have some settled in with the Sister."

"Quite right," I replied," but it will be well for me to have a little talk with you."

"Now, I tell you what it is, Mister," replied the patient. "It's no use any of your coming talking to me. I belong to the Sister's religion, and that's enough."

"Exactly, and so do I. I am a priest and that religion – the Catholic religion: and I have come to see what I can do for you."

He would not however be satisfied until he called the Sister and learned from her that all was right and proper. While I instructed him, something or another I told him seemed too much for his good will.

"Oh, how come now," he said, "you don't expect me to believe that!"

"Yes," I said, "that is what the Catholic Church teaches, and we are bound to believe it."

"Well," he replied, "we'll see. Here, Sister!"

The sister came, and the patient addressed her saying, "Sister, this man tells me so and so. Is that true?"

"Oh, yes," said the Sister smiling; "quite true."

"Do you believe it, Sister?"

"Yes, certainly; we all believe it." "Very well," he said, turning to me, "all right, I believe it. Go ahead, Mister; what next?"

The man's language may seem flippant and offhand; but he was thoroughly in earnest, and received everything I told him: it was however necessary to make a few appeals to the Sister now and then, and when she confirmed what I said, he accepted it once and finally. He only remarked once, "He says some very hard things, Sister!" But he took all the hard things in directly as he had the Sister's word. In the end I baptized him; though it might be said perhaps to be rather in fidem Sororus, *than* fidem Ecclesia *(in the faith of the Sisters rather than in the faith of the Church).*[87]

Father Bannon moved to Memphis with the trans-Mississippi Army and accompanied it on its railroad trip to Corinth, Mississippi. The Battle of Shiloh had opened the lid to the South, and the Union wanted to immediately take advantage of the opening. Corinth was the perfect place to begin. One rail line ran north to south through Corinth, terminating in the north at Chicago, Illinois, and in the south at Mobile, Alabama. An east-west line ran through Corinth connecting Memphis, Tennessee with Richmond, Virginia, and with a spur going to Atlanta, Georgia.

Early blood was drawn when General Sterling Price caught General William Rosecrans' Union army napping at Iuka, 24 miles east of Corinth. The federals fled, leaving their supplies behind them, giving the rebels an opportunity to feast on rarities, including, according to Father Bannon, mustard, ketchup, and vinegar. But the feast was short-lived; Grant ordered a counterattack and two divisions under General E. O. Ord struck from the northwest as Rosecrans returned from the southeast.

Price made a successful withdrawal from Iuka and joined up with

---

87   William Barnaby Faherty, S. J. *Exile in Erin: A Confederate Chaplain's Story: The Life of Father John B. Bannon.* Saint Louis: Missouri Historical Society Press. 2002. PP. 78–80.

Confederate forces under Earl Van Dorn at Ripley, some 20 miles southwest of Corinth. Van Dorn was still smarting from his defeat at Pea Ridge and was looking to redeem his glory.

The assault on Corinth did not redeem Van Dorn's glory. It was another bloody affair without effect. Price had success on the Confederate left flank and took the first fortifications, driving all the way into the city of Corinth. Van Dorn's right flank stalled and went no further. It was yet another case of eighteenth-century tactics against nineteenth-century weaponry. The rifled musket had a range that made no sense for troops to assemble on the battlefield in lines or columns. And the butcher's bill at the Second Battle of Corinth showed it. The Union lost 315 killed and 1,812 wounded, while the Confederates lost over 2,000 killed and wounded. At that time in military medical history, when 80% of amputees died in surgery, to be wounded was almost as bad as being killed.

After the battle, Father Bannon was almost captured while tending to the wounded in an ambulance wagon. Instead, he made his way to Vicksburg, Mississippi, with what was left of Price's army, having lost 500 men at Corinth. Price himself was called to Richmond, where he was dispatched west of the Mississippi, not to see his Missourians again.

Father Bannon arrived at Vicksburg on January 2, 1863. Neither he nor anyone else could have known that 1863 would be the bloodiest year in this bloody war, featuring simultaneous battles at Vicksburg, Mississippi, and at Gettysburg in Pennsylvania. Father Bannon joined his First Missouri unit at Grand Gulf near Vicksburg. On the last Sunday of March, 1863, he said Mass for the soldiers, giving communion to 43 of them. That evening he conducted Vespers by the light of a campfire when word came they were about to be attacked by federal gunboats. Three boats blasted away at the First Missouri fortifications. The rebels returned fire, but little damage was done to either side. The Confederate shells could not penetrate the ship's iron sides, and the Union shells inflicted little damage on the Confederate earthworks. The only casualties were two Confederate artillery men who died when their parrot gun exploded. Father Bannon buried both men nearby.

Ulysses S. Grant had his mind set on capturing Vicksburg; it was the last holdout on the Mississippi River. When the gunboat artillery assault on Grand Gulf failed, Grant sent 23,000 men to land south of Grand Gulf to try a land assault. Confederate General John Bowan had but 5,500 Confederates to confront the Yankees. They fought throughout May 1 and into the night, but the weight of the Union arms was too great and the Confederate defenders abandoned Grand Gulf, slowly making their way to Vicksburg, stopping on the north side of Bayou Pierre. The little Bayou failed to hold the Union forces for long, but it served as a place where Father Bannon's courage would shine.

The following account is an incident recorded in Father Faherty's *Exile in Erin*.

Upon one occasion when both armies were stationed and entrenched on either side of the river ... He was on the extreme right of the Confederate lines. He learned that an officer had been mortally wounded on the extreme left and was anxious to see a priest. Father Bannon immediately mounted his horse and before the firing had ceased, started to gallop more than a mile to the position at which the officer was stationed. His commanding figure, of course, enabled him to be recognized, and troops on both sides, Federal and Confederate, struck by his heroism, started up from their trenches, ceased firing, and cheered him loudly. The same recognition of his devotion and courage was repeated on his return journey.[88]

Throughout May 1863 the Union grip on Vicksburg grew tighter and tighter. The strategy became known as "the Python policy." The city was under an extreme siege as artillery pounded the city all day long and Union snipers shot at anything that moved.

The Confederate wounded were taken to a school building and nursed by six Sisters of Mercy. These were not Sister-nurses though. They were teachers and had opened a school in 1859, coming from Baltimore. These were joined by three Sisters of Charity who stole their way into the besieged city just before Grant closed the noose. Another incident during the siege speaks of the tender mercies of the sacraments in the heat of battle.

Within the lines of Vicksburg during the siege, we were under a tremendous sun, and a tremendously hot fire, and had to live for six weeks on wretched rations of mule meat, that I went one day to visit the ward for the mortally wounded. This ward was naturally not so well cared for as the others, for the cases were all hopeless as far as nursing and surgery went; but for my purposes they were perhaps more hopeful than

---

88   William Barnaby Faherty, S. J. *Exile in Erin: A Confederate Chaplain's Story: The Life of Father John B. Bannon*. Saint Louis: Missouri Historical Society Press. 2002. P. 107.

many others. On this occasion I noticed a group which struck me more than usual. A wounded man, about 40 years of age, lay insensible on one of the beds, and two other soldiers, one about the age of the dying man, the other a lad, but both bronzed with hard service, were standing sad and silent by his side. I went over to them and asked the elder of the two if the wounded man was a relative.

"He is my brother," was the reply, "and this boy's father." They were all three Patriot Soldiers, as the first Southern volunteers were called; they served in the ranks at their own expense, and took not a farthing of pay.

"I fear," I said, "that there is no hope of his life."

"Do you think so?" said the brother anxiously; and turning to the lad he added, "How should we tell your mother?"

"Well," I said, "perhaps he was prepared for death. Did he profess any religion?"

"No – but he thought a great deal about religion, and was fond of hearing preaching."

"Do you know if he was ever baptized?"

"He was not. But I have heard him say quite lately that he wished he had been; and that if God spared him through this war, he would get himself baptized at the end of it."

"Well," I replied, "it is a pity that if he wished for baptism he should die without it. From what you tell me he certainly believed in God. Did he believe in the Trinity?"

"Yes, he did."

"Did he believe that Jesus Christ was God?"

"Of course he did."

"Well, I'll tell you what I think, I think you ought not to let him die without being baptized, since he wished for it himself, and now cannot help himself. Besides it would be a consolation to his wife and all his family at home to know that he was baptized before he died. It would take off some of the pain of losing him."

After saying so much I went away; I left them to talk the matter over between them. It is often well not to seem to push things, but to allow something to come spontaneously to from the other side, though it may be an answer to one's own suggestion.

I visited some of the cases and came back after an interval. I saw the two were in some perplexity.

"I am a Catholic priest," I said, "but if you wish it I will myself offer

to baptize your brother; for from what you tell me I find in him all the conditions requisite for me to do so in his present state. Think it over, and let me know."

I then left the ward. It was not long however before the two men came to seek me, and finding me in one of the corridors of the hospital, the elder said, "Mister, we think he ought to be baptized. And we should like you to baptize him rather than anybody else, for all the boys speak well of the Catholic priests and Sisters."

"Very well," I said," I will keep to my word."

We went back to the bedside, and taking off the damp cloth that was laid over the dying man I prepared to baptize him. It was an affecting thing to see those two rough soldiers dropped to their knees instinctively, and see the tears roll down their bronzed cheeks as I administered the sacrament.

"Mister," said the brother, seizing my hand when I had finished, "I should like to be a Catholic too, if you will have me. If you will only teach me all about it, I will be thankful to you forever."

The dying man never recovered his senses; and the brother became a Catholic. The younger man did not offer himself at once with his uncle, and the surrender of the town took him out of my sight, but I trust his case was only reserved for more worthy hands than mine.[89]

On July 3, Father Bannon saw Generals Bowan and Pembleton riding into the Union headquarters under a flag of truce. The next day, Vicksburg surrendered, along with its 15,000 men. Some were sent as prisoners of war to northern prisons. Most were exchanged for Union prisoners or paroled. Father Bannon was paroled. He was called to Richmond to meet with President Jefferson Davis. His life was about to take a dramatic twist.

At Richmond, Father Bannon reported to Bishop John McGill. There he also met Secretary of the Navy Stephen Malloy, the man who had secured for Father Bannon a commission as a Confederate chaplain, elevating him from his role as a volunteer chaplain to the Missouri militia. President Davis wanted to send Father Bannon to Ireland to counter Federal recruiters there. It seems that the Union had devised a scheme whereby agents posing as railroad recruiters would convince young Irishman to come to America to build railroads. But

---

89   William Barnaby Faherty, S. J. *Exile in Erin: A Confederate Chaplain's Story: The Life of Father John B. Bannon.* Saint Louis: Missouri Historical Society Press. 2002. PP. 112-113.

once they arrived, the fictitious railroad disappeared and they were lured into joining the army. The whole enterprise was funded by those drafted into the Union Army, but given permission to hire substitutes. The clueless Irish lads were the substitutes. Father Bannon's mission was to expose the fraud.

All of this played into the mind and attitude of the Rebel chaplain. He knew that Know-Nothing violence plagued the Church in America, mainly in the North. He regarded many on the Union side as freethinkers and religious skeptics. The Union Army represented the heavy-handed pressure of the industrialized North.

The Confederacy transferred Father Bannon from the Army to Special Services and gave him $1,200 in gold to carry out his mission. The priest's delicate canonical state was given some status when Bishop McGill authorized the mission. Father Bannon, as a priest of the Archdiocese of Saint Louis, was in canonical limbo as Archbishop Peter Richard Kenrick never recognized his absence and therefore did not authorize his excardination.

Father Bannon snuck through the Union blockade and made his way to Bermuda. He then sailed to Halifax, London, and finally Dublin. There he told stories of Union desecration of Catholic churches and schools. Indeed, in Saint Louis, federal authorities seized Christian Brothers College on Eighth and Cerre Street, turning it into a federal prison along with Dr. McDowell's medical school across the street.

Twelve thousand posters were printed and sent to parishes all throughout Ireland explaining Father Bannon's views on the Civil War in America. At a funeral attended by many Irish clergy, Father Bannon was given the opportunity to speak directly about the Southern cause.

After a visit to Cork, Father Bannon was dispatched to Rome to meet Pope Pius IX. Both sides had courted the pontiff for an endorsement, but both sides went away disappointed.

Father Bannon accompanied Bishop Patrick Lynch of Charleston, South Carolina. A tender story followed, which shows the sense of humor possessed by both "Pio Nono" and John B. Bannon.

Bannon bent his knee to kiss the papal ring as all the others had done. As he straightened up to his great height, with his great black flowing beard, the expression of the Pope's face denoted wonder, then admiration.

Motioning the two cardinals to stand aside, the Pope said, "That I may better see cet homme magnifique.*"*

Of course Father Bannon felt twice as tall as he actually was. The Pope saw that he had caused this display of vanity, and the expression on his face changed. In a stern voice he demanded, "Who gave you permission to wear that beard?"

Momentarily flustered, Father Bannon relied on his Irish wit. Bowing low before the Pope, he said, "Holy Father, I am only a poor Confederate chaplain. What would become of me if in camp, I had one half of this enormous beard shaved off, and the bugle should ring out, to horse to horse, the Yankees are here? I, the poor priest, should have to ride away like a fool, with half of my beard gone."

A heavenly smile gradually crept over the face of Pius IX, as he said, "My son, you may wear your beard."[90]

Father Bannon eventually shaved off his beard and entered the Jesuit novitiate at Milltown Park near Dublin. It was December 26, 1864, and Father Bannon was 35 years old. Father John B. Bannon spent the rest of his life as a Jesuit serving in Ireland. It is speculated that he met with Archbishop Kenrick when the Archbishop visited Ireland in June 1867 and again in September 1868 on his trip to Rome. Such was suggested by a close friend, Captain Joseph Boyce.

Dublin was also visited by Father Patrick Ryan, Vicar-General of the Archdiocese of St. Louis. Though no record is made of their encounter, both priests were in Dublin at the same time and both would have stories to tell each other, as Ryan had been made chaplain for the Confederate prisoners at the Gratiot Street prison at the request of Archbishop Kenrick.

Father Bannon, Confederate chaplain and Confederate agent, then a Jesuit priest, served Saint Francis Xavier Parish in Dublin for the next fifty years. Father John B. Bannon died on July 14, 1913, having experienced 83 years of a most extraordinary life.

Our other Saint Louisan, Franz Sigel, also had adventures after Pea Ridge. His performance on the second day of the Pea Ridge battle gave him a reputation as a Union general who could win battles, something few Union commanders could claim. He was transferred to the East and given command of an Army Corps. There Sigel witnessed the shoddy way the Federals treated his German soldiers. One division, under General Ludwig Blecker, had marched for six weeks in

---

90   William Barnaby Faherty, S. J. *Exile in Erin: A Confederate Chaplain's Story: The Life of Father John B. Bannon.* Saint Louis: Missouri Historical Society Press. 2002. P. 139.

the Allegheny Mountains, had worn out their shoes, and were short on rations. When the men sought to loot the landscape, Blecker was cashiered by the War Department.

Sigel had no high opinion of his immediate commander, General John Pope. In one letter he wrote that Pope was affected with "looseness of the brains as others with looseness of the bowels."[91] Things came to a head on August 9, 1862. The federal troops were attacked at Cedar Mountain by the legendary Thomas Stonewall Jackson. Pope was hard-pressed while Sigel kept his men in the rear, waiting for a supply train to bring them a hot meal. When Pope raged, Sigel finally sent his men forward, arriving on the battlefield at dusk, just in time to give cover to the Union soldiers retreating from Jackson's assault.

Later it was learned that the courier Pope sent to tell Sigel to advance had been captured by the Confederates. Sigel could not be held guilty of ignoring orders he had never received. The Battle of Cedar Mountain was a bloody encounter on both sides. Jackson lost 320 dead and 1,466 wounded, while Pope lost 314 dead and 1,062 wounded. But it reminded the Federals that Thomas Jackson was a dangerous foe who could surprise his enemy at any time.

And on August 27, Jackson did surprise his enemy. Early that morning he took Manassas Junction, setting the scene for a second battle there. The contest opened on August 29, as a reluctant Pope with 75,000 men went against Jackson's 24,000. But the battle turned against Pope when General James Longstreet arrived with another 30,000 Confederates. Pope mismanaged the battle so badly that General Halleck ordered the army to retreat back to Washington, D.C. Sigel was given orders to reorganize his Corp of 15,000 men, now designated as the Eleventh into three divisions. It was nicknamed "the German Command," as the division commanders were Julius Stahel, Adolph Steinwehr, and Carl Schurz. More and more, Franz Sigel grew in the opinion that his transfer to the east had more to do with politics and less to do with military command. The Lincoln administration was using Sigel as a poster boy to keep German-Americans engaged in the war and voting Republican.

This opinion seemed to be borne out, as Sigel was sent to Reading, Pennsylvania, to campaign for the Republicans and to denounce the Copperheads, politicians who came to oppose the war. Only then was

---

91   Stephen D. Engle. *Yankee Dutchman: The Life of Franz Sigel*. Baton Rouge: Louisiana State University Press. 1993. P. 129.

he allowed to resume command of the Eleventh Corp, and that under the close scrutiny of General Halleck.

A further Union defeat at Newmarket on May 15, 1864, left Sigel's reputation in tatters. Worse, he seems to have performed badly in the field, giving conflicting orders, sometimes in English and at other times in German.

Franz Sigel felt he was mistreated by the Union command, that there was a prejudice against him because he was German and not a West Pointer. He commented that he had to fight two enemies at once, one in the front and one in the rear.[92] Finally, on May 4, 1865, Sigel resigned his commission and returned to civilian life. Sigel engaged himself in Republican politics, but like his Saint Louis counterpart Father John Bannon, he never returned to Saint Louis. His took up residence in New York City. He died on August 22, 1902. Though he became a bitter enemy to men who had once served with him, like Carl Schurz, the outpouring of appreciation for his service was witnessed at his funeral. An estimated 25,000 people lined the streets to view the funeral procession. Honorary pallbearers came from the units he had led in the Civil War as well as comrades from the 1848 Baden uprising. Schurz was present and delivered an oration, but broke down with emotion.

For years afterward, when German-American veterans came into Saint Louis taverns and declared, "I fight mit Sigel," bartenders would respond, "Pytem! You pay noting for your lager!"[93]

Father John Bannon and General Franz Sigel experienced the Civil War in two fundamentally different ways. Meanwhile, back in Saint Louis, Archbishop Peter Richard Kenrick endured the national tragedy in a profound silence. His Vicar General Father Patrick Ryan reflected on this: "He kept aloof from politics and abstained for a time from reading the newspapers, because he believed that, in the particular circumstances of Missouri as a border state, the interest of religion would best be forwarded by prudent silence."[94]

This prudent silence did not please Secretary of State Seward, who tried to persuade Roman authorities to remove Kenrick from his see.

---

92   Stephen D. Engle. *Yankee Dutchman: The Life of Franz Sigel*. Baton Rouge: Louisiana State University Press. 1993. P. 208.
93   Rev. John Rothensteiner. *History of the Archdiocese of St. Louis. II* Saint Louis: Blackwell Wielandy Co. 1928. P 232.
94   Ibid. P. 212.

Father Ryan further observed: "...But Mr. Seward's little bell did not tinkle in the Vatican."[95]

Kenrick was also the object of Frank Blair's rage. Blair had attempted to use Father Peter De Smet as a recruiting tool for the Union army by making him a chaplain. When the Archbishop blocked this, Blair used his considerable influence in Washington to punish Kenrick. In the end he backed off, realizing that any attempt would be futile. The man who caused General Harney and General Frémont to be dismissed from command in the West was powerless against the Lion in the Fourth City. While the Archbishop himself proved powerless to restrain Father Bannon from becoming a Confederate chaplain, he worked tirelessly to protect his priests in Saint Louis. Father John O'Sullivan, pastor of St. Malachy, was targeted by federal military officials because of his pro-Southern statements. Before he could be arrested, Archbishop Kenrick transferred him to Alton, Illinois, where Bishop Junkers gave him a parish in Springfield. When the Provost Marshal requested that a federal flag be flown from the steeple of the cathedral, Archbishop Kenrick replied, "No other banner may be placed there, for already there stands one, which alone shall stay, the banner of the church, meaning the cross."[96]

After the battle of Shiloh, Saint Louis was inundated with wounded and prisoners of war. Besides City Hospital, which cared for the Federal wounded, and Saint Louis Hospital, run by the Sisters of Charity caring for the Confederate wounded, and later Quarantine Hospital and a military hospital at Benton Barracks, other smaller hospitals sprang up. This included Immaculate Conception Parish, where the facilities were given over to the Sisters of Charity.

Father Patrick Ryan, pastor of the Church of the Annunciation and Vicar General, was also assigned by the Archbishop to act as chaplain to the prisoners at Gratiot Street military prison. There he eventually baptized 600 soldiers. The prison was originally Dr. McDowell's Medical College, founded and operated by Dr. Joseph Nash McDowell. The good doctor was brilliant but eccentric. He was an outspoken Southern sympathizer, and his facility was raided by Federal troops on May 30, 1861. To their surprise, the troops found two small cannons, which McDowell said he fired off only on the Fourth of July.

---

95   Rev. John Rothensteiner. *History of the Archdiocese of St. Louis. II* Saint Louis: Blackwell Wielandy Co. 1928. P 213.
96   Ibid. P. 213.

The raid so shocked McDowell that he and his son Drake fled south, bringing their cannons with them. A second son, Max, stayed in Saint Louis to recruit for the Southern cause. He was later captured and imprisoned in the inhumane Myrtle Street prison, the former holding pen for the slave market.

The Federals seized McDowell's College and turned it into the Gratiot Street Prison after it served briefly as a barracks. Fifty workmen prepared the facility for its new purpose, and fifteen former slaves were sent into the basement to remove three wagon loads of human bones, which had been used for anatomical studies. On December 24, 1861, some 1,200 Confederate prisoners of war were crowded into the prison. To these would be added political prisoners and Union defectors.

When the facility proved to be too small for federal needs, they moved the guards next door to occupy Christian Brothers College. The school was just nine years old and struggling from one crisis after another. Many of the students were withdrawing to join opposite armies. When the Brothers' community lost their chaplain, Father Renauld, they petitioned Archbishop Kenrick for another. He declined, arguing a shortage of priests. The Brothers responded by telling him that they would leave the city rather than be without a chaplain. The Archbishop then pointed out that the deed on the Cerre Street property was written in such a way that the Brothers could not sell without the Archbishop's permission. They were caught.

And worse, the Brothers found themselves neighbors to the Federal prisoner of war facility and now forced to quarter Union troops sent to guard the prison. Classes were interrupted by noise and especially disturbing were rifle shots fired at escaping prisoners. Finally, the school itself was confiscated and classrooms on the upper floors were used for sniper pits. Only in 1884 would Christian Brothers College be compensated for the Federal occupation of its campus.

Father Ryan was offered a commission in the Federal Army as a paid chaplain. He refused and continued to visit the Gratiot Street Prison without compensation. Other priests joined him, including Father Patrick Feehan, who later was named Bishop of Nashville, even as Ryan became the Archbishop of Philadelphia.

The war brought havoc to the rest of the state, too. Father John Hogan of Chillicothe spoke of the sacking of a Catholic Church in Macon City, as pews, altars, and the wooden floor were taken to be used as fuel for a local Union encampment. This happened in 1864, as the Confederate forces from Glasgow threatened attack.

When the war ended, conflict did not. The November election of 1864 included contests for the presidency of the United States, the governorship, state and federal representatives, and delegates for a new Missouri constitutional convention. Two issues were paramount for this convention: abolition of slavery in Missouri and creating a way to reward the loyal and to punish the rebel. Already introduced for the election of 1864 was a Test Oath, which required the electorate (that is, white male adults) to swear loyalty to the Constitutions of the United States and of Missouri. As a result, 52,000 fewer votes were cast in 1864 than in 1860. Abraham Lincoln won the election of 1864, and Thomas C. Fletcher, a Civil War hero, easily took the governorship of Missouri. Indeed, the Republicans swept the field in both houses of the legislature and for the constitutional convention. These Republicans were dominated by a majority called the Radicals (locally called "The Charcoals" because they burned with zeal to punish the rebel).

The constitutional convention met at the Mercantile Library in Saint Louis and on July 6, 1865, voted to amend the Missouri Constitution to outlaw slavery. One is reminded that the Emancipation Proclamation of 1863 freed only the slaves in the rebellious States, so Missouri slaves were not freed until 1865. There followed that night a sixty-gun salute by the Federal troops and a fireworks display; the streets of Saint Louis were filled with a joyful throng of both blacks and whites. But when it came to the question of black suffrage, things got ugly. William Greenleaf Elliot, who prayed at the convention, "Thanks be to God for the day that light has now come out of the darkness," had a contrary opinion of giving blacks the right to vote. He urged the convention delegates to require that voters demonstrate an ability to read and write, regardless of the language, "thus reducing the present mass of ignorant voters."[97]

Charles Drake, the leader of the Missouri Radical Republicans, further demogogued against the foreign-born and foreign-inclined, a thinly-veiled reference to Catholics. He pressed for a broader interpretation of disloyalty to include anyone who gave aid, comfort, or support to persons engaged in any such hostility.

Allies of the Radicals began to break away because of the bigotry

---

97   Louis G. Gerteis. *Civil War St. Louis*. Lawrence: University of Kansas Press. 2001. P. 311.

exhibited. The Germans, who had been so supportive of the Republicans, were repelled by the Radicals. Isidor Bush, a prominent Saint Louis Jew, co-founder of B'nai El Congregation and delegate to the convention, objected to the constant use of the word "white" in constitutional wording. Drake's bigotry and prejudice were on display. He favored the Union and favored emancipation, but was unwilling to imagine a truly color-blind society.

The convention, still under radical influence, instructed Governor Fletcher to replace all judges and even sheriffs throughout the state. Called "the ousting ordinance," it gave the governor broad powers to interpret who should be ousted and who should be retained.

In a high-profile case, two Missouri Supreme Court Justices, John Dryden and William Bay, refused to step down, calling "the ousting ordinance" unconstitutional. They were physically removed from the bench by Saint Louis City police as 700 militia men stood guard on the streets to quell any public protest. The Supreme Court was then reconstituted by Fletcher appointees.

The new Constitution came up for a vote on the June 6th ballot. Drake tilted the odds in his favor when he got Union soldiers registered as Missouri citizens. Not only did soldiers from Jefferson Barracks vote, but also those at Camp Douglas in Illinois and even the Union garrison in Little Rock, Arkansas. Saint Louis went 80% against the new Constitution, and the opposition would have carried the vote statewide by a margin of 1,000 votes. However, the military vote, when factored in, passed the radical Constitution by 2,000 votes. It would take a legal showdown to reverse this action.

Alexander J. P. Garesché refused to take the test oath. He was a practicing attorney who had been rounded up at the Camp Jackson affair in May 1861. Though paroled, he felt harassed by federal authorities and departed for Columbia, South Carolina. His wife soon joined him with their four children. She served as a nurse for the Confederate wounded and also for several black workers who were victims of a powder magazine explosion.

After the war, Garesché returned to Saint Louis to practice law, challenging the constitutionality of the Test Oath. The Missouri Supreme Court, the one appointed by Governor Fletcher, ruled against Garesché. His appeal to the United States Supreme Court was not reviewed by the court, and so his challenge to the Test Oath was not successful.

It was in the realm of religion that a second challenge would be launched. Many Protestant clergy in Missouri were caught in the trap. They had shown clear Southern sympathies during the conflict; so had some Catholic priests. Regardless, most Catholic clergy followed the example of Archbishop Kenrick and refrained from political statements. Now Kenrick would act decisively. Father Rothensteiner summarized his position clearly: "They found in the Archbishop of Saint Louis a man whom they could not bend nor break: at no time in his life did Peter Richard Kenrick more strikingly show forth the leonine qualities of his character, than in his opposition to the infamous test oath required by the so-called Drake Constitution."[98]

The Test Oath went further into the soul and psyche of a citizen: demanding not just loyalty in act and word throughout the war, but even a private desire to see the South triumph or any sympathy for those in rebellion. Eventually 36 ministers and priests would be brought before grand juries, indicted for refusing to take the Test Oath; all refused to vacate their pulpits in the meantime. Governor Fletcher fumed, "Religious liberty is a political right." He predicted court victories over these recalcitrant clergy and threatened to enlarge the penitentiary in order to house these criminals. Two Catholic priests played starring roles in the unfolding of the challenge to the Test Oath.

In the west, Father John Hogan of Chillicothe, and in the east, Father John Cummins in the Mississippi River town of Louisiana, were the standouts, though all Catholic priests in the state refused to take the Test Oath. Fathers Phelan of Edina and Hilner of Boonville were briefly arrested. Father Hogan's case is best told in his own words, as he described how the deputy sheriff, named Drury, tried to moderate the arrest but was cleverly manipulated by the priest.

On the last day but one of the year 1865, which was Saturday, my modest young chorister, riding an elegant horse, drew up at the gate before my cottage. Dismounting, he passed gracefully on foot through the grassy lawn, amid cedars and arbor vitae that led up to the door. I saw him as he advanced. His dress and manner were faultless, but his bland smile had left him, and his face was as solemn and woebegone as if he had come to invite me to his father's funeral. Hastening to meet him, I said: "Drury dear, how are you; and why are you so grave and serious today?"

"Have you not heard the bad news?" said he.

98   Rev. John Rothensteiner. *History of the Archdiocese of St. Louis. II* Saint Louis: Blackwell Wielandy Co. 1928. P. 215.

"No," said I, "what is it?"

"You have been indicted," said he; "the Grand Jury have found against you, for having preached without having taken the test oath. Garry and I are afraid the constable will take you to jail, as he may do at any moment; and to prevent this disgrace we have thought it better to call upon you without delay, and to have you sign a bond before your appearance. But you need not go to court until Term time, which will be the third Monday in May next."

"Thank you, Drury," said I; "the news is not the worst possible. Garry and you take much of the harm out of it. And, so you tell me, my friend Garry Harker, the sheriff, has sent you here with all possible speed, so as to be first to do me a favor?"

"Yes," said he. "And have you the bond?" said I. "Yes," said he, "here it is."

"Thanks be to Garry," said I; "it is very kind of him to be so thoughtful of me. Drury, please wait here a minute until I return from the next room."

"At your pleasure," said Drury, bowing politely.

Having softly closed the door between myself and Drury, I quickly dressed in full canonicals – soutane, surplus, stole, birette; then taking a large crucifix in my right hand, and in my left a large folio Bible, which I swung over my shoulder, I opened the door and advanced toward Drury, saying to him in a low but rather commanding voice: "Now, sir, I am ready for you; come along." Instantly there was a scene. Drury rose to his feet, and with horrified face and outstretched hands, seemed to fall into the role of Hamlet before the ghost, though his lips spoke not a syllable.

"Angels and ministers of grace defend us. Be thou spirit or goblin? Thou comest in such a questionable shape. I will speak to thee, O, answer me. What may this mean? Say, why is this?"

"Drury," I said, "I am a priest; I plead guilty; I confess that I preach the gospel without authority from the state to do so; and if I have to go to jail for it, you will have to take me there. That's what's the matter."

"But," said Drury, "if you please, go to the courthouse without me. You will please take that street, and I will take this, and when we meet at the courthouse, we will fix up this bond there."

"Drury," said I, "you were never ashamed of me before, now you will not walk with me. What have I done to you that you are so displeased with me? If you go without me, you know you will have to come after me again."

"But, Reverend Father," said Drury, "please ride my horse and I will walk."

"Oh, not so, dear Drury; this canonical dress is not becomingly worn on horseback. Rather, do you ride and I will walk with you." So we paired, side-by-side. He on horseback, I, in the name of the Lord. O, the crowds, the crowds they gathered up, and followed us from all sides. I feared, as there was anger visible, and excitement all around, that there would be trouble. But who could think of interfering when it was seen that Drury and I were friendly and when it was very well known that we were dear friends. Yet at one time on the march along the street, with hundreds of people at our heels, there was danger, as an old Negro lady moaned out: "Oh Lor' have mercy, there is Father Hogan going to jail, and Drury McMillan has him prisoner." But Drury was fond of me, and I was fond of Drury. So, I went with him to the courthouse, and signed the bond. We bade each other goodbye. He went to his home. I, too, went home to change my canonical dress for less ghostly attire. Then I went to the depot to take the train for Cameron, where I was to say Mass the following day – this Sunday of the month, the last day of the year 1865.[99]

Father Cummings was not so bold and not so fortunate. On Sunday, September 3, 1865, the young priest preached at his parish. On Tuesday he was arrested and held in jail for a week before a trial where he was convicted of violating Article III, Section 9 of the Missouri State Constitution. By October of that year, the Missouri Supreme Court, the same court that denied Garesché, also ruled against Father Cummings.

The case was referred to the United States Supreme Court, which, this time, agreed to hear it. Legal expertise began to gather behind the beleaguered priest. Of all people, Frank Blair, leading Republican and Pro-Union supporter, refused to take the Oath. He argued that since he was involved in the attack on Camp Jackson, he had attacked his state. His brother, Montgomery Blair, agreed to argue Father Cummings' case before the U.S. Supreme Court. He was joined by Alexander Garesché, who could not practice in Missouri but could in a federal court. Further joining the team was Reverdy Johnson, who had argued against Blair in the case *Sandford v. Scott*, as well as David Field, brother of Supreme Court Justice Stephen Field.

In a 5 to 4 decision, the Court ruled for Father Cummings. The majority declared the Test Oath to be unconstitutional, as it acted as a bill

---

99   Ed. Crystal Payton. John Joseph Hogan. *On the Mission in Missouri & Fifty Years Ago: A Memoir.* Springfield: Lens & Pen Press. 2009. PP. 104 – 105.

of attainder and was an *ex post facto* law, that is, it punished a citizen for something the citizen did prior to the deed being declared illegal. The four dissenting justices were all Lincoln appointees.

The Cummings victory blunted the Radical agenda somewhat. It proved to be a victory for religious liberty, though it was decided on narrower, constitutional grounds. It was also an expensive victory. The original fine levied against Father Cummings was $500. The legal defense ran closer to $10,000, all of it paid for by Archbishop Kenrick.

Again the words of Father Rothensteiner: "In effect it was a triumph of religious liberty over bigotry and fanaticism. The Drake Constitution and its infamous test oath had to go into innocuous destitute and final extinction. Archbishop Kenrick's warning: 'Noli irritare leonem' had found its perfect exemplification."[100]

---

100   Rev. John Rothensteiner. *History of the Archdiocese of St. Louis. II* Saint Louis: Blackwell Wielandy Co. 1928. P. 219.

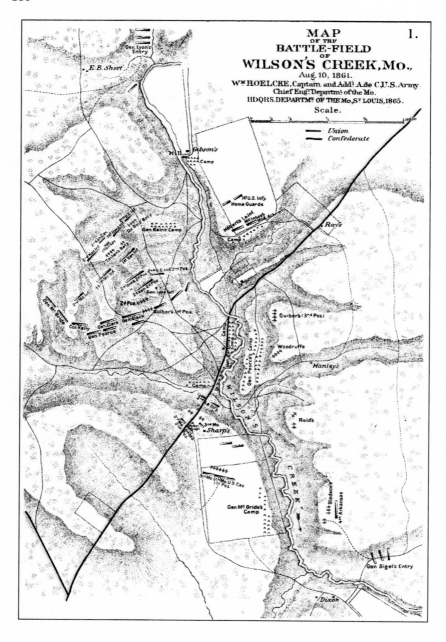

Modified map of the Battlefield of Wilson's Creek from Atlas to accompany the Official Records of the Union and Confederate Armies by the U.S. War Department (Washington, D.C.: Government Printing Office, 1891) on Internet Archive at https://archive.org/

Elkhorn Tavern in Pea Ridge, Arkansas, circa 1886. Image from Library of Congress Prints and Photographs Division in Washington, D.C. Digital ID: HHH AR0001. photos.010297p

Letter from Archbishop Peter Kenrick to Father Jacob Meller in Jefferson City, MO, September 15, 1865. Archdiocese of St. Louis Archives and Records.

St. Louis
September 15, 1865

Rev. Dear Sir,

I am sorry to learn your arrest, but am glad that you gave bail. I have every confidence that when the case comes before the Supreme Court, the test oath will be declared unconstitutional, as it has already been declared by the Circuit Court of Ray Co. in this State. You are not the only one who has had to suffer annoyance on account of refusing to take the Oath. Rev. Mr. Cummings of Louisiana was indicted by the Grand Jury of Pike Co., last week, and was tried and found guilty. Refusing to give bonds for the result of an appeal to the Supreme Court, he was confined in Bowling Green Jail, where he remained from Friday last until, perhaps, yesterday. On learning the fact I sent Rev. W. Kielty to the place for the purpose of having him released, and taking an appeal to the Supreme Court. I have just learned from a lawyer of this city who was in Louisiana and Bowling Green, that the parties who had Rev. W. C. indicted are much embarrassed by his refusal to give bail, and that they are more anxious than himself to have him liberated. Rev. W. Cronin of Hannibal was arrested last Tuesday, but liberated on giving bail. Here no one as yet has been arrested, nor is it likely that the Grand Jury will find any indictment in the matter. I was sorry to read in this day's paper a report of an explanation made by Rev. B. Donnelly of Kansas City, in which he stated that he would not take the Oath but that neither would he preach or solemnize marriages. I hope that a letter from me written last Friday, and which he could not have received before Monday last, will cause him to outmove manfully, and to meet the difficulty rather than avoid it. This will be the course pursued by the Catholic Clergy throughout the State, and it will at once bring the matter to a fore. I believe that the result of our passive resistance will be triumphant, as it no doubt already has gained us many friends.

I remain, Rev. Dear Sir, Your obedient servant,
+Peter Richard

Transcription of opposite letter.

Dr. Simon Pollak, no date. Image from the Bernard Becker Medical Library, Washington University School of Medicine. ID VC323035.

Bishop Patrick Ryan, 1888. Oil painting by artist George Calder Eichbaum, a popular portrait artist in Missouri. Owned by Archdiocese of St. Louis Archives and Records.

Chapter Seven

1866

Even while civil matters regarding Father Cummings' trial and incarceration raged, Archbishop Peter Richard Kenrick had ecclesiastical matters to deal with. While the American Civil War was in its last year, Cardinal Barnabó wrote to all the Archbishops of America and Canada, warning them of a rash of Spiritism spreading across their lands. Also known as necromancy, Spiritism was the belief in the possibility of communicating with the dead.

Though there were instances of this practice in Saint Louis, Archbishop Kenrick decided to ignore the warning and wrote a reply to the Cardinal, quoting from the early Church Father Tertullian. The Archbishops had been asked to consult with their suffragan bishops, but Archbishop Kenrick had not done so. A pointed response came from Rome, of which Kenrick told Archbishop Spalding that the Cardinal had "rapped him over the knuckles." Indeed, in the next few years, the Archbishop of Saint Louis would receive several more Roman "rappings", each souring him with the Roman Curia.

When the idea of a Plenary Council to be held in Baltimore surfaced, Archbishop Kenrick wrote approvingly to Archbishop Spalding. Such a Council would be a public sign of unity among American Catholics, in contrast to the devastating effects the slavery issue and the Civil War had on Protestant denominations. He wrote, "We are the only body whose organization has not suffered in the ordeal through which the country has passed."[101]

Despite the frequent correspondence between the Archbishop of Saint Louis and the Archbishop of Baltimore, tension bubbled just below the surface. Rumor spread that Kenrick might be named president of the upcoming Baltimore Council, but Spalding dismissed the idea. He wrote to Bishop Purcell of Cincinnati, "There was not the slightest danger of your neighbor in Saint Louis being named president of the

---

101 Samuel J. Miller. "Peter Richard Kenrick: Bishop and Archbishop of St. Louis: 1806-1896." *Records of the American Catholic Historical Society of Philadelphia*. Vol. 84. No. 1-3, 1973. P. 72.

Council..."[102]

Even before the Council formed, Kenrick and Spalding had differing ideas which surfaced. Spalding suggested the participation of a theologian from Rome; Kenrick objected that it would taint the tenor of the gathering, as a Roman theologian would have undue influence without knowing anything about the American Catholic scene.

Kenrick suggested that vicars apostolic and superiors of religious congregations be included in the deliberations, if not the votes. He also proposed that the method of recommending names to Rome for episcopal honors should be revamped. He called the present system a failure, perhaps reflecting on the long vacancy of the See of Nashville after the resignation of Bishop Whelan. He felt the polling of bishops was inadequate because they did not know priests outside of their own diocese. Better that the recommendations came from priests within the vacant see, perhaps by a Cathedral choir, though Archbishop Kenrick doubted that Rome would ever allow such a thing. He felt the influence of the Sacred Congregation was too great in matters of naming bishops and told Spalding, "This appears to be carrying centralization to excess, and taking from the bishops the exercise of that discretion they ought to presume to have."[103]

Archbishop Kenrick also wanted the question of ownership of diocesan property to be put on the Council agenda. He felt that it was disadvantageous for a bishop to control all the assets of his diocese, leaving the general public with the mistaken notion that Catholic bishops were rich. He complained of the heavy financial responsibilities he bore and added, "No one in his senses would accept the office of Archbishop of St. Louis, if he were to assume my responsibilities."[104]

When the agenda for the Plenary Council of 1866 was published, Peter Richard Kenrick found little evidence that his suggestions were considered. The first item was to bring "uniform discipline" within the American Church. Next, the present method of recommending names for bishop was retained, though Archbishop Kenrick called this "the

---

102   Samuel J. Miller. "Peter Richard Kenrick: Bishop and Archbishop of St. Louis: 1806-1896." *Records of the American Catholic Historical Society of Philadelphia*. Vol. 84. No. 1-3, 1973. P. 73.

103   Archives of the Archdiocese of Baltimore (AAB) Kenrick to Spalding. St. Louis. May 1866 as cited in Samuel J. Miller. "Peter Richard Kenrick: Bishop and Archbishop of St. Louis: 1806-1896." *Records of the American Catholic Historical Society of Philadelphia*. Vol. 84. No. 1-3, 1973. P. 75.

104   Ibid. P. 75.

worst method." Concerns about feasts and establishment of seminaries and care for the newly freed African-Americans filled in the rest of the agenda. The senior Archbishop in America, and the seventh longest-serving Archbishop in the world, had just been sidelined.

Archbishop Kenrick brought with him to Baltimore three priests as his theologians: Fathers Joseph Melcher (his Vicar General), Patrick Ryan, and Charles Ziegler. The sessions began on October 4, 1866.

In the first congregation, Archbishop Kenrick made his presence felt. He was invited to draft a greeting to be sent to Pope Pius IX by telegraph. He also made three interventions.

The second congregation saw Kenrick's first defeat. He had proposed that mitered abbots have a vote in the assembly. Instead, the Council gave them only consultative votes.

In the third congregation, Archbishop Kenrick's suggestion was adopted that the Council deal only with disciplinary concerns, leaving to a special committee doctrinal issues. But even here, Kenrick's attitude toward the Roman Curia, and by extension, Archbishop Martin Spalding, was one of growing suspicion. He feared that any doctrinal issue to be resolved by the Council would merely be done at "the nod of the Apostolic Delegate" and bowed to by the bishops.

Kenrick's proposal to allow abbots' full participation was rejected in a 32 to 45 vote. He blamed this either on the bishops' ignorance of what was at stake or the vigorous opposition mounted by Martin Spalding. Thereupon, Kenrick announced that he would not sign any Council decree that was not drawn up in the conciliar form and clearly approved by a majority of the assembled bishops. Again, Kenrick implied that Spalding and the Roman Curia were attempting to hijack the Plenary Council with pre-packaged proposals. Relations between the two Archbishops became strained.

Archbishop Kenrick was selected to celebrate the solemn Mass on Sunday, October 14, but he immediately began a further resistance in the seventh congregation on the question of consulting suffragan bishops. Samuel J. Miller made the following observation:

A certain element of sheer pig-headedness is suggested by this posture. Unlike many men, Kenrick seemed to have been unable to desert a position once taken. He could have, as many did, worked to modify the decrees which were presented to the bishops, but he chose to stick to principle, which in this case was undeniably a good one, amounting to nothing less than the full exercise of what is now known as collegiality.

His great difficulty lay in his inability to do what could be done in the authoritative situation and wait for a better day. His conduct at Baltimore anticipated his reaction to a comparable situation later at Vatican I.[105]

At the tenth and eleventh congregation, Archbishop Kenrick was active again. His proposal for missionary bishops to choose their field of lifelong service passed 25 to 19. He also proposed an extension of dispensation authority to Vicars General in extraordinary circumstances and support for the American College in Rome. He was selected to preach at the closing session and chose as his theme Saint Paul's text, "Faith comes by hearing, and hearing by the word of God." (Romans 10:17) Kenrick used this as a launching point to assert that bishops have a special responsibility for preaching the Gospel and that this commission came from the Lord and was directed to all of the apostles as a body, not just as individuals. Therefore, the college of bishops bears this universal responsibility. Those who listened carefully to Peter Richard Kenrick's words heard a stark contrast to Martin Spalding's opening remarks, which placed the same mission first at the feet of Peter and his successors and secondly at the feet of the bishops in communion with the Pope.

At the Council's final session, Kenrick's conduct caught the attention of Rome. Cardinal Barnabó, in a letter to Bishop Patrick Lynch of Charleston, spoke of the "improper disturbances" of Peter Richard Kenrick. The Bishop of Chicago, Saint Louisan James Duggan, was asked by *Propaganda Fide* to send his observations of the interplay between Kenrick and Spalding at the Council.

William McCloskey, Rector of the North American College, wrote to Bishop Purcell of his admiration for Kenrick's courage. "... I have always thought and spoken of him as a prelate worthy of the early age of the Church, an Archbishop so elevated above the regions of self that in these days he finds few to understand or appreciate him."[106]

More and more, Rome found itself interested in Saint Louis affairs. In November 1866, *Propaganda Fide* became involved in an issue regarding the Bishop's bank. When a depositor, Patrick McDonald, died and willed that his parents should receive his $100 deposit, Archbishop Kenrick failed to pay the bequest, seemingly because there was no

105   Samuel J. Miller. "Peter Richard Kenrick: Bishop and Archbishop of St. Louis: 1806-1896." *Records of the American Catholic Historical Society of Philadelphia.* Vol. 84. No. 1-3, 1973. P. 79.
106   Ibid. P. 80.

written will, only the hearsay of the family. The family took the matter to Rome. Cardinal Barnabó wrote Kenrick, expressing his incredulity that the Archbishop would compromise his reputation over such a trifling matter.

Three days later, an even more irritating letter arrived in which Cardinal Barnabó, expressing even greater incredulity that the Archbishop of Saint Louis should so disgrace himself by unseemly conduct at the Council of 1866. He speculated that Kenrick's actions "perhaps rose from the fact that your Amptitude was not at all pleased with the selection of the Metropolitan of Baltimore as president of the Synod..." and concluded, "...now, therefore, it behooves you to defend the behavior which you have exhibited from these incriminations and completely free your name from this heavy stigma, because I wish this to be brought about as soon as possible by the Sacred Congregation."[107]

Kenrick had opportunity to make that report in person to Cardinal Barnabó on his 1867 visit to Rome. Pope Pius IX had invited the Catholic bishops of the world to join him in Rome to celebrate the eighteen hundredth anniversary of the martyrdom of Saints Peter and Paul. On May 27, 1867, Archbishop Kenrick left in the company of Father Patrick Ryan. They travelled first to Boston; then the two booked passage to Ireland for a brief visit. From there they went to Rome.

Pope Pius IX felt beleaguered in Italy and saw a beleaguered Church suffering there, as well as in Germany, in France, in England, and elsewhere. After the terrifying events of 1848, the Roman Pontiff stiffened the defenses of the Church to confront the attacks of modernity and the soon-to-appear agnostic ideologies which would dominate the Western history of the late nineteenth and twentieth centuries. Pius would turn to Marian devotions and apparitions, the celebration of the canonization of the Japanese martyrs, the remembrance of Saints Peter and Paul, a Syllabus of Errors, and finally an ecumenical council, to steel the Church through the conflicts ahead.

After attending the Saints Peter and Paul Memorial with 500 fellow bishops, Archbishop Kenrick spent a few weeks at the American College and then began his journey home via a visit to Dublin. There he delivered a speech which made him famous to the Irish worldwide.

---

107   Congregatio de Propaganda Fide (APF) Barbarò to Kenrick. Rome. Nov. 16, 1866, as cited in Samuel J. Miller. "Peter Richard Kenrick: Bishop and Archbishop of St. Louis: 1806-1896." *Records of the American Catholic Historical Society of Philadelphia*. Vol. 84. No. 1-3, 1973. P. 81.

"Ireland differs from other nations in this, that while they have given martyrs to the Church, she is the martyr-nation of the world."[108]

Kenrick and Ryan returned to Saint Louis on June 23, 1868, and immediately the Archbishop found himself in another financial controversy, with Rome again paying close attention. Kenrick had come to the opinion that it was inopportune for the Ordinary to be the sole holder of wealth of his diocese. For Kenrick, that included the Bishop's Bank. He intended to divest himself of the Bank and turn it over to competent lay leadership. He wrote a pamphlet entitled "Temporal Administration of the Churches Served by the Secular Clergy of the County of Saint Louis."

Rumors, though incorrect, began to float about that Archbishop Kenrick was facing insolvency. These were fueled by one of Kenrick's own priests, Father William Wheeler, pastor at Saint Michael's Parish. Saint Michael's was one of the parishes which had borrowed money from the Bishop's Bank and had signed a proviso that, if the diocese faced financial difficulties, it would call in the loan at any time.

Father Wheeler evidently had a flair for the dramatic in his letter writing. In the same letter wherein he speculated on the Archbishop's financial embarrassment, he demanded that parish priests have the right to elect their own bishops, taking off "their girlish pants and putting on men's britches." He complained that "hard-working, active and zealous priests" were being passed up for episcopal honors in favor of "the obsequious wire pullers with influential ladies at his back..."[109]

Despite the success of the Bishop's Bank and the extraordinary contribution of the Thornton bequest, Archbishop Kenrick believed that diocesan solvency ultimately rested on the free will offerings of the faithful, and this lagged behind expectations in Saint Louis. So the Archbishop tried a program he himself had long resisted and often criticized: pew taxes. The Archbishop instructed each parish to designate two laymen, one as treasurer and the other as a secretary, to collect and record revenues from a five cent pew tax, ten cents for a High Mass. Charging a tax at the door would accustom the laity to their

---

108   John J. O'Shea. *The Two Kenricks: Most Rev. Francis Patrick, Archbishop of Baltimore. Most Rev. Peter Richard Kenrick, Archbishop of St. Louis*. Philadelphia: John McVey. 1904. P. 311.

109   Manuscript Collection, University of Notre Dame (MCUND), Wheeler to McMaster. St. Louis. Oct. 19, 1868, as cited in Samuel J. Miller. "Peter Richard Kenrick: Bishop and Archbishop of St. Louis: 1806-1896." *Records of the American Catholic Historical Society of Philadelphia*. Vol. 84. No. 1-3, 1973. P. 85.

obligation to support the Church. The parish would keep the bulk of the revenue, with a modest 1/30 to go to the Archdiocese as a *cathedraticum.*

It did not take long for Archbishop Martin Spalding to pounce on this practice. Already he had written a sour note to the Archbishop of Cincinnati regarding the Archbishop of Saint Louis: "We are all prepared for his opinion on the Baltimore decrees, which is little edifying and does not amount to much."[110]

A struggle between Kenrick and Spalding over the See of Chicago erupted when Kenrick's man, Bishop James Duggan, had to be removed for reasons related to a mental breakdown. Kenrick proposed as a replacement the President-Rector of St. Mary's of the Lake Seminary, John McMullen, but lost out to Spalding's Vicar General, Thomas Foley. Spalding wrote of his victory in a letter to Purcell, "Roma locuta est." Regardless, McMullen administered Chicago in 1879 and became Bishop of Davenport two years later.

It was the pew tax issue that caused *Propaganda Fide* to ask Martin Spalding to investigate the Saint Louis situation. The result was another rap on the knuckles from Rome, demanding that the faithful not be charged to attend Mass. There was no enquiry made of Archbishop Kenrick, to discover his motives. While Spalding's letters to *Propaganda* were written in Italian or Latin, many of the other bishops' letters were in English, and there was evidence that no one at *Propaganda* read that language, as they had to have translations made at the American College.

Samuel J. Miller concludes that distrust between Peter Richard Kenrick and the Curia had become a reality on the eve of the Vatican Council. "In short, this understanding of American conditions, linguistic handicaps, and Kenrick's stand at Baltimore in 1866 all may have combined to convince *Propaganda* that Kenrick was a dangerous character."[111] One must add to this mix the cold feelings between the Archbishop of Saint Louis and the Archbishop of Baltimore, a state of affairs which would worsen in the years ahead.

Viewed from Rome, the events of the 1840s, 1850s and 1860s had a special foreboding in them. The Church was under assault from

---

110   MCUND, Spalding to Purcell. Oct. 10, 1868, as cited in Samuel J. Miller. "Peter Richard Kenrick: Bishop and Archbishop of St. Louis: 1806-1896." *Records of the American Catholic Historical Society of Philadelphia.* Vol. 84. No. 1-3, 1973. P. 86.
111   Ibid. P. 88.

secular forces and autocratic governments with agendas which would harm the Church. This would have to be resisted by greater unity within the Church, but that was not the perspective of the Archbishop of Saint Louis. These two views would clash in the titanic struggle which was the First Vatican Council.

Cardinal Alessandro Barnabó. First Vatican Council Photograph Album. The Catholic University of America, American Catholic History Research Center. Digital ID VaticanI-P02R4D-Barnabo.

Bishop of Wheeling, Vincent Whelan. First Vatican Council Photograph Album. The Catholic University of America, American Catholic History Research Center. Digital ID VaticanI-P10R3B-Whelan.

Archbishop of Baltimore, Martin Spalding. Frontispiece from *The Life of the Most Rev. M. J. Spalding, D.D.* by John Lancaster Spalding (New York: The Catholic Publication Society; Baltimore: J. Murphy & Co., 1873) on Internet Archive at https://archive.org/

Chapter Eight

A VIEW FROM ROME

By 1848, Pope Pius IX was powerless. On April 29, Cardinal Antonelli and the whole government resigned. More chaos followed, and the Pope called upon the services of Count Pellegrino Rossi, the former French ambassador to the Roman See. Count Rossi quickly consolidated authority of the Department of the Interior and Finance and was about to become the Chief of Police for the city of Rome. These moves toward centralization of authority caused fear in some circles. But that all changed on November 15, 1848, with the assassination of the papal Secretary of State. As Rossi's carriage entered the courtyard of the Chancery for a meeting with the new parliament, he noticed an angry crowd. Rossi also saw only the Civic Guard present, which meant trouble. Stoically, he left the carriage and walked toward the Chancery. Luigi Brunetti, son of the demagogue Ciceruocchio, ran forward and stuck a dagger in Rossi's neck. The young man had been planning the assassination for days, practicing on cadavers.

Pope Pius was shocked and abandoned. Both his lay and clerical staff took to the hills for their own safety. The next morning there was a massive demonstration at the Quirinale. The Pope, surrounded by Catholic ambassadors, met with leaders and agreed to hear their demands if the crowd was disbanded. Instead, there was greater violence. Several Swiss guards were injured. Msgr. Palma was shot dead as he stood near a window. Even the newly formed radical government under Strebini feared for the Pope's safety. He demanded that the Swiss Guard be disbanded to be replaced by the Civic Guard. On November 16, for all practical purposes, the Pope was a prisoner in his own palace.

Suddenly Rome woke to discover the Pope gone. He had been rescued by several Catholic ambassadors and their families and spirited away to Gaeta. Meanwhile, the radicals formed a government and sought to legitimize it with an election for early 1849. Pope Pius responded with a monitory from Gaeta. Some brave priests read it from the pulpit while others posted it on walls. It called for a boycott of the upcoming vote, and it worked. Many refused to vote, and others spoiled their ballots. In Rome, for instance, 23,000 out of the 60,000 votes cast were illegible. At Sinigallia, the Pope's hometown, only 200 voted out of 27,000 eligible. At Frascati, 90 votes were cast, but 52 of them were blank. Regardless, the elected assembly was even more hostile to the Church. On November 9, 1849, the parliament voted to end the temporal powers. In their eyes, the Papal States ceased to exist. The vote was 120 yes, 10 no, and 12 abstentions.

By now Cardinal Antonelli was back with Pope Pius IX and in charge, calling on France, Austria, Spain, and the kingdom of Naples to return the Pope to Rome.

Garibaldi, Mazzini, and Strebini had shown Pope Pius the consequences of liberalism. He left Cardinal Antonelli to concentrate on temporal affairs, and more and more, Pius became a Pope of prayer.

In March 1849, a conference was called at Gaeta. Attending were representatives of Austria, France, and Spain. Sardinia-Piedmont was not invited. With the Austrian Army slowly moving south toward Rome, Louis Napoleon decided to act. On April 24, 1849, French troops landed by sea under General Nicholas Oudinot. Troops from the kingdom of Naples began to move north to support the French. Shortly after, 4,000 Spanish reinforcements also arrived.

Republican Rome braced itself for an attack. It was defended by two groups, the Civic Guard regulars under old General Roselli, and by irregulars under Garibaldi. The noose tightened as Bologna fell to the Austrians in May. By early June a professional siege was underway, and on July 2, 1849, Rome surrendered as Garibaldi fled. The allied troops were not well received. Shouts of "Death to Pope Pius IX and the priests" rang out in the streets.

The Pope stayed at Gaeta, disturbed by the events happening in Rome. Mazzini was allowed to stay in Rome for a month. The tricolor was flown over Castel Sant'Angelo. Even his recent liberators, the French, sent a note telling him to reform his government when he returned. When the French pressed for greater lay participation in papal government, Cardinal Antonelli pointed out that of the 5,127 members of the government, only 104 were priests. When the French demanded a general amnesty for the revolutionaries, Pope Pius quoted the Code Napoleon, which debunked the idea.

After he was assured the Romans would welcome him back and the Republican rabble-rousers were gone, and having secured a loan from Baron Rothschild, Pope Pius IX thanked King Ferdinand for his hospitality and returned to Rome on April 12, 1850. He received a polite reception. There was a procession from Saint John Lateran to Saint Peter's Basilica. There the Pope took up residence in the Vatican Palace. The Quirinale had been trashed and was set aside.

Pope Pius instituted reforms in a *motu proprio* of September 1849 and spurred economic progress. Railroads were extended. The Vatican post office was normalized. Downtown Rome received gas lighting. To respond to urban needs, even the city administration grew. By 1856, 7,125 people were employed, 289 of them clerics.

Nonetheless, the Papal States were subjected to a withering propaganda campaign, painting them as corrupt, inept, and cruel. Many Italian revolutionaries had fled to England and stoked anti-Catholic fires there. An in-depth study by the French ambassador countered these slurs, reporting the opposite.

Another area of progress was in ancient archaeology. Giovanni Baptiste de Rossi discovered the catacombs of Callixtus. The Forum, the Colosseum, and many early Christian churches were given new facelifts. "Pio Nono" loved to walk, visiting hospitals, schools, prisons, and a state-of-the-art cholera ward at the hospital of Santi Andrea.

But what was happening in Piedmont broke his heart. Count Camillo Cavour controlled Parliament in the liberal constitutional monarchy of the Kingdom of Sardinia-Piedmont. In November 1854, he passed the Law of the Convents. It abolished all religious orders except the Sisters of Charity and the Sisters of Saint Joseph and "those Orders and Communities dedicated to public instruction, preaching, or the care of the sick which are mentioned by name in the list..."[112] A large seminary was seized. The salaries of bishops and archbishops were regulated. Monks and nuns were called "useless," "medieval," and "anomalous in modern society."[113] The *Risorgimento* was clearly anti-Catholic, reflecting the radicals' call for "a free Church in a free State." King Victor Emmanuel was powerless to stop it. His frustration was mixed with grief when the Queen Mother Maria Teresa died, followed shortly by the death of his wife Queen Marie Adelaide, followed immediately by the death of his brother, the Duke of Genoa.

The Law of Convents had been enacted purportedly as an economic measure, but when the Piedmontese bishops offered to raise one

---

112   E.E.Y. Hales. *Pio Nono: A Study in European Politics and Religion in the Nineteenth Century.* Garden City: Image Books. 1962. P. 184.
113   Ibid. P. 184.

million lire to relieve the state budget, Prime Minister Cavour turned it down and redefined the issue as a social reform concern. "The claustral habit of abstinence from work exercises a very bad effect upon industry, it renders labor less respectable and less respected."[114] Such was his view. He saw monks not only as useless but actually harmful.

Following immediately the Law of the Convents was the introduction of a new bill, the Matrimonial Law. When Pope Pius IX protested this new bill, King Victor Emmanuel sent a secret letter to him.

Your Holiness should know that it is I who prevented the Senate from passing the matrimonial law, that it is I who will now do what is possible to prevent the passage of that of the Convents. Perhaps within a few days this ministry of Cavour will collapse, and I shall nominate one from the right, and make it a condition, sine qua non, *that it brings me as soon as possible to a complete adjustment with Rome. (Do me the kindness of helping me.) I for my part have always done what I could. (Those words to Piedmont have not helped us in this, I fear lest they have ruined everything for me.) I shall try to prevent the law from passing, but help me, as well, Holy Father.*

Please burn this piece of paper.[115]

Added to the hostile legislation in the Piedmontese Parliament, Count Cavour now plotted a war against Catholic Austria. In the summer of 1859, a brief, disastrous war was fought by the Austrians on one side and the French and Piedmontese on the other. In the end, Piedmont got a little of what Cavour wanted, and when the Austrians left Bologna, all Emilia-Romagna was open to brigands and revolutionaries. Cardinal Antonelli sent General Schmidt and 2,000 Swiss Guards to pacify the area, but they were of little help. Tuscany ousted its beloved Grand Duke Leopold. The Duke and Duchess of Parma and Modena fled with the Austrians. Only the French had the manpower to bring order out of the chaos in Romagna, and they refused to come.

Enemies everywhere surrounded Pope Pius IX. Garibaldi invaded Sicily in May after wreaking havoc in Romagna. Mazzini was in Florence and all Umbria was in revolt, as was the Marches. Austria was gone; France was two-faced. England was using its diplomacy to try to keep Spain, Portugal, Belgium, and Bavaria from aiding the Pope. Even the King of Naples was helpless, as he was fighting for his life against

114   E.E.Y. Hales. *Pio Nono: A Study in European Politics and Religion in the Nineteenth Century.* Garden City: Image Books. 1962. P. 187.
115   Ibid. P. 189

Garibaldi.

The state of affairs continued to deteriorate with the arrest of the Cardinal Archbishop of Pisa and the Bishop of Bologna. Both had refused to allow their priests to sing a *Te Deum* on the anniversary of the Piedmontese Constitution. Even when the arch-nemesis Count Camillo Cavour contracted an intestinal infection and died in May 1861, there was no respite. His successor, Baron Bettino de Ricasoli, was just as anti-Church as Cavour had been. Napoleon III joined the tormentors, reintroducing the Organic Articles in France, demanding the right of the French sovereignty to influence choices of bishops and exert control over the publication of papal bulls.

To counter all of this opposition, Pope Pius introduced a three-pronged strategy to bolster the defenses of the Church by assembling bishops in Rome. First, he would invite the bishops of the world to come to the canonization of the Japanese martyrs. Then he would invite them again to return to celebrate the eighteen hundredth anniversary of the martyrdoms of Saints Peter and Paul. Finally, he would call an ecumenical council.

The canonization of the Japanese martyrs in 1862 drew forty-three cardinals, five patriarchs, fifty-two archbishops, and 186 bishops, including 50 French whom Napoleon's government had tried to prevent from coming. Added to this were 4,000 priests and 100,000 laity. The Pope used this as an opportunity to critique modern trends. He called upon the bishops to defend Catholic doctrine and reassess the revolutionary and liberal principles, the Spirit of '89, the Religion of Man.

As a balance against the revolutionary and liberal principles condemned by Pope Pius IX, a new rallying point was to be established for devout Catholics. During his year at Gaeta, Pius became convinced that the key to the defense of the Catholic Church rested in reliance upon the Blessed Virgin Mary. It was in her title of the Immaculate Conception that he found confidence.

In 1830, on November 7, a Sister of Charity had had a second apparition of the Blessed Virgin Mary. Saint Catherine Labouré described a vision of Mary crushing a snake under her feet, holding a golden globe with a small cross, with rays of light surrounding her. In the light was the inscription "O Marie, conçue sans péché, priez pour nous qui avons recours à vous."[116] A medal was struck with this image in 1832,

---

116   "O Mary, conceived without sin, pray for us who have recourse to you."

the Miraculous Medal. By Catherine's death in 1876, one billion such medals had been distributed.

In 1854, the bishops of the United States petitioned to have the Immaculate Conception as the patroness of their country. After consulting a commission of cardinals and theologians, Pope Pius issued the encyclical *Ubi Primum*, asking advice of the world's bishops. Five-hundred ninety-three bishops wrote, 583 of them endorsing a definition of the Immaculate Conception. Pope Pius IX assembled a bevy of theologians to work on the document, and on December 8, 1854, before fifty-three cardinals, forty-three archbishops, and ninety-nine bishops, the largest assembly of prelates since Trent, Pius himself read the decree, the Bull *Ineffibilis Deus,* to the dignitaries and to a gathering of 150,000 faithful.

This dogmatic declaration seems to have been ratified by Mary herself. In 1858, in the little village of Lourdes, France, on March 25, Mary told the seer her name was *Que soy era Immaculada Councepciou*: I am the Immaculate Conception.

Pope Pius IX continued his assault on hostile secularism with an encyclical, *Quanta Cura*, promulgated on December 8, 1864. His intention was to target governments which subverted the Church, authors who subordinated religion to reason, and those who held that all religions lead to salvation. Accompanying the encyclical was the Syllabus of Errors, warning of evil men and the designs of nations to subvert the Church. "Since the throng of its propagandists has grown enormously, these wicked groups think that they have already become masters of the world and that they have almost reached their pre-established goal. Having sometimes obtained what they desired, and that is power, in several countries, they boldly turn the help of powers and authorities which they have secured to trying to submit the Church of God to the most cruel servitude, to undermine the foundations on which it rests, to contaminate its splendid qualities; and, moreover, to strike it with frequent blows, to shake it, to overthrow it, and, if possible, to make it disappear completely from the earth."[117]

The Syllabus of Errors contained eighty statements, but the most volatile was the last one, warning readers against "progress, liberalism and modern civilization." This was widely misinterpreted. In England, progress meant the Great Exhibition of 1851, modern chemistry

---

117   Quanta Cura, *Syllabus of Errors.* Number 80. Paragraph 3.

labs, the internal combustion engine, Bessemer steel mills, and Victoria Station. Liberalism meant Robert Peel's reforms, the Great Reform Act of 1832. France also misunderstood the eightieth statement, much of France having been won over to the "Principle of '89," a constitution, centralization of authority in Paris, central planning, and rational scientific answers. In America, notions of liberalism meant freedom from oppression and arbitrary government, free enterprise, and innovation.

Therefore, the Syllabus of Errors was a public relations disaster in the Western countries. The Pope had tried to critique the Italian situation: the Piedmontese government and its assault on the Church. By "progress", Pope Pius IX meant progressivism and collectivism. By liberalism, he saw the evolution into radical revolutions. And his critique of modern civilization was a prophetic warning against the kinds of countries which would be created by Adolf Hitler, Benito Mussolini, Joseph Stalin, and Mao. The storms of dissent were not quieted until Bishop Dupanloup of Orleans published a small pamphlet, "The September Convention and the Encyclical of December 8," which explained each of the 80 errors outlined in the Syllabus.

One story illustrates the concern that Pope Pius IX had for Catholics during his pontificate. A visitor to the Vatican remarked to the Pope, "One thing is sure, Holy Father, whatever the storms and massive floods, the barque of Peter can never be overwhelmed, can never be sunk." Pius replied pensively, "But what about the crew?" He was thinking of the liberal and half-hearted Catholics about to abandon the ship.

After successfully celebrating the canonization of the Japanese martyrs and again drawing a large gathering of bishops and laity for the 1800th anniversary of the martyrdom of Sts. Peter and Paul in Rome, Pope Pius IX turned his attention to the formation of a council which would defend the Church in the age of godless, revolutionary liberalism. The idea of an ecumenical Council had long been in the mind of Pope Pius IX. In 1849, while still at Gaeta, he told Cardinal Lambruschini, a realist who had served Pope Gregory XVI as Secretary of State, that a council would be needed to address certain contemporary errors and restore discipline within the Church.

On December 6, 1864, the Pope met with fifteen cardinals in a secret consultation about the calling of an ecumenical council. Thirteen said yes, while one dissented. A final cardinal as much as said, "You're the Pope; you decide." In March 1865, a preparatory commission was established, and in April the Prefect of the Congregation of the Council wrote thirty-six European bishops. All but one was enthusiastic for a council. By September 1865, five commissions began meeting.

On June 29, 1869, the Bull *Aeterni Patris* announced a council to be convened on December 8, 1869, to counter "a concourse of calamities." Invited were 700 residential bishops, nuncios, Vicars Apostolic, prelates of the Curia, auxiliary and missionary bishops, about 250 of them, Abbots General, and generals of congregations and monastic congregations. Added were 61 Oriental Rite bishops. Pius also invited "all the bishops of Oriental Rites who were not in communion with the Apostolic See," the Orthodox, Copts, Nestorians, and Jacobites.

As the bishops began to arrive in Rome, there was great excitement. The last ecumenical council had been closed 306 years earlier. There was a sense of security that had been won on the battlefield by General Kansler and his Papal troops. On November 3, 1867, 2,913 Papal Zouaves approached Garibaldi's troops as they maneuvered southbound, in an action they dubbed "Rush Rome." The papal troops were badly outnumbered, with Garibaldi counting between 9,000 and 10,000 men. Despite this, Kansler's troops routed the revolutionaries just as a French reinforcement of 2,000 arrived on the battlefield. Garibaldi withdrew into the town of Mentana, then fled. Around 1,000 of the Garibaldi revolutionaries were killed or wounded. The rest surrendered. Papal losses included 30 dead and 100 wounded. The French counted two dead, 86 wounded, and one missing in action.

On November 6, there was a triumphant return to Rome with the French claiming victory, while battle reports showed they arrived only at the last moment of the struggle. Regardless, the Council fathers felt secure with a French garrison remaining in Rome.

To make sure all the bishops who wanted to attend could come, Pius ended up paying for forty percent of the Council fathers' expenses. At one moment he quipped that it was still an open question as to whether the Council would declare the Pope infallible or fallible, but his main question was whether at the end of the Council he would be insolvent.

Several European newspapers opened subscriptions to help pay for the Council expense. The first meeting was held on December 2, 1869. Five hundred bishops and others joined the Pope. The Vatican Council had two issues to consider. The first was a Constitution dealing with the errors of the day, promulgated on April 24, 1870 under the title *Dei Filius*. Four propositions were laid out as doctrines Catholics should believe: A. God is the creator of all things; B. The sources of revelation; C. The certainty of Faith; and D. The compatibility of faith and reason. The Constitution was adopted unanimously.

It was the second schema, *Ecclesia Christi*, which caused all the heartburn. This was introduced on January 20, 1870. Fifteen chapters presented the Church's nature and the powers and properties over and against modern ecclesiastical heresies. The Church was defined as the mystical body of Christ, a spiritual society, but also a visible society. Toward the end, the question of papal primacy was considered, but papal infallibility was not mentioned. The document ended with a consideration of the error of separation of Church and State. Specifically, it was the question of society receiving moral guidance from the Christian Church. The State needed to respect the moral, religious, and natural laws regarding marriage and families, especially regarding children and education.

Regardless, two trans-language groups began to form around the question of papal infallibility. Those in favor of a definition, known as the Majority, came mainly from Italy, Spain, Austria, Ireland, and Latin America. Those against a definition, called the Minority, came mainly from Belgium, Netherlands, and Switzerland; there were also large blocks from France, England, the United States, and the German states. The Minority gathered around Archbishop Ketteler of Mainz and Rauscher of Vienna, as well as Darboy of Paris and Bishop Dupanloup of Orleans. Adding his voice to the Minority was Peter Richard Kenrick of Saint Louis.

In the end, the original schema was rejected and re-fashioned. Into this vacuum came the debate over infallibility.

At one point, German Archbishop Ketteler ordered a case of pamphlets entitled *Quaestio* to be delivered for distribution. The thesis of the pamphlet stated that because the Church is a limited monarchy and the Pope has to share power with bishops, infallibility only comes in union with the bishops. The case of pamphlets was delivered to the Master of the Sacred Palace, who showed them to the Pope. Pius then called in Archbishop Ketteler and rebuked him for handing over weapons to the Pope's enemies. The Pope asked that the bishop pray with the case of pamphlets before him, with a crucifix, and make the decision whether to distribute the booklets or to burn them. Ketteler distributed the pamphlets, though he declared he did not agree with the thesis, only that he wanted to let the question be studied.

Tempers heated and words were exchanged that needed to be moderated. One exchange took place between Bishop Dupanloup and the Pope himself. The Bishop of Orleans wrote to the Pontiff:

Most Holy Father:

My name is not pleasing to you; I know it, and it is my sorrow. But for all that, I feel myself authorized and obliged, in a profound and inviolable devotion of which I have given so many proofs to your Holiness, to open my heart to you at this moment.

The report is confirmed that many are soliciting your Holiness to suspend suddenly our important works and invert the order of the discussions, in order to bring before the Council on the spot, abruptly, before its time and out of its place, the question of infallibility. Allow me, most Holy Father, to say to your Holiness: nothing could be more dangerous.

This question has already set Europe on fire: the fire will become a conflagration, if by the violent haste it seems that, at all costs and by a change in the natural order of things forestalling the hour of Providence, the thing is being carried by assault...

To this Pio Nono replied,

Venerable brother:

Your name is no less pleasing to us now than in the past, nor do we love you less, or esteem less than formerly the gift that God has bestowed upon you. But our paternal affection for you compels us, when you are stiffly dissenting from most of your venerable brothers and from the greatest part of the clergy and the Catholic people of the whole world, warn you not to wish to be wise in your own eyes, or to rely on your own prudence; for you know that all errors and heresies have arisen from the fact that their authors thought they were wiser than others, and would not acquiesce to the common opinion of the Church. It is right for the Fathers at the Council to put forward clearly difficulties they think stand in the way of any definition; but it is not right to strive by all means to bring all over to one's way of thinking: especially as we know the Council is under the guidance of the Holy Ghost, and that nothing can be defined that is not true and revealed, or that is not for the good of the Church. We say this to you with all the more confidence, in that for many years we have known you to follow the simplicity of faith of believers and to be quite differently minded than you are now. Return, brother, I pray you, to the golden simplicity of little ones.[118]

On April 27, by way of Cardinal Bilio, Pope Pius IX announced a new Constitution specifically dealing with papal infallibility and primacy, *Consitutio Prima de Ecclesia Christi*. It would be delivered to the Council on May 9. It was debated from May 14 to June 3. The debate was heated and finally broke off briefly.

The debates were renewed again. The Council presidents called for a vote on July 13. Six hundred and one voted yes, eighty-eight voted against the constitution, and sixty-three voted yes with some changes. Fifty of the Fathers had boycotted the vote entirely. The majority had argued that infallibility is not granted to the Pope by the Council, but rather the Council recognizes papal infallibility. By July 16, 1870, sixty of the Minority left Rome. The Constitution *Pastor Aeternus* passed 535 to 2. A *Te Deum* was sung and *placet* votes, that is, yes votes, were solicited from the absentees, and all submitted, except the two who had voted no, Bishops Edward Fitzgerald of Little Rock, Arkansas and Aloisio Riccio of Sicily.

The Council was sent into recess until November 11, but they never came back. On July 19, France and Prussia went to war. The French garrison was removed. On September 20, King Victor Emmanuel ordered his troops into the Papal States and into Rome itself. Facing the inevitable, the Pope refused an invitation to evacuate on the French warship *Orénoque* and instead turned to prayer.

When the Piedmontese envoy, San Martino, assured the Pope of protection by King Victor Emmanuel, Pio Nono roared out that the Piedmontese government was full of "whited sepulchers and vipers," and that he would not surrender Rome to them. As the ambassador made a hasty retreat for the door, Pius added, "But that assurance is not infallible!"[119]

---

118   E.E.Y. Hales. *Pio Nono: A Study in European Politics and Religion in the Nineteenth Century*. Garden City: Image Books. 1962. Pp. 314-316.
119   Ibid. P. 329.

Archbishop of Mainz, Wilhelm Ketteler. First Vatican Council Photograph Album. The Catholic University of America, American Catholic History Research Center. Digital ID VaticanI-P13R3D-De-Ketteler.

Pope Pius IX with First Vatican Council attendees. Clockwise from bottom center: Pope Pius IX, Cardinal Rudiger, Cardinal Rauscher, Archbishop Dupanloup, Cardinal Bonaparte, Archbishop Manning, Cardinal Antonelli. Center: Archbishop Paul Melchers. From New York Public Library Digital Collections. Digital ID 1813624.

208

Pope Pius IX with a few First Vatican Council Cardinals. From New York Public Library Digital Collections. Digital ID 1813644.

Chapter Nine

KENRICK GOES TO ROME

On November 1, 1869, Peter Richard Kenrick met his Council *paritus,* or theological expert, Father Constantine Smith, in Dublin and greeted him with the salutation, "Descendus de coelo!" Smith was a brilliant priest, an Irishman trained at St. Mary's of the Barrens in Perryville. But Kenrick would rely on his own seminary training at Maynooth, reinforced by twenty-six years of episcopal leadership, to guide his deliberations in Rome.

Peter Richard had enrolled in the Royal College of Saint Patrick's at Maynooth in 1827, at the age of twenty-one. The seminary offered the standard fare of theological, philosophical, and language studies. But what made Maynooth special in the 1820s was the same windfall that benefited the Church in America: the French clergy fleeing revolution. Four French priests joined the faculty at Maynooth, the most prominent being Louis De Lahogue of the Sorbonne. He was professor of dogmatic theology and authored several textbooks which set the standard in theological classes.

These priests brought with them a strong sense of Gallicanism, often referred to as conciliarism. This ecclesiology posited that the bishops of the Church were "the indispensable guardians of the faith."[120] Whether residing in their diocese or gathered in synod or council, the bishops were infallible once they had moral unanimity. De Lahogue argued certain criteria for an ecumenical council. It must be called by a legitimate Pope, with invitations extended to all bishops in ordinary jurisdiction. There must be a critical mass of bishops attending, though the figure was not set; and at its close, the council must promulgate decrees and be approved by the entire Church.

Several textbooks used at Maynooth supported this ecclesiology. *Tractus de Ecclesia* was published by a colleague of De Lahogue, Louis Bailey. Bailey, also a Frenchman, argued that unity in the Church con-

---

120   Samuel J. Miller. "Peter Richard Kenrick: Bishop and Archbishop of St. Louis: 1806 – 1896." *Records of the American Catholic Historical Society of Philadelphia.* Vol. 84. No. 1-3, 1973. P. 8.

sisted of unity in faith, sacraments, and governance, and in a visible head, that is, the Roman pontiff. He argued a Gallican sort of infallibility in the Church, an infallibility which resides primarily with the Church universal and secondarily in the Supreme Pontiff. De Lahogue wrote his own text, *Tractus de Ecclesia.* For him, unity rests in unity of doctrine and less in governance. This reversed the opinion of the Tridentine Dominican theologian, Melchior Cano, who had argued that conciliar infallibility was derived from papal infallibility; that is, the council could not err because the Pope cannot err and that it is he who called the council.

De Lahogue questioned Cano's proposition, and his textbook no doubt had an influence on young Peter's mind. Did papal primacy imply inerrancy? And was the Pope superior to the general councils? De Lahogue argued that even speaking *ex cathedra,* the Pope was not infallible nor was he superior to a council. The French scholar quoted Bellarmine, Bossuet, and Tournely as his authorities. Kenrick's rector, Bartholomew Crotty (1813-1833), when asked about De Lahogue's ecclesiology, defended his professor and said that the doctrine of papal infallibility as an article of faith was "an absurd opinion."[121] Furthermore, the vice president of Maynooth, Father Michael Montague, stated that ultramontanism and papal supremacy had never been taught at Maynooth.

One sliver of modified ultramontanism came from the observation of another professor, Anglade, who voiced the opinion of most of the Gallicans, "that if tomorrow the Pope and the Council together declared the Pope infallible then it would be an article of faith binding on all good Catholics."[122] In the end, this teaching would be the safety net which kept Peter Richard Kenrick in the Catholic Church after his Vatican Council experience.

What Maynooth gave Peter Richard Kenrick was what others have called mitigated Gallicanism. Pure Gallicanism held that the King of France was invulnerable to papal sanctions and excommunication. This was eliminated under the Irish circumstances. What was left was a high esteem for the office of the Catholic bishop who was the guaran-

---

121   Samuel J. Miller. "Peter Richard Kenrick: Bishop and Archbishop of St. Louis: 1806 – 1896." *Records of the American Catholic Historical Society of Philadelphia.* Vol. 84. No. 1-3, 1973. P. 10.
122   London, 1827. *Eighth Report of the Commissioners for Maynooth.* As cited in Ibid. P. 10.

tor of the Catholic Faith, a belief reinforced by Kenrick's many years as bishop as well as the few years he served as an aide to his brother, the Bishop of Philadelphia.

With these attitudes, Peter Richard Kenrick entered into the charged milieu of the pre-Council days. He found fellowship in the ideas of the Dean of the Sorbonne theology faculty, Henry Maret, a mitigated Gallicanist. Not distant in thought were the liberal French Catholics led by Charles de Montalembert, allied to England's Lord Acton and Germany's Ignaz Döllinger. These took offense at Pius IX's condemnation of certain modern trends such as freedom of press, religious liberty, and democracy. Archbishop Kenrick would stand alongside the Bishop of Orleans, Felix Dupanloup.

The genesis of the Vatican Council can be traced all the way back to 1864 with the publications of *Quanta Cura* and the Syllabus of Errors. Pope Pius IX spoke to the Cardinals about the need for an ecumenical council, the first since Trent. He suggested topics, and two of the twenty-one spoke in favor of a declaration of papal infallibility; thus, from the beginning this concern was tied to a potential council. Later Pius polled several bishops, and eight of the thirty-four mentioned infallibility. The topic was in the air. Even the other twenty-six spoke of the need for a statement regarding the primacy of the Roman See. This became the rallying point for the ultramontanes, those who took papal supremacy to new heights. Included in this group were Louis Veuillot, editor of *L'Univers*, Cardinal Manning of Westminister, and the Jesuit editors of *Civiltà Cattolica*.

Other topics for the upcoming council seemed to have surfaced, but they were sucked under by the vortex of activity around the question of papal infallibility. Not to be discussed were ways to bring schismatics back to the Church, improvements in clerical life, discipline and religious orders, a universal catechism, reform of canon law, relations between Church and state, and better coordination of mission activities.

As the American delegation arrived in Rome, there was a clear distinction between the Roman-educated prelates and the Maynooth and Sulpician men. Martin Spalding of Baltimore, Philadelphia's James Wood, and Natchez' Elder took the Roman view. On the other side were Peter Richard Kenrick of Saint Louis, Richard Whelan of Wheeling, Verot of Saint Augustine, Edward Fitzgerald of Little Rock, and William McCloskey of Louisville.

These were generally joined by the inopportunists, who argued that this was not a good time to promulgate any bombastic statements about papal authority, and who feared above all that the Syllabus of Errors might be recognized as doctrine. These included most of the English bishops, Joseph Strossmeyer of Croatia, and Thomas Connolly of Halifax.

On December 8, 1869, the feast of the Immaculate Conception, the Council opened with peals of bells, cannonade, and a solemn procession of the Council Fathers into the north transept of Saint Peter's Basilica. Archbishop Kenrick, seventh oldest Archbishop in the Catholic world, was seated near Pope Pius IX and could look out upon the face of John MacHale, dogmatic theology professor, serving at Maynooth even before Peter had attended, Cardinal Barnabó, with whom the Archbishop had many difficult dealings, and Cardinal Cullen of Dublin, who had been a supporter of Kenrick as a young priest.

The rules to govern the Council were almost Germanic. The origin was the work of Bishop Carl Joseph von Hefele of Rottenburg, a scholar of previous councils. He was determined to keep the machinery of this council clean and efficient. In doing so he gave the Roman Curia an edge in centralization. This was a red flag for bishops who arrived at the council with the conviction that their authority came from an unbroken line of apostles to bishops. These were men who guarded the apostolic freedom which they sensed was now being hindered.

The first general assembly met on December 10, 1869. It was announced that a ballot had already been secured of the names the Pope had appointed to the Congregation to receive proposals. Archbishop Kenrick objected and sent a note to one of the five council presidents, asking that the ballot be delayed until the second general session so that the Council Fathers could get to know each other. Coincidentally, on the papal ballot was the name of Martin Spalding. Croatia's Strossmeyer joined the protest, but it was overruled.

Soon sides began to form. One group met at Villa Caserta, the Redemptorist motherhouse. The convener was Bishop Dupanloup of Orleans. Others included the followers of the Bishop of Malines, Victor Descamps, Kenrick, Strossmeyer, and Bernard McQuaide of Rochester. Their proposals were ultimately rejected.

On the other side, pro-papal Fathers rallied around Edward Manning, a convert who had become the Archbishop of Westminister. He went so far as to brand the other side as heretics, declaring "they come to the council to be heard and condemned, not to take part in the for-mulation of doctrine."[123] Joining this group were Spalding of Baltimore and Alemany of San Francisco.

Both sides squared off, aware of the high stakes involved. Man-ning's group represented the centralizing monarchial model while Dupanloup stood for the collegial, arguing that it was the traditional, historical type and would avoid the dangers of the new centralized experiment.

As both sides hardened, they found cause in the question of papal in-fallibility. The anti-infallibalists came as a sort of loose coalition. Some rejected the doctrine outright; some saw it as inopportune for this time and place. Some saw it as a political nightmare. To these groups were added Cardinal Jacques Mattieu, Archbishop Georges Darboy of Paris, Cardinal Prince Friedrich zu Schwartenberg of Prague, Joseph Othmar von Rauscher of Vienna, Lajes Haynald of Kolosca, and Janos Sinor of Ezstergom. Lord Acton, John Dahlberg, was a strong support-er of this faction, even lending his villa for their meetings. He was also the vital liaison to Church historian Ignaz Döllinger of Munich.

The first schema was submitted to the Council Fathers on Decem-ber 10, and discussions began on December 28. *De doctrina catholica* was a difficult document, with eighteen chapters. The document's complicated nature drew criticism, including from Kenrick. But be-low the surface, other forces were at work. By December 1869, it was clear that one faction, the Majority, would maneuver the Council for a statement on papal infallibility, while the Minority would seek ways to thwart that path. A third party emerged, trying to find a compromise. Regardless, on February 23, 1870, the Council Fathers received the schema *De ecclesia Christi,* and on March 6 the second part, *De infal-libilitate Romani Pontificis,* was distributed.

By April 27, a vote was taken only on *De ecclesia.* It passed unani-mously with 667 votes, though eight, including Kenrick's, were regis-tered under protest. In his customary slicing rhetoric, Peter Richard Kenrick voiced his opposition:

Another point which at least to me is laughable is the frequency of anathema in the several canons... I know this formula, borrowed from the apostles John and Paul, is consecrated by perennial usage but I have

---

123   Samuel J. Miller. "Peter Richard Kenrick: Bishop and Archbishop of St. Louis: 1806 – 1896." *Records of the American Catholic Historical Society of Philadelphia.* Vol. 84. No. 1-3, 1973. P. 94.

no desire to conceal my view that consideration must be taken of the customs of our times in which the average ear will hardly bear in precautions of this sort. It is not out of place to imitate the example of St. Paul, who was accustomed to be all things to all men since he counted all as a gain. The condition of the Church in this age is not such that it can hold men to their duties by fear of penalties; it ought to attract rebellious sons to its fold by a suitable means and keep these members of its family to their duty by displaying the wealth of its inherent goodness rather than repeated threats of punishment.[124]

Early in 1870, Peter Richard Kenrick published a 42-page tract, *De infallibilitate pontifica,* to explore the ideas of the schema *De ecclesia Christi* which had been handed out on February 23. Samuel J. Miller noted, "Regardless of the consequences for his future career, he wanted to lay his mature, thoughtful reflections before the Fathers of the council and indeed before the world itself in the most forceful manner."[125] The brochure was a scholarly piece attempting to show that papal infallibility did exist when the Pope was confirmed by the Episcopal college, but was not infallible without their assent. Kenrick's arguments sought to show the stand-alone papal infallibility argument could not be grounded in Scripture, Church tradition, patristic writings, council decrees, and even reason. Kenrick also stated that such an assertion would diminish the rights of the bishops. For instance, Kenrick conceded that Matthew 16:17-19 shows Peter alone receiving the keys of the kingdom from Jesus, but countered that John 21:12 showed the authority to forgive sins was shared by the apostles/bishops.

Regarding the early Church Fathers, Catholics often turn to Irenaeus of Lyon and his description of Rome as *potestiorem principalitatem* as a recognition of papal supremacy among the Christian Churches. Kenrick argued that Irenaeus was referring to the *city* of Rome, not the papacy, as the capital of the empire, an argument found more often in the Protestant camp.

Furthermore, Kenrick argued that recognition of the Pope as the source of the Church only came as late as the Council of Trent. Finally, he saw the twist of logic: if the Pope could speak infallibly on matters *de fide,* he alone could decide what matters were and were not *de fide.*

---

124   Samuel J. Miller. "Peter Richard Kenrick: Bishop and Archbishop of St. Louis: 1806 – 1896." *Records of the American Catholic Historical Society of Philadelphia.* Vol. 84. No. 1-3, 1973. PP. 101-102.

125   Ibid. P. 103.

Kenrick also dismissed criticism that the exercise of sole papal authority had already been exhibited in the 1854 definition of the doctrine of the Immaculate Conception. The Archbishop of Saint Louis pointed out that this doctrine had been widely, if not universally, held for many centuries and that Pope Pius IX had been moved to announce the doctrine after a wellspring of petitions reached his desk, compelling him to act. And in so acting, the Roman pontiff had not diminished the rights of the bishops and the universal Church.

In a final chapter, the author used the Council of Jerusalem of 70 A.D. to show collegiality at work in perfect harmony with Peter's role as head of the church. In emulating Jerusalem, later councils gave the Fathers the time needed to deliberate and discern the will of the Holy Spirit. To act impulsively by papal *fiat*, the Church ran the risk of not listening to the Holy Spirit and thus suffering grievously as a result.

By April 1870, the Fathers of the Vatican Council were grappling with the notion of papal infallibility; as the sides hardened, attacks turned *ad hominum* and spilled out of the Council chambers into newspapers. Bishop Dupanloup wrote a lengthy letter to the Bishop of Malines and intimated that Peter Richard Kenrick's brother, Archbishop Francis Patrick Kenrick, now deceased, would have stood against a definition of papal infallibility. Francis Patrick Kenrick's successor, Martin Spalding, took exception to this observation and replied in the negative one month later. Spalding's response seemed to give credence to a rumor circulating in Rome that the Archbishop of Baltimore was over-exerting his role as the leader of America's Prime See to make himself the spokesman for the American hierarchy.

The Bishop of Orleans responded to Spalding's response, pointing out misstatements in Spalding's April 4 letter. Dupanloup drew Peter Richard Kenrick into the argument when he stated that Kenrick understood his brother's ecclesiology better than Spalding. Beneath his smooth rhetoric, Dupanloup chastised the Archbishop of Baltimore. "After having read it I am sure, Msgr., you will regret having called a palpable travesty of the truth a situation which, you see, is discovered to be simply simple truth according to the evidence of the man who merits being believed above all others in interpreting the thought of Msgr. Kenrick."[126]

---

126   Samuel J. Miller. "Peter Richard Kenrick: Bishop and Archbishop of St. Louis: 1806 – 1896." *Records of the American Catholic Historical Society of Philadelphia.* Vol. 84. No. 1-3, 1973. PP. 112-113.

Peter Richard penned two letters within days of each other, expressing opposite sentiments. In one letter to Archbishop Martin Spalding, he apologized for having appeared in public to disagree with Spalding, assuring him, "I will always endeavor to maintain friendly relations." The other letter went to Dupanloup and came to be published in the French journal *L'Univers*, a letter in which the Archbishop of Saint Louis denied Spalding's interpretation of his brother's views and the right to speak for the American hierarchy. The letter descended into nastiness when Kenrick remarked, "Those who have the honor of enjoying the company of the amiable Archbishop of Baltimore were, like your Grandeur, mistaken about his being an inopportunist and perceived clearly (*bien et nettement*) the change which took place when the venerable prelate found himself a member of two conciliar depositions."[127]

A critic of Peter Richard Kenrick, Bishop Modeste Demers of Vancouver, speculated that Kenrick's hard line stemmed less from his interpretation of his brother's position on papal infallibility and more on his "financial difficulties… known to all" and even "an agony of the mind" which plagued him. These observations were unfair and false but showed the depth to which many of the participants of the Vatican Council had descended "*de coelo*," as Kenrick had predicted to Father Constantine Smith even before the Council began.

The formal debate on infallibility opened on May 14, 1870. Five days later, Cardinal Cullen of Dublin attempted to do what Archbishop Spalding had been accused of regarding the American hierarchy. Cullen claimed to speak for the Irish hierarchy, supporting papal infallibility and accusing the Irish minority of disloyalty. He then added Peter Richard Kenrick's name into the mix. This was an unnecessary attack on one who many years earlier had been the recipient of Cullen's solicitude and kindness. Archbishop Kenrick asked for permission to respond from the floor at the Council but was denied. Indeed, he was frozen out of the debate, denied any chance to deliver an address. On June 4, he resolved to speak no more at the Council. Lord Acton speculated to historian Döllinger that the Archbishop of Saint Louis went into silence because he no longer recognized the Council as legitimate, a speculation which was not factual.

---

127   Mansi, VII, 1366-1373. As cited in Samuel J. Miller. "Peter Richard Kenrick: Bishop and Archbishop of St. Louis: 1806 – 1896." *Records of the American Catholic Historical Society of Philadelphia*. Vol. 84. No. 1-3, 1973. PP. 113-114.

Actually, Kenrick had decided on another course of action. If the Council authorities would deny him the right to speak and explain his views, he would do so instead in writing. What resulted was a tract: *Concio Habenda Et No Habita*.

The tract was published in Naples through the efforts of Lord Acton. Once published, it was widely distributed to the Council Fathers while other copies made their way to the general public, though only academics could read the remarks, as the pamphlet was written in Latin. If delivered as an address, it would have run about four hours long. Unlike the booklets ordered by Archbishop Ketteler of Mainz, which ended up in the Vatican post office, *Concio* came directly to Archbishop Kenrick, who had the books distributed. *Concio* clearly outlined Kenrick's views, but it also confirmed his stature as a *bête noir* in Vatican circles for years to come.

The basic premise of the tract was set out on the first page – a kind of double infallibility, each dependent on the other. The Pope was infallible, but so are the Pope and the bishops when gathered together. Kenrick cited Matthew 18:19-20, "Go, teach all nations," pointing out Jesus' exhortation was not to Peter alone, but to Peter and the disciples with him. Regarding the bishop individually and episcopacy collectively, Kenrick observed:

The individual bishops, taken singly, received, by the ordinance of the College itself, only an ordinary local jurisdiction in their several dioceses. The bishops taken universally, and the universal jurisdiction; not in the sense exactly that the universal jurisdiction is made up by the sum of the local jurisdictions; but that the bishops universally, whether dispersed and separated from each other, are united in a general council, constitute the apostolic college.[128]

When interpreting Matthew 16, "Thou art Peter and upon this rock I will build my church," Peter Richard Kenrick ignored the Protestant position that the Lord was speaking to all the apostles. Clearly Jesus used the second-person singular. Kenrick then tried to show that the "rock" was not Peter professing the faith, but the faith professed by Peter. Thus, it was not the person of Peter or by extension the office of the Pope which was elevated by Jesus, but the Faith itself. Yet at one point, *Concio*'s author affirmed primacy while rejecting domination.

---

128   Samuel J. Miller. "Peter Richard Kenrick: Bishop and Archbishop of St. Louis: 1806 – 1896." *Records of the American Catholic Historical Society of Philadelphia*. Vol. 84. No. 1-3, 1973. P. 117.

Kenrick feared that the papal infallibility definition would leave the Pope as the sole power in the Church and demote bishops to mere creatures of the Pope.

Kenrick then threw down the challenge which he would later be forced to take back up. "I boldly declare that that opinion, as it lies in the schema, is not a doctrine of faith, and that it cannot become such by any definition whatsoever, even by the definition of a council."[129] The tract ended with a plea to form a committee to seek a compromise definition, or failing that, to put off the definition until it was properly studied and a consensus could be formed.

The final vote on papal infallibility came on July 18, 1870. Kenrick and fifty-nine other bishops made themselves absent, even while they had joined others in the morning to sign a final petition to the secretary of the Council trying to stay the vote. Instead, a steady stream of bishops cast their affirmative votes over a three-hour period. By noon, 535 bishops cast affirmative votes. Only two voted against.

The document read that "the Roman pontiff, when speaking *ex cathedra*, that is, when in discharge of the office of pastor and doctor of all Christians, by virtue of his supreme apostolic authority he defines a doctrine regarding faith or morals to be held by the Universal Church, by the divine assistance promised to him in blessed Peter, is possessed of that infallibility with which the divine Redeemer willed that his Church should be endowed for defining doctrine regarding faith and morals; and that therefore such definitions of the Roman Pontiff are here reform of all of themselves and cannot come from the consent of the Church."[130]

The council broke up shortly after this vote due to the political instability in Italy caused by the Franco-Prussian war. Archbishop Peter Richard Kenrick returned to Saint Louis on December 15, nearly six months after he left Rome. Avoiding public view, he traveled in Spain and spent a short time in Philadelphia before coming home. Regardless, he was the subject of great interest among his fellow bishops.

A committee of bishops in Rome examined in detail *Concio* to find any element of heretical thought. In September, while Rome was un-

---

129   Samuel J. Miller. "Peter Richard Kenrick: Bishop and Archbishop of St. Louis: 1806 – 1896." *Records of the American Catholic Historical Society of Philadelphia.* Vol. 84. No. 1-3, 1973. P. 118-119.
130   Giuseppe Alberigo et al. (eds.), *Conciliorum Oecomenicorum Decreta* (Basel etc. 1962, 792) as found in Ibid. P. 121.

der siege by a Piedmontese army and Garibaldi's irregulars, Archbishop Barnabó found time as Prefect of *Propaganda Fide* to urge Bishop John Hogan of Saint Joseph to persuade Kenrick to make a quick public endorsement of the decree on infallibility. Cardinal Filippo de Angelis sent letters to each of Kenrick's suffragans, urging them to tell the Archbishop that *Concio* had been condemned but that this condemnation would remain secret if Kenrick publicly accepted the decrees of the council. Correspondence was initiated between Martin Spalding and Cardinal Cullen over Kenrick's next moves. The Rector of Saint Charles Borromeo Seminary in Philadelphia reassured *Propaganda* that Kenrick was ready to recant.

This most delicate request was made through the diplomatic and rhetorical skills of the Vicar General, Patrick Ryan. On January 2, 1871, a reception was held at Saint John the Evangelist Parish to welcome back the Archbishop. He barely spoke, but let Ryan assure the assembly that the Archbishop had the interest of the Church in mind when he took his principled stand, that his opposition cost him long-standing friendships, and that his motives were pure. Samuel J. Miller observed, "The Archbishop's reply was a model of brevity."[131] He replied that he accepted the verdict of the council, that the Pope was infallible, because he always believed the councils were infallible. If an infallible council could declare that the Pope was infallible, then the Pope was infallible. "Simply and singly on that authority, I yield obedience and full and unreserved submission to the definition concerning the character of which there can be no doubt as emanating from the council, and subsequently accepted by the greater part even of those who were in the minority on that occasion."[132]

Kenrick continued to correspond with Lord Acton, explaining his adherence to the council decrees in simple fashion, as he explained them to his Saint Louis flock. He told the English lord that he had been asked to repudiate *Concio* but would refuse to do so. He did not write Pius IX directly nor take part in demonstrations showing support and solidarity for the Pope, who had just been denied his temporal powers

---

131   Samuel J. Miller. "Peter Richard Kenrick: Bishop and Archbishop of St. Louis: 1806 – 1896." *Records of the American Catholic Historical Society of Philadelphia.* Vol. 84. No. 1-3, 1973. P. 123.
132   John J. O'Shea, The Two Archbishops Kenrick, pp. 332-3, as cited in John Rothensteiner. *History of Archdiocese of St. Louis.* St. Louis: Blackwell Wielandy Co. 1928. P. 314.

by the Piedmontese army.

When Archbishop Kenrick wrote to *Propaganda* for some dispensations in January 1871, he added to Cardinal Barnabó that he had made a public statement regarding the adherence to the decrees. To this the Cardinal told Peter Richard Kenrick of his joy at receiving this news and suggested Archbishop Kenrick write Pope Pius IX informing him.

When pushed by Cardinal de Angeles, Prefect of the Congregation of the Index, to repudiate *Concio*, Kenrick responded that he had done as much when he stated publicly on January 2nd his acceptance of the Council decree. The Vatican decided not to press the case further, though *Concio* was given special condemnation. It was never publicly repudiated specifically, and Kenrick never wrote Pope Pius IX. Even Archbishop Martin Spalding counseled patience in this regard. Any further measures to push Kenrick were bound to make matters worse. This advice made its way via the Bishop of Toronto to Cardinal Barnabó.

Regardless, pettiness still tinged the ongoing relations between the Vatican and the Archbishop of Saint Louis. When commemorative medals of the Council were sent to Archbishop Spalding in June 1871 to be distributed to the attending Council Fathers, instructions were added that the medals destined for Kenrick of Saint Louis and Domenec of Pittsburgh were not to be given until specific public statements of adherence would satisfy *Propaganda*. Later, they requested copies of newspaper articles which reported on Kenrick's public statements.

On June 25, 1871, while the Catholic world celebrated the twenty-fifth anniversary of the election of Pope Pius IX as Supreme Pontiff and Saint Louis prepared its own procession and festival, Peter Richard Kenrick left town, giving his Vicar for German affairs, Father Henry Mühlsiepen, the uncomfortable task of trying to explain the Archbishop's absence.

Chapter Ten

LIFE AFTER THE VATICAN COUNCIL

The decade of the 1860s began with the contentious election of Abraham Lincoln, leading to secession and Civil War. The decade ended with Peter Richard Kenrick at a contentious ecumenical council, in which the Archbishop of Saint Louis ended up clearly holding a minority position.

This would not be a decade of parish founding and church building. Indeed, only 12 parishes were established during the 1860s. The first was dedicated on December 26, 1860: Saint Boniface in the German south side. Previously, the Germans in the area gathered with young Father Gamber, the assistant pastor at the newly erected Saints Mary and Joseph Parish. Each Sunday they used the church for their 8 A.M. Mass. Archbishop Kenrick encouraged the newly ordained priest to rally the community to establish their own parish. This the people did, purchasing a large lot on Michigan Street. Besides a new church, the eager congregation built a rectory and a school, hiring a lay teacher until the School Sisters of Notre Dame arrived. Father Gamber stayed less than one year, after which he returned to his hometown near Mainz, Germany. He left so suddenly that his successor, Father E. A. Schendel, discovered that the rectory had no furniture. The church walls had yet to be plastered, a bell tower stood with no bell and a steeple had no cross on top. Instead, Father Schendel found lots of debt for work finished but unpaid for. The Archbishop intervened and solved the parish's financial woes until it was established on firm footing. That came because the German parishioners were generous and they had solid, high-paying jobs at the Carondelet Iron Works, building Union gunboats.

Father Schendel served as pastor of Saint Boniface for 35 years, adding an improved school building in 1865 and a Sisters' convent three years later. He even built a hospital, but it was lost tragically in a fire.

The Archdiocese would see only one other parish founded during the war years, another German parish: Holy Cross in Baden, in 1864. Baden was a sparsely populated area six miles north of Saint Louis, annexed to the city in 1876. Toward the Mississippi River, it was swampy land, but westward it rose to forested hills. Its main feature was a road that ran from the city of Saint Louis north to a ferry landing owned by Edward Hall, which crossed the Missouri River at Portage des Sioux.

As the German population grew northward from Bremen, where Most Holy Trinity was located, people gathered for Mass at the Carmelite convent at the old Clay Farm, which later became Calvary Cemetery. Father Caspar Doebbner convinced these German Catholics to purchase land and establish their own parish. This they did, buying two acres from Friedrich Kraft, an early settler from Baden-Baden, Germany, who named the area after his hometown and then became the local postmaster.

The parishioners cleared the land themselves, cut and hauled stone and sand, built the foundation of the church, and fired their own brick. On May 3, 1864, a small church was dedicated, though the congregation rapidly outgrew the building. The parish split in 1872, with Irish members forming Our Lady of Mount Carmel Parish just a few blocks away. In 1909, the 54-year-old structure was again found inadequate to the size of the parish and a fine Gothic church replaced it.

The population of Baden continued to grow, dominated by single-family dwellings "on the hill," and commerce expanded along Broadway and Halls Ferry Road. Heavy industry hovered near the riverbank, draining the swampy land and providing steady jobs for the local residents.

As peace returned to the region after the Civil War, three city parishes and one rural parish were established in 1865. Holy Rosary was founded in Warrenton, Missouri, while the three new city parishes catered to the needs of the growing German population. Saint Teresa of Avila was built on North Grand Avenue. Its brick Byzantine architecture reflected the classical scholarship of its founding pastor, Father Francis Gallagher. The project of erecting a parish began a year earlier, when Father James O'Brien sent a circular letter to Catholics in the area encouraging them to organize a parish. Shortly after that, Father O'Brien left the scene for three years, eventually taking residence in Cape Girardeau. Father Gallagher served Saint Teresa for ten years until health problems caused him to resign. His successor was young Father William Brantner, who helped the parish school grow to 300 pupils. He died at the young age of 40, after serving the parish for 17 years.

In South Saint Louis two parishes were organized for the Germans, Saint Henry and Saint Nicholas. Saint Henry would be destroyed in the 1896 tornado, but before that it would boast of a fine church, an accommodating rectory, and a school serving 200 children. St. Nicholas of Myra was founded by Father Nicholas Staudinger. On the occasion of laying the cornerstone, Archbishop Kenrick presided, preaching the sermon in German. The parish grew rapidly from 50 families to over 300. In 1870, the Sisters of Saint Joseph took over direction of the school. The second pastor arrived in 1876: Father Caspar Doebbner, founder of Holy Cross Parish in Baden. Between the two assignments, he had been on loan to the diocese of Vincennes. Father Doebbner died just two years later and Father Joseph Schaefers arrived, bringing with him a shrewd financial mind, which was needed to settle the large parish debt he had inherited. In time, Father Schaefers retired the debt and built the parish hall and rectory. When the neighborhood saw a shift in population as Germans moved away and African-Americans moved in, the next pastor, Father Herman Adrian, turned over the school building to the Jesuits and the Sisters of the Blessed Sacrament to run a school for Black children.

African-American Catholics were to receive their own parish in 1872. Father Ignatius Panken, a Jesuit, was named pastor of Saint Elizabeth Parish. Vinegar Hill Hall, formerly a Baptist Church, was purchased and renovated. On May 18, 1873, the building was dedicated by coadjutor Bishop Patrick Ryan and included a procession of 10,000 Saint Louis Catholics to celebrate the event. But the interracial harmony was soon squashed by the Archbishop. Saint Elizabeth was to serve all Black Catholics in the city, but when Father Panken inquired about non-blacks also attending, Archbishop Kenrick, through Father Panken's Jesuit superior, instructed the priest to refuse the sacraments to any white person who attempted to attend Saint Elizabeth's.

This order brought considerable hardship, especially to Black Catholics, as the ruling segregated them from other parishes, ethnic and otherwise, in the city. When Carondelet was annexed to the City of Saint Louis, for instance, its sizable black Catholic population was directed to join Saint Elizabeth's, some 50 city blocks away. Under this neglect, the Black Catholic population dwindled, many joining with Black Protestants migrating from the South.

In 1866, four parishes were founded. One, in Union, Missouri, was dedicated to the Immaculate Conception. Over the next 14 years, three other parishes would receive the same patroness. Also in 1866, a downtown parish, Holy Angels, was founded by Father Michael Welby on land donated by John Dillon. It was located at LaSalle and St. Ange and prospered for the next 40 years, until most of its parishioners abandoned downtown in the early twentieth century. During its heyday, Holy Angels counted as many as 1,300 parishioners; but it had no parish school. Neither Father Welby nor his successor, Father Francis Kielty, favored parochial education, making them anomalies of their time.

That same year, 1866, around 35 German-speaking families in Saint Ferdinand's parish in Florissant petitioned Archbishop Kenrick to allow them to found a parish and school where their language would be spoken. Thus the parish of Sacred Heart, Florissant, was founded with Father Ignatius Panken, S. J., the future founder of Saint Elizabeth's parish, as their first pastor. Two and a half acres were purchased for the parish grounds. The land was rough and a large gully ran through it. First to be constructed was the school, as it was the catalyst for the new parish. The school house was completed in September 1866. The men of the parish laid the foundation themselves and furnished building materials.

By that time the foundation of the church was laid, but a harsh winter set in and delayed construction until spring. The church was finished by September 1867, just as Father Panken was transferred. The parish grew rapidly and the school expanded. It was conducted by two Sisters of Saint Joseph and a layman who taught the boys. Half of the day classes were conducted in English and the other half in German. Within six years the enrollment overwhelmed the facility, and a second building was built for the boys.

For the remainder of the decade, only four more parishes were founded, mostly in rural areas: Immaculate Conception in Old Monroe, Saint John Lateran in Imperial, and Saint Maurus in Biehle. The only urban church was Saint Francis De Sales, founded in 1867.

By that time, Saints Peter and Paul had grown to be a huge parish under the leadership of Father Franz Goller. In the westernmost part of the parish boundaries, some 35 families wanted to be given a parish of their own. They met at the home of their ringleader, Van Mierlo, and purchased property against the wishes of Father Goller and without the knowledge of the Archbishop. Having contracted to build a church for $12,500, they contacted the Vicar General Father Melcher, who interceded for them with Archbishop Kenrick. Surprisingly, the Archbishop agreed and allowed Father Melcher to lay the cornerstone of Sacred Heart parish in September 1867. Graciously conceding to the new reality, Father Goller attended the ceremony. Construction went on pace so that Christmas Mass could be offered at the new facility.

Christmas that year proved to be a disaster. The new pastor, young Father Louis Lay, celebrated Mass in an almost vacant church. Bad weather kept many home, while other families resisted leaving their beloved Saints Peter and Paul. The walls were still unplastered. The altar was just a set of boards on a stand. There was no heat. After the first Mass, Father Lay told the other two gatherings to go to Saint Anthony's or Saints Peter and Paul.

Things improved in the spring and Father Melcher, now Bishop-elect of Green Bay, dedicated the church in the spring of 1867. With time the parish grew to 800 parishioners, and a fine rectory was built for Father Lay. Regardless, internal conflicts and a staggering debt caused the priest to resign as pastor. Eventually that role fell to Father Peter Wigger, a Westphalian immigrant. He spent his entire priesthood as pastor of Saint Francis De Sales. He addressed the debt, built a school, brought in the Franciscan Sisters of Oldenburg to conduct the school, and still found time to edit a journal, *Herold des Glaubens*. Beyond all of that, Father Wigger brought his brother and three nephews to Saint Louis, and all four would serve as priests in the Archdiocese.

The founding of these parishes, mainly for German speakers, demonstrates continued growth of the German population in Saint Louis during the 1860s. Saint Boniface on the south side, Holy Cross in Baden, Saint Teresa of Avila on North Grand, Saint Henry and Saint Nicholas on the near south side, Saint Elizabeth to accommodate black Catholics citywide, Holy Angels downtown, Sacred Heart in Florissant, and Saint Francis De Sales were joined by six rural parishes. The population of Saint Louis grew from 161,000 at the beginning of the Civil War and hit 310,000 by the 1870 census. City boosters called Saint Louis the Fourth City, as only New York, Philadelphia, and Brooklyn had larger populations. But the boast was a hollow one meant to slight Chicago, which had gone from a beloved daughter of Saint Louis to an unabashed rival. Chicago's population had tripled in that same time period, holding a census position of 298,000.

Chicago's natural location, as discussed earlier, predisposed it to be one of America's great cities. Located on the south side of the Great Lakes, it was a natural gathering spot for lumber and grain from the

North. It was the northernmost spot where railroads could be built, the lakes acting as natural barriers. In winning the bridge race when the Gasconade failure of 1855 doomed Saint Louis and the Rock Island success paved the way West for Chicago, the contest was thrown all the more in Chicago's favor when Saint Louis teetered between the Union and the Confederacy, whereas Chicago never wavered.

With the construction of the Illinois and Michigan Canals, Lake Michigan was connected to the Illinois River. The canal project swelled the population with Irish laborers. In its first four months of operation, the canal helped ship nearly 35,000 barrels of flour and 95,000 bushels of wheat to Saint Louis. The creation of the Board of Trade, the extension of the telegraph, Cyrus McCormick's reaper factory, iron foundries, grain elevators, and a new livestock operation all gave Chicago an edge on the future.

But Saint Louis would have its own one last day of glory as America's Fourth City, if only through a little skullduggery. The 1870 federal census figures for Saint Louis were delayed in publication until the Chicago numbers were reported. Chicago could complain, but it had to wait ten more years: in 1880, Saint Louis counted 350,000, while Chicago reached a half million. Joseph Pulitzer's *Post-Dispatch* questioned the accuracy of 1870's census. *The Republican* wondered at the school populations, noting Saint Louis had a lower school-age census than in cities smaller than the Fourth City. Regardless, Saint Louis boosterism was relentless as Saint Louis Catholics joined in by building bigger and bigger churches with higher and higher steeples. Entering the Gilded Age, everyone seemed set for a bright future. But hidden challenges lay ahead.

The Mississippi River had been one of the key reasons for the founding of Saint Louis, but by the post-war era, it was seen as a barrier to commerce. To move goods and people across the river, Saint Louis relied on ferries. Since 1820, one company, the Wiggins Ferry Company, held a monopoly on the business. Such Saint Louis notables as Samuel Christy, Bernard Pratte, and John O'Fallon owned stock in the company. By 1865, the firm owned three transfer boats and most of the Illinois-side shoreline opposite Saint Louis. Wiggins' warehouses and railroad terminals dotted the landscape. By 1872, Wiggins Ferry installed rail lines at Chouteau Avenue and Mound Street so rail cars could be on-loaded on one side of the river and off-loaded on the other. The barges could accommodate 450 rail cars a day.

But winters played havoc with river traffic. In the winter of 1865-

66, the Mississippi froze, making traffic impossible for twenty-seven days. The next winter was worse: thirty-eight days. In the winter of 1867-68 the river was frozen for forty-one days; the river was closed to traffic, causing coal shortages in the city and threatening other commerce, especially cotton processing.

Saint Louis had become the third-largest cotton market in America, just behind New Orleans and Savannah, Georgia. Cotton was shipped from the South, less by steamboats and more by railroad. In Saint Louis, the cotton was cleaned and then compressed for transfer to textile mills in the northeast. The Saint Louis Compress Company, founded in 1873, used hydraulic presses to compact five-hundred pound bales into nine-inch bundles, so fifty such loads could be placed in a single rail car.[133] Nearly a half-million bales were processed annually by 1880, and these needed reliable railroad transportation, which Wiggins Ferry Company could not provide. All this spurred conversation about a railroad bridge at Saint Louis which could span the Mississippi.

One such bridge had been successfully constructed at Rock Island, Illinois. A wooden drawbridge linked Chicago with the western markets in 1855. By 1868, further bridges spanned the Mississippi at Quincy, Clinton, and Dubuque.

Opposition to a Saint Louis bridge came, logically, from Wiggins Ferry Company, but also from Chicago business interests. Chief among these was Boomer & Blackstone, the architectural firm that had built the successful Rock Island Bridge the same year they built the bridge over the Gasconade River, the bridge which tragically failed on its inaugural day in 1855.

In the end, the bridge at Saint Louis would be built by a most unlikely player, James B. Eads. Eads had made his reputation building ironclad gunboats for the Union during the Civil War, but he knew the Mississippi River unlike any man alive. Eads had designed his own diving bell capable of descending to depths of 65 feet. He used it for salvage operations and had dived more than five hundred times.

Eads was assisted by two German engineers, Henry Flad and Charles Pfeifer. They chose a site at the foot of Washington Avenue where the river was the narrowest, 1,500 feet. Boomer & Blackstone entered a competing bid, designating a spot where the river was 1,700

---

133   James Neal Primm. *Lion of the Valley: St. Louis, Missouri 1764-1980.* Saint Louis: Missouri Historical Society Press. 2010. P. 277.

feet wide. The Chicago firm intended to build a five-span bridge, proposing to place the piers on the riverbed. Eads' proposal called for a three-span bridge with the piers driven all the way down to bedrock. Eads understood that the riverbed of the Mississippi was not impervious and was therefore unreliable as a foundation for a bridge.

The Eads proposal attracted financial backing from New York City, and finally Boomer & Blackstone gave up their bid to join Eads in the project. Eads' intuition about the riverbed proved correct. He had to dig 68 feet through sand and debris to find bedrock. The feat was unprecedented. The foundation piers would stand sixteen stories high. Six hundred men worked in air chambers to complete the piers. Fourteen men would die of the mysterious disease called caisson disease, or "the bends". But on May 24, 1874, 25,000 people had the stroll of their lives by walking across Eads Bridge. The bridge had been tested by coal cars and locomotives and even an elephant! On July 4, 1874, the bridge was officially opened, celebrated by 200,000 and a fourteen-mile parade.

There was, however, a hidden price to pay for the construction of Eads Bridge. As part of the project, a tunnel over 1,600 yards long was dug from Washington and Third to the Mill Creek Valley. This rendered unstable the foundation of Immaculate Conception Church on Eighth and Chestnut, and the building had to be abandoned. The story of Immaculate Conception has some interesting twists and turns and influenced the location to be chosen for the New Cathedral.

Immaculate Conception was founded by Father James Duggan and consecrated on December 11, 1853, by Father Anthony O'Regan. Both men would serve as bishops of Chicago. Father Duggan's assistant was Father John Bannon, who was made pastor of Saint John the Apostle before abandoning his post to become a chaplain for the Confederate army. When Duggan became bishop of Chicago in 1859, Father Patrick Feehan succeeded him as pastor and served the parish throughout the war years until he was named bishop of Nashville, Tennessee in 1865. Father Feehan's years were marked by exceptional acts of charity for the poor and for wounded soldiers, as well as for prisoners of war. He helped the Sisters of Charity establish a small hospital in his parish to care for the soldiers.

There was a quick succession of pastors until Father Francis Patrick O'Reilly took charge, only to discover the foundation failure caused by the tunnel serving Eads Bridge. Archbishop Kenrick gave

Immaculate Conception Parish property at Jefferson and Locust, some sixteen blocks west of the old location. The land had been donated by Anne Lucas Hunt, who hoped to persuade the Archbishop to build a new Cathedral at that site. Kenrick was distracted by the Civil War, the Drake Test Oath (which led to the arrest of several of his priests), and by his intense involvement in the Vatican Council.

Again, Anne Lucas Hunt stepped forward and gave a donation to build a modest wood frame church, no doubt hoping that the arrangement would be temporary and a new cathedral would eventually be built there. Immaculate Conception was the home parish of the old Creole elite of Saint Louis, but their influence had definitely waned. The neighborhood around the church became clogged with businesses and industry. Eventually, Kenrick's successor, Archbishop John Kain, would close the parish and sell the property to help fund his plans for a new cathedral on fashionable Lindell Boulevard.

Besides moving Immaculate Conception, the Archdiocese established eight more rural parishes and five urban ones. Serving mainly farming communities were Assumption in O'Fallon, Saint Aloysius in Spanish Lake, Saint Lawrence in Lawrenceton, Our Lady Help of Christians in Weingarten, Saint Monica in Creve Coeur, Saint Joseph in Bonne Terre, Immaculate Conception in Saint Mary, and Saint Francis of Assisi in Luebbering.

Further afield in territory, which would later become the diocese of Jefferson City, twenty-nine parishes would be founded, added to the sixteen which already existed there. These new parishes served ethnic communities, especially German farmers and Irish railroad builders. The very act of establishing these parishes was a defiance of the turmoil and horrors of the Civil War and the guerrilla fighting which plagued much of rural Missouri.

The busiest year for parish founding came in 1860, when Saint Boniface in Brunswick, Saint Peter in Marshall, and Holy Family in Sweet Springs were erected. During the war itself, Immaculate Conception in Montgomery City (1861), Saint Patrick in Jonesburg (1861), Saint Patrick in Rolla (1862), and Our Lady Help of Christians in Frankenstein (1863) were founded. No parish was opened in 1864. But in 1866, Saint Boniface in Koeltztown, Saint Mary in Glasgow, Saint George in Linn, Saint Vincent (later Saint Patrick) in Sedalia, and Saint Joseph in Palmyra were opened.

The City of Saint Louis also saw parish growth after the war. In 1871, around one hundred families pledged $5,000 to establish Saint

Agatha. In 1872, Saint Elizabeth was founded for Black Catholics, and Our Lady of Mount Carmel separated the Irish from the Germans of Holy Cross. In 1873, "Maria Hilf," Our Lady of Perpetual Help, was set up in the College Hill neighborhood, so named because it contained a farm owned by Saint Louis University. The founding pastor was Father A. J. Stroomberger, who had founded Saint Agatha only two years earlier. In 1874, another German parish was founded, Saint Augustine's, on the corner of Hebert and Lismore Streets in the old Fairgrounds neighborhood.

Besides parish building, the Archdiocese was graced in 1871 with the founding of Saint John's Infirmary at Twenty-Third and Locust by the Sisters of Mercy. The congregation had been in Saint Louis for fifteen years, teaching schools and caring for the poor. But some of the Sisters learned nursing skills from having served an Irish regiment in the Crimean War, then in the American Civil War, and more recently in the Franco-Prussian War. The demand for medical service quickly outgrew the Infirmary, and a larger hospital was built on the same location.

The first half of the 1870s saw lots of other activity in Saint Louis. The Mill Creek sewer was completed in 1872, allowing for drainage and rain run-off. It eventually ran three miles long and measured twenty feet wide and fifteen feet high. All Saints Episcopal Church added to the cityscape in 1874, as well as the Merchants' Exchange Building on Third and Pine. It was considered one of the grandest buildings in the city, and its Exchange Hall became the home of the annual Veiled Prophet Ball.

1875 was celebrated with the opening of Sumner High School, part of a reform movement in Saint Louis public education. The *Saint Louis Globe-Democrat* began publishing, joining some sixteen other daily newspapers; there were as many in German as in English.

1875 also witnessed the Great Saint Louis Ice War in January. The river had again frozen over, always a thorn in the Wiggins Ferry Company's side. An entrepreneurial young man named Tim Hickey decided to harvest the ice for storage in the deep caves below Saint Louis. He hired workers who cleared away the snow and river debris. They planned on returning the next day to cut the ice. To their surprise, the Hickey crew found that someone had cut the ice the night before. When the poachers returned for more, fistfights broke out. Hickey and his men were at first driven off, but they recruited more men, promised a princely wage of $1.50 a day, and armed themselves with some rusty pistols. Hickey's force of fifty drove off the opponents and harvested the rest of the ice.

More peaceful excitement came with the royal visit of King Kalakaua of Hawaii. He had paid a diplomatic visit to Washington, D.C. and was on his way to San Francisco before returning home. Saint Louis fêted the king and he was entertained by General William Tecumseh Sherman, Henry Shaw, and Mayor Theophile Papin.

Next to the opening of Eads Bridge, the most significant contribution of Saint Louis boosterism got very little publicity indeed. In December 1875, a book entitled *Pictorial St. Louis: A Topographical Survey in Perspective, AD 1875* was published. It was the brainchild of Richard J. Compton, a publisher of sheet music in Alton, Illinois. Compton had a passion for perspective mapping, that is, drawings of cities as seen from the sky, a bird's-eye view. This sort of drawing had been popular for centuries, but Compton envisioned something far more dramatic: a street-by-street, house-by-house detailed sketch of Saint Louis, right down to every tree and shrub.

Compton hired Camille N. Dry, who had done perspective maps on a small scale in other cities. Dry rented a hot-air balloon and positioned it on the Illinois side of the river, and over the year drew one hundred and ten "plates." Included in this oversized book were details and descriptions of most of the buildings depicted in the plates, one hundred and twelve pages long. Compton paid for the project by selling subscriptions to the businesses and factories and apartments in the sketches. A subscription meant your building would be identified by number, and a description would be included. At publication time the massive book, the first of its kind, was sold for a hefty $25.00, the equivalent of $340.00 today.

Compton's *Pictorial St. Louis* remains the best artifact of life in 1870s Saint Louis. It includes railroads, insurance firms, retail distributors, sugar refineries, confectioners, and factories. Breweries and jewelry stores were featured. The forty-nine public schools were identified, and the narrative boasted of a bevy of 700 teachers in the system. The book pointed out the thirty Catholic churches and stated that another 167 existed beyond the city. It called Saint Louis "the most eminently Roman Catholic city in America," with 250 priests, sixty seminarians, and approximately 300,000 Catholics. A full page was devoted to the history and design of the cathedral. Churches of various faiths were shown and described. Curiously, there was no mention of the vibrant Jewish community in Saint Louis.

Compton's book compared Saint Louis favorably to other American cities. He showed that in 1870, manufacturing amounted to $335 million in New York City and $322 million in Philadelphia, while Saint Louis created $158 million in goods compared to Chicago's $92 million. New Orleans produced a mere $10 million. Saint Louis had financial capital in excess of $20 million in its banks, while Chicago had just $14.5 million. Even in vital statistics, a booster would find Saint Louis a healthier place to live. The death rate in the Fourth City was 14.45 per thousand. Chicago had a death rate of 20.29 per thousand, and the New Orleans mortality rate topped them all at 30.73 per thousand.

Richard J. Compton published a book which gave the most complete snapshot of any city in America, but he could not see into the future. Within a year, the city of Saint Louis would split from the county in the Great Divorce. And within two years, the city would experience the worst general strike in the history of the country.

Before considering the separation of City and County and the Great Strike of 1877, it would be good to take a survey of the state of religion in Saint Louis, via the information furnished by Richard J. Compton's excellent book.

Preeminence is given to the Catholic community due to its size. An estimated 300,000 Catholics lived in the Archdiocese, which encompassed the entire State of Missouri except the new Diocese of Saint Joseph.

Baptists were speculated as being the largest Protestant denomination, with eight or ten congregations and ten to twelve ordained ministers serving around 3,000 congregants. The inexact nature of Compton's report contrasts with his meticulous accuracy regarding Catholics. His treatment of Presbyterians is even more inexact and even anecdotal, emphasizing the founding dates of the Presbyterian Churches; 1816, two; 1817 and 1818, one each.

Compton mentioned the arrival of Methodism, first by an Alton visitor to Florissant, Reverend John Clark, in 1810, and the establishment of a congregation in 1821 by Reverend Jesse Walker, who built a large congregation over the years. The split of the congregation over the question of slavery saw two branches: The Methodist Episcopal Church favoring the Union and the Methodist Episcopal Church South favoring the Confederacy. By 1875, the Northern branch had prospered with five or six large churches. The Southern branch was not mentioned in Compton's report.

Episcopalians were noted as having among their number the wealthiest Saint Louisans. Prominent among the religious edifices of the city were Saint George Episcopal at Beaumont and Chestnut, a new structure erected in 1874 at a cost of $160,000. Trinity Episcopal was located at Eleventh and Washington, home of the Episcopal bishop of Missouri, though the building was not yet completed, interrupted by the Civil War and plagued with slow construction afterwards. Seven other smaller Episcopal congregations were also named.

The Congregational and Unitarian Churches were noted. The First Congregational Church at Tenth and Locust was founded in 1852, when 67 members of the Third Presbyterian Church left to be joined by nine others. This came under the inspiration of Dr. Truman M. Post, who had been invited to Third Presbyterian as a minister with a four-year contract. In 1852 he preached a discourse which triggered the exodus, declaring, "In a city where all varieties of religious creeds and orders, from Mormonism to the Papacy, were asserting themselves in distinctive organizations, it seems strange that that only should be excluded which came with the *Mayflower* to the New World."[134]

Here, too, the Civil War battered membership as pro-Southern congregants left. In 1867, some of the most prominent members left to form The Pilgrim Church, while others formed the Webster Grove Church. The collapse of the front wall of the church further distressed Dr. Post's congregation which, in 1875, numbered a mere two hundred, after a heyday of 650 earlier.

The saga of the First Congregational highlights the evolving and devolving nature of Protestant bodies, Saint Louis not being an exception.

In the case of First Presbyterian and the creation of Second Presbyterian, it was a matter of overcrowding. The church at Fourteenth and Lucas Place grew to 250 members and sought to reduce its size. Twenty-five members formed Second Presbyterian in 1832, but returned in 1837 when a larger worship space was built. Yet a year later, in October 1838, sixty-four were sent to reestablish Second Presbyterian, and in 1842, eighty-five members of that growing congregation left to form Third Presbyterian, which was decimated by Dr. Truman M. Post

---

134   Richard J. Compton, *Pictorial St. Louis: A Topographical Survey in Perspective AD 1875.* 1876. P. 82.

when he led the majority of congregants into Congregationalism. By 1875, additional Presbyterian congregations included Central Presbyterian, Walnut Street Presbyterian, and Pine Street Presbyterian.

On the corner of Ninth and Olive stood The Church of the Messiah, founded by Rev. Dr. William Greenleaf Elliot. Also the founder of Washington University, Dr. Elliot served as pastor there for thirty-seven years. The church conducted a school for poor children of the neighborhood. The church was valued in 1875 at $150,000, but the neighborhood was changing in such a way that Compton speculated a move would be necessary in a few years.

A daughter church of The Church of the Messiah was The Church of the Unity, located near trendy Lafayette Park. It was small, prosperous, and home to both a Sabbath School and the Literary Society.

Compton gave a brief account of the German Protestant congregations. Perhaps they declined to join in his initial subscriptions for the publication. He notes four houses of worship with a combined membership of 1,200 and the existence of Concordia College, a theological seminary for the German Evangelical Lutheran Church.

A distinction was made for the German Evangelical Churches, five in number, and Saint Mark's English Evangelical Lutheran Church, erected for a mere $15,000. Compton noted also the First German Baptist Church on Fourteenth and Carr, a small house of worship which built a church in 1863 and had recently overcome its debt.

Compton mentioned that there were four Jewish congregations in Saint Louis, but identified only one: Congregation "Scherrish" Israel, renting space on Sixth Street. For African-Americans, the only entry was the Eighth Street Colored Church, though later Compton would speak of Saint Elizabeth's for Black Catholics.

Richard Compton's 1875 survey of Catholic churches is a rich treasure trove of information. There is no evidence that Father Rothensteiner made use of this information when assembling his two-volume history of the Archdiocese, so Compton's book offers a unique and interesting secular perspective.

Richard Compton's introduction to Catholic churches and schools is indeed laudatory. In the flowing prose of the day, he speaks of early pioneer efforts uncovered by mid-century progress. "The engineer, in opening up new streets to the north, south or west, ever and anon ran across some humble place of worship which the weather-beaten cross on its summit told him was Catholic, and which some self-sacrificing father the church had erected years before. To this spirit of improvement and advancement may be attributed the Catholicity of St. Louis to the present day."[135]

Pictorial St. Louis turns its attention to the many educational, medical, and charitable works of the Catholic Church. "Nor is it in her temples alone that the Roman Catholic Church excels. Her school houses, attached to every parish – for where you find a church, you invariably find a school – are among the finest in the land; her convents and universities of learning are renowned throughout the world; her eleemosynary institutions, for the care of the orphan, the sick, the lame, the blind, the helpless and unfortunate of God's creatures, are the admiration of all Christian denominations; and for these things the whole of Christendom rises up, and with one accord pronounces her blessed. These institutions are scattered broadcast over St. Louis, another proof of the spirit of advancement which actuates the bosom of this Church."[136]

One further paragraph is worth quoting at length. Here Compton makes the point that Saint Louis is unique among American cities, as it is particularly hospitable to Catholics and open to Catholic participation in civic and commercial affairs.

The Roman Catholics of St. Louis are to be found in every important branch of industry, leading in many of the great manufacturing interests which go to make her the vast metropolis she is; representing vast amounts of wealth and capital, owning property in every nook and corner of the city, holding honorable positions in all the learned professions, on the bench, at the bar, in medicine, and the fine arts, filling some of the most responsible offices in the midst of the people and moving in the choicest circles of society. Differing from many other cities in America, in St. Louis it is no disqualification in the eyes of protesting denominations that a man bend his knee in the confessional or receives the eucharist under but one form. No religious prejudices of any kind debar the son of the Church of Rome for any position in our municipal government, or from any circle of private society.[137]

Pictorial St. Louis portrays twenty-five city parishes and renders drawings on the various plates of the churches, their schools, and

135   Richard J. Compton, *Pictorial St. Louis: A Topographical Survey in Perspective AD 1875*. 1876. P. 115.
136   Ibid, P. 115.
137   Ibid. P. 118.

their rectories.

Annunciation Church was located at Sixth and Lasalle, erected in 1861 at a cost of $100,000. It was built by Patrick Ryan, future coadjutor of Saint Louis and Archbishop of Philadelphia. Outstanding was a colonnade of Corinthian columns supporting the arched roof. The three altars were of Italian marble, and it housed an oil painting of the marriage of Joseph and Mary, a gift from King Louis XVIII of France to Bishop Du Bourg. Attached was Annunciation Free School, conducted by the Brothers of the Christian Schools for some 172 boys. Some 200 parish girls attended a free school on the property of the Sacred Heart Convent.

Saint Alphonsus Parish, Grand at Easton, was founded by the Redemptorist Fathers. The church, later dubbed "The Rock Church," was noted as being "an imposing building of limestone, Gothic in architecture, with a transept." At the time of the drawing, it was just two years old.

The Church of the Assumption was found on Sidney Street, near Seventh. Its pastor was Father Constantine P. Smith, who had served as theological expert, or *peritus*, to Archbishop Peter Richard Kenrick at the Vatican Council. Earlier, Father Smith had been promised the pastorship of Immaculate Conception, but that church building was compromised structurally during the construction of a tunnel to service Eads Bridge. Later, he would found Saint Agnes Parish in 1891 from part of Assumption Parish. Assumption was closed in 1951.

On Twenty-Second and Hebert, Saint Augustine's Church was erected. It was two stories, made of brick and included a basement, used by the parish school as well as the first floor. A chapel was located on the second floor. The church was erected the year of the pictorial book. It closed in 1982. The Sisters of the Precious Blood conducted the parish school for around 200 children.

Saint Bridget of Erin Parish was eighteen years old, located at Jefferson and Carr. The congregation had around 5,000 members, and the school was conducted by the Christian Brothers and the Sisters of Saint Joseph. Around 300 boys attended in one building, and around 450 girls attended in a new building, which boasted a hot water boiler system. It was an Irish-only parish for the remainder of the nineteenth and early twentieth century, and adjusted to become Black Catholic in mid-century, serving the Pruitt-Igoe settlement for five decades. The parish closed in 2003.

Saint Bonaventure was a short-lived parish serving the Italian immigrant community. Founded in 1871 at Sixth and Spruce, it was purchased from Saint John Episcopal and served the spiritual needs of an estimated 5,000 Italian Saint Louisans until the neighborhood deteriorated in 1883. Saint Bonaventure has the distinction of having been located between home plate and second base in the present Saint Louis Cardinals stadium!

The Saint Louis Cathedral received a full-page description of her history and architecture in Compton's book. Its school was free to all, operated by the Sisters of Loreto, with attendance around 300. Financially, the parish received support from the rest of the Archdiocese.

The Church of the Holy Angels at St. Ange and Chouteau, made of brick, was Gothic in design. Compton mentioned the parish had no school, and its children attended Annunciation school, seven city blocks to the west.

Sacred Heart was at the corner of Twentieth and University Streets. Though founded in 1871, it still used a temporary wooden building while a permanent structure was planned. Sacred Heart closed in 1978.

Saint John the Evangelist was afforded an essay of great detail, describing the Romanesque architecture of the structure at Sixteenth and Chestnut. Compton mentioned the incredible artwork in fresco by Hoffman and added, "In every respect, Saint John's is a credit and ornament to our city." The school housed some 450 children under the watchful eyes of the Christian Brothers and the Sisters of Saint Joseph. One error in the description appeared when Father John Bannon, the pastor who left the parish to serve in the Confederate army, was identified as Father Raemon.

Saint Malachy, at Clark and Summit, was called an imposing brick Gothic with the most handsome frescos in the city. The girls' school was called Saint Philomena's Asylum and School, conducted by the Sisters of Charity of Emmitsburg. It also served as an orphanage. In 1875, there were 325 students in the school, with 92 orphans as well as other boarders. The boys' school of 220 was conducted by the Christian Brothers. Saint Malachy was closed in 1959 after 101 years of service.

Saint Michael Parish was called "a neat one-story brick structure" on North Eleventh Street. The founder was the famed John Hogan, by 1875 the Bishop of Saint Joseph, Missouri. The school served around

250 children under the direction of the Sisters of Loreto. Saint Michael's was closed in 1975.

Saint Francis Xavier, 1875, was still located downtown on Ninth Street. It was described as Romanesque, a brick structure, with a capacity of 3,000. Its school held 415 boys under lay direction and 280 girls under the Sisters of Loreto.

Saint Lawrence O'Toole was on the southeast corner of Fourteenth and O'Fallon. Compton wrote, "It is a handsome brick edifice of the mixed Gothic style of architecture, which never fails to attract the attention of even the most unobservant." The present church cost $75,000 and served a parish of 6,000 members. The school was a philanthropic gift of Mrs. Jane Chambers, while the lot on which the church sat was a gift of Jane Graham, a member of the Mullanphy family. Around 500 children attended the school conducted by the Christian Brothers and the Sisters of Saint Joseph. Compton lauded the founding pastor, Father James Henry, a native of County Caven, Ireland, for "his indomitable energy and perseverance in the cause of his church and religion." This was a reference to a pitched battle fought by parishioners of various parishes under Father Henry's leadership to protect their churches from a Know-Nothing mob. Several people were injured on both sides, while the leader of the Know-Nothings, a man nicknamed "Violet," was killed in the heat of the battle. Two years later, Father Henry was commissioned to build Saint Lawrence O'Toole, replacing the rubble left by an 1864 tornado. The picture which appeared in Plate 42 of *Pictorial Saint Louis* was the third structure. The parish was closed in 1948.

Another Irish parish on the north side was Saint Patrick's, at Sixth and Biddle. It, too, was of Gothic design, 120 feet deep and 75 feet wide with a 190-foot spire. The main altar was Italian marble, "noted for its exquisite workmanship and one of the most costly in America." The parish had 15,000 members. The school was run by the Christian Brothers and the Sisters of Saint Joseph, but Compton did not include enrollment figures.

Saint Teresa of Avila was a relatively small parish of 400 located on Grand and Parsons. As yet it had no school. It was closed in 2003.

The oldest German parish in Saint Louis was Saint Mary of Victories at Third and Mulberry. It had episcopal roots, as the cornerstone was laid in 1843 by Bishop Andrew Blanc of New Orleans and consecrated by Bishop John Simon, later the Bishop of Buffalo. Its rectory was the residence of Vicar General Henry Mühlsiepen and Chancellor

Henry van Der Sanden. The school of 600 was conducted by the School Sisters of Notre Dame.

Saints Peter and Paul, "this magnificent structure," is "one of the most elaborate churches west of the Alleghenies." Its grounds ran the block of Allen Avenue between Seventh and Eighth Streets. Compton spoke of its "beauty and imposing grandeur," the rich flood of light through the tall stained glass windows under a vaulted roof seventy feet high. The church sat 3,000 and cost an estimated $150,000. The creator of this remarkable church was Father Franz Goller, whose name Compton misspelled as "Galler." The book mentioned a school of 1,200 children under the direction of eight School Sisters of Notre Dame and lay teachers.

At Ninth and Park was Saint Vincent's Church, "a massive brick edifice of the Roman style." It was unique in parochial governance, as it had a pastor for the English portion, Father Hennessy, and a pastor for the Germans, Father Uhland. The school also had two departments based on native tongue. The Christian Brothers taught the boys, and the Sisters of Saint Joseph taught the girls. The schools were intended to be bilingual, as classes were conducted in both English and German.

A Bohemian church, Saint John Nepomuk, was located at Soulard and Rosati. It was a Gothic brick edifice, 64 feet wide and 114 feet deep. The church sat 600 and cost an initial $30,000. The land was donated by a French priest, Father Renaud. The school of 300 was conducted by the School Sisters of Notre Dame.

Compton highlighted three other German parishes. Saint Joseph, at Eleventh and Biddle, had received a donation of land from Mrs. Anne Biddle. The church was built in two phases. The first part was the 110 feet by 55 feet structure, which proved to be too small for the congregation. In 1865 Father Joseph Weber, S. J. added to the church, making it 130 feet by 85 feet. The Romanesque building cost $123,000 and the main altar alone cost $10,000. Around 1,200 German Catholics attended Saint Joseph in 1875 and were served by a staff of four Jesuit priests.

The parish school for Saint Joseph's stood on Eleventh Street between Cass and O'Fallon, three buildings of three stories each. The school accommodated over 1,000 students and was conducted by the School Sisters of Notre Dame.

Saint Nicholas, on Twelfth and Christy, served German Catholics also. The church and grounds were assessed at $110,000 and the school at $24,000.

At Nineteenth and Monroe stood Saint Liborius Church, of brick Roman style architecture. The church stood 90 feet long and 60 feet wide and served nearly 500 families. Around 500 children attended Saint Liborius School, directed by the School Sisters of Notre Dame. The parish closed in 1992. The church was mothballed, while the school is a juvenile detention center, and the convent serves the Catholic Worker movement as Karen House.

Remarkably, one of the most impressive German parishes, Most Holy Trinity, was neglected entirely in Richard Compton's survey.

The final Catholic parish covered in Compton's work was Saint Elizabeth, at Franklin and Morgan (now Delmar). Compton noted, "It is a handsome little structure, Gothic, and of brick, and was for many years known as the Ashbury Methodist Church..."[138] The parish sponsored a school of 120 children, taught by secular teachers. The pastor was a Jesuit, Rev. Ignatius Pankan. Saint Elizabeth was closed in 1951, but was revived when Saint Engelbert on Schreve Avenue closed in 1994. The congregations of Saint Engelbert and Most Holy Rosary, at Margaretta and Clarence, were combined to form Saint Elizabeth, Mother of John the Baptist Parish, a predominately African-American Catholic parish.

Of the twenty-five parishes depicted in Richard Compton's *Pictorial Saint Louis,* the Old Cathedral, Saint John the Evangelist, Saint Francis Xavier (now at Grand and Lindell), Saint Mary of Victories, Saints Peter and Paul, Saint John Nepomuk, as a chapel of ease, Saint Joseph (the shrine), and Saint Nicholas continue to serve the Archdiocese of Saint Louis. Only Saint Bonaventure was closed in the nineteenth century. All the others closed in the turmoil of the 1960s and 1970s.

---

138   Richard J. Compton, *Pictorial St. Louis: A Topographical Survey in Perspective AD 1875.* 1876. P.123.

Father James Henry, no date. Archdiocese of St. Louis Archives and Records.

Father Henry Mühlsiepen (front, second from left) and Father Henry Van der Sanden (front, second from right) sit together at an unknown event. Fr. Mühlsiepen became Vicar-General for German, Bohemian, and Polish Catholics. Fr. Van der Sanden became Chancellor. Archdiocese of St. Louis Archives and Records.

Chapter Eleven

TURBULENT TIMES AND CREATIVE GROWTH

Pictorial St. Louis, the extraordinary book which included drawings of every street, building and tree in Saint Louis in 1876, was like a snapshot showing a mid-American city in full progress in growth and prosperity. What it could not show were the pools of anxiety, anger, poverty, and hopelessness seething just below the surface.

Two issues would dominate the last half of the 1870s in Saint Louis: the Great Divorce of City and County and the General Strike of 1877. Three causes are often given for the separation of the city from the county: infrastructure costs, tax inequities, and differing politics. Each deserves attention.

The paving of roads became a serious topic in the 1870s. From colonial times forward, the city had a bad reputation for impassable roads, particularly after a rain storm. Mud and animal feces churned up as wagons, horses, and people made their way down these streets, which had no sidewalks.

An insufficient answer was found with the quarrying of the bluffs above the riverfront. Doing so allowed for the city to expand a hundred yards or so closer to the levee, which led to the disastrous results of the great fire of 1849. This provided material with which to pave the streets, but the bluff limestone was of poor quality. Under any weight of a wagon or horse it pulverized, turning to dust in dry weather and to a gray goo when it rained. Called macadam, it was cheap and easy to lay but required sprinkling trucks to keep the dust down and demanded frequent repairs.

Geography and politics played into the decision of where to place the roads and how to maintain them. The center corridor was always prime real estate for the city. The three original blocks, Place des Armes, Laclède's homestead, and Place d'Eglise continued westward up to Broadway, then over the meadow to the Jefferson ridge, across the plain to the Grand ridge and, by the late nineteenth century, to the Skinker ridge, an area of fine neighborhoods and elegant homes. Business executives and office workers could live in this upscale region and quickly get downtown using the nickel trolleys.

Less successful were the wards south of Mill Creek. The dwellings of these wards were mainly compressed apartment housing that was not connected to the heart of the city except for Broadway (then Carondelet Street) and the Seventh Street streetcar.

Adding to the sense of inequity was the fact that the limestone used for south Saint Louis streets was of even poorer quality than much of the rest of the city, and had to be repaired or replaced every few months. Some south city streets rarely got sprinkled at all, while fashionable Lindell Boulevard received three sprinklings a day during dry weather.

The south side also had more difficult terrain to deal with. When Chippewa Street was laid, neighbors petitioned to have their streets, Missouri and Indiana, joined to it, only to find that the necessary grade for the two streets would be eight to ten feet higher than their property.[139]

The very idea of contemplating a road system beyond Skinker into the hinterlands of Saint Louis County was enough to cause nightmares.

And yet the road system paled in comparison to the challenges of drainage and sewers. Pierre Laclède's decision to place his village at the spot he chose was pure genius. It was strategically located on America's most important river, the Mississippi. It was within easy reach of the Missouri, the Illinois, the Kaskaskia, and the Meramec. Its bluffs made it immune to flooding. It was uninhabited, though the commercial partners, the Osage, were nearby. Its forests provided lumber and wild game. But it also had stagnant pools of water, creeks, and ravines which scarred the landscape, and it had sinkholes. Even the series of rises which ran parallel to the river impeded rainwater from escaping freely to the rivers.

As the population grew, human waste became an issue, accumulating in personal privies and cesspools. Violent storms would wash these out, carrying the vilest debris down gutters and into the rivers which surrounded Saint Louis on three sides.

The city street commissioner, Henry Kayser, thought the solution was to allow the naturally forming sinkholes to fill up and drain by way of underground fissures. He experimented with one prominent sinkhole at Ninth and Biddle. But the hole did not drain. Residents complained of the smell, dubbing the hole "Kayser's Lake," and noted "a very ugly body of water, which in the summer changed to a yellow-

---

139   Eric Sandweiss, "Paving St. Louis's Streets." *Common Fields: An Environmental History of St. Louis.* Saint Louis: Missouri Historical Society Press. P. 101.

green, and (which) emitted vapors freighted with chills, fever and death."[140]

After the 1849 cholera outbreak, the city council arranged for a twelve-foot main to be constructed to drain Kayser's Lake. The new commissioner, Samuel R. Curtis, put no faith in Kayser's fissure theory and began to construct the Biddle Street sewer, though it meant cutting a tunnel through the Broadway Avenue ridge, which proved to be forty feet of solid rock.

The development of a comprehensive sewer system introduced by an 1850 city ordinance was to prove to be a challenging engineering feat, but Saint Louisans could count themselves fortunate in comparison to their rival in Illinois. Unlike Saint Louis, with its series of rises parallel to the Mississippi River, Chicago sat on a plain of hard-packed clay which did not drain well. Human waste gathered in privy vaults, which leached into nearby shallow wells. The cholera epidemic of 1854 killed six percent of Chicago's population which, unlike Saint Louis, had no hospital. Waste made its way to the Chicago River, where it combined with the discard of tanneries, packing houses, and glue factories. The river was said to be "greasy to the touch."[141] Unlike Saint Louis, which even with its terrain complications tended to assist the flow of water and waste downhill to fast-flowing rivers, Chicago's river barely moved as it inched its way to Lake Michigan, where the river water mingled with the lake only to be sucked up into the intake pipes of the city's public waterworks.

Chicago's solution was a breathtaking engineering feat, literally raising the entire city by as much as ten feet to create a gravity flow that Saint Louis took for granted. It took George Mortimer Pullman and his crew twenty years, raising buildings one by one to increase the grade. Most remarkable was the raising of the Matteson House, a five-story structure. It took 1,200 men and 5,000 jack screws to accomplish the feat.

As monumental as this task was, the second solution was even more audacious: to reverse the flow of the Chicago River. The objective was to cause the Chicago River to flow from east to west into a canal linked to the Illinois River. This was achieved by Ellis S. Ches-

---

140   Scharf, History of St. Louis City and County, as cited in Katherine T. Corbett, "Politics of Sewers in St. Louis." Ibid. P. 111.
141   Donald L. Miller, *City of the Century: The Epic of Chicago and the Making of America.* New York: Simon & Schuster. 1996. P. 125.

brough when he deepened the bottom of the canal and installed powerful pumps at Bridgeport.

Saint Louis' engineering feat was the construction of the Mill Creek sewer, which extended over five miles and thirty blocks from the river toward Grand Avenue. The Mill Creek sewer and the Rock Branch sewer were connected to thirty-three miles of secondary sewers carrying waste and rainwater to the river.[142] West of Grand Avenue, where fashionable housing was going up, there were no public sewers. Instead, the developers built their own Pine Street sewer. Prior to that, the waste of the wealthy made its way to the River des Peres, giving it a bad reputation that persisted into the first half of the twentieth century.

As with the question of road construction, the question of sewer extension was not even entertained for the county.

One bright spot for sewer construction, as well as fire prevention, came with the settlement of a western region of the city called Cheltenham. The land had gone through many hands in Saint Louis history. It began as a 5,700-acre Spanish land grant to Charles Gratiot. By 1830, mountain man William Sublette owned much of it, and Derrick A. January owned the remainder. Sublette's land came into the possession of real estate genius Thomas Allen, who deeded it to an Englishman, William Wible. It was he who named the area Cheltenham, after his British birthplace.

Cheltenham did not remain an idyllic wilderness for long. Just before the Civil War, a kind of clay formed from loess was discovered there. That particular kind of clay would make the best brick and tile and pipe in the world. Immediately firms formed to take advantage of this Paleozoic treasure. Charles P. Chouteau organized the Evans and Howard Fire Brick Company and William Greenleaf Eliot, besides founding Washington University, came to own the Hydraulic Brick Company.

The brick, tile, and pipe industry attracted German miners, who were later overwhelmed by Italians from Lombardy and Sicily. Saint Louis brick built the cities of the Midwest plains. Saint Louis pipe answered their drainage and sewer needs, and Saint Louis tile roofs made cities safer from devastating fires.

As much as Saint Louisans refused to extend their expansive in-

---

142   Katherine T. Corbett, "Politics of Sewers in St. Louis." *Common Fields: An Environmental History of St. Louis.* Saint Louis: Missouri Historical Society Press. P. 118.

frastructure, which served 300,000 out into the county with a mere 30,000 residents, they chafed under the burden of a tax structure which they found inequitable. In 1867, the power to assess and collect taxes in the City of Saint Louis was given to the county court, as the city was part of Saint Louis County. The real reason rested in politics. The city population was quickly returning to the fold of the Democratic Party. In fact, in 1876, the Party would hold its national convention in Saint Louis. This shift displeased the Radical Republicans who controlled the Missouri legislature, and they bestowed taxation powers on the county court, which was stacked with fellow Radical Republicans. In 1869 the county collected nearly $2 million from city taxpayers, while the city government had to make do with fees and licenses which netted it a mere $300,000.[143]

Tempers flared, and at one point publisher Joseph Pulitzer got involved in a shooting at the state capitol in which a county officer was wounded. Pressure mounted and two separate paths to a solution were proposed. One called for the city to take over the county, in which the city limits would be extended to take in the entire county. Those who feared the expenses of infrastructure expansion opposed that path.

The alternative was total separation. This path was opposed by the county, and it could not win a majority of the Saint Louis legislators. Only in 1873, when the legislature was controlled by the Democratic Party, did the city have an opportunity to solve its taxation problems either through consolidation or separation. But city politics prevented a move. A mayoral election gave City Hall to Arthur Barret, who narrowly defeated a German independent named Henry Overstolz. But Barret died shortly after taking office. The Democrats put up a banker, James H. Britton, who also beat Overstolz in this second election. However, this time the vote was so fraudulently rigged that Overstolz demanded an investigation. After several months of inquiry and testimony, the city council awarded the election to Henry Overstolz. He would oversee the two key events of the late 1870s: the Great Divorce and the General Strike of 1877.

A board of thirteen elected freeholders was instructed to draw up a city charter which would separate the city from the county. They created a mayoral office which had a four-year term, but they failed to

---

143   James Neal Primm. *Lion of the Valley: St. Louis, Missouri, 1764-1980*. Saint Louis: Missouri Historical Society Press. 2010. P. 299.

win back the city's control of its own police department, lost during the opening days of the Civil War. The city boundaries were set just west of the Skinker rise, tripling the size of the city to just over sixty square miles.

The proposal was put on an August ballot and failed. Opponents included most of the county citizenry, the leadership of both political parties, and office holders who would see their positions disappear if the scheme were adopted. Proponents included the newspaper *Republican,* German newspapers, and business interests. A cry went up about foul play, and an investigation showed widespread fraud in the city vote. When the tainted ballots were discarded and three precincts were set aside as incapable of reform, the scheme and the charter both passed. The Great Divorce had happened. The Missouri Secretary of State ordered county officials to vacate their offices in the city, and the city assumed the whole of the county debt. The fate of the City of Saint Louis was sealed.

Henry Overstolz would soon have more to worry about than hard feelings on the part of county residents. Trouble was brewing on a national level. The uncontrolled growth of the post-Civil War era caused economic booms and busts, fueled by a lust for profits and followed by panics of doom. The Panic of 1873 was the worst. Capital had flowed into speculative projects from railroad schemes to new factories to mines and to family farms. Investors looked at success stories like that of Cyrus H. McCormick, whose simple idea of a reaper created a giant industry in which he sold over 40,000 reapers a year. Each reaper stimulated wheat production, doubling the acreage of production in just a few years. To advance sales, McCormick allowed farmers to put a down payment on a machine and to defer payments until they turned a profit. But the process led to overproduction, surplus, and falling prices for wheat.

On the high end of merchandizing, multi-millionaire Potter Palmer created a shopping experience especially for women of means, the Palmer House. The-six story department store featured parking spaces for carriages, satisfaction-guaranteed purchases, and even home delivery service. "Palmer's aim was to turn shopping, as it already was at Paris' Bon Marché, from a necessary weekly chore to a delightful daily pastime."[144]

---

144   Donald L. Miller, *City of the Century: The Epic of Chicago and the Making of America.* New York: Simon & Schuster. 1996. P. 140.

But the peace and pleasure of a visit to the Palmer House was in stark contrast to what the businessmen and bankers woke up to one day when they learned of the failure of New York's Jay Cooke and Company. The shock sucked into bankruptcy another 5,000 firms. Unemployment lines turned into riot zones in New York City.

The nation did not recover from the downturn of 1873. Overproduction drove prices down, and firms seeking to avoid bankruptcy attended to the one elastic expense they could control: wages. It was in the railroad industry that labor reaction was most severe. When Baltimore and Ohio Railroad cut wages ten percent and laid off workers, railroad workers who had already been living in stressful conditions for several years called for a strike. In July 1877, the company sought to hire substitutes but the strikers reacted with violence, beating up the new hires and destroying property.

Maryland's governor, John Lee Carroll, great grandson of Charles Carroll, signer of the Declaration of Independence, sent the state militia to Cumberland. When this failed to abate the labor violence, he called on President Rutherford B. Hayes to send in federal troops. Soldiers from Fort Henry arrived in Baltimore even as naval vessels entered the bay and landed marines. By August 1 the workers were subdued, though the population seethed under the heavy-handed acts of the government done on behalf of the railroad ownership.

In the Midwest events unfolded differently. On July 22, 1877, the threat of a railroad strike made its way to the yards of East Saint Louis. That day the strikers closed down all rail traffic, and in desperation the mayor of East Saint Louis deputized the strikers and gave them the task of protecting the peace and property. Surprisingly, the leadership of the strike took the task seriously, closing down taverns and enforcing law and order.

In Saint Louis, the strike was taken up by the Workingman's Party. This small socialist party of perhaps a thousand members had been organized in Philadelphia in the summer of 1876. It was dominated by German socialists, who made up over sixty percent of its membership and most of its leadership. Seizing on the unrest in the railroad industry, the socialists sought to broaden their range by bringing in other trade unions in sympathy with their fellow workers. There were perhaps two thousand workers in Saint Louis organized into some twenty-two trade unions, many of them German.[145] To broaden the appeal even further, the leadership of the Workingman's Party sought to recruit the thousands of unskilled Irish and African-American workers. These took to the streets, joined nationwide by as many as a million strikers from Baltimore to Pittsburgh and now, on July 23, to Saint Louis.

A mass meeting was held at Lucas Market, attended by at least five thousand people. Speakers whipped up the crowd with demands for an end to child labor and for an eight-hour day.

That day, a Monday, was followed by two days in which crowds of workers went from factories to bakeries to breweries and demanded that they close down. In fear, most did, and Saint Louis came under the grip of the first General Strike in American history.

Negotiations between Mayor Overstolz and strike leader Albert Currlin, conducted at City Hall and spoken in German, went nowhere. The newspaper *Republican*, a Democratic Party organ, demanded a stiff reaction calling for volunteers to form a citizen's militia to take back the city.

On the afternoon of July 25th, the first rift in the unity of the strikers appeared. It came along racial lines. A group of Black levee workers led a demonstration, but the German leadership of the Workingman's Party disassociated itself from the action. Thereafter, the German and Irish portion of the General Strike had nothing to do with the Black workers.

On Thursday the crowds grew so restive and radical that even the socialist leadership refused to take the podium. Just one day before, it seemed that Saint Louis was in the grip of a Midwest equivalent of the Paris Commune. Factory owners in Carondelet organized a rally to form a Committee of Public Safety, but it was overwhelmed when strikers attended and had sufficient numbers to elect one of their own as chairman. One angry orator hinted at a guillotine to dispatch opponents. Others wanted weapons and talked about seizing Four Courts, which housed the police department and jail. Some demanded a move on the Federal arsenal, evoking memories of the 1861 Camp Jackson affair.

It should be recalled that many of these strikers were Civil War veterans, hardened men and capable of using weapons if put in their hands.

---

145   Stephen L. McIntrye, "Communist Progress: The Workingman's Party and St. Louis Educational Politics, 1877-1878." *Missouri Historical Review*. October 2000. P. 25.

On Friday afternoon, civil authorities acted. Police cavalry sortied out of Four Courts to be joined by six hundred civilian militia under A. J. Smith, a Union Civil War general, and John S. Marmaduke, a Confederate Civil War figure. They were supported by some three hundred federal troops of the Twenty-Third Infantry, recently brought to the arsenal. The mayor's forces surged up the streets to Schuler Hall on Biddle Street and arrested seventy-three strikers there, as the leadership of the socialists fled into the woodwork. One militia man was injured by his own bayonet when he fell off a ledge. It was the only bloodshed in the General Strike of 1877.

Eventually, Currlin and the other leaders were arrested and put on trial, but as there was no violence and only minimal property damage, the cases were dismissed. Regardless, the Strike of 1877 had consequences beyond a labor dispute. It shook the Workingman's Party to its core. It split labor along racial lines. It drove a wedge between Irish Catholics and secularist Germans, and the next battlefield was to be found in the Saint Louis public schools.

On September 3, 1877, the Workingman's Party held a rally at Lucas Market, which attracted several thousand people. Speakers encouraged their listeners to vote in the upcoming school board election in October. The audience seemed to listen, as the socialists scored five wins of the twenty-eight city wards.

This election result came as a shock to William Torrey Harris, the superintendent of city schools. He was a strong opponent of the strike of the past summer and feared the ascension of socialists to the school board would derail his efforts to reform education and reverse the progress made to date.

The goal of Workingman's Party candidates was to bring educational resources to working-class children. They saw Harris' emphasis on building high schools as an elitist move to cater to the rich and middle class. Statistics seemed to bear this out: while half of all city public school children in grade schools were from working-class families, that number dwindled to twenty-one percent in the high schools. Even more so, only six percent of high school students came from families of unskilled workers.[146]

The socialists were critical of the high costs of high school buildings and of the hiring of expensive teachers from elite eastern univer-

---

146   Stephen L. McIntrye, "Communist Progress: The Workingman's Party and St. Louis Educational Politics, 1877-1878." *Missouri Historical Review*. October 2000. P. 27.

sities. They wanted the money to go to a different reform movement in education: kindergartens. Introduced by Saint Louisan Susan Blow in 1873, these schools were generally run by volunteers trained by Blow. The socialists wanted a kindergarten in every school, as well as gymnasiums and free textbooks. Only with these changes would children of working-class families have a chance to better themselves and maintain their health.

The socialists soon found they had new opposition, and not just from bourgeois interests behind William Torrey Harris. Many Catholic parishes had established schools. As it became clearer by the day that the general public refused to support sectarian education, the parochial schools which served the Irish and German working-class families could only survive and prosper by heroic sacrifice. Hundreds of sisters, brothers, and priests poured their lives into Catholic education, and families of modest means had to find a way to pay the tuition.

Opposition to the socialists, most of whom were German and from the skilled trades, came to coalesce around Irish Catholic Democrats. The Democratic Party in Saint Louis, led by ward bosses, formed a secret order called The Dark Lantern Society. It was dominated by the boss of bosses, Edward Butler, who manipulated affairs in the city's First Ward and made spoils money on a city horse-shoeing monopoly for his blacksmith shop, as well as a garbage removal monopoly for his brother-in-law.

The Dark Lantern Society purposely confused the political landscape by putting up so-called Workingman's Party candidates in clearly Democratic wards, thus infiltrating the German leadership with Irish candidates. This frustrated the socialists, who adamantly opposed any public funding of parochial schools.

Of the five Workingman's Party representatives elected to the school board in October 1877, two were Irishmen: John O'Connell and Thomas Mockler. The others were two Germans and an Englishman.

At the first board meeting, the five Workingman's Party representatives proposed that the city provide free textbooks to all city school pupils. The motion was defeated fifteen to nine. At the same February 12, 1878 meeting, Michael Glynn, a school director, presented a petition with thousands of signatures asking that Gaelic be introduced in the public schools. The German language had been introduced as early as 1864 to Saint Louis Public Schools, assumed as a maneuver to entice German Catholics to withdraw their children from parish schools.

Clearly the Gaelic proposal was not meant to draw Irish Catholic children to the public schools. It was meant to drive a stake into the heart of the Workingman's Party, to separate once and for all the Irish Catholic workers from the German secularists. And it worked. O'Connell and Mockler voted for the proposal; the other three Workingman's Party operatives broke party unity and voted against it. Now Irish board members joined the two Irish Workingman's Party members in questioning the teaching of German in the public schools.

Behind Michael Glynn's devious proposal, it seems, was the hand of Father James Henry. He was the founding pastor of Saint Lawrence O'Toole Parish on Fourteenth and O'Fallon. A native of County Caven, Ireland, Henry came to America and was ordained by Archbishop Peter Richard Kenrick on January 6, 1853. He had protected his first assignment, Saint Patrick's, from a Know-Nothing mob bent on burning down the church. He proved to be an indefatigable pastor, enlarging Saint Lawrence only to see it destroyed by a tornado. In the summer of 1865, he completed another church for Saint Lawrence by going from door to door begging for funds. He then added a school staffed by Sisters of Saint Joseph. Upon his death in 1891, Philadelphia's *Catholic Standard and Times* eulogized him, declaring, "Father Henry was known and beloved not only in his own diocese, but throughout the whole country. Every movement for the spread of religion and the advancement of his fellow countrymen had in him a zealous champion."[147]

It is probable that Father Henry was more than an innocent bystander in the language controversy that engulfed the Workingman's Party. He served as treasurer of the Irish Catholic Benevolent Union, which raised money for Catholic schools. He himself opened two parochial schools and raised money so poor Catholic children could go to those schools. The language controversy completely alienated the Irish-American workers from the socialists.

The Workingman's Party changed its name for the upcoming election and called itself the Socialist Labor Party. It fielded six candidates, five of whom were German. Only one was Irish and he favored dropping German language studies in the public schools. The Party did well in two wards, the Seventh and the Fourteenth, both predominately German. Michael Glynn, the man who started the language controversy with his petition to introduce Gaelic, won as a Democrat in

---

147   Rev. John Rothensteiner. *History of the Archdiocese of St. Louis. II* St. Louis: Blackwell Wielandy Co. 1928. P. 195.

the Fourth Ward. German secularists blamed their bad luck on the Jesuits, "the sons of darkness."[148] The intellectual elitism of the socialists now drove off Irish working-class voters even as they had previously driven off African-American workers, giving Father Henry the victory he sought.

Yet the late 1870s were not filled only with labor issues of the various classes and political issues of separation of city and county. The 1870s saw the creation of two major parks which would bless the landscape of Saint Louis. Henry Shaw donated land for Tower Grove Park in 1868 and adorned it with a statue of William Shakespeare ten years later. Nearby, Shaw built a country estate he named Tower Grove. He surrounded it with a seventy-five-acre garden designed and maintained by world-renowned botanist Dr. George Engelmann. Eventually, Shaw's estate would be bequeathed to the City of Saint Louis and become the Missouri Botanical Garden.

The second great park came from a land purchase by the city. For $800,000, a tract of nearly 1,400 acres was bought, which ran south of prestigious Lindell Boulevard from Kingshighway to Skinker Boulevard. All but three hundred acres were heavily forested; hence the name, Forest Park. The purchase was not without its critics, who thought it too far from the center of the city. Yet at its opening on June 24, 1876, Saint Louisans were delighted with its beauty. As the city moved further west the park proved less remote, and it provided the necessary fairgrounds for the Louisiana Purchase Exposition of 1904.

One week before the opening of Forest Park, Saint Louis newspapers were abuzz about another way to keep cool in the city's hot and humid summers: the invention of air conditioning. At the Goodyear Rubber Company at Fourth and Locust, a motor in the basement pumped cool air through tubes which were to run through the rooms on the higher elevations. The rather complicated design was meant to mimic the hot water boilers and radiators. Instead of pumping hot water or steam, this system delivered cool air from the basement. The system proved no match for a Saint Louis summer, and the idea was soon abandoned.

The next year, on November 22, 1877, Saint Louisans experienced another technological breakthrough, this time with commercial consequences. That evening a concert was scheduled. George Durant, a

---

148   Stephen L. McIntrye, "Communist Progress: The Workingman's Party and St. Louis Educational Politics, 1877-1878." *Missouri Historical Review.* October 2000. P. 40.

salesman for a new invention, the telephone, made arrangements for telephones to be installed in various parts of the city, including the residence of William Tecumseh Sherman. Another phone was installed in the concert hall. At the appointed time, connections were made and perhaps for the first time ever, a broadcast, via the telephone, was made. Besides astounding the crowds of listeners, the event familiarized hundreds with the telephone, a device previously found only in a few offices and even fewer homes.

Earlier in the month of November, the city hosted the Tom Thumb Company, an entertainment troupe of little people. Eleven months later, Saint Louisans entertained themselves with the creation of the Veiled Prophet Ball and Parade. The elite of Saint Louis dressed in their finest to receive the shadowy monarch from Khorassan. The entourage included a royal barge which was accompanied by brightly illuminated floats and scores of torchbearers marching on foot. The annual Agricultural and Mechanical Fair was held at the same time as the Veiled Prophet Ball and Parade, so thousands more visitors to the city were drawn to line the streets of Saint Louis.

At 8 P.M. the parade pulled up to the Merchant's Exchange Building. The Veiled Prophet entered the decorated trading floor of the exchange building, to be greeted by Saint Louis debutants. The annual event would have something for everyone: a spectacular parade and fireworks for the city's plebeians and a socialite's ball for the patricians.

In 1879, Saint Louis found itself host to many visitors, one famous and the others desperate. The famous guest, Walt Whitman, was the brother of the city water commissioner, Thomas Jefferson Whitman. Walt Whitman was already a famous poet in 1879. He stayed at Planter's House downtown and raved about the restaurant's food. He also found the western part of the city most commodious. That favorable critique was balanced by a complaint about the city's air, full of coal fumes and dust, no doubt raised by industry and from the macadam roads which plagued the city.

The other visitors arrived six month earlier than Whitman, and they kept on coming. Thousands of southern blacks decided over a period of several months to emigrate out of the South and move to Kansas.

The causes were many. Since emancipation, the plight of the former slaves had not improved considerably. Though they received the vote, could run for office, and feel some sense of security during Reconstruction, that era ended in 1877. Federal troops were withdrawn. State and local governments were rapidly returned to the Democratic Party, and vigilante organizations like the Ku Klux Klan were spreading terror at night. Economic doldrums and the rumor of free land in Kansas were all that was needed to spark the exodus. Between April and July of 1879, an estimated 15,000 to 20,000 southern Blacks made their way to Kansas.[149]

The hoax was a cruel fraud played upon these poor people, many of whom had spent their life savings to book passage on steamboats or trains to Saint Louis.

The first sign of a crisis came on March 11, 1879, when 280 Blacks arrived in Saint Louis on the steamer *Colorado*. They became known as "The Exodusters." By the end of the month, the number swelled to 1,400, soon depleted to one thousand, as four hundred had continued their journey to Kansas.

First to help the travelers were Saint Louis Black residents. Charleston H. Tandy took it upon himself to solicit aid from families and businesses. He prevailed on churches to provide shelter. Eventually, around eight hundred Exodusters found temporary shelter. A committee drawn from Black congregations aided them in continuing their journey west. A steamer was hired to take them as far as Kansas City. The *Joe Kinney* loaded some four hundred and fifty on board, most paying their own fare. Another one hundred and fifty were aided by churches. The Immigrant Relief Committee of the Colored Churches cared for over five thousand travelers, raising money from local citizens, both Black and white, as well as from wealthy donors in the East.

Even so, a dispute broke out in the committee over organization and finance. J. Milton Turner formed his own Colored Refugee Relief Board, which provided for immediate relief to be followed by transportation out west. Turner was well connected, as he had served on the Missouri Equal Rights League as early as 1865. Missouri Blacks had not been given the right to vote, but Turner and others worked closely with the Radical Republicans to try to gain the franchise which would only come in the ratification of the Fifteenth Amendment in 1870. Regardless, J. Milton Turner's contacts with powerful politicians aided his efforts.

Meanwhile, Charleston Taney tapped every means possible to aid

---

149   Suzanna M. Grenz, "The Exodusters of 1879: St. Louis and Kansas City Responds." *Missouri Historical Review*. Oct. 1978. P. 55.

the Exodusters. He called upon the Mullanphy Emigrant Relief Board, funded from the estate of Bryan Mullanphy. The response was that, according to the bylaws of the organization, the funds could help individual families but not colonies on the move. After a spirited debate the Board agreed to help families on a case-by-case basis, if they could show they had the financial means to settle in Kansas.

One Mullanphy board member was Mayor Henry Overstolz. While recognizing the horrible circumstances which southern Blacks had to endure, he favored aiding only those families which had $300 with which to settle in Kansas. As mayor he convinced the Board of Health to provide free medical attention to the travelers. But when the question arose about using the city's quarantine hospital as a temporary shelter for the Exodusters, the motion failed. The Saint Louis solution to the Exoduster crisis was to treat the worst cases with food and medical supplies and to move the thousands westward as quickly as possible. Even multimillionaire Jay Gould agreed to lend his Kansas Pacific Railroad to transport the immigrants free of charge.

A better reception was found in Kansas City, Missouri. Mayor George M. Shelly took a personal leadership role in addressing the needs of the immigrants. It was their own intransigence that hurt them. The Exodusters had fallen victim to "Kansas fever," a longing to settle down in Kansas and in no other place. When efforts were made to find temporary work for the men to provide for their families, most refused the stigma of working, even as a free man, in a former slave state.

Eventually, by the summer of 1879, it became widely known throughout the South that the Kansas promise was a fraud. "Kansas fever" broke and no more southern Blacks joined the migration.

Saint Louis proved to be an unwilling host to thousands of Blacks seeking a better life. Its answer was to give them immediate assistance and then to move them out. The response spoke volumes about race relations in 1870s Saint Louis. J. Milton Turner relied heavily on the Republican Party to advance the cause of Blacks in Saint Louis, but he let it be known that the Black vote would not be taken for granted. Black Democratic clubs existed in at least two wards. Black civil rights in Saint Louis were observed, but not universally. The city hospital admitted Black patients, but in a segregated ward. Blacks were welcomed at the public libraries, but not at swimming pools or tennis courts. Hotels and restaurants were closed to Black patrons, but in a limited way higher education was open to Black students. In

1889, Walter M. Farmer graduated from Washington University's Law School, even as Albert Burgess, a graduate of the University of Michigan Law School, was admitted to the Saint Louis bar in 1877. Other Black students were admitted to Washington University, though in a very limited number.[150]

Some Black students attended Christian Brothers College on Kingshighway. Their presence only became an issue at the time of their graduation. When it became known that two African-American students would take part in the graduation ceremonies, several white families threatened to boycott the event. The college president, Brother Paulian, responded by offering to mail the diplomas to the white students who refused to attend. The president's strong stance caused the opposition to collapse, and the graduation ceremony took place without a hitch.

Much of the progress of Black Catholics at Saint Elizabeth's Parish came from the work of the Oblate Sisters as well as the longtime pastor, Father Ignatius Panken, S. J., who served from 1872 to 1894. Along with his duties as pastor, Father Panken was Archbishop Kenrick's spiritual director during these years.

The 1870s closed in Saint Louis with a flourish. Two new parishes were established, Saint Cronin's in 1878 on the near south side, for the Irish, and Saint John's in Bismarck, Missouri. The first half of the 1880s would see nine more parishes open in the Saint Louis area, most of them rural, even as other parishes opened to serve the growing Catholic population throughout the Archdiocese. Besides opening parishes, Saint Louis proved to be at the heart of Catholic evangelization in America's heartland in another impressive way. It was, as historian Father Barnaby Faherty called it, "a cradle of bishops."[151] When Archbishop Kenrick left Saint Louis to attend the Third Plenary Council of Baltimore, he took with him Father Franz Goller, pastor of Saints Peter and Paul Church, and Father Thomas Bonacum. The Archbishop certainly did not know that he was about to lose the latter, who would be made the founding bishop of Lincoln, Nebraska. He became one among many.

First to be separated from Saint Louis was the diocese of Dubuque, created after the Third Provincial Council of Baltimore in 1837. Before

---

150   L. O. Christensen. *Missouri Historical Review*. Jan. 1984. P. 134.
151   William Barnaby Faherty, S. J. *Dream By The River: Two Centuries of Saint Louis Catholicism: 1766 – 1967.* Saint Louis: Piraeus Publishers. 1973. P. 108.

that time, the region was ministered to by Jesuit Father Charles Van Quickenborne. He stayed only one year, 1833, to organize Irish immigrants into a fledgling Catholic community. Two years later, Dominican Father Samuel Mazzuchelli arrived to renew the work. Mathias Loras was named the first bishop of Dubuque. He recruited Fathers Joseph Cretin and Anthony Pelamourges to join him, as well as four French seminarians. When they arrived at their diocese, which included all of Iowa, Wisconsin, and part of Minnesota, they found only one priest there, Father Mazzuchelli. Bishop Loras quickly ordained the four seminarians, though three of them would abandon him to return to France.

Bishop Loras, a native of France and a friend of John Vianney, a seminary student of Ambrose Maréchal, future bishop of New York, was a tireless worker. He bought land west of Dubuque for a mere $1.25 an acre and sold it at a profit to put his diocese on firm financial footing. He invited the Sisters of Charity (BVM) to his diocese and convinced Irish monks to found a monastery at New Melleray, populated by twenty-two monks. Soon Loras could count on thirty-eight priests, freeing up two priests to serve as missionaries to Indians in Minnesota.

When his health failed, Bishop Loras received help from Trappist monk Clement Smyth, who was named his coadjutor. After Smyth became the second bishop of Dubuque, he brought the Saint Vincent de Paul Society to his diocese and established schools under the leadership of the Visitation nuns and the School Sisters of Notre Dame.

Two controversies rocked the diocese in its early years. The first had to do with ethnic jealousy. When Bishop Loras founded Holy Trinity Parish for the Germans of Dubuque in 1849, the Irish complained until he built Saint Patrick's Church. However, unlike Holy Trinity, the Irish parish was a dependency on the cathedral of Saint Raphael. This practice was called "succursal" churches, a common practice throughout the United States. In a huff, the Irish refused to support their parish through a pew tax. Bishop Loras threatened to remove the priest from the parish and, with that, the pastor sided with his congregation against his bishop. In the end, a reconciliation took place and eventually Saint Patrick became a full-fledged parish.

The second controversy took place under Bishop Smyth. He was one of the few American bishops who spoke forcefully against slavery in the days leading up to the Civil War. He was a strong advocate for the Union when war came and an open critic of his fellow bishops for not openly opposing slavery.

When Bishop Smyth died in 1865, Saint Louis made another contribution to the Dubuque diocese. Father John Hennessy was named the third bishop of the diocese. He had served as rector at the theological seminary in Carondelet. Bishop Hennessy served thirty-four years as bishop of Dubuque, during which time he caused three motherhouses of sisters to come to Dubuque. In 1879 he attracted the Sisters of Mercy to build Saint Joseph Hospital and found Loras College. He worked tirelessly for Catholic education and came to see one hundred and thirty-five parish schools founded, serving over 16,000 children. As his old Archbishop was nearing death in Saint Louis, Hennessy himself was named Archbishop of Dubuque in 1891. He could boast of an Archdiocese with 203 priests and nearly 615 religious sisters.

But Hennessy's tenure as bishop of Dubuque was not without its conflicts and controversies. Early on, he picked a fight with the principal of a local public school. Orentes A. Brownson, Jr., the son of the prolific author convert, ran a school that was Catholic in all but name. Ten of his twelve teachers were Catholic and most of the student body was Irish Catholic. Bishop Hennessy denied sacraments to the children and forbad the sisters from teaching them catechism. He was the most strident of any American bishop regarding parochial education.

Even more, Bishop Hennessy soured his relationship with a congregation of teaching sisters, the BVMs. When their superior, Sister Gonzago McCloskey, inherited an annuity from her brother's estate, the bishop demanded that it go to him instead. Sister Gonzago refused and the bishop ordered her out of the city. He then ordered the whole community to leave Saint Raphael's Parish, where they had been teaching since their invitation by Bishop Loras. Hennessy filled the gap by inviting Visitation nuns to take their place.

But most troubling of all were the accusations that Bishop Hennessy used diocesan funds for his own purposes. One historian intimated that the bishop had lavished funds on his brother, his sister, and two nieces, who later came to live with him in his episcopal residence. He supported the Roman education of a nephew who later was ordained a priest and, at the time of his death in 1900, had an estate worth over a million dollars.[152]

The Archdiocese of Saint Louis made remarkable contributions to

---

152   M. Jane Coogan. "Dubuque's First Archbishop: The Image and the Man." *Records of the American Catholic Historical Society of Philadelphia.* March-December 1981. P. 83.

Chicago as well. As noted earlier, the first priest to serve in Chicago, Father John St. Cyr, was sent there by Bishop Rosati in 1833. The first bishop of Chicago was an Irishman, William Quarter. The second was a Jesuit brought from Saint Louis, James Oliver Van de Velde. He had been part of the Belgian band recruited by Father Nerinckx in his clandestine visit to Europe. Van de Velde built on the early foundations of Bishop Quarter and added an orphanage and a hospital run by the Mercy Sisters. When he became ill, Van de Velde was transferred to the Diocese of Natchez for a more moderate climate, but unfortunately he died there two years later, of yellow fever.

The third bishop of Chicago had Saint Louis roots also. Bishop Kenrick had recruited Anthony O'Regan to be rector of the diocesan seminary. He held this post for a number of years and seemed perfectly happy. When Chicago became vacant, O'Regan refused the episcopal honor offered him. Over time he yielded to considerable pressure. Peter Richard was reluctant to lose him and had to be urged by his brother Francis Patrick, Archbishop of Baltimore.

O'Regan was consecrated on July 25, 1854 in the Cathedral in Saint Louis. But Chicago proved to be a bad fit for him. He quarreled with his clergy, and in less than three years went to Rome to tender his resignation. Bishop O'Regan never returned to America, but died in London in 1866.

The fourth bishop of Chicago was also a Saint Louisan, James Duggan. Duggan was born in Ireland, had studied at Maynooth outside of Dublin, Archbishop Kenrick's alma mater, and had come to Saint Louis to be ordained a priest of the Archdiocese. During the ten years he was in Saint Louis, he served one year as interim rector of the diocesan seminary while Peter Richard Kenrick waited for Father O'Regan to become free to take the rector-presidency.

In 1857, James Duggan was consecrated bishop and made Archbishop Kenrick's coadjutor. He was then shipped off to Chicago as administrator when Bishop O'Regan left. In a letter to Peter Richard, his brother Francis Patrick urged swift, clear action: "The matter is urgent, so as not to let the diocese of Chicago go headlong to ruin."[153] In early January 1859, Rome approved of Bishop Duggan as Ordinary of Chicago.

At first things went very smoothly. Parish schools began to sprout

---

153   Rev. John Rothensteiner. *History of the Archdiocese of St. Louis. II* St. Louis: Blackwell Wielandy Co. 1928. P. 129.

up. The Benedictines, Redemptorists, and Religious of the Sacred Heart came to Chicago, as did the Sisters of the Good Shepherd. Five parishes were erected. Duggan chose wisely priests of high caliber for his administration.

But upon Bishop Duggan's return from the Second Plenary Council of Baltimore in 1866, his erratic behavior caught everyone's attention. On the advice of friends, he took treatment at Carlsbad in Germany. It did not work. When Bishop Duggan returned to Chicago, he quarreled violently with his clergy and withdrew faculties from several of them. In April 1869 the bishop was removed to an asylum in Saint Louis, where he lingered for nearly twenty years, bereft of his senses.

Chicago's fifth bishop did not have Saint Louis roots. He had been chancellor of the other Kenrick Archdiocese, Baltimore. Bishop Thomas Foley arrived in his see on March 10, 1870. Nineteen months later the great Chicago Fire of 1871 gutted the city.

Only one inch of rain had fallen since July. The "City of Wood" was completely parched. Even the tar-paper roofs bubbled under the unusual heat and the blistering prairie winds from the northwest. The city of over 300,000 was protected by 185 firefighters and seventeen steam engines drawn by teams of horses. Both men and horses were exhausted on October 8, having just battled a seventeen-hour blaze.[154]

The diocese of Chicago lost seven churches with schools and rectories in the Great Fire. Fireproof buildings replaced the tinderbox structures. Dioceses around the United States sent aid. More religious congregations came to Chicago: the Franciscans, the Servites, Resurrectionists, and Vincentians. Bishop Foley erected twenty-five new churches, seven academies, and several more institutions before his death in 1879. Even with the early separation of southern Illinois into the diocese of Quincy and later Alton, and the establishment of the diocese of Peoria in 1872, the diocese of Chicago boasted of three hundred parishes served by over two hundred priests.

Bishop Foley was succeeded by Bishop Patrick Feehan of Nashville, Tennessee. Here was yet another Saint Louis connection. Feehan left Ireland, an alumnus of Maynooth, to be ordained in Saint Louis by Archbishop Kenrick in 1852. He replaced O'Regan as rector of the seminary when the latter went to Chicago as bishop. Feehan later served as pastor of Saint Michael's on the near north side and as pastor of Immaculate Conception before being named Bishop of Nash-

---

154   Donald L. Miller. *City of the Century.* P. 145.

ville. In 1880, Chicago was elevated to the honor of becoming an Archdiocese. At the time of his death in 1902, Archbishop Feehan counted a presbyterate of 538 priests serving 298 parishes.

During the lifetime of Archbishop Peter Richard Kenrick, Saint Louis was a cradle of bishops, as we have witnessed in Dubuque and Chicago. Saint Louis also provided four founding bishops – Green Bay in 1868, Kansas City, Kansas in 1877, Wichita in 1887, and Lincoln that same year.

Other bishops had Saint Louis connections, though some were brief and tenuous. In 1847, John Timon, C. M. was named bishop of Buffalo, New York and shepherded his diocese through the Civil War, raising the federal flag over his episcopal residence while refusing to fly it over his cathedral. Jesuit John Baptist Miège was named administrator in 1851 of the Vicariate Apostolic of the Indian Territories and Father James Whelan became coadjutor of Nashville in 1859. He was succeeded by Patrick Feehan, who later became Archbishop of Chicago.

Patrick J. Ryan became coadjutor of Saint Louis for Archbishop Kenrick, but was later made Archbishop of Philadelphia. Prior to that, John Hogan was made bishop of Saint Joseph, Missouri (later Kansas City-Saint Joseph) in 1868. Michael Domenec, C. M. educated at Saint Mary's of the Barrens, became bishop of Pittsburgh in 1860; Stephan Ryan, C. M., also a Saint Mary's alumnus, was made bishop of Buffalo in 1868. John Odin, C. M. became Vicar Apostolic for Texas and later was named Archbishop of New Orleans, shepherding that see through the terrible years of the Civil War. The bishop of Monterey, California and Los Angeles was Thaddeus Amat, C. M., who had a brief encounter with Saint Louis.[155]

Father Joseph Melcher, who had recruited forty seminarians and priests from Germany and the Ursuline Sisters from Hungary, was named founding Bishop of Green Bay in 1868. He had come to Saint Louis at the invitation of Bishop Joseph Rosati and was sent by Bishop Kenrick to create a parish in Mattis, south of the city. There he was for-

---

155   Historians have mistakenly claimed other bishops for Saint Louis, but this record should show that the following had no Saint Louis connection: John McGill of Richmond, 1850; Clement Smyth of Dubuque, 1857; George Carrell, S. J. of Covington, Kentucky, 1853; Thomas Grace, O. P. of Saint Paul and James O'Gorman, Vicar Apostolic of Nebraska.

gotten, an intellect of high quality and a former chaplain to a European court, until Kenrick needed a theological expert, a *peritus*, to attend a Baltimore Council with him. Melcher served as pastor of Saint Mary of Victories Parish and was Vicar General for the German-language part of the Archdiocese of Saint Louis.

When Bishop Melcher arrived in Green Bay, he found only a small wooden church as his cathedral. Its formal name was Annunciation of the Blessed Virgin Mary, but locals simply called it "The German Church." A truly beautiful cathedral would have to wait for a later bishop, Francis Xavier Krautbauer. Melcher busied himself with founding parishes and inviting religious communities and missionary priests to his diocese. These included the Servite Fathers, who came in 1870, and the Sisters of Saint Felix.

During his time as Bishop of Green Bay, Bishop Joseph Melcher embroiled himself in two controversies. The first landed him in civil court due to his support of one of the priests he had recruited from Poland.

Father Joseph Dabrouski was from the region around Lublin. His father died when he was twelve but his mother saw to his education. After studies in Lublin, Dabrouski studied mathematics at the University of Warsaw. There he became involved in the 1863 uprising against the Russian Tsar. Wounded in battle and with a price on his head, Dabrouski fled first to Dresden, Germany, then to Switzerland and finally to Rome. He studied at the Collegium Polonicum and was ordained in 1869. Dabrouski met Bishop Melcher, who was attending the Vatican Council, and was recruited to come to Green Bay to serve the growing Polish immigrant population.

In his farewell visit to his mother, Father Dabrouski met the Sisters of Saint Felix, and with the encouragement of Bishop Melcher, invited them to come to Green Bay.

After spending a few months in Milwaukee, Father Dabrouski was invited to become the pastor at "Poland Corner," a small community of Irish, German, and Polish immigrants. The young priest found that Poland Corner was dominated by saloon keepers, and he vigorously preached against the abuses these men encouraged.

Tensions became so severe that Father Dabrouski and several parishioners dismantled their little church and rebuilt it two miles away on twenty acres donated for that purpose. He called the place Polonia. As he continued to rail against the saloon keepers from his new location, the community continued to be in turmoil. In 1872, the tavern owners struck back by suing the priest and Bishop Melcher, who supported him. The case eventually made its way to the Wisconsin Supreme Court, wherein the bishop and priest prevailed.

Melcher's second controversy had to do with a mystic in his diocese. A lay woman who styled herself Sister Adele claimed to have witnessed apparitions of the Blessed Virgin Mary. Marie Adele Joseph Brise was brought to America by her Belgian parents, who purchased a 240-acre farm near Red River, Wisconsin. While working on the farm at the age of twenty-eight, Adele believed the Blessed Virgin appeared to her, standing between two trees. The following Sunday Adele saw a second apparition. This time Mary told her to teach catechism to children.

Adele donned a religious habit and invited several local women to join her "Sisters of Good Help." In 1859 she built a small chapel, a convent, and a school, called Saint Mary's Academy. Adele's reputation grew due to her piety and her zeal for teaching children the elements of their faith. She also seemed to have had other mystical powers. The day of the Great Chicago Fire, a similar conflagration occurred near Green Bay; it was called the Peshtigo Fire. Acre after acre was consumed and local people fled to Sister Adele. She took a crucifix and walked out to the fire. People who witnessed it swore she turned back the blaze singlehandedly. She was also credited with several cures.

With time, the Shrine of Our Lady of Good Help drew unwanted attention. As pilgrims streamed there, vendors set up stands to sell food and beer and trinkets. Sister Adele was powerless to stop them, but Bishop Melcher was alarmed and become involved. Without a full inquiry, he ordered the convent and the school closed. An interdict was placed on the chapel, and Adele was threatened with excommunication if she so much as spoke about her apparitions. The bishop ordered Adele to lock up her buildings and bring him the keys.

This Adele obediently did, but reminded the bishop that without the school the children would not be instructed in the Faith, thus endangering their immortal souls. Bishop Melcher was so moved by Adele's plea that he restored her and her school, where she continued her work until her death in 1896. After an investigation into the authenticity of the apparitions, Bishop David Ricken declared them authentic in December 2010. Bishop Melcher's reconsideration proved correct.

A second Saint Louis priest to become a founding bishop was John Hogan. In 1868, he arrived in Saint Joseph to find his little "cathedral" in sore need of repair. A nearby creek regularly flooded the structure, and wild pigs made it their home. Hogan once exclaimed, "We should give the pigs a prize for church attendance." Eventually, a worthy church was erected.

Nine years later, as Kansas City grew due to the railroad, and a railroad bridge was spanned across the Missouri River, Rome created the diocese of Kansas City and made Bishop Hogan its founding bishop in 1880. For thirteen years he also administered Saint Joseph, until the two dioceses were merged.

Further west, Saint Louis priest John Joseph Hennessy became the first bishop of Wichita, Kansas in 1887. He replaced Father James O'Reilly of Topeka who had been named bishop but died before his consecration.

Hennessy was brought to America by his parents at the age of three. He attended Saint Louis Cathedral School and Christian Brothers College before entering theological studies at the Salesianum in Milwaukee. He was ordained at the age of twenty-two, requiring a special papal dispensation because of his youth.

Archbishop Kenrick sent Hennessy to Iron Mountain as pastor of a parish which stretched all the way to the Arkansas border. There he built six churches for his widely dispersed Catholic communities. Hennessy founded a convent at Arcadia in 1877 for the Ursuline nuns and founded the Catholic Railroad Men's Benevolent Union. In 1878, his acquaintance with the Christian Brothers was renewed when he became procurator of the Catholic Protectory for Boys in Glencoe, Missouri, later the provincial motherhouse of the province as well as the formation house. For eight years, Hennessy served as *de facto* pastor of Saint John the Evangelist Parish, for all intents and purposes, Archbishop Kenrick's co-cathedral. He proved to be indefatigable. He was editor of the *Saint Louis Youth Magazine*, the secretary of the Saint Louis Orphan Board, spiritual director for the Saint Vincent de Paul Society, and treasurer of the Archdiocesan clergy fund.

At Wichita, Bishop Hennessy brought the same zeal and passion for work. There he found only 8,000 Catholics in his diocese. The future looked bleak. There were only three churches in the diocese and many people were leaving Kansas, moving south to the Indian Territory (later Oklahoma) to escape repeated droughts. Despite setbacks, Bishop Hennessy soldiered on and eventually erected a fine cathedral, which was dedicated by Cardinal James Gibbons in 1912. Bishop Hennessy died in 1920 at the age of seventy-one.

The same year John Joseph Hennessy was made bishop of Wichita, Father Thomas Bonacum founded the diocese of Lincoln, Nebraska. He too had been brought to Saint Louis as a child from County Tipperary, Ireland. He studied at Saint Vincent College in Cape Girardeau and finished studies at the University of Würtsburg, Germany. After his ordination, Father Bonacum served briefly at Saint Peter's Parish in Gravois, later Kirkwood. For three years he was pastor of the small parish in Indian Creek; he later spent three years at Cuba, then three years at Rolla. It was his work at the Third Plenary Council of Baltimore in 1883 that won him the admiration of the American bishops. Thereafter, Father Bonacum was named founding bishop of Lincoln at the age of forty.

The one controversy Bishop Bonacum engaged in during his twenty-three years as bishop had to do with prohibition. Lincoln had a strong lobby attempting to limit and, if possible, prohibit alcoholic beverages. Two organizations were most active, the Anti-Saloon League and the Women's Christian Temperance Union. But the controversy split along religious, ethnic, and social class lines. "The Dries" were church-goers, mainly Baptist, Methodist, Presbyterian, and Congregationalist. "The Wets" were also church-goers, mainly Catholic, Lutheran, and Greek and Russian Orthodox.

"The Dries" tended to be old-stock Americans, while "The Wets" were recent arrivals: Irish, German, Czech, Greek, and Russian.

"The Dries" saw "The Wets" as undermining traditional American values, as many of the prohibitionists hailed from the more affluent parts of society: owners of businesses and commercial leaders of Lincoln. They had no idea of the role a public house played in the ethnic communities, a place of socializing, a place where drinking beer or wine or enjoying a shot of spirits was part of the overall dining experience.

Bishop Bonacum stepped into the issue by writing an open letter to Governor Ashton Shallenberger in 1919. He proposed a "daylight law" in which alcoholic beverages could be sold during the hours of daylight. This, he hoped, would appease "The Dries" while curbing the abuses of "The Wets." Eventually, his daylight idea caught on. The city of Lincoln passed such an ordinance and it later became the template for a state law. Bishop Thomas Bonacum died in 1911 at the age of sixty-four.

As much of the 1870s seemed like turbulent yet creative times with the City-County divorce, the General Strike of 1877, contested elections for school boards, and issues of language and ethnicity, the next decade was even more creative, with the founding of many parishes, and also turbulent, with the renewed questions of language and assimilation of large waves of immigrants in America.

Bishop John Hennessy of the Diocese of Dubuque. Archives of the Archdiocese of Dubuque.

Chapter Twelve

MORE PARISHES AND MORE LANGUAGES

In the four years prior to Archbishop Kenrick's attending the Third Baltimore Council, there was a wave of parish founding, mainly in rural areas. In 1880 Holy Cross was founded in Cuba, Missouri, though it would not have a resident pastor for nearly forty-four years. Later the parish opened a school in 1928, the first Catholic school between Pacific and Springfield.

1880 also saw the founding of Sacred Heart in Bevier, a mission of Immaculate Conception in Macon. It remained a small Catholic enclave until 1890, when Italian immigrants came to work in the nearby coal mines.

Closer to Saint Louis was the founding of Immaculate Conception in Dardenne Prairie. The area had been settled by French Canadians prior to the Louisiana Purchase and named after a founding family. By the 1820s, Virginians and Kentuckians, many of them Catholic, moved along the creek, mainly on the western side. As the population grew, new parishes were established: Saint Paul in 1854, Old Monroe in 1867, O'Fallon in 1872, and Cottleville in 1880, as well as Immaculate Conception in the village of Dardenne.

That same year, 1880, Father John Nordmeyer founded Saint Mary's Church in Moselle, Franklin County. Father Nordmeyer was a native of Osnabruck, Germany, as was the pastor of nearby Neier, Father Herman Nieters. These parishes served the needs of the German farmers of the region; many of them, like Saint Anthony in Sullivan, Holy Martyrs of Japan in Japan, Holy Trinity in Bean, and Immaculate Conception in Owensville, waited for many years to get a resident priest.

In 1881, Father David Phelan founded Saints John and James in Ferguson. The first church was dedicated by Bishop Ryan and was the spiritual home of ten Catholic families. In 1882, the Fathers of the Precious Blood came to Sedalia to found Sacred Heart Church, serving German Catholics who had been attending Saint Vincent's in Sedalia. Shortly after that, the Sisters of the Precious Blood arrived from Ohio to open a school.

Meanwhile in Saint Louis, the non-German Catholics who had been attending Saint Anthony's petitioned to establish their own parish, Saint Thomas of Aquinas. The next year Rev. John J. Hennessy, the future founding bishop of the Wichita diocese, laid the cornerstone. The founding pastor, Father David Doherty, stayed one year minus a day. His successor, Father Martin Brennan, built a rectory and a school in his six and a half years there.

In 1883, two more parishes were established, Saint Theodore in Flint Hill and Our Lady of Sorrows in Mary's Home, south of Jefferson City. Saint Theodore was a mission parish for the next twelve years, the tiny community assembling for Mass in a wood structure served by priests from nearby parishes. At Mary's Home, the little German community was brought together by the pastor of Saint Elizabeth, Father Cosmos Seeberger, a Precious Blood Father. Each week he crossed the Osage River to offer Mass in a small frame church.

One Sunday, Father Seeberger heard parishioners refer to the village as Morgan, after the owner of the local tavern who had secured a post office for the people. The priest was enraged and denounced the designation from the pulpit, insisting that the honor of the town's name should go to the Blessed Virgin Mary. The idea stuck and people began calling the village Mary's Home.

A school was added in 1889, and after a disastrous fire destroyed the church in 1907, local Catholic farmers searched their land for stone and erected a fine white stone church, which stands today.

Also in 1883, Polish Catholics living in Krakow left Saint Gertrude Parish to found Saint Anne in the tiny village of Clover Bottom. The migration tells a tale of ethnic solidarity. Poles who had settled in Washington, Missouri, found themselves overwhelmed by Germans moving into the region. So they founded their own parish five miles south of Washington. They named the village Krakow. There they built a small church and a school. Because they had no resident priest, the people had to settle for a Jesuit who would visit from Washington on weekdays. Eventually Father Alexander Mathauschek, S. J. was assigned to the Poles of Krakow. The priest served the community for eleven years, except for 1886, when he was brought back to Washington. His lasting legacy was a fine church building. By then the Jesuits left the area entirely, turning over Washington to the Franciscans and Krakow to the Archdiocese.

By then the Poles were again overwhelmed by Germans. Their pastors had names like Rimmele, Niederkorn, Keller, and Fugal: far too

German for Polish tastes. That is what prompted twenty Polish families to found Saint Anne in Clover Bottom. By 1900, Saint Anne had a church and a school and a Franciscan pastor, Father Dominic Czeck. Even so, Germans began moving in around Clover Bottom, too, and the Polish founding families found themselves outnumbered by thirty German families.

In 1884, Saint Patrick's was established in Clarence, not far from Macon. It served both German and Irish immigrants in the area. Further east in Monroe City, Holy Rosary Parish was founded to serve the English and Irish Catholics there. As in so many instances, Holy Rosary would not have a resident priest for seventeen years.

In the four years from 1880 to 1884, the Archdiocese opened at least seventeen parishes; many of them served the spiritual needs of ethnic groups: German, Irish, Polish, and old-stock English Catholics from Maryland, Virginia, and Kentucky. In the previous decade over a million and a half immigrants had come to America, mainly from England, Ireland, and Germany. In the 1880s, that number nearly doubled to 2.7 million, plus another 900,000 from Italy, Austria-Hungary, and Russia.

One response to an inquiry of a Rhinelander shows the cause for so many coming from Germany. An officer of the *St. Raphaelsverein* asked the man in Hamburg and got this mix of economic and religious freedom motivation:

My landlord gave us free lodging and 23- 30 pfennig a day for wages. For this my whole family had to labor on Sundays as well as weekdays. We were obliged to do our own chores during free hours and on Sunday afternoons. If we asked permission to go to Church on Sunday, then the man abused us ... every time and said: "You won't always need to be running after the priest if you find yourselves in the alms house." And so I am going to America. My acquaintances write from there that they have such good conditions, and on Sundays as many as wish to may go to Church. My children shall not imitate my slavery.[156]

Bismarck's persecution of Catholics ended in 1878, but the aftermath of the *Kulturkampf* remained. These immigrants arrived at ports along the eastern seaboard or in New Orleans. But most did not stay there. They flooded into the "German Triangle": Saint Louis, Cincinna-

---

156   St. Raphael's Blatt, I (Jan. 1886), p. 7 as cited in Colman J. Barry, O.S.B. *The Catholic Church and German Americans*. Milwaukee: The Bruce Publishing Company. 1952. P. 7.

ti, and Milwaukee. Many of these new immigrants brought with them the scars of the *Kulturkampf.* Imperial officials had accused them of being unpatriotic because they were Catholic. Their reaction was to emphasize their love of fatherland as well as their love of the Catholic faith. Thus, when they came to America, these Germans had a strong blend of fatherland and Catholicity. Many feared that to lose one would be to lose the other.

This apprehension was lost on English-speaking American Catholics generally. Since most did not read or speak German, they were unaware of the assault on German Catholics by German socialists and free-thinkers who had come to America after the 1848 revolution. Indeed, the inviting voice of German Lutherans was always present, too.

Advice even came from the king of Bavaria, Ludwig. When he endowed a missionary effort for sisters to come to America, he warned them, "I shall not forget you, but stay German, German! Do not become English."[157]

This advice ran contrary to many American bishops, who wanted to Americanize their Catholic immigrants as quickly as possible. History also played a role in their attitudes. They had experienced the terrible years of nativist attacks on the Church and its institutions. Even in Catholic Saint Louis there had been an attempt to torch at least one church, and a Know-Nothing mob forced the closure of Saint Louis University's medical school for over a half century. Would this large influx of Catholic immigrants resurrect the demon xenophobia?

These bishops who strove for quick Americanization included the militant John Ireland of Saint Paul, John Keane of Dubuque, John Hughes of New York, Michael O'Connor, Dennis O'Connell, third Archbishop of Milwaukee and, most importantly, Cardinal James Gibbons of Baltimore. Their suspicions were heightened all the more after a series of incidents which seemed to indicate an aggressive attitude on the part of the Germans.

The first incident came to be called the Abbelen Affair. Archbishop John M. Henni was nearing old age and sought to have a coadjutor named, one who could become the next Archbishop of Milwaukee, the northernmost point of the German Triangle which included Saint Louis and Cincinnati. He was the only German among these Archbishops, and wanted to be replaced by another German.

157　Colman J. Barry, O.S.B. *The Catholic Church and German Americans.* Milwaukee: The Bruce Publishing Company. 1952. P.11.

A terna of suggested names included Bishops Francis Xavier Krautbauer of Green Bay, Michael Heiss of La Crosse, and Joseph Dwenger of Fort Wayne, all Germans. This terna was carried to Rome by Father Peter Abbelen.

One priest in Milwaukee, Father George Willard, caught wind of the mission to find a German successor for Henni and wrote Cardinal Gibbons to alert him. Gibbons in turn consulted Archbishop Williams of Boston and Bishop Foley of Chicago, and suggested Bishop Spalding of Peoria be considered, as he spoke German but was thoroughly American.

Archbishop Henni's terna was rejected in Rome as he had failed to consult his suffragan bishops. So in August 1878, Archbishop Henni assembled all the bishops of the Milwaukee province. This time Dwenger's name was dropped and Spalding's added. When John Lancaster Spalding heard that his name had been added to the Milwaukee terna as a possible coadjutor to Archbishop Henni, he flatly refused. Eventually, Bishop Michael Heiss received the honor in 1880. It was a German victory.

What really irritated the Americanizers among the U. S. bishops was the accusation made by Father Abbelen that "a great many Irish priests" were holding German priests and parishes in a subordinate place, defining them as chapels of ease or succursal churches. He cited Saint Louis as an example. It is true that Archbishop Peter Richard Kenrick made this his practice. As he read the decrees of the Council of Trent, there would not be two co-equal parishes in the same territory. Yet it was the Archbishop's wish to serve the spiritual needs of his German-speaking flock that led him to establish German parishes. He saw no other way out of the dilemma than to create succursal parishes within the boundaries of established English-speaking parishes. Regardless, Abbelen's criticism unfairly cast a bad light on an Archbishop who had done everything possible to aid the German immigrants.

When Father Abbelen arrived in Rome to press his concerns, a firestorm erupted, fueled by the bombastic rhetoric of Bishops Ireland and Keane, who were in Rome on other business. Bishop Keane wrote Cardinal Gibbons, calling Abbelen "this secret emissary of a clique of German bishops among us."[158] The two bishops went to Cardinal Simeoni of *Propaganda Fide* to counter Abbelen's petition and to warn him

---

158   John Tracy Ellis. *The Life of James Cardinal Gibbons: Archbishop of Baltimore. 1834 – 1921. Volume I*. Milwaukee: The Bruce Publishing Company. 1952. P. 349.

that if this secret got back to the American bishops, it would tear the American episcopacy asunder.

Back in America, Cardinal Gibbons hesitated. He knew how complex the problem was. In his own Archdiocese, Gibbons recognized the difficulties of combined language groups at Saint Joseph's Parish in Washington, D. C. When the sermons were preached in German, many parishioners left Mass. Yet when sermons were preached in English, no one left. It turned out that the German speakers were of the second generation and knew enough English to understand the priest.

In Philadelphia, Archbishop Ryan turned a parish over to the Italians when they became the majority. He then ordered the English speakers to go to another parish, but this threw the parish into a tailspin. The pastor begged the Archbishop to leave the English speakers in his parish, as the Italians could not support it alone. In the end, the parish of Saint Mary Magdalen dei Pozzi remained bilingual.

After much politicking by both sides, *Propaganda* made its decision. As described by John Tracy Ellis, "The decision gave sanction to the practice of accommodating the foreign language groups in more than one parish in the same neighborhood, the designation of certain pastorates as irremovable rectorships, and the restriction of the children of families of a foreign nationality within the limits of that nationality's parish, so long as they live in their parents' home and providing it be understood that the parents were free to send their children to any Catholic school of their choice."[159]

But this would not be the end of the language controversy. Archbishop Heiss made an off-handed comment to the *Milwaukee Sentinel* that a gathering of German priests in a convention in Chicago was probably going to recommend the creation of more German bishops for America. He was referring to the *Deutsch-Amerikanische Priesterverein* gathering in September 1887. Then Bishop Elder of Cincinnati got information, which he passed on to Cardinal Gibbons, that Bishop Katzer of Green Bay was maneuvering to have a German named bishop of Detroit. Instead, upon the death of Archbishop Michael Heiss of Milwaukee, Katzer got the appointment. Earlier, Archbishop Ireland had written Cardinal Gibbons, declaring that Katzer was "thoroughly

---

159   John Tracy Ellis. *The Life of James Cardinal Gibbons: Archbishop of Baltimore. 1834 – 1921. Volume I*. Milwaukee: The Bruce Publishing Company. 1952. P. 359.

unfit to be an Archbishop."[160]

Nor would the Americanizers be pleased with the developments in Cleveland. On April 13, 1891, Bishop Gilmour, Gibbons' ally and confidant, died and was replaced eight months later by Ignatius F. Horstmann from Philadelphia. Further trouble was brewing by a move on the part of an immigrant aid society, the *St. Raphaelsverein,* based in Hamburg, Germany.

In 1882 Pope Leo XIII encouraged a Swiss Catholic layman, Peter Paul Cahensly, to coordinate efforts to aid Catholic immigrants coming to America. The tool to bring about this cooperation was the *St. Raphaelsverein,* which held its second international congress in Liège, Belgium, in September 1887. In the next few years, Cahensly was successful in gathering support from powerful figures in Europe, including Emperor Franz Joseph of the Austro-Hungarian Empire. He consulted with John Bosco, founder of the Salesians, and met Bishop Giovanni Battista Scalabrini of Piacenza. It was the bishop's vision to found a missionary seminary to train Italian priests for service to Italian immigrants in America. The Irish had done something similar at All Hallows Seminary.

At a Lucerne, Switzerland meeting of the European societies on December 9 and 10, 1890, the delegates drew up an overall plan to address the needs of European immigrants in America. It became known as the Lucerne Memorial, and was hand-delivered to Pope Leo XIII by Peter Paul Cahensly. Its contents would outrage the Americanizing bishops.

The memorial called for separate churches for each national group. If a group could not support itself, it should find a parochial home among the English-speaking Catholics, but at least one priest assigned to that parish should be able to serve the needs of the immigrants. Parochial schools should be established where each nationality could preserve its language and heritage. Mutual aid societies should be founded to discourage immigrants from seeking out non-Catholic or anti-Catholic societies like the Freemasons.

The memorial proposed that same-language bishops should be appointed to sees with large nationality representation. And several European seminaries should follow the example of All Hallows Seminary and the efforts of Bishop Scalabrini. The signers suggested that *St.*

---

160   John Tracy Ellis. *The Life of James Cardinal Gibbons: Archbishop of Baltimore. 1834 – 1921. Volume I.* Milwaukee: The Bruce Publishing Company. 1952. P. 364.

Raphaelverein be placed under the leadership of a cardinal-protector.

When news of the Lucerne Memorial was reported to the press, it became a bombshell. Nor were all the reports accurate. It was reported that the memorial was the work of Peter Paul Cahensly, when he was merely the messenger. He was misquoted as saying, "The Irish bishops in the United States only nominate Irish priests, who do not know the languages spoken by the immigrants."[161]

The press coverage fueled the controversy. Archbishop John Ireland of Saint Paul unloaded on an Associated Press reporter. "What is the most strange feature in this whole Lucerne movement is the impudence of the men in undertaking to meddle under any pretext in the Catholic affairs of America. This is simply unpardonable and all American Catholics will treasure up the affront for future action. We acknowledge the Pope of Rome as our chieftain in spiritual matters and we are glad to receive direction from him, but men in Germany or Switzerland or Ireland must mind their own business and be still as to ours."[162]

The Archbishop ended his comments with a personal assault on Cahensly. "Indeed, Mr. Cahensly and his supporters are somewhat excusable when they see in America naught else, or little else, than foreigners or foreign domination. This is largely, they perceive, the case in politics. Why should it not be, they ask, in religion? When we will be more American in civil and political matters, there will be fewer petitions from vereins in America and conferences in Lucerne for the foreignizing of Catholics in America."[163]

Archbishop Ireland was joined by other American bishops trying to move Cardinal Gibbons to answer the Lucerne Memorial. But they had little to fear. Cardinal Gibbons' quiet diplomacy secured a letter from the Secretary of State, Cardinal Rampollo, at the direction Pope Leo XIII, assuring the American prelates that the Lucerne Memorial would not be enacted and that events should develop in America according to the wishes of the bishops there.

Two coincidences convinced Cardinal Gibbons to lay to rest for good the phantom of Cahenslyism. On July 11, 1891, the Cardinal had a chance encounter with U. S. President Benjamin Harrison. The two

---

161   Colman J. Barry, O.S.B. *The Catholic Church and German Americans.* Milwaukee: The Bruce Publishing Company. 1952. P. 137.
162   Ibid. P. 140.
163   Ibid. P. 140-141.

happened to be vacationing at Cape May, New Jersey. They walked along, talking of various interests, until they approached the residence where the President was staying. Harrison invited Cardinal Gibbons to continue the conversation, which turned serious. President Harrison was aware of the Lucerne Memorial, and it bothered him. He told Cardinal Gibbons he appreciated the Cardinal's public comments about the affair and hoped that the bishops in America would be in harmony with "the political institutions and sentiments of the country."[164]

This conversation was fully reported by Cardinal Gibbons in a letter to Cardinal Rampolla, and he released to the press a similar report of the visit with the President, as well as the general contents of Rampolla's previous letter.

The second coincidence gave Cardinal Gibbons the opportunity to state clearly the Americanists' views. Archbishop Katzer of Milwaukee had denounced Cahenslyism in a pastoral letter. He also invited Cardinal Gibbons to confer the pallium, the sign of the Archbishop's authority. The date was set for August 20, 1891.

At Saint John's Cathedral in Milwaukee, over seven hundred bishops and priests of every hyphenated Catholic community gathered to hear Cardinal Gibbons' sermon. The words were gentle and encouraging and absolutely uncompromising about the unity of the Church in America. No Balkanization would be tolerated, which could sow seeds of discord and disunity.

Gibbons spoke: *"Let us unite hand-in-hand in laboring for the Church of our fathers. The more we extend the influence of the Christian religion, the more we will contribute to the stability of our political and social fabric ... Next to love for God, should be our love for our country. The Author of our being has stamped in the human breast a love for one's country, and therefore patriotism is a sentiment commended by almighty God Himself...*

The Catholic community in the United States has been conspicuous for its loyalty in the century that has passed away; and we, I am sure, will emulate the patriotism of our fathers in the faith.

Let us glory in the title of American citizen. We owe our allegiance to one country, and that country is America. We must be in harmony with our political institutions. It matters not whether this is the land of our birth or the land of our adoption. It is the land of our destiny...

---

164   Colman J. Barry, O.S.B. *The Catholic Church and German Americans.* Milwaukee: The Bruce Publishing Company. 1952. P. 157.

When our brethren across the Atlantic resolve to come to our shores, may they be animated by the sentiment of Ruth, when she determined to join her husband's kindred in the land of Israel, and may they say to you as she said to their relations: "Whither thou has gone, I also shall go – where thou dwellest, I also shall dwell; thy people shall be my people, and thy God my God. The land shall receive thee dying, in the same will I die, and there will I be buried."[165]

---

165   James Cardinal Gibbons. A Retrospect of Fifty Years. (New York, 1916, II pp. 148-155, as cited in Colman J. Barry, O.S.B. *The Catholic Church and German Americans.* Milwaukee: The Bruce Publishing Company. 1952. P.163.)

St. Gertrude Parish in Krakow, MO, circa 1895. Rev. John J. Noelker Glass Plate Negatives Collection, Archdiocese of St. Louis Archives and Records.

English Parish Boundaries in the City of St. Louis

By Decree of 1896 December 14

Our Lady of Mount Carmel

St. Edward

Holy Name

Holy Rosary

St. Mark

Our Lady of Good Counsel

Visitation

St. Matthew

St. Rose

St. Theresa

Sacred Heart

St. Michael

St. Paul

St. Leo

St. Lawrence O'Toole

New Cathedral

St. Alphonsus

St. Bridget

St. Francis

Immaculate Conception

St. Patrick

St. Malachy

St. John

Old Cathedral

St. Cronan

Holy Angels

Annunciation

St. James

St. Kevin

St. Vincent

St. Agnes

Assumption

Holy Innocents

St. Thomas of Aquin

Sts. Mary and Joseph

St. Columbkille

Note: Some of the city parishes extend beyond the city limits, but only such part of these parishes is here given as lies within the city limits.

Archdiocese of St. Louis Archives and Records.

German Parish Boundaries in the City of St. Louis

By Decree of 1897 February 2

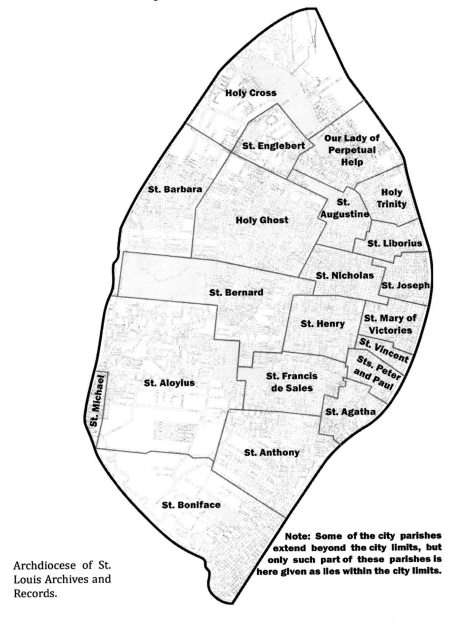

Note: Some of the city parishes extend beyond the city limits, but only such part of these parishes is here given as lies within the city limits.

Archdiocese of St. Louis Archives and Records.

Chapter Thirteen

WHIRLWINDS OF CHANGE

Father Franz Salensius Goller had been a student at the University of Tübingen when he met Father Joseph Melcher on one of the Vicar General's recruiting tours. Goller became a Melcher man and came to finish his seminary studies in America, being ordained by Archbishop Peter Richard Kenrick on November 1, 1855, along with Casper Doebbner. Goller was a learned scholar familiar with Augustine, Aquinas, and Bonaventure. But his first two assignments were disasters.

Father Goller lasted less than one year at Most Holy Trinity, tormented by a dictatorial pastor. Archbishop Kenrick removed him to Saints Peter and Paul, where he was again persecuted by a jealous pastor and his loyal staff. When the young, diminutive priest sought the advice of the Archbishop, rather than move Goller again, Kenrick removed the pastor and made Goller pastor of Saints Peter and Paul. Goller was twenty-five years old and would serve the parish for the next fifty-two years. He paid off the debt, built one of the most beautiful churches in Saint Louis, and operated a very successful school with 1,300 children counted among its alumni at the time of Father Goller's death in 1910, in their number twenty-two priests and one hundred and sixty religious sisters.

In 1884, Archbishop Kenrick chose Fathers Franz Goller and Thomas Bonacum to accompany him to the Third Plenary Council of Baltimore as *pariti*, theological experts. Bonacum so impressed the attending prelates that his name was set forth to be the founding bishop of the diocese of Lincoln, Nebraska. Goller would make his mark by encouraging legislation mandating Catholic schools in every parish.

Topics for the Council began in a rather mundane fashion. It was suggested that, if the local bishop wished, seminarians would be encouraged to take summer vacations. Cathedral chapters were rejected but irremovable rectors could be established upon the action of the local bishop. The decision came regarding the care of infirmed and elderly priests. Various means of fundraising were discussed. Trade unions, a national collection for an apostolic outreach to African-Americans, and the question of providing Italian priests for the increasing number of immigrants from Italy all occupied the attention of the Council. In addition, a committee was commissioned to explore the construction of a catechism common for all Americans. Over time the *Baltimore Catechism* was published and widely used throughout the nation.

In all, the Council was attended by fourteen archbishops, fifty-seven bishops, seven abbots, thirty-one religious congregation superiors, and eighty-eight *periti*. The Council fathers voted on three hundred and nineteen pieces of legislation. Nearly twenty-five percent of this legislation dealt with education, particularly that in parochial schools. So strident was the majority that one decree mandated a school for every parish and recommended that a pastor who failed to follow the decree within two years be removed from his parish.

Father Goller's role in the school legislation won him both admirers and detractors. While his long tenure at Saints Peter and Paul won him widespread acclaim, and his parish high school was one of the first in the nation, it was Goller's activity on behalf of preserving German language and culture which endangered his reputation, allowing him to be unjustly characterized as a Cahenslyite.

Goller was an active founder of the *Deutsch-Amerikanischer Priesterverein,* The German-American Priests Society, when it held its first meeting in February 1887 in Chicago. Sixty-five German priests, including Vicar General Henry Mühlsiepen, sought to replicate the German *Katolischentage*. Father Goller was named chairman of the central committee. It was in this capacity that he spoke against a proposal by Bishop John Lancaster Spalding and Bishop Martin Marty of the Vicar Apostolic of the Dakotas. They believed that the *Priesterverein* should broaden itself to invite all American Catholics to participate. To this Goller responded that it would water down the society and weaken the German language. Bishop Marty retorted that such multilingual "confabs" were common in Silesia and Switzerland. The question was remanded to a special committee which concluded that the *Priesterverein* should meet annually and that an attempt should be made to find common ground with other Catholic groups, but that for the present each group should meet in its language category.

Father Goller's name became associated not only with the organization of the *Deutsch-Amerikanischer Priesterverein,* but also with some unguarded and intemperate comments made by some of the priest members. The same guilt-by-association smeared Vicar General Mühlsiepen.

All it took was one outrageous act by a German-American priest in Saint Louis to cause charges of Cahenslyism to surface. The culprit was Father William Faerber. He had been the founding pastor of Saint Vincent de Paul Parish in Dutzow in 1865 and assistant to Vicar General Mühlsiepen at Saint Mary's in Saint Louis. He became the pastor the next year. While he was at Dutzow, a mission parish was erected in Augusta. Sunday Mass was celebrated in Dutzow every Sunday but one per month. On that one Sunday, Father Faerber and the Dutzow congregation travelled to Augusta to attend Mass with that congregation. The custom worked well to everyone's pleasure and continued all the way into the early twentieth century.

Saint Mary of Victories was one of the grand old parishes in the Archdiocese, but was in decline as Father Faerber took over and Mühlsiepen moved to the Ursuline convent to become the spiritual director for the nuns. Bordering the east of the parish was the Mississippi River, to the north the cathedral, itself surrounded by warehouses and office buildings. To the west were the flourishing parishes of Saint Henry and Saint Nicholas. The southern part of the parish had been the old Frenchtown from colonial days. Long since, these cabins and homes had given way to warehouses and office buildings. The lack of residential property caused a rapid decline in parish membership. The very future of the parish seemed to hang in the balance.

To break the freefall, Father Faerber purchased property on Morrison Avenue near Twelfth Street. He proposed to build a new church there. The only problem was that the property was in Saint Vincent de Paul Parish, his neighbor to the south! Father Faerber's scheme was to draw the German-speaking members of Saint Vincent to the German-language Saint Mary of Victories Church, leaving Saint Vincent de Paul as an English-only parish. His plan even won the approval of Vicar General Mühlsiepen.

The project became a contest of wills between Fathers Faerber and Mühlsiepen on the one side and the Vincentians on the other. They argued to Archbishop Kenrick that Saint Vincent's had always been a trilingual parish, accommodating French, English, and German tongues. To disrupt the parish by allowing Father Faerber's scheme to advance would destroy the harmony of Saint Vincent's and financially endanger its existence. The Archbishop sided with the Vincentians. Not content with the verdict, Father Faerber appealed to Rome, only to be rejected by Cardinal Simeoni of *Propaganda Fide*.

The church move scheme was not the only one to raise eyebrows about Father William Faerber. He was editor of *Pastoral Blatt*, a periodical in German with articles of interest for German clergy. Generally, the paper dealt with pastoral and liturgical issues, interspersed with theological and historical topics. Now it became a forum for criticizing what Father Faerber referred to as "forced Americanism."

One article in *Pastoral Blatt,* by Benedictine Father Innocent Wappelhorst on the need for Catholic schools to counter the "godless or so-called public schools," caught the attention of the readership. By July 1884, eighty-two priests had signed a petition criticizing the succursal status of foreign-language parishes. It was forwarded to Cardinal Simeoni of *Propaganda Fide* by Vicar General Mühlsiepen. By now, Father Mühlsiepen had acquired two designations that gave him status. Many referred to him as "the apostle of the Germans in Missouri" and others imprudently called him "the unconsecrated bishop of St. Louis."[166] Mühlsiepen was quick to point out that the petition was not aimed at his Archbishop, who often expressed his displeasure at English pastors abusing the succursal status of non-English parishes. The petition was aimed at those pastors.

Cardinal Simeoni turned over the issue of the petition to the Archbishops of the United States, most of whom were taken by surprise. Archbishop Patrick Ryan of Philadelphia assured Cardinal Gibbons that nowhere in America were German Catholics treated with greater respect and encouragement than in Peter Richard Kenrick's Archdiocese. But he too added that something had to be done to rein in the English-language pastors who abused their authority. The topic would be discussed at the Third Baltimore Plenary Council, particularly in regards to another wave of Catholic immigrants beginning to surge into America: the Italians. The commission assigned to address the issue did not discuss the German petition. The issue would fester for the next several years in America and in Rome and eventually became a question of the pace of Americanization, which was eventually accepted as inevitable.

One final attempt to slow the Americanization process and to protect German Catholic culture was made by Father Franz Goller. He used the upcoming golden jubilee of Archbishop Kenrick's episcopal consecration to hatch the scheme.

---

166   Colman J. Barry, O.S.B. *The Catholic Church and German Americans*. Milwaukee: The Bruce Publishing Company. 1952. P. 54.

Father Goller wanted to raise money to pay for the trip of Roman seminarian and noted historian Paul Marie Baumgarten to attend the festivities in Saint Louis. Baumgarten was to carry a congratulatory letter from His Holiness Pope Leo XIII. On the surface, that was what was to happen. But Goller planned for a grand tour for Baumgarten of German Catholic communities all throughout the United States. He would be seen as a Roman emissary to German-American Catholics. The whole affair had to be shrouded in secrecy until the tour began. Vicar General Mühlsiepen was brought into the scheme and insisted on secrecy as well.

But secrecy was not maintained. Baumgarten confided the whole plan to Countess Marianne Kinsky, who informed Monsignor Denis O'Connell, a confidant of Cardinal Gibbons. O'Connell leaked the information to the New York press, and on Baumgarten's arrival in New York City he was given a copy of *The New York Herald*; the paper speculated that the Baumgarten visit was a ruse to cover a grand tour which meant to re-enkindle Cahenslyism. The visitor read the article and reacted with two words: Denis O'Connell! The Baumgarten mission had been doubly foiled. Not only were his real intentions made known before he even began his grand tour, the Vatican declined to give him the papal congratulatory letter which would have increased his status. Instead, he was travelling as a private person.

Worse, in Buffalo a speech which Baumgarten had decided not to deliver was stolen from his hotel room and published in the *Buffalo Courier*. He was dissuaded from reporting the incident to the police to avoid creating even more harmful publicity. Instead, Baumgarten gave an interview to a journalist in which he distanced himself from Peter Paul Cahensly and the Lucerne Memorial.

Father Goller watched his plans disintegrate, but he tried one last time to turn the tide. Over the years, Goller had grown very fond of Archbishop Kenrick, who had saved his priestly career twice during his early years. Archbishop Kenrick also admired Father Goller for his parochial work, his bright intellect, and his dedication to Catholic education. It seemed only logical that the opening address of the golden jubilee would be given by Father Franz Goller. With so many dignitaries flocking to Saint Louis, it was a grand opportunity to shine.

The little priest began his address by thanking Peter Richard Kenrick for his many years of service to the thousands of immigrants who came to his diocese. He praised the immigrants themselves for the courage and initiative to come to America. Goller noted eloquently, "If you rejoice in the fact America is great and glorious and free today, that the United States forms the most prosperous, and most enlightened, and the most powerful empire of the world, then you owe heartfelt thanks and praise to the adopted sons and daughters of America. Do not call them foreigners, for they are true Americans."

Father Goller then went to the heart of the matter regarding Americanization and ethnic differences. "We have a country, but we are not yet a nation in the full sense of the term: we are, as it were, 'the rudis indigestaque moles' of our mother, and we disdain to become a mere second edition of John Bull. A grander destiny awaits us. From the 'disjecta membra' of many tribes and peoples we are gradually forming a new national type: we are absorbing the noble traits of various foreign nationalities. A hundred, perhaps more, years must roll on ere the typical American will be produced, embodying in himself the common sense and business capacity of the Anglo-Saxon, the patient research of the German, the keen wit of the Celt, the brilliant dash of the children of France, the childlike piety of Catholic Italy: but when he does make his appearance, all the world will recognize in him the ideal man."[167] Father Goller then turned to the Archbishop and added: "Archbishop Kenrick discovered in Catholic immigration, not a danger to the Republic, but a priceless acquisition." One last Latin quote nailed Goller's case shut. He said Kenrick's noble principle was always, "In necessitas, unitas, in dubiis libertas, in omnibus caritas."[168]

The address was a stunning attack on the Americanizers, every bit as strong as was Cardinal Gibbons' defense of Americanization at Archbishop Katzer's pallium Mass. Later, Archbishop Michael Corrigan of New York gave a toast which defended the Americanizers, and Archbishop John Ireland of Saint Paul pontificated: "We recognize in civil matters no other power than the authorities in Washington, and in religious matters no other power than the Pontiff of the Vatican."[169] While the comment seemed innocent enough, it reminded the audience that some had conflated the Lucerne Memorial and Cahenslyism with certain European governments wishing to preserve the ethnicity

---

167   Colman J. Barry, O.S.B. *The Catholic Church and German Americans.* Milwaukee: The Bruce Publishing Company. 1952. P. 172. (A rude and disorderly mass, Ovid/scattered fragments, Horace)

168   "In necessity unity, in diversity liberty, in all things charity."

169   Ibid. P. 174.

of their emigrants.

Other than these exchanges, the rest of the golden jubilee of Peter Richard Kenrick's episcopacy was pure celebration. Attendance was bolstered by sixty bishops and Archbishops. $50,000 was raised for a new Archbishop's residence on fashionable Lindell Boulevard. A memorial sermon was delivered by Archbishop Ryan of Philadelphia, who spoke fondly of the many years he had shared with Archbishop Kenrick as his Vicar and as his coadjutor. "I spent the first seven years of my priestly life in his house, and knew him intimately for thirty-two years of my life in St. Louis."[170]

Archbishop Ryan spoke of two of the most extraordinary moments of courage in Kenrick's life. "His courage was shown on several occasions during the Civil War. His absolute refusal to take the test oath as a condition for permission to preach the Word of God and for other sacred functions, which oath he believed to be unconstitutional, and which the Supreme Court of the United States afterwards declared to be so, and his command to his clergy not to take it, great as were the penalties, showed a fortitude that few in those trying days possessed. Another instance of his courage was his action at the Vatican Council in regard to the definition of the infallibility of the Pope, and his subsequent submission to that dogma."[171]

The Archbishop went on to speak of Saint Louis as the source of Catholic evangelization in America's heartland. "The See of St. Louis held originally in its jurisdiction not only the State and Territory of Missouri, but beyond these, south to Louisiana and Texas, west to the Rocky Mountains, north to the sources of the Missouri and the Des Moines and east to the tributaries of the Illinois and the Wabash. From this territory Little Rock was made a see in 1843; Santa Fé and Saint Paul in 1850, Leavenworth in 1851, Alton and Omaha in 1857; Green Bay, La Crosse, St. Joseph and Denver in 1868, Kansas City in 1880; Davenport in 1881, Wichita, Cheyenne, Concordia and Lincoln in 1887. These sees were erected and Bishops appointed for them by the efforts and labors of the Archbishop of St. Louis. Also, it was by his efforts and recommendations that four of these were raised to the rank of metropolitan sees and suffragans appointed to them, namely, Mil-

---

170   John J. O'Shea. *The Two Kenricks: Most Rev. Francis Patrick, Archbishop of Baltimore. Most Rev. Peter Richard, Archbishop of St. Louis.* Philadelphia: John J. McVey. 1904. P. 350.

171   Ibid. P. 352.

waukee in 1875, with Green Bay, La Crosse, Marquette and Sault Ste. Marie as suffragans, Santa Fé likewise in 1875, with Denver and Tucson as suffragans, Chicago in 1880, with Alton, Peoria and Belleville as suffragans, St. Paul in 1888, with Jamestown, Duluth, St. Cloud, Sioux Falls and Winona as suffragans. Five Archbishoprics and twenty Bishoprics in less than fifty years."[172]

Toward the end of his address, Archbishop Ryan returned to the Test Oath and Kenrick's opposition to it. It was clearly a government violation of freedom of conscience and an attempt to exert state control over religious bodies. Ryan compared it to the Jacobin Civil Constitution of the Clergy in revolutionary France. Then he mixed his metaphors and compared Kenrick to General Helmuth von Moltke, victor of the Franco-Prussian war.

"A few words more and I shall have done. In 1865, on April 1, an April Fools' convention, following the madcap ideas of the French infidels, enacted a Missouri 'Civil Constitution of the Clergy,' forbidding them, under pain of fine and imprisonment, to preach or teach, or hold property in trust or otherwise, unless by writ of privilege from the Missouri Jacobins. As I have said, this was not a Missouri idea. It was an imported craze. Missouri but once in its life got all into a madhouse, and that was once too often for its good name and its good sense."

Ryan compared Missouri to the Church in France, in which 7,000 priests and four bishops took the Jacobin oath, but here in Missouri not a one signed on. Then he turned to Von Moltke. "In the last great Franco-Prussian war there was one grand old general who did not go to the battlefield. He stayed at home in his office. With the maps of the battlefields open before him, he gave his orders. He was a master of strategy. In the Missouri campaign we, too, had our Von Moltke. So far as I know he never went out to see what we were doing, but we knew what he meant, and he knew what we meant, and we all thought we meant right. That was enough."

Archbishop Ryan thundered on. "Accordingly, we arrayed ourselves for battle with unbroken front to the enemy. Radicals to the right of us, radicals to the left of us, radicals before us, radicals behind us 'volleyed and thundered.' 'You rascals,' said the radicals to us, 'why don't you obey the law of your country?' Our Von Moltke for once spoke up.

---

172   John J. O'Shea. *The Two Kenricks: Most Rev. Francis Patrick, Archbishop of Baltimore. Most Rev. Peter Richard, Archbishop of St. Louis.* Philadelphia: John J. McVey. 1904. P. 360.

'That is no law. You owe it to your God and to your country to uphold religion and liberty.' The Supreme Court of the United States said, just as our Von Moltke said: 'That's no law; that's tyranny.'"[173] It was raw meat and the audience loved it.

The jubilee culminated with a grand parade of civic organizations and Catholic societies. There were fireworks and transparencies, something like an early slide show. The parade included 20,000 marchers joined by 50,000 onlookers. Dignitaries included Governor David R. Francis and Mayor Noonan. All this the old Archbishop watched from the comfort of his new episcopal residence. Other festivities included concerts by the Christian Brothers College orchestra, school groups chanting songs, and an assembly of girls led by the Sisters of Saint Joseph, demonstrating sign language. Peter Richard Kenrick was moved to tears. Asked to speak, he could only reply, "I cannot; this is simply overwhelming. Say something for me," as he turned to his beloved Archbishop Patrick Ryan.[174]

The Lion of the Fourth City would roar no more. After the jubilee celebration, the Archbishop's health deteriorated rapidly. He was eighty-five years old and needed help, and he knew it. But his plans for a coadjutor would be foiled in the last five years of his life.

Archbishop Kenrick's golden jubilee had revealed to everyone the frailty of the octogenarian. He had lost his coadjutor when Ryan was named Archbishop of Philadelphia. The Father Faerber affair had strained his relations with Vicar General Mühlsiepen, at least for a while. Meanwhile there was much work to do. Kenrick presided over 6,000 confirmations a year. He ordained fifty-five priests in the seven years prior to his jubilee, consecrated two bishops, and invested Cardinal Gibbons in Baltimore. In the midst of all this activity, the old Archbishop came to rely more and more on his second Vicar General, Father Philip P. Brady.

Philip Brady was born in Ireland and brought to America at the age of two. He was schooled at Saint Vincent Seminary in Cape Girardeau. After ordination, he served briefly in Lexington, Missouri and New Madrid before becoming pastor of Annunciation Church in Saint Louis. There he was named Vicar General, replacing Ryan in 1884, and

---

173   John J. O'Shea. *The Two Kenricks: Most Rev. Francis Patrick, Archbishop of Baltimore. Most Rev. Peter Richard, Archbishop of St. Louis.* Philadelphia: John J. McVey. 1904. P. 363.
174   Ibid. P. 385.

became pastor of Saint John the Evangelist.

Historian Father Rothensteiner had a harsh assessment of the man Archbishop Kenrick came to rely on more and more. "He was not a man of profound scholarship or of oratorical power. His health had been impaired by the privations and exposures of missionary life in the swamps of southeast Missouri. The qualities of character fitted him better for a subordinate position rather than for the high and arduous duties of an Archbishop. At least, that was the opinion of his fellow priests, who must have known him well."[175]

Archbishop Kenrick had other ideas. When the Archbishops of America gathered for a meeting in New York City, Kenrick excused himself and sent Vicar General Brady as his representative. It was November 1892. Brady submitted a letter to the assembly, which was joined by the new Apostolic Delegate Cardinal Satolli. In the letter, Kenrick requested that Father Brady be named his coadjutor with right of succession. The letter placed Father Brady in a very compromising position before the Archbishops of America. Worse, it ignored the procedure for naming Archbishops adopted at the Third Baltimore Council.

The Council's regulations called for a terna of names to be proposed by a committee of diocesan consultors and irremovable rectors. This list would be submitted to the bishops of the province, who could accept or reject the candidates. If objecting, the bishops had to state their reasons why. The list would then be forwarded to Rome.

This procedure could not be followed in Saint Louis because in the eight years since the Council, Archbishop Kenrick had named no consultors nor irremovable rectors. And that put everyone in a bind. The American Archbishops suggested that the priests of the Archdiocese of Saint Louis act as a body and create a terna. A letter was sent to all pastors instructing them on the process. But the priests of Saint Louis had already done so; three days before Father Brady submitted Kenrick's letter to the Archbishops in New York, forty-four priests, all pastors, had signed a petition submitting the names of Bishop John Joseph Kain of Wheeling, Bishop John Lancaster Spalding of Peoria, and Bishop Edward Fitzgerald of Little Rock as episcopal candidates for Saint Louis. Among the signatures were those of Father Constantine Smith, Kenrick's *peritus* at the Vatican Council and founding pas-

---

175   Rev. John Rothensteiner. *History of the Archdiocese of St. Louis. Vol. II.* Saint Louis: Blackwell Wielandy Co. 1928. P. 532.

tor of Saint Agnes Church, Father Franz Goller, pastor of Saints Peter and Paul and long-time friend of the Archbishop, and Father William Faerber, who had caused such an uproar when he tried to move Saint Mary of Victories into Saint Vincent de Paul Parish. Significantly, the pastor of Saint Michael's Parish, Father Andreas Eustace, signed, the Archbishop's own nephew.

When the petition became public, the rift in Saint Louis clergy became public also. The two camps, pro-Brady and pro-anybody else camps, seemed to have settled for the pastors' terna. *The Western Watchman*, the Archdiocesan newspaper, called it a Truce of God, referring to the medieval custom of cessation of combat during certain holy days. The whole affair weighed heavily on Father Brady's spirit. He returned to Saint John's, his parish. Rothensteiner notes that he "bore up bravely under his disappointment; for the Archbishop's confidence in him never wavered. But the knowledge that his brethren in the ministry had not only ignored him in their petition for a coadjutor, but had actually arraigned him before the tribunal of Rome, as one unworthy of the high dignity, at last broke his spirit."[176] Father Philip Brady died on March 5, 1893, at forty-five years old. Archbishop Ryan traveled to Saint Louis to preach at Father Brady's funeral. But his was a double mission of mercy. He lingered in Saint Louis for a month to be at the side of the bereaved Archbishop Kenrick.

And Kenrick had more to mourn. He had recently buried his beloved niece, Elizabeth Eustace, who had kept house for him for many years. A cousin, Jane Eustace, died, and not long after the coadjutor petition affair, his nephew, Father Andreas Eustace, died. Peter Richard Kenrick was left in the last few years of his life with only one faithful old companion, his butler Thomas Franklin, who before the Civil War had been his slave and house servant.

Shortly before Father Brady's death, Archbishop Kenrick suffered a brief but severe illness. The source of the sickness is shrouded in mystery, but Rothensteiner notes "it affected his mind in such a way, that he was rendered incapable of administering the affairs of the Archdiocese."[177]

Meanwhile, events moved inexorably toward his replacement.

Rome appointed Bishop John Joseph Kain as coadjutor of the Arch-

---

176   Rev. John Rothensteiner. *History of the Archdiocese of St. Louis. Vol. II*. Saint Louis: Blackwell Wielandy Co. 1928. P. 582.
177   Ibid. P. 583.

diocese of Saint Louis. In an unprecedented show of support, twenty-two Saint Louis priests traveled to Wheeling to congratulate him and escort him to his new home.

Arriving in Saint Louis, Bishop Kain was faced with a dilemma and made an error in judgment which plagued him for the next three years: where to live? He had been offered a suite of rooms at the new Kenrick Seminary. It had been established in 1892 by Archbishop Kenrick and was in the care of the Congregation of the Mission, the Vincentians. Previously, the Archdiocesan seminarians had studied at Saint Vincent's in Cape Girardeau or at the Salesium in Milwaukee; a few studied in Baltimore or even in Rome. When the Archdiocese reacquired the old Visitation Convent at Cass and Nineteenth Streets, the Archbishop decided it was time for the Archdiocese to have its own seminary. Its success showed in its numbers. Within ten years, twenty-five dioceses enrolled their men at Kenrick. Its student body numbered one hundred and forty-five.

While a suite at the seminary would not have been ideal for the new coadjutor, the alternative was a disaster. Kain decided to move into the episcopal residence with Archbishop Kenrick, who Rothensteiner observed "had not taken kindly to or did not recognize the fact that he had a claimant in his house."[178]

Each day Bishop Kain would rise, take breakfast, and attend to Archdiocesan business at the residence. He then left for the day, receiving hospitality from various pastors. Each evening he would return to the residence where Peter Richard Kenrick posted his coat of arms on the front door. Entering the house, Kain would glance up and see the warning "Noli irritare leonem!"

But in the end, the Lion had to be irritated. When Rome named Kain administrator of the Archdiocese, Kenrick refused to turn over the temporalities. Kain resorted to taking him to civil court. Nor did things improve when Rome made John Joseph Kain Archbishop of Saint Louis and demoted Kenrick to a titular Archbishop of Marcionopolis, an ancient ruin in Bulgaria.

John Joseph Kain was not an unknown entity to the priests of Saint Louis. Two prominent pastors, the brothers James and Michael Mc-Cabe, had studied with him in Baltimore. With one exception, Kain's priestly and episcopal career had been stellar. He was ordained for

---

178   Rev. John Rothensteiner. *History of the Archdiocese of St. Louis. Vol. II.* Saint Louis: Blackwell Wielandy Co. 1928. P. 583.

the diocese of Richmond in 1866 and made pastor of a parish that included eight counties in West Virginia and four in Virginia, all ravaged by war.

Kain's tireless efforts, his financial acumen, and his irrepressible spirit caused his reputation to soar. Within nine years of his ordination, Father Kain was named bishop of Wheeling, West Virginia. It was mission land, nearly 30,000 square miles with a sparse Catholic population, only one in twenty residents. There were thirty-five diocesan priests, aided by a few Capuchins. The Sisters of Saint Joseph administered a hospital in Wheeling while the Visitation nuns ran a small school out of their convent and the Sisters of Divine Providence conducted an orphanage.

Bishop Kain tried to improve his lot at the expense of Richmond. He wrote Rome suggesting that the diocesan boundaries between Wheeling and Richmond be identical to the state boundaries between West Virginia and Virginia. As it was, seventeen Virginia counties were in his diocese while eight West Virginia counties were under the guidance of Bishop Gibbons of Richmond. The shift would bring the heaviest Catholic population of the Richmond diocese into Wheeling's orb, while enlarging Richmond's territory without adding to the Catholic count. Kain had not consulted Bishop Gibbons before making the proposal, no doubt knowing that Gibbons would not approve of it. Indeed, Bishop Gibbons did oppose the change and rallied Archbishop Bayley of Baltimore to his side. Gibbons won the day but the debacle did not hurt the friendship between Kain and Gibbons, which grew stronger as the years passed.

Now John Joseph Kain was Archbishop of one of the most important sees in America. He had two hundred and fourteen diocesan priests, one hundred and twenty-seven priests of various Orders, one hundred and seventy-four parishes with churches, ninety-four missions with churches, twenty-seven chapels with daily Mass, and another thirty-five stations. On March 4, 1896, Archbishop Peter Richard Kenrick died at his residence, attended only by his longtime servant, Thomas Franklin. Archbishop Kain was now his own man.

For the second time in five years, Saint Louis played host to a large number of bishops gathering to honor the Lion: first to celebrate his fiftieth anniversary of his episcopal ordination and now to honor him in death. The funeral was presided at by Cardinal James Gibbons. In the sanctuary were Archbishops Ryan of Philadelphia, Kain of Saint

Louis, Feehan of Chicago, Ireland of Saint Paul, Katzer of Milwaukee, and Elder of Cincinnati. These were joined by Bishops Ryan of Alton, Hennessy, Scannell, McClosky, Foley, Heslin, Janssen, Cotter, and Rademacher. Attending also were an army of priests and some 30,000 mourners.

Father Rothensteiner reflected on this man who so dominated the bulk of nineteenth-century Saint Louis, this Lion in the Fourth City: "He was ever the friend of the oppressed, the weak and the needy, although he made no great to-do about his charities. He sometimes passed a gentle censure on a priest as a means to introduce his praise. He was the embodiment of Sidney's gentleman: 'High erected thoughts seated in a heart of courtesy.' Thus Archbishop Kenrick lived, blending the interior Christian life with exterior duty of a Catholic bishop. He was a distinguished orator; his preaching was direct and paternal; and as Archbishop Ryan said, 'He preached with a power, a logic and an unction, that convinced the intellect and touched the heart. He knew his duties well and fulfilled them; he knew his rights and always maintained them.' On the American Church he left the indelible impress of his individuality, that of a really great man. This perfect consistence of character, simple, dignified and beautiful, was Archbishop Kenrick's most valued gift to his beloved archdiocese of St. Louis and to the people of the entire territory of his early days."[179]

But mourning was short-lived. The next month witnessed a visit by Cardinal Francisco Satolli, the newly appointed Apostolic Delegate to the United States. He was the first to serve in that capacity. In years past, an American bishop would be appointed as temporary Apostolic Delegate for the Baltimore Plenary Councils. Indeed, Archbishop Kenrick served in that role in 1854. But after Rome was inundated with petitions and requests from priests trying to have decisions by their bishops annulled or reversed, it was decided that a permanent Apostolic Delegate was needed to represent the Vatican. This move had been resisted by several American bishops as an unnecessary infringement upon their episcopal authority, but after Cardinal Gibbons realized opposition was fruitless, he cooperated fully with Rome's wishes.

Cardinal Satolli arrived in Saint Louis on April 8, 1896. The next morning witnessed a solemn High Mass at which Father David Phelan,

179   Rev. John Rothensteiner. *History of the Archdiocese of St. Louis. Vol. II.* Saint Louis: Blackwell Wielandy Co. 1928. P. 594-595.

founder of Saints John and James Parish in Ferguson, preached. Later a banquet was held at Kenrick Seminary, which included an address in perfect Latin by Father Franz Goller. This was followed by a recitation of a Latin ode by Father Frederick Holweck, future co-founder of the Archdiocesan Historical Society. One hundred and eighty-four attended the feast.

Various tours of Catholic institutions around the city followed. The greatest surprise, a Goller coup, came when the Cardinal entered the sanctuary of Saints Peter and Paul church. The magnificent Gothic structure was filled to standing room only by the entire parochial student body of fourteen hundred children. This was a three-dimensional display of Catholic education at its finest; the size of the student body was impressive. To add a German twist, the children sang to the Cardinal hymns in German. Afterwards, Father Goller delivered another oration in Latin.

Two days later, on Sunday, Cardinal Satolli visited Calvary Cemetery to pray at the grave of Archbishop Peter Richard Kenrick. On Monday morning, the Apostolic Delegate returned to Washington, D. C.

While the visit was a success, its preparation had stirred an unnecessary controversy. Originally, the reason for the visit was to impose the pallium on Archbishop Kain. It had been scheduled for an earlier date, during Lent. At a February meeting of priests at Kenrick Seminary, Archbishop Kain suggested a grand banquet to honor Cardinal Satolli and celebrate the arrival of the pallium, the white wool band that signifies the authority of an Archbishop. In the conversation, the Archbishop allowed himself the indiscretion of a remark slighting the memory of Archbishop Kenrick. Father Charles Ziegler, a native of Sainte Genevieve and indefatigable pastor of Saint Malachy, had earlier spoken against a banquet which would come during Lent. Now his anger rose when he heard the memory of the old Lion besmirched. Father Ziegler, who had been the very first to sign the priests' petition to bring Kain to Saint Louis, rose and faced Archbishop Kain. "I hope the pallium celebration will be a great success, but the reception of the Cardinal a great fiasco." [180] The presbyterate split on the vote: forty-three backed the Archbishop while thirty-seven voted with Ziegler.

Nor was this incident the first time Archbishop Kain crossed swords in his new realm. In April 1894, he ordered a letter be read from all

---

180   Rev. John Rothensteiner. *History of the Archdiocese of St. Louis. Vol. II.* Saint Louis: Blackwell Wielandy Co. 1928. P. 601.

the pulpits calling the *Western Watchman* "a paper utterly unfit to be brought into a Catholic home."[181] One week later another letter was read throughout the Archdiocese rescinding the previous missive. It seems the editor, Father David Phelan, had sufficiently apologized to Archbishop Kain to receive his forgiveness.

The pallium investiture took place after Cardinal Satolli's visit. On May 10, 1896, twenty-five Archbishops and bishops joined Cardinal Gibbons in the cathedral for the event. For the first time now, Kain was master of his own Archdiocese. He had witnessed the continued expansion of the Archdiocese without much control over events. Indeed, with the death of Father Brady, the Vicar General, and the incapacity of Archbishop Kenrick, and with the affairs of the Archdiocese constantly being contested between the two prelates, developments regarding the Catholic Church in Missouri seemed to happen automatically.

In 1891, Archbishop Kenrick approved a plan to erect Saint Anne Parish, but expanded it into the territory which had been served by the Redemptorists at Saint Alphonsus on Grand Avenue. This was the brainchild of Father John Tuohy. He began with a small chapel just blocks away from Saint Alphonsus. Later, under the pastorate of Father O. J. McDonald, the site for the church was placed at Whittier and Page, a respectable distance. Father Tuohy was then installed by Archbishop Kain as pastor of the grand old parish of Saint Patrick in 1896.

Kain's first year in Saint Louis, while still coadjutor, must have been mind-boggling. Three rural parishes were established in 1893 along with five urban ones. On September 12, Nativity Church was blessed in Belgique, Perry County. Here was a colony of Belgian and Dutch Catholics who had migrated with their priest, Father D. L. De Ceunyuck. Representing Bishop Kain, who had just arrived at his new home on August 3, was the Archdiocesan chancellor, Father Henry van Der Sanden, on whom Kain would come to rely heavily.

Van Der Sanden had immigrated to America from the Netherlands in 1857. He continued his priestly studies at the Archdiocesan seminary in Carondelet and was transferred to Saint Vincent's Seminary in Cape Girardeau when Archbishop Kenrick consolidated seminary studies there in 1858. Van Der Sanden was ordained on June 3, 1860 and was immediately assigned as pastor to a small Belgian enclave in Bollinger County, Vinemount. Violence visited Vinemount during the

---

181   Rev. John Rothensteiner. *History of the Archdiocese of St. Louis. Vol. II.* Saint Louis: Blackwell Wielandy Co. 1928. P. 601.

Civil War when three young men were brutally murdered by Confederate guerillas. By then, Father van Der Sanden had been reassigned to Jefferson City, then Kirkwood, and finally, in 1874, he became the chancellor of the Archdiocese. His later role in preserving the historical documents of the Archdiocese was invaluable.

Bishop Kain himself blessed the new parish of Saint Aloysius in Baring, Missouri, on November 13, 1893, travelling to northern Missouri between Edina and Memphis. The other rural parish was Guardian Angels in Oran.

In the city, Holy Innocents was erected on the near south side. To the north was Saint Matthew's on Kennerly and Sarah, made up of around one hundred English-speaking families. German Catholics lived in the area but attended Mass at Holy Ghost on Taylor and North Market. The founding pastor was Father Joseph Shields. He experienced unprecedented growth in what had been a sparsely populated area. By 1902, when Saint Matthew opened a parochial school, it counted nearly twelve hundred families with a school enrollment of seven hundred children guided by a community of fourteen Sisters of Saint Joseph. Like Saints Peter and Paul in the Soulard area, Saint Matthew's was a powerhouse for vocations, counting eighteen priests and seventeen sisters among its alumni.

Within months Saint Mark's Parish was established on Page and Academy, not far from Christian Brothers College on North Kingshighway. Later, during the 1904 World's Fair and the International Olympics held in Saint Louis (the People's Olympics), Saint Mark's fielded a soccer team, which won an Olympic medal. Even so, the team was denied the medal for decades because they did not represent a country.

Saint Edward's was built at Clara and Maffitt by Father Edward J. Wynne, who had previously served in three rural sites. Father Wynne gathered in some two hundred and fifty families to found his parish. The last of the urban parishes to be founded was Saint Barbara's. The founder was Father John Schramm, who followed the Irish method of establishing a parish. Historically, while German Catholics typically gathered together to purchase property, establish their community, and petition for the erection of a parish to which a priest would be assigned, the Irish model was to give the priest a free hand to go out and gather in parishioners. In the case of Saint Barbara, Father Schramm was sent to purchase land at Etzel and Goodfellow and then scout out German Catholic families. Vicar General Mühlsiepen preached the first

Mass on June 4, 1893, as the parish had grown to one hundred and fifty families. Father Schramm served Saint Barbara's and was quick to set up a parochial school there.

While 1893 saw the establishment of three rural and four urban parishes, 1894 counted four new parishes, three rural and one urban. Father Joseph Conrad came from Clear Creek to establish Saint Joseph's Parish in Pilot Grove. The area had been settled since the 1820s but had no church until he arrived. Father Conrad also began a school staffed by Benedictine Sisters. With time, Saint Joseph's drew in nearby Catholics from Martinsville, Nelson, and Clear Creek itself. It is one of only two Catholic parishes in Cooper County, the other being at Boonville. In Jonesburg, Saint Patrick's, though in existence for seventeen years, got its first resident pastor in 1894, Father B. H. Schlathoelter. He died within three years and was replaced by Father H. J. Shaw, who left within a year. Stability came with Father M. Collins, who served until December 1903 when he was succeeded by Father J. T. Tuohy, who had given Archbishop Kain considerable headaches earlier.

At New Haven, a new church in honor of the Assumption was established by Father Sevecik. Catholics had been worshiping there since 1863, when a small church was blessed by Archbishop Kenrick and assigned as a mission to the Jesuits in Washington. Father Sevecik was a resourceful priest. He demolished the old chapel but saved the material for a fine new church and a spacious rectory. The changes brought murmuring protests from his parishioners, who proved to be uncooperative. Father Sevecik relied on Saint Louis benefactors to help him. He did much of the construction himself, including the carpentry and bricklaying. He presided at New Haven for ten years. Thereafter, the parish went into physical decline, as Father Sevecik's successor was ill most of the time. A revival would only come in 1920 with another powerhouse, Father Francis Schiller. It was through his remarkable leadership that the people of New Haven rallied together and raised $18,000 for a new church. The final church to be built in 1894 was Our Lady of Good Counsel, a daughter of Saint Michael's Parish. While Father Patrick O'Donahoe founded the parish of nearly seven hundred families, it had little chance for growth. Its boundaries were only two city blocks wide, running east of Broadway to the lumberyards near the river.

1895 saw only one parish erected: Saint Joseph's in Canton, Missouri. Like many of the parishes of rural western and central Missouri, a Catholic presence preceded the founding of a parish by many years. A wooden structure served as a mission for this river town as early as 1841, with a brick building replacing it in 1869. The area had been visited by Father Lefevere as early as 1837. The question of a school for Saint Joseph's is interesting. Father Rothensteiner states that the parish never had a school.[182] In another part of his history of the Archdiocese, he says there was "noteworthy progress" of a school under the direction of the Ursuline nuns.[183] Both comments are contradicted by a history of the Jefferson City diocese, where it is mentioned that Saint Joseph, Canton conducted a school between 1904 and 1916, closing twelve years before Father Rothensteiner published his seminal two-volume history of the Archdiocese of Saint Louis.[184]

In 1896, only Saint Joseph's in White Church, Howell County, was founded. The community traced its history back to the migration of several German families from Rhineland, Missouri. In 1872, these families climbed into covered wagons and moved southwest. At one point in the expedition, disease raged among the people and several animals died. The people decided to go no further and settled near the town of Peace Valley, with its little white Methodist church.

The people called their little settlement White Church and built homes as well as a Catholic church for themselves. Attracting a priest proved difficult. One came from Poplar Bluff for a while, but that proved too difficult a journey for him. Another was sent as a resident priest from Saint Louis, but he found the area too remote and life too demanding, so he returned to the city. Father Mühlsiepen visited White Church at Easter to bring the people their sacraments. Finally, in 1895, Father John Waltherman arrived to set the parish on solid footing. The new pastor awoke to an unpleasant surprise his first day in the parish: a violent storm had erupted the night before and the bedroom of his little cabin was flooded. Father Waltherman stayed only two years but was present to host Archbishop Kain and Father Mühlsiepen on their episcopal tour of Howell County in 1896.

As discomforting as a flooded rectory may have been for Father Waltherman in 1895, another weather event marked the next year as

---

182   Rev. John Rothensteiner. *History of the Archdiocese of St. Louis. Vol. II.* Saint Louis: Blackwell Wielandy Co. 1928. P. 379,
183   Ibid. P. 678.
184   Loretta Pastva, SND. *Proclaiming the Good News in the Heart of Missouri.* Strasbourg: Éditions du Signe. 2005. P. 55.

one of the most tragic in Saint Louis history. May 27, 1896 was an exceptionally hot day in Saint Louis and by 4 P.M. the sky turned an ominous black with areas of green. Those with barometers would note a plunge in air pressure. Tornadoes were not uncommon in Saint Louis, and a few citizens began looking for shelter.

Suddenly, storm clouds revealed a funnel, which touched ground at Arsenal Street just east of Hampton Avenue. The twister was near the site of the City Poor House, which sheltered around thirteen hundred of the city's elderly and indigent. Even as chimneys were blown away and walls collapsed, remarkably no serious injuries were reported. Next to be hit was the Female Hospital, where the roof of one wing was blown away. The tornado traveled east, crossing Kingshighway, churning a diagonal path through Tower Grove Park. There it destroyed hundreds of trees, but as before, it took no human lives. That luck was about to change. The next building hit was the Liggett and Myer Tobacco Company. Ironworkers were caught off-guard as they were building an addition to the building. Many were blown away from their perches; others fell to the ground to be crushed beneath tons of brick and steel. At least ten men lost their lives there that day.

The tornado's path then crossed Grand Avenue and sped through Compton Heights, churning its way to Jefferson Avenue. At this point it entered the tony Lafayette Park neighborhood. Lafayette Park, the first constructed in Saint Louis, was the pride of the city. Tall, narrow, stately homes looked out onto the park from every direction. In minutes, the park was a rubble of twisted trees surrounding a foundation which had once been a bandstand.

The next victim of the great tornado was City Hospital with its four hundred patients. Walls and roofs were blown away. The crematorium was destroyed. A few patients were sucked out of their rooms and hurled like dolls. George Wilson had been in his room on the second floor. He was pulled out and, incredibly, landed on his feet. Without a second's delay, Wilson ran for cover in the hospital's basement. Remarkably, no one was killed or seriously injured at the hospital.

Such could not be said about the next neighborhood, the Soulard area. At Seventh and Rutgers the Mauchensheimer Building collapsed. Seventeen people were killed there and another six died across the street.

Now the tornado reached the riverfront, which was crowded with twenty steamboats and ferries and tugs. A sort of shantytown coexisted with the commercial vessels, as poor people made homes of all sorts of floating craft. All of these were battered into rubble. One steamboat, *The Anchor Line*, was picked up like a little toy and crashed onto the Illinois shoreline. There was no accounting for the lives lost in the shanty boats. Bodies disappeared into the Mississippi River. The best estimate is that as many as one hundred and fifty were killed there.

At least one humorous incident brought a sense of humanity to the disaster. One of the ferry boats to be tossed about was a Wiggin's boat, the *Andrew Christy*. It was hit by several other boats out of control on the river. Finally, a wharf boat slid by, grazing the side. Someone on the wharf boat called out to a crewman on the *Andrew Christy* and asked if he wanted to join them. He called out, "Yes. Wait till I get my dog." Then both man and dog jumped to safety on the wharf boat.[185]

On Eads Bridge, William Swoncott was driving eastward the #17 train for the Chicago and Alton Railroad. He witnessed the carnage on the riverfront and realized the storm was heading his way. The engineer called for increased steam and the train sped as fast as it could toward the Illinois side of the river. The #17 was around two hundred feet from the east side when the tornado struck Eads Bridge at the east tower. The top course, the pedestrian and wagon roadway, collapsed sending tons of debris onto the railroad level. Because of the fast thinking of engineer Swoncott, only the last baggage cars were destroyed. The passenger cars were thrown to their side and several people sustained injuries. But no one was killed.

Now East Saint Louis felt the brunt of the tornado. The police station and court house were destroyed. A jury sitting at trial escaped with just minutes to spare. The rail yards were devastated. Of the thirty-five workers at the Saint Louis, Vandalia and Terra Haute railroad depot, fifteen were killed instantly.

And then it was over. People began to emerge from underneath the rubble. They came out into the rain, which continued to pour. Some gathered in little clusters. Some began searching for loved ones. Some merely stood or sat stunned.

On the 28th, efforts got underway to recover the bodies of the dead and to take them to the city morgue. Crowds of loved ones became so large the police had to restore order and establish lines in which

---

185   Julian Curzon. *The Great Cyclone at Saint Louis and East Saint Louis, May 27, 1896.* Carbondale: Southern Illinois University Press. 1997. P. 328.

people could walk past bodies for identification. A facility which could house several hundred now homeless, the Good Shepherd Sisters residence (which had been abandoned when the sisters moved their work into the county on Gravois Road), was pressed into service. Patients were transferred from the ruined City Hospital to that facility. Stories circulated about how city inmates at Four Courts screamed for help and ran from the exercise yard into the relative safety of their cells when the tornado struck.

It seemed the tornado targeted churches; or perhaps because Saint Louis had so many churches, it was natural they would be disproportionately hit. Of the forty churches struck by the great tornado of 1896, four were Catholic. Saint Vincent de Paul had the least damage: shingles and ornaments torn from its steeple, an estimated damage of around $3,000. Saint Henry and Annunciation Church were less lucky, sustaining damages of $10,000 and $18,000, respectively. The worst hit among all the damaged churches in Saint Louis was Father Goller's pride and joy, Saints Peter and Paul. The damage there was estimated at $30,000.

Over eight thousand buildings were damaged or had to be destroyed in the clean-up which followed. Property losses ranged as high as $10,000,000. At least one hundred and forty people lost their lives, though the toll was certainly much higher as scores of shanty boat residents disappeared into the river, the bodies within never recovered. One effect of the great tornado was to spur some of the wealthiest families to move westward; while many rebuilt around Lafayette Park, even more sought new homes in the west. In the western part of the city, exclusive neighborhoods with private streets had developed in the 1870s. These provided homes for railroad executives, mayors, bankers. In contrast, even before the Great Tornado of 1896, less elegant housing was being constructed near Lafayette Park, west on Lafayette Street and south on Jefferson Avenue. The park itself was often filled with loud, fun-loving crowds, changing the atmosphere of the neighborhood. Many residents used the tornado as an excuse to abandon the old neighborhood and seek out new, fashionable neighborhoods on the West End. With construction of electric street cars in the 1890s, it was less important for executives and professionals to live close to downtown. More often, narrow gauge railroads fanned out from Grand Avenue and Olive into Florissant and Normandy, making country living possible on large estates. Catholic churches were soon to follow.

In 1898, there were three parishes founded on the outskirts of the city. Father Francis Brand purchased the Murdock estate and erected a small, frame church, Saint Michael's. Murdock was a native of Great Britain. Moving to Saint Louis, he settled beyond the city itself on a large estate he named Shrewsbury, after his British hometown. Father Brand stayed only two years at Saint Michael's, opening a school conducted by the Ursuline nuns. His replacement stayed only two years. Then Father Charles Einig gave the parish stability by serving as pastor there for nearly nine years.

In the Tower Grove Park area, it became obvious that parishes were needed for the growing population. South of the park, Holy Family was founded when Father J. F. Reuther was transferred from rural Saint Monica in Creve Coeur. He celebrated his first Mass on November 10, 1898, in a chapel in an old home he rented on Wyoming Street. The Mass was sparsely attended and as Father Reuther walked the streets of his parish, drawing a census, he found only one hundred and seventy-three Catholics there, many of whom had abandoned the Faith and were not inclined to come back. Refusing to be discouraged, the priest soldiered on, opened a school under the direction of the School Sisters of Notre Dame, and purchased property on Humphrey Street.

In 1900, Holy Family School came under the direction of the Precious Blood Sisters, and the parish census increased dramatically as Catholic families in the Soulard area moved from Saints Peter and Paul Parish, from their crowded tenements to single-family brick homes surrounding Holy Family Church. Father Reuther remained pastor there until his death in 1927, just six weeks after the dedication of a grand Romanesque church made of gray granite. North of Tower Grove Park, Saint Margaret of Scotland was founded. Father James O'Brien rented a storefront on Russell and Vandeventer. He lived in the apartment above the store. With time and canvassing the neighborhood, as Father Reuther was doing at Holy Family, Father O'Brien drew together a congregation of English-language Catholics. He was slower to establish a school though, waiting until 1911. Father O'Brien remained pastor of Saint Margaret's, building a beautiful Gothic church on Flad, until his death in 1922.

Archbishop Kain caused the erection of three other parishes in the last years of the nineteenth century, each beyond Saint Louis. In 1897, Holy Ghost Church was founded in Centralia. The community there had been served by visiting priests as far back as the days of the legendary Father John Hogan, in 1859.

In the northeastern-most corner of Missouri, a parish was founded in Kahoka, Clark County. Father Brand, fresh from founding Saint Michael's in Shrewsbury, was given the task of establishing another Saint Michael's. He built a church there but used it more as a base for travel rather than as a permanent residence. Father Brand spent four and a half years bringing the sacraments to a scattered Catholic flock in Wayland, Chambersburg, and Mudd Settlement as well as occasional visits to Memphis, Hitt, Avela, Neva, Acesto, Athens, Saint Francisville, Alexandria, Wyaconda, Neeper, and Medill. He travelled by horseback, in buggy, and even by rail. Sometimes Father Brand resorted to a handcar to get to the most remote parts of his parish. One further parish was founded at New Bremen, now Ozora. Father Martin Bahr, a native of Sainte Genevieve, became the founding pastor and served there nearly five years before being transferred.

A project near and dear to the heart of Archbishop Kain was the erection of a new cathedral for his Archdiocese. Archbishop Kenrick had made no secret of his dislike for Bishop Rosati's cathedral, calling it "an injudicious combination of ancient style and modern innovation." Instead, he had Saint John the Apostle and Evangelist built in such a way as to be a church worthy of episcopal ceremony, while the rectory could accommodate a bishop or two.

Yet, by the time of the Civil War, Saint John's too had been swamped with urban clutter. In 1863, the ever-generous Anne Lucas Hunt gave the Archbishop a spacious lot on the southeast corner of Jefferson and Locust for the erection of a new church, perhaps a new cathedral. But the Archbishop's attention had turned to battling the State of Missouri over the Drake Amendment with its Test Oath. Then he became embroiled in the definition of papal infallibility at the Vatican Council. So the lot stood vacant until 1874.

In that year a wooden frame church was built, again with a gift from Anne Lucas Hunt. No doubt, in her mind, this modest structure was only temporary until the issue of a new cathedral surfaced. The Church of the Immaculate Conception downtown had been structurally damaged during the building of Eads Bridge and had to be abandoned. Attending Immaculate Conception was what remained of Saint Louis' Creole elite, though they no longer dominated the city's civic or political affairs. The property intended for the new cathedral now became home for the Church of the Immaculate Conception, with around one thousand parishioners.

Archbishop Kain was determined to build a new cathedral even further west on one of the most fashionable streets in Saint Louis, Lindell Boulevard. He purchased property between Lindell and Maryland and erected a modest church there, calling it the New Cathedral Chapel. He himself sketched drawings of a Roman-style basilica and began raising funds for the project. He predicted the cathedral would cost a million dollars but said, "We have a right to think, to hope and to expect that a great and noble building will be erected commensurate at once with your civic pride, your Catholic Faith, and your generous giving."[186] Two events blocked Kain's path to building a new cathedral: the first was the tornado of 1896 and the second was the Archbishop's deteriorating health.

Archbishop Kain realized it would be unseemly to begin construction on a million-dollar cathedral with so many parish churches and schools damaged by the tornado. He seemed to know that his dream would not be fulfilled in his lifetime. Regardless, the Archbishop wrote into his will that all of his personal wealth and possessions should go toward the cathedral building fund.

In the meantime, Kain prepared himself for a long European tour. The chief purpose was to make his *ad limina* visit to Pope Leo XIII and to deliver to him the results of the Third Synod of Saint Louis, held in September of 1896.

Two hundred and nineteen priests joined Archbishop Kain in this Synod, with thirty-five excused absences. Here the decrees of the Third Plenary Council of 1884 were finally applied. Every parish was to provide for the Catholic education of its children, and parents were reminded that they were required to enroll their children in a Catholic school. The penalty for failing to do so was potentially a refusal of absolution in confession. Children were to receive First Communion between the ages of ten and fourteen and were encouraged at that time to make a pledge of abstinence from strong drink until the age of twenty. The pledge was to be made personally to the pastor. In addition, German, Polish, and Bohemian parishes were raised to equal status as English-language parishes, removing once and for all any threat of Cahenslyism. However, members of such national parishes

---

186   Rev. John Rothensteiner. *History of the Archdiocese of St. Louis. Vol. II.* Saint Louis: Blackwell Wielandy Co. 1928. P. 640-641.

were free to join English-language parishes if they lived in the parish boundaries and were fluent in English.

When a Board of Consultors was established, also mandated by the Plenary Council of 1884, eyebrows were raised when Fathers Goller and Walsh were not included. It was explained that both had been named irremovable rectors, along with thirteen others, so they would join the six consultors in forming the electoral college of the Archdiocese, which would make episcopal recommendations to Rome. Aging Father Mühlsiepen was reconfirmed as Vicar General. Father Henry van Der Sanden remained as Chancellor; Father Frederick G. Holweck, a founding member of the Archdiocesan Historical Society, was named Censor Librorum. The Synod ended with a flurry of decrees encouraging the practice of the Forty Hours Devotion, establishment of sodalities and Saint Vincent de Paul Conferences for each parish, and the prohibition of membership in secret societies. Late-night dancing was also condemned. The cathedraticum, the tax on all parish income for support of the Archdiocesan administration, was set at five percent.

On July 31, 1897, Archbishop John Joseph Kain left with two priests for Europe. First they visited Ireland, Scotland, and England, then the trio went on to Antwerp, Cologne, Paris, Lourdes, Marseilles, Genoa, Pisa, Florence, and Rome. Along the way, Kain made note of churches and cathedrals, drawing inspiration for his own project.

The Archbishop met with Pope Leo XIII on November 22. But he had other things on his mind. Father John Thomas Joseph Tuohy had made a name for himself after returning to Saint Louis after a two-year sabbatical at Catholic University in Washington, D. C. He took over Saint Anne Parish, which intruded into the territory of the Redemptorist parish Saint Alphonsus. Affairs remained at an impasse until Tuohy was named pastor of the once-prestigious Saint Patrick's in 1896.

A financial mismanagement caused the Archbishop to remove Tuohy from his pastor's position at Saint Patrick's. But the Archbishop was now in Europe and Tuohy refused to vacate the rectory. The task of removing the hot-headed priest fell to Vicar General Mühlsiepen. The Vicar General moved with great caution and caused the Archbishop to express his frustrations in a letter to a friend. "Father Mühlsiepen seems to be inclined to give the reverend gentleman all the time he asks for, and Father Tuohy was not at all backward in asking for it."[187]

The Tuohy affair made its way into the local newspapers. The priest gathered lots of support with twelve hundred men signing a petition asking that the affair be settled to the approval of both sides. A thousand women then sent their own petition to the Apostolic Delegate. Some six hundred Italians from the neighborhood sent a petition. Finally, Father Mühlsiepen launched his own assault, telling newspapers of Father Tuohy's mismanagement of funds, failure to pay bills, and failure to keep sacramental records at his previous parish. On April 13, 1898, Archbishop Kain, having returned to Saint Louis, took the witness stand to testify against one of his own priests, Father John Timothy Joseph Tuohy. In the end, Judge Richard B. Haughton ordered Tuohy to vacate Saint Patrick rectory within twenty days. Instead, Tuohy wrote the Apostolic Delegate, Cardinal Sebastian Martinelli. In response, the Apostolic Delegate wrote Archbishop Kain asking that the affair be settled to the satisfaction of all parties. Kain had tried to entice Tuohy to take the position of pastor at Edina, but he would not budge, even when a civil judgment went against him. Slowly, his supporters began to desert him and come to the Archbishop's camp.

Kain wrote Martinelli, warning him that he was being duped by "a first-class trickster." Kain now wanted the priest removed to a monastery to do penance. Martinelli wanted a private, amiable settlement. In the end, Tuohy solved the dilemma by taking an extended leave from active priesthood. He would return to the Archdiocese after Kain's death and serve as pastor of Jonesburg until his death in 1919.[188]

Meanwhile, the toll of administration was becoming more and more obvious on Archbishop Kain. In the summer of 1899, Kain went east to vacation in Atlantic City and to visit some of the places where he had once served. He spent time with his old friend, Cardinal Gibbons. While out east, Kain experienced an attack of vertigo which lasted an entire day. After some rest, the dizziness abated and he returned to Saint Louis to assume his duties.

In April 1900, Archbishop Kain again left Saint Louis for Rome. Again he traveled with two priests. In Rome he delivered a list of candidates proposed by the bishops of his province for the Archdiocese

---

187   Rev. John Rothensteiner. *History of the Archdiocese of St. Louis. Vol. II.* Saint Louis: Blackwell Wielandy Co. 1928. P. 609.

188   William Barnaby Faherty, S. J. *Dream by the River: Two Centuries of Saint Louis Catholicism: 1766 – 1967.* Saint Louis: Piraeus Publishers. 1973. P. 134.

of Dubuque. First on the list was Archbishop Keane. On his way home, Archbishop Kain had occasion to be surprised by the rumor that had circulated back in Rome. He wrote from Ireland: "I see, by the way, that they are stealing a march on me. Someone sent Father Tracy a clipping from P. D. announcing that Father Harty was to be the Auxiliary-Bishop of St. Louis. This was news to me, but queer things are sometimes done at Rome."[189] The rumor turned out to be untrue, but as Kain's health continued to fail him, the idea of episcopal help became fixed more and more in his mind.

In October 1902, Kain appealed to Cardinal Gibbons for an auxiliary bishop. He was unable to hold a pen in his right hand. He instructed two of his priests to write letters on his behalf. His doctor, John P. Boyson, also wrote a letter. The Cardinal immediately wrote Rome, but no response came. Kain petitioned that Father Joseph A. Connelly assist him, but he got no reply from Rome. He tried again, naming Father Jeramiah Harty. Again Rome did not reply. In desperation, Archbishop Kain called a meeting of the consultors and irremovable rectors and asked for a terna to propose a coadjutor. The list was then sent to the bishops of the province. The final terna listed Coadjutor Bishop John J. Glennon of Kansas City first. Bishop Edward Dunne of Dallas and Saint Louis native Bishop John Hennessy of Wichita filled out the list. The original terna drawn up by the consultors and rectors placed Glennon second and did not name Hennessey at all. The provincial terna was circulated to the American Archbishops, who approved the list. Archbishop Riordon of San Francisco was most enthusiastic for Glennon, as was Cardinal Gibbons. This time Rome acted quickly. On April 17, 1903, Pope Leo XIII, his own death merely weeks away, named John Joseph Glennon as coadjutor of Saint Louis with the right of succession. Glennon was forty years old.

Upon the arrival of Bishop Glennon in Saint Louis, he was named Archdiocesan administrator. On May 3, 1903, Archbishop Kain, now relieved of responsibilities, traveled to Baltimore with one other priest at his side. They took up residence at Saint Agnes Sanitarium. There the Archbishop lingered until his death on October 13, 1903. Archbishop John Joseph Kain was sixty-two years old. Father Rothensteiner was brutally honest in his assessment of the Archbishop who ruled a mere seven years and eight months since the Lion had died.

---

189   Rev. John Rothensteiner. *History of the Archdiocese of St. Louis. Vol. II.* Saint Louis: Blackwell Wielandy Co. 1928. P. 611. (P. D. is the Saint Louis Post-Dispatch)

"He was not exactly a loveable character: his appearance and manner of speech seemed to preclude familiarity; yet he craved warm loyalty and whole-souled regard. The multitude of priests and laymen who came in contact with him still treasure his memory, the memory of a high minded prelate, a faithful and kindly priest, a strong, fearless and sincere man."[190]

As Saint Louis and its Archdiocese entered the twentieth century, both would rely more heavily on the resources which had come to the Rome of the West in the nineteenth century. With notable exception of the Italians, and later the Lebanese, Saint Louis would witness no great immigrant wave, unlike Chicago, Detroit, and Cleveland. It would attract few new religious congregations to add to the many societies already here. The population would shift westward, but not grow. Industries would come and others leave. Great questions of politics, the environment, of securing a certain quality of life amid wars and depressions, would challenge the creativity of the city and the Church. Corruption under Boss Butler, the devastating trolley strike of 1900, and the squalor of slums would plague the city. Leaders like Mayor Rolla Wells and "Holy Joe" Volk and David R. Francis were about to emerge. But first, Saint Louis decided to throw itself the biggest party in its history: the World's Fair of 1904.

---

190   Rev. John Rothensteiner. *History of the Archdiocese of St. Louis. Vol. II.* Saint Louis: Blackwell Wielandy Co. 1928. P. 632.

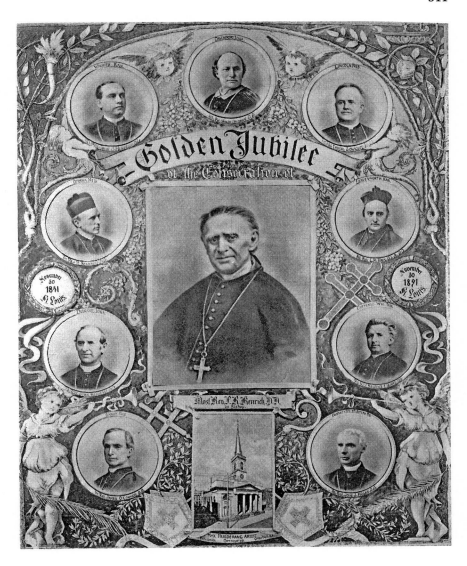

This illustration commemorates Archbishop Kenrick's 50th anniversary as bishop in St. Louis, with small portraits of bishops who participated in the celebration. Clockwise from bottom-left: James O'Connor of Omaha, John Hennessy of Dubuque, R. Scannell of Omaha, John J. Hennessy of Wichita, Henry Cosgrove of Davenport, Thomas Bonacum of Lincoln, L. M. Fink of Leavenworth, Maurice F. Burke of the Cheyenne-Wyoming Territory, and John J. Hogan of Kansas City-St. Joseph. Archdiocese of St. Louis Archives and Records.

Father David S. Phelan, no date.
Archdiocese of St. Louis Archives and Records.

Archbishop John Joseph Kain. Archdiocese of St. Louis Archives and Records.

ST. LOUIS, MO., June 1, 1896.

REV. DEAR SIR:

The calamity, which has befallen our city, has rendered many families homeless and destitute. Humanity and religion call on us to come to their relief. I therefore appeal to you and your good people in behalf of the sufferers. Those who have been spared, should give a thank-offering for their preservation. You will therefore invite your people on next Sunday, or as soon after as possible, to contribute to a fund for the benefit of their stricken brethren. Send at once the amount you may receive to the President of the Upper Council of St. Vincent of Paul Conferences, J. T. Donovan, 700 Chestnut Street, St. Louis. The Conferences are working in conjunction with the Relief Committee, so that you are assured of a judicious distribution of your alms amongst the deserving.

Donations of clothing and furniture are also solicited. These articles may be sent either to the respective Parish Conferences, or to the Relief Committee, Room 126, Chamber of Commerce, entrance on Chestnut Street.

Yours truly in Christ,

✝ JOHN J. KAIN,

Abp. St. Louis.

Circular letter from Archbishop Kain to pastors in the Archdiocese regarding the tornado of 1896. Archdiocese of St. Louis Archives and Records.

CHURCH OF STS. PETER AND PAUL, SEVENTH STREET AND ALLEN AVENUE

CHURCH OF ST. JOHN OF NEPOMUK, SOULARD AND ELEVENTH STREETS

Photographs from book *Pictured Story of the Tornado* (St. Louis: Southern Age, 1896)
on Internet Archive at https://archive.org/

The path of the tornado, which traveled from west to east, may be traced by darkened portion of map.

THE ROUTE OF THE
GREAT CYCLONE
AT ST LOUIS
MAY 27TH 1896.

Map of the path of damage through St. Louis of the great tornado of 1896. From the book *The Great Tornado* (St. Louis: Graf Engraving Co., 1896). Archdiocese of St. Louis Archives and Records.

BIBLIOGRAPHY

General

Baily, Thomas A. and David M. Kennedy. *The American Pageant.* Lexington: D. C. Heath & Co. 1979.

Curtis, Susan. *Dancing to the Black Man's Tune: A Life of Scott Joplin.* Columbia: University of Missouri Press. 1994.

Curzon, Julian, ed. *The Great Cyclone at St. Louis and East St. Louis, May 27, 1896.* Carbondale: Southern Illinois University Press. 1997.

Erwin, James W. *Guerillas in Civil War Missouri.* Charleston: The History Press. 2012.

Marks, Geoffrey and Beatty, William K. *Epidemics: The Story of Mankind's Most Lethal and Elusive Enemies – from Ancient Times to the Present.* New York: Charles Scribner's Sons. 1976.

Miller, Donald L. *City of the Century: The Epic of Chicago and the Making of America.* New York: Simon & Schuster. 1996.

Seagraves, Anne. *Soiled Doves: Prostitution in the Early West.* Wesanne Publications.

Swain, Gwyneth. *Dred and Harriet Scott: A Family's Struggle for Freedom.* Saint Paul: Borealis Books. 2004.

Local and Regional

Arenson, Adam. *The Great Heart of the Republic: St. Louis and the Cultural Civil War.* Cambridge: Harvard University Press. 2011.

Burnett, Robyn and Ken Luebbering. *German Settlement in Missouri: New Land, Old Ways.* Columbia: University of Missouri Press. 1996.

Castel, Albert. *General Sterling Price and the Civil War in the West.* Baton Rouge: Louisiana State University Press. 1996.

Christian, Shirley. *Before Lewis and Clark: The Story of the Chouteaus, the French Dynasty that Ruled America's Frontier.* New York: Farrar, Straus and Giroux. 2004.

Compton, Richard J. *Pictorial St. Louis: A Topographical Survey in Perspective AD 1875.* Saint Louis: Compton and Company. 1876.

Engle, Stephen D. *Yankee Dutchman: The Life of Franz Sigel.* Baton Rouge: Louisiana State University Press. 1993.

Faherty, S. J., William Barnaby. *Exile in Erin: A Confederate Chaplain's Story, The Life of Father John B. Bannon.* Saint Louis: Missouri

Historical Society Press. 2002.

Gerteis, Louis S. *Civil War St. Louis*. Lawrence: University of Kansas Press. 2001.

Hodes, Frederick A. *Rising on the River: St. Louis 1822 – 1850*. Tooele, Utah: Patrice Press. 2009.

Hurley, Andrew, ed. *Common Fields: An Environmental History of St. Louis*. Saint Louis: Missouri Historical Society Press. 1997.

Piston, William Garrett and Richard W. Hatcher III. *Wilson's Creek: The Second Battle of the Civil War and the Men Who Fought It*. Chapel Hill: The University of North Carolina Press. 2000.

Primm, James Neal. *Lion of the Valley: St. Louis, Missouri, 1764 – 1980*. Saint Louis: Missouri Historical Society Press. 2010.

Sandweiss, Eric. *St. Louis: The Evolution of an American Urban Landscape*. Philadelphia: Temple University Press. 2001.

Sandweiss, Lee Ann, ed. *Seeking St. Louis: Voices from a River City, 1670 – 2000*. Saint Louis: Missouri Historical Society Press. 2000.

Stadler, Frances Hurd. *Saint Louis Day by Day*. St. Louis: The Patrice Press. 1990.

The Catholic Church

Barry, O. S. B. Colman J. *The Catholic Church and German Americans*. Milwaukee: The Bruce Publishing Company. 1953.

Brennan, Lawrence, Timothy Dolan, James Dryden, Robert Finn, Bernadette Snyder and Michael John Witt. *Archdiocese of St. Louis: Three Centuries of Catholicism: 1700 – 2000*. Strasbourg: Éditions du Signe. 2001.

Callan, R. S. C. J., Louise. *Philippine Duchesne: Frontier Missionary of the Sacred Heart: 1769 – 1852*. Westminster: The Newman Press. 1957.

Davis, O. S. B. Cyprian. *The History of Black Catholics in the United States*. New York: Crossroads. 1990.

Ellis, John Tracy. *The Life of James Cardinal Gibbons: Archbishop of Baltimore, 1834 – 1921*. Vol. I and II. Milwaukee: The Bruce Publishing Company. 1952.

Faherty, S. J. William Barnaby. *Dream by the River: Two Centuries of Saint Louis Catholicism, 1766 – 1967*. Saint Louis: Piraeus Publishers. 1973.

Faherty, S. J., William Barnaby. *The St. Louis German Catholics*. St. Louis: Reedy Press. 2004.

Hales, E. E. Y. *Pio Nono: A Study in European Politics and Religion in the Nineteenth Century*. Garden City: Image Books. 1962.

Killoren, S. J. John J. *"Come, Blackrobe:" De Smet and the Indian Tragedy*. Norman: University of Oklahoma Press. 1994.

Magaret, Helene. *Giant in the Wilderness: A Biography of Father Charles Nerinckx*. Milwaukee: The Bruce Publishing Company. 1952.

O'Shea, John J. *The Two Kenricks: Most Rev. Francis Patrick, Archbishop of Baltimore. Most Rev. Peter Richard, Archbishop of St. Louis*. Philadelphia: John J. McVey. 1904.

Payton, Crystal, ed. *On the Mission in Missouri & Fifty Years Ago: A Memoir. Two Irish-American Classics by John Joseph Hogan, Pioneer Priest*. Springfield: Lens & Pen. 2009.

Rothensteiner, John. *History of the Archdiocese of St. Louis*. Vol. II. St. Louis: Blackwell Wielandy Co. 1928.

Spalding, Thomas W. *The Premier See: A History of the Archdiocese of Baltimore, 1789 - 1989*. Baltimore: The Johns Hopkins University Press. 1989. P. 175.

Witt, Michael John. *I. Phil: The Journey of a Twentieth-Century Religious*. Winona: Saint Mary's Press. 1987.

Articles

Brandt, Patricia. "'A Character of Extravagance:' Establishment of the Second Archdiocese in the United States." *The Catholic Historical Review*. October, 2003.

Capizzi, Joseph E. "For What Shall We Repent? Reflections on American Bishops, Their Teaching and Slavery in the United States." *Theological Studies*. 65. 2004.

Coogan, M. Jane. "Dubuque's First Archbishop: The Image and the Man." *Record of the American Catholic Historical Society of Philadelphia*. March-December 1981.

Gollar, C. Walter. "Catholic Slaves and Slaveholders in Kentucky." *The Catholic Historical Review*. January 1998.

Grenz, Suzanne M. "The Exodusters of 1879: St. Louis and Kansas City Responds." *Missouri Historical Review,* October 1978.

McIntrye, Stephen L. "Communist Progress: The Workingman's Party and St. Louis Educational Politics, 1877 – 1878." *Missouri Historical Review*. October 2000.

Miller, Samuel J. "Peter Richard Kenrick: Bishop and Archbishop of St. Louis: 1806 – 1896." *Record of the American Catholic Historical Society of Philadelphia*. Vol. 84. No. 1 – 3, 1973.

INDEX

Deutsch-Amerikanische Priesterverein, 274, 283
Deutsches Institut, 146
Diocesan Synod, Second, 96
Doebbner, Fr. Caspar, 41, 95, 222–223
Doherty, Fr. David, 270
Domenec, C.M., Fr. Michael, 220, 263
Doyle, John, 102
Duggan, Fr. James, 147, 189, 192, 228, 261–262
Dwenger, Joseph, Bishop of Fort Wayne, 273

Eads Bridge, 228, 231, 236, 302, 305
Elder, Bishop, 211, 274, 295
Eliot, Rev. William Greenleaf, 5, 6, 8, 111, 160, 246
Elkhorn Tavern, 156, 181
Emerson, Irene Sanford, 110, 112–113, 117
Eustace, Fr. Andreas, 292
Everhart, John, 88

Faerber, Fr. William, 284–285, 290, 292
Fathers of the Precious Blood, 269
Feehan, Bishop Patrick, 173, 228, 262–263, 295
Fittman, Fr. John Christopher, 100
Fitzpatrick, Thomas (wagonmaster), 63, 70, 73
Flathead Indians, 63, 67
Florissant Indian School, 52, 61, 65
Fort Tecumseh, 57
Franciscan Sisters of Oldenburg, 225
Free Soilists, 118–120, 127, 130

Gallagher, Fr. Francis, 38, 222
Gamber, Father, 221
General Strike of 1877, 232, 243, 247, 250–251, 268
German "Forty-Eighters", 146, 149
German Saint Vincent Orphan Society, 5, 39–40, 99
Gibbons, Cardinal James, 27, 266, 272–278, 285–287, 290, 294–295, 297, 308–309, 318
Gilmour, Bishop, 275
Goller, Fr. Franz Salensius, x, xi, 23, 41, 92, 94–96, 224–225, 239, 258, 282–283, 285–287, 292, 296, 303, 307
Gratiot Street Prison, 137, 161–162, 169, 172–173
"Great Divorce" (of City and County), 232, 243, 247–248
Great Fire of 1849, 11, 13–15, 26, 39–40, 42, 85, 89, 91, 243, 262

CPSIA information can be obtained
at www.ICGtesting.com
Printed in the USA
FSOW02n1829191016
26342FS